AT THE CUTTING EDGE

AT THE CUTTING EDGE

The Crisis in Canada's Forests

Elizabeth May

Foreword by Farley Mowat
Afterword by Glen W. Davis

Sierra Club Books San Francisco

The Sierra Club, founded in 1892 by John Muir, has devoted itself to the study and protection of the earth's scenic and ecological resources—mountains, wetlands, woodlands, wild shores and rivers, deserts and plains. The publishing program of the Sierra Club offers books to the public as a nonprofit educational service in the hope that they may enlarge the public's understanding of the Club's basic concerns. The point of view expressed in each book, however, does not necessarily represent that of the Club. The Sierra Club has some sixty chapters coast to coast, in Canada, Hawaii, and Alaska. For information about how you may participate in its programs to preserve wilderness and the quality of life, please address inquiries to Sierra Club, 85 Second Street, San Francisco, CA 94105.

Library of Congress Cataloguing in Publication Data available upon request.

ISBN 0-87156-952-3

The text of this book is printed on 100% recycled paper using vegetable-based inks.

Electronic formatting: Rena Potter

Printed in Canada

10 9 8 7 6 5 4 3 2 1

Dedication

This book is dedicated to our eco-heroes Wayne McCrory (born in 1942) and his sister Colleen (born in 1950). They have lived in the small village of New Denver in British Columbia's Slocan Valley for most of their lives, and have spent most of their adult lives working as full-time environmentalists. In 1975, Wayne was one of the founders of The Valhalla Wilderness Society, and since 1978 Colleen has been chairperson. Colleen is also Victoria Cate May's godmother.

The Valhalla Wilderness Society focuses on wilderness, forest and wildlife protection. The society spearheaded the eight-to-twelve-year struggles to create the 49,800-hectare (123,006-acre) Valhalla Provincial Park (1983), the 44,902-hectare (110,908-acre) Khutzeymateen Grizzly Sanctuary (1992) and the 79,500-hectare (196,365-acre) Goat Range Provincial Park (1995).

Wayne McCrory is a professional biologist and ecosystem research expert who specializes in bears. He has worked on numerous government studies across British Columbia and serves on the government's grizzly bear science committee. At the time that Wayne was primarily involved in the Khutzeymateen Valley, Colleen found time to be one of the leading figures in the effort to create the 149,500-hectare (369,265-acre) South Moresby National Park Reserve (1987), now called Gwaii Haanas. In 1989 Colleen founded Canada's Future Forest Alliance, which led to her Canada: Brazil of the North campaign (1992), designed to publicize and change Canada's inadequate forest practices.

Since 1988, Wayne and Colleen have been working on the proposed 300,000-hectare (741,000-acre) Spirit Bear Park on the central British Columbia coast, which includes part of Princess Royal Island. (The spirit bear, or Kermode bear, is a rare white black-bear.)

Colleen McCrory is the public personality of this dynamic duo and of the society. She has won the Governor General's Conservation Award (1984), the Fred M. Packard International Parks Merit Award (1988), the Equinox Award for Environmental

Achievement (1990), the United Nations Global 500 Award (1992), and the Goldman Environmental Prize (1992) for her involvement in grassroots environmentalism.

In 1997, Wayne McCrory resigned as a director of the Valhalla Wilderness Society. On 2 October Wayne became involved in a protest against logging practices near his home in the Slocan Valley. This action led to his arrest on a logging road. His trial is pending.

Contents

PART III   WHERE DO WE GO FROM HERE?   219

Acknowledgements

Many, many people have played a role in making this book a reality. Initially, Sierra Club's Boreal Forest Committee, chaired by Rosemary Fox, envisioned a report on Canadian provincial forest regulation, wood supply and the impacts of industrial forestry on biodiversity. The idea was taken to the broader membership of the Club at an annual general meeting in the summer of 1995, approved, and grew like topsy. Several workshops were held to determine what kind of information should be pulled together, reaching what audiences and with what message. Researchers were contracted to seek out the relevant data and histories from every jurisdiction.

In thanking everyone, I have to start with those who generously provided financial assistance, for without their support nothing would have been possible. Glen Davis has played a *sine qua non* role for many Canadian environmental books. He has not only donated considerable financial resources to this book, but spent countless hours as an editor and critic and contributed the afterword. David Bronfman and the Bronfman Foundation have also provided extremely generous assistance. Martin Rudy Haase not only donated personally, but also offered encouragement to the overall project (and to the author in her more despondent moments!). The Seagull Foundation in Nova Scotia made the research in the Atlantic provinces possible. The Bickert Foundation also provided significant support.

In these tough times for Canadian publishers, my thanks for getting this book before the Canadian public go to Anna Porter, Key Porter Books, and especially my editor, Michael Mouland. Thanks to Sierra Club Books in San Francisco, and especially Jim Cohee, for helping us reach the consumers, for whose benefit our forests are clear-cut, and all the great activists south of the border.

My mentor, friend, inspiration and toughest critic, Farley Mowat, knows how much I love him and, I hope, knows how grateful I am for his support and for taking the time to write a foreword for this book.

Our researchers all helped tremendously and gave generously of their time and knowledge, for very little remuneration: Greg Mitchell (Newfoundland), Charlie Restino (Nova Scotia), Gary Schneider and Ruth Richman (Prince Edward Island), Matthew Betts (New Brunswick), Pierre Dubois (Quebec), Lorne Johnson (Ontario), Don Sullivan, (Manitoba), Joys Dancer (Saskatchewan), Karen Baltgailis and Erin McGregor (Alberta), Jim Cooperman (British Columbia), Juri Peepre and Laurel Jenkins (Yukon). As well, numerous people read drafts at various stages and provided useful comments and corrections. The author is extremely grateful to Ron Burchell, Don Huff, Vicky Husband and Merran Smith—all key forest activists within the Sierra Club of Canada.

Much help was received from the following friends and colleagues: Martin von Mirbach, Geoff May, John May, Russell Diabo, David Coon, Michael Fitzsimmons, Brennain Lloyd, Susan Gibson, Gaile Whelan-Enns, Suzanne Hilton, Wayne McCrory, Colleen McCrory, Geoff Quaile, Grand Council of the Cree, Algonquin of Barriere Lake, Barbara Robson, Senator Mira Spivak, Senator Pat Carney, Adriane Carr, John McInnis, Stan Rowe, Ray Travers, John Broadhead, John Cartwright, Doug True, John Caraberis, Maude Barlow, Steve Shrybman, Herb Hammond, Ben Parfitt, Tzeporah Berman, Tim Gray, Trevor Goward, Luc Boutilier and Henri Jacob.

Mike Klassen and Rita Morbia were of great help, assisting with fact-checking and editing within the Sierra Club office. And last, but not least, eternal thanks go to Erica Konrad who over-saw the whole project, coordinated and compiled research, helped edit, chased down footnotes and photographs, and managed to fit in a honeymoon. (Thanks also to Mike Bowick for not divorcing her.)

As is always the case, any mistakes are my own. Due to the rapid shifts in ownership and logging rates, the situation may well have changed by the time this book reaches the public. The tone of voice and opinions expressed are also my own, although the Sierra Club of Canada generally has the same view.

The "forest book" has occupied much of my daughter's life. As she is now six, Mommy has been "busy writing the book" for what must seem an eternity to her. So all my love and thanks go to my sweet and patient Victoria Cate, for whom I hope there will always be forests.

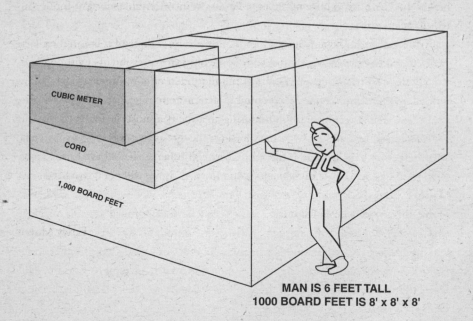

MAN IS 6 FEET TALL
1000 BOARD FEET IS 8' x 8' x 8'

Foreword

Our species has demonstrated a singular and ever-expanding ability to eradicate its fellow species, and to erode the support system upon which life itself depends. We are clever creatures. Yet for all our vaunted brilliance we seem incapable of realizing that our prime endeavor, making money, will not enable us to go on eating, and breathing, or in fact, existing.

Nowhere is our tendency to trash this planet for short-term gain more obvious than in what we have done, and are doing, to the forests. Their ongoing destruction at our hands is not only an ecological abomination in itself, it may well be a huge wooden nail in our coffin. And yet the forest industry responsible for this degradation seems to be immune to reason. Furthermore, it has been able to distance itself from the damage it does, at least partly through the connivance of government at all levels. The butcher has become sacrosanct.

What Elizabeth May has done in this book is to shine a new and powerful light on what modern industrial forestry is really all about. By dissecting the Byzantine computer models, double-speak, and selected scientific data used by the industry to conceal its crime, she reveals not only a naked Emperor, but an evil one. Her hope, and mine, is that revelation of the smoke-and-mirror charade employed to justify the destruction of the forests may help shock the nation into acting now to save what remains of the forests . . . and ourselves. She shows us that the long-term costs of allowing the rape to continue are so horrendous as to be almost inconceivable, not just for us, but for all life on earth.

The forest industry will hate this book. But it cannot pretend it is based on false premises, or that its argument is just another ideological expression of environmentalism. The book is thoroughly grounded on a mountain of government-generated, as well as independent, data which inexorably demonstrate that, beyond the rhetoric, the forest industry is culpable of committing an atrocity against the living earth. This book sounds much the same warning signal for the forests that was sounded by committed environmentalists about the East Coast cod fisheries. If we have learned anything from that ecological, human and economic tragedy, we will not fail to heed what May tells us, and take preventive action.

Now. Before it is indeed too late.

Farley Mowat

Introduction

The potential for the human population to gorge itself, consuming at a rate that would leave it scraping the bottom of the resource barrel, was highlighted in the early 1970s in such books as Paul Ehrlich's *The Population Bomb* and the Club of Rome's *Limits to Growth*.

The warning signs were clear. We would run out of oil, run out of coal. We started talking about the importance of conserving non-renewable resources.

The irony is that we were unaware of a far more immediate threat: that we would run out of trees and fish, first.

One can forgive the theorists of that time for assuming that our problems lay with the preservation of non-renewables. After all, the conservation of *renewable* resources was axiomatic. It was in the campaign for sustainable use of forests that the conservation movement began.

Over a hundred years ago, the Sierra Club's founder, John Muir, joined with the founder of the Yale School of Forestry, Gifford Pinchot, to expound the theory of forest conservation. Muir wrote: "The forests must be, and will be, not only preserved, but used; and like perennial fountains be made to yield a sure harvest of timber, while at the same time all their far-reaching [aesthetic and spiritual uses] may be maintained unimpaired."[1]

Gifford Pinchot led the movement for forest conservation in the 1890s in the United States, while Bernard Fernow led the movement in Canada. The term "sustainable-yield forest management" can be dated to those times. The goal was simple—the efficient use of natural resources. Never cut more in one year than can be replaced naturally; scientific principles, scientifically applied.

Ultimately, John Muir and Gifford Pinchot parted company. Pinchot's utilitarian view was incompatible with Muir's fierce devotion to wildness. Pinchot wrote: "The object of our forest policy is not to preserve the forests because they are beautiful or because they are refuges for the wild creatures of the wilderness . . . but the making of prosperous homes. . . . Every other consideration comes as secondary."[2]

As leading ecologist Aldo Leopold, an early graduate of the Yale School of Forestry, wrote of his work with Pinchot, "a stump was our symbol of progress."[3]

As we face the new millennium, a fundamental question needs to be asked: Are we capable of sustaining renewable resources?

Around the world, it is the renewables that are in scarce supply. According to the United Nations, of the world's seventeen major fisheries, thirteen are collapsed or collapsing. Deforestation around the world has global implications—not only in the diminishing stores of firewood for the burgeoning populations of the developing nations, but in the reduction of our planet's ability to cope with the ever-increasing release of carbon into our atmosphere. Forests have acted as sinks, containing these greenhouse gases that would otherwise enter the atmosphere. Could we be felling and burning at rates significant enough to affect the global climate?

We have learned nothing in Canada from the disastrous mismanagement of the immense marine resources of our East Coast fishery. One of the richest fisheries in the world, with legendary abundance that hundreds of years ago made it difficult for ships to ply the waters or come to harbor for the sheer pressing mass of cod, has all but disappeared.

The evidence of over-fishing is clear enough. But, beyond the shallow public pronouncements of "too many fishermen chasing too few fish," there are a number of lessons worth noting. Technology was the driving force behind the collapse of the fishery. New, highly efficient draggers, with nets capable of scooping up twenty 747s' worth, wasting as much as they caught, scraped the ocean floor year round. With radar, sonar and a ship's bridge that would have done the starship *Enterprise* proud, these draggers could keep at it until they hunted down the last fish. Thus, the technology exceeded the ecosystem's ability to recover.

This massive harvesting power was matched by overcapacity in the fish plants. A bonanza of new fish processors throughout Newfoundland created constant pressure to keep up the volume of the catch, no matter what the ecological consequences. All this was buttressed by government subsidies and a corporate dedication to short-term profits.

Of course, our fishery was regulated. It has been said that the roughly $9 billion spent on fisheries management between the extension of Canada's territorial limit to 320 kilometres (200 mi) in the late 1970s and the collapse of cod stocks was an investment in the best system in the world. We had access to extensive scientific expertise. Catches were specified on the basis of theories of conservation and sustainable harvest.

But there were problems. The commitment of the government scientists to their own models was so strong that early warning signs were discounted. When the small inshore fishers complained that the cod were gone, it was assumed that these people, who had fished for generations, simply were not good at it. Bigger boats, with better sonar and radar, were seen as the answer. Thus, technological solutions and science outweighed the voice of experience.

As the fishery began to collapse around them, the scientists and, more to the point, the ministers who set quotas and catch rates went into a state of denial.

Recently, Greenpeace ran a newspaper ad that depicted a clear-cut, running as far as the eye could see. Below was this caption: "They said we'd never run out of cod, either."

This book examines whether Canada's forests are at risk of going the way of the cod. It questions whether a century's worth of evidence suggests that, faced with an unrestricted profit motive operating in the near term, long-term ecological values are inevitably compromised.

Ultimately, the question addressed here is of vital concern to the thousands of Canadians who make their living in the forests or in the forest-products industry. It is not a debate about the environment versus jobs. It is about the fact that, as the case of the East Coast fishery has proved, without a healthy environment there can be no jobs.

They said we'd never run out of cod, either.

Stop Clearcutting Canada.
GREENPEACE

I

AT THE
CUTTING EDGE

1

Canada:
A Forest Nation

Canada's forests have always seemed inexhaustibly vast—the endless forest is part of the national mythology, and the wealth it represents is one of the cornerstones of the country's economy. Canada is the world's largest exporter of wood and wood products, and produces a third of all the newsprint used in the world; 369,000 Canadians are directly employed, and an additional 511,000 indirectly, in cutting down the forests and converting them to pulp, paper, chips and lumber.[1] In the truism of the politicians, "Canada is a forest nation"—a huge geographical area that was once nearly completely forested, and even now, after centuries of clearing for settlement and logging for economic growth, still has fully 10 percent of the world's forests within its borders. British Columbia alone contains more temperate forest wilderness than anywhere else in North America.[2] For most of our history it has been easy to believe that it doesn't matter how many trees we cut down: there will always be more.

But Canada is "a forest nation" in another sense. Forests balance the climate, protect fresh water, purify the air and provide food and shelter to a myriad of other species. They generate wealth for Canadians in ways that have nothing to do with cutting them down. Billions are made through tourism, fishing, hunting, trapping, and other forest subsistence activities, all of which are heavily dependent on healthy forests. All of these forest functions have real economic value, although the economics of *forests* in Canada is always presented as the economics of *forestry*.

A 1997 report from the World Resources Institute (WRI) puts Canada's role as a forest nation in a global perspective. WRI set out to map the last remaining primary forests, identifying all "frontier forests" that still exist in large, intact ecosystems. Of all the world's remaining frontier forests, 25 percent are in Canada's boreal region.[3] Nearly half of Canada's huge land mass is forested, a total of 417.6 million hectares.[4]

These big numbers can be misleading. Of that 417.6 million hectares, only

236.7 million hectares are considered "productive" or commercial forest land, although the meaning of such terms varies from province to province.[5] Yet many Canadians still believe in the myth of inexhaustibility. The expanse of forest from coast to coast has instilled in them the sense of an endless and ever-self-renewing resource. The same belief drove the over-fishing of the Grand Banks off Newfoundland, until the fish were gone, and the industry collapsed.

When technology was limited to cross-saws and axes, the ability to annihilate ecosystems was limited as well. But despite the primitive technology, historically, Canadian logging did alter ecosystems. The practice of "high-grading," taking the best and leaving weaker trees and less valuable species behind, eroded the wealth of large ecoregions. But it was not until recently, when the industry began to use large-scale mechanized equipment, that logging operations became capable of fundamentally altering whole landscapes. The myth of inexhaustibility, the curse of the cod fishery, persists. Governments continue to offer incentives to lure new industrial development to their province. Primary jurisdiction over forests is vested in provincial governments. Provincial natural resource bureaucracies are tasked with producing reassuring statistics to prove that, even if it takes "creative accounting," Canada has enough forest remaining to maintain its industry—at least on paper.

Giving away the forest

Each province has its own way of giving away its wood to forest companies. Like the fishery, Canada's forests are largely a publicly owned resource. And as in the East Coast fishery, the allocation of harvest rights over a common property resource is essentially a form of privatization. When you hear MacMillan Bloedel talking about the threat a national park represents to the timber supply, or see the compensation that industry demands—and gets—if publicly owned forest is set aside for such a park, it is easy to forget that industry, for the most part, does not own the forest it logs. Leases are cheap. Industry never pays anything like the true commercial value of the forest it converts to cash, let alone its larger value in ecological services, habitat and biological diversity.

Our economics are badly skewed. We subsidize short-term gain—logging the forest and building the mills—while long-term interests, the sustainability of the resource itself, and all other future values are heavily discounted. If the importance of the forests' role in maintaining global climate was properly valued, and weighed against the actual costs of reducing that ecological gold mine to pulp, logging in Canada would be drastically reduced.

Compared to other forest-industry-dependent nations, Canada has very little forest

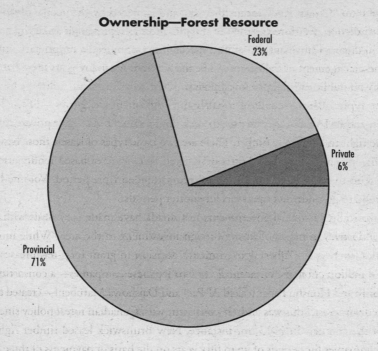

Ownership—Forest Resource

Federal 23%

Private 6%

Provincial 71%

land in private hands. Only 6 per cent of Canada's forest is privately held, compared to roughly 70 percent private ownership of forests in the United States and Sweden.[6]

While some provinces have significantly more privately owned forest, the reality is that the vast majority of Canadian forest is owned by the Crown. For the non-Canadian reader, this may sound perfectly delightful. Visions of Her Majesty taking tea in a glade of tall pines come to mind.

CANADA'S FORESTS (1996)

Total Area	997.0 million ha
Land Area	921.5 million ha
Forest Land	417.6 million ha
Productive Forest Land	236.7 million ha (1995)
Area Logged	1,011,328 ha (1995)
Volume Logged	183.1 million m³ (1995)
Annual Allowable Cut	232.9 million m³ (1995)

SOURCE: Natural Resources Canada, Canadian Forest Service, *State of Canada's Forests 1996-1997* (Ottawa, 1997).

The term "Crown land" means that the land is owned by the people of Canada, with jurisdiction over forests vested in the provinces as representatives of the people. Thus, in theory, Canadians can exert a special interest, indeed a proprietary interest, over the management of their forests. The irony is that for many years there has been virtually no public oversight of forest policy.

The types of leases come in a baffling profusion of categories—TFLs, TSAs, CAAFs, and FMAs. But they all pretty much do the same thing—give private companies the right to cut public timber. There are two basic types of leases: those based on a specific *area* and those based on a designated *volume*. Area-based tenure arrangements tend to go to large companies over an extended time period. Volume-based leases tend to go to smaller operators for shorter periods.

Historically, provincial governments in Canada have made cozy deals with large forest industries in hopes of luring foreign investment to the area. While modern examples, such as the Alberta government's decision to grant long-term leases over nearly 6 million cubic meters annually to two Japanese companies—a consortium of Mitsubishi and Honshu Paper (called Al-Pac) and Daishowa Marubeni—created alarm and media interest,[7] this was entirely consistent with Canadian forest policy since the turn of the century. In 1913, for instance, New Brunswick leased timber rights to forest companies for periods of up to fifty years on the basis of payments of three cents per hectare.[8] Newfoundland offered ninety-nine-year renewable leases, with no stumpage for pulpwood, and with water and mineral rights thrown in for good measure. These leases still apply.

What does the public get out of this? Surprisingly little—unless you subscribe to the belief that "what's good for MacBlo is good for Canada." Two types of repayments occur: first, the actual price paid at the time the lease is negotiated, or sometimes annually as "rent"; and second, payment for the volume of wood cut from the leased land, described as "stumpage." The initial cost of a lease is usually minimal. The Tree Farm Licence (TFL) held over critical ecosystems of the Queen Charlotte Islands in British Columbia by Western Forest Products was purchased in the 1930s for $35,000. To protect those ancient forests from industrial exploitation, and place them within what is now a national park, tens of millions of dollars had to be paid in "compensation."[9]

The price paid for stumpage in Canada has historically been low. This is part of the ongoing dispute between U.S. forest industries and Canadian exporters. The American firms claim, and not without reason, that Canadian forest products are heavily subsidized: low stumpage rates—cheap trees—are either part of our "competitive advantage" or our ongoing "undervaluing of our forests." It all depends on how you look at it.

Stumpage rates paid by forest companies in most provinces have historically been much lower than the costs of running the provincial forest departments. U.S. rates are much higher; for example, in 1994 B.C. charged as little as $22 per cubic meter, while south of the border the price was $111.[10] The same pattern can be found across Canada, with stumpage in Quebec at $5 per cubic meter and in the eastern U.S. at $16.[11] While stumpage rates varied west to east, depending on the commercial value of different forest types, the pattern consistently reflected lower costs north of the border.

Despite such advantageous arrangements, forest industry spokesmen traditionally complain about "insecurity of tenure." They argue that longer-term leases are required, and on more favorable terms, if the industry is to be induced to reinvest. There is a certain persuasiveness to the argument. With forests requiring anywhere from forty to eighty years, depending on the ecosystem, before another round of logging can be undertaken, private companies argue that it is only logical that if they had a long-term stake, such as they would have in their own land, they would be more likely to take responsibility for the future productivity of the forest.

It is true that small, privately held woodlots in Canada have historically been better managed, more diverse and healthier than Crown lands. At least one Canadian environmental group has argued for privatizing Crown lands to obtain better forest management.[12] But in the 1990s, it is no longer axiomatic that private property rights will create a commitment to the well-being of any particular place. In a world of stateless capital and transnational companies bestriding the globe like so many Colossuses, it no longer follows that ownership promotes values of responsibility and good stewardship. If shifting operations to Indonesia or Brazil is less costly than regrowing a Canadian forest, nationalism will not be the factor that drives the business decision. As explained by MacMillan Bloedel's new president, Thomas Stephens, at the ribbon-cutting of a new $1.3 billion pulp mill in Indonesia, B.C.'s wages and forestry rules "can't be tolerated in a world where free-market forces will determine the winners and the losers."[13]

"What? Me worry?"

Some voices in industry have been raised against the outdated assumptions on which Canada's logging rates are based. The head of the Forest Group Ventures Association of Nova Scotia told a legislative committee in March 1997, "It's time to wake up . . . We're in a crisis." John Roblee explained that without accurate inventory information, and with no regulations to ensure that cut levels are not exceeded, the province's industry was unsustainable. "Add her up, folks," he said. "We don't have the data of what is leaving the province by rail, by truck and by boat. It's going on twenty-four hours a day . . . It's just clear-cutting."[14]

Governments continue in a state of denial, avoiding the uncomfortable conclusion that a series of "local" wood shortages and province-wide wood-supply deficits may actually constitute a national crisis. The only level of government capable of providing the "big picture" of Canada's forests, the federal government, is loath to do or say anything critical of either the provinces or the industry. The federal government and all the provinces have established the Canadian Council of Forest Ministers (CCFM) comprising all the ministers with forest responsibility. Collectively, they have produced statements of principle, a Forest Accord, and Criteria and Indicators for Sustainable Forest Management. Reading such documents, a reasonable person might fairly be convinced of a deep and abiding commitment to ecological values across Canada. But the reality in the forest is far different. Even if the federal government were truly concerned about provincial levels of overcutting, Canada's interminable political instability means that the provinces cannot be criticized, only capitulated to. Political contributions and traditional influence guarantee that the forest industry is immune to criticism despite its "cut and run" approach to Canada's forests.

While federal agencies do much useful work in other international fora and in forest science, budget cutbacks have reduced the impact of these efforts. Through the 1980s, the federal government role in forests expanded somewhat through funding programs for intensive silviculture in partnership with the provinces. But those came to an end in the mid-1990s. In fact, the federal government's participation in forest management, which was never large, has become even more circumscribed. It now acts primarily as a propaganda arm of Canada's forest industry, helping to protect Canada's trade in forest products from nasty rumors of environmental malfeasance. Canada's 1997 report to the United Nations Commission on Sustainable Development went so far as to offer the web site address of the British Columbia forest industry lobby, the Forest Alliance of B.C., as a reliable source of information about sustainable development in Canada.[15]

Even international negotiations for a binding convention to arrest global deforestation have been co-opted by the trade-protection lobby. According to former federal Minister of Natural Resources Anne McLellan, one beneficial effect of such a convention would be to silence environmental critics. "It's [the convention] to ensure we're not held hostage to environmental terrorism," she said in early 1997.[16]

While the federal government pumps out propaganda claiming that forestry in Canada is sustainable, the reality on the ground is far different. As a national average, approximately 90 percent of all territory logged in Canada is clear-cut, and 90 percent of it is virgin forest.[17] The area logged annually has steadily increased. From under

500,000 hectares in 1950 to 600,000 hectares in 1970, to the 1995 total of just over one million hectares, Canada is constantly reaching into previously unlogged areas to meet the demand for wood.[18] The voracious appetite for forest products pushes new roads into wilderness, felling areas that had been pristine.

The fact that nearly all the cutting is in the natural forest makes it clear that Canada is converting forest ecosystems to fiber farms, and that no tried-and-true reforestation techniques have been established. There is no track record of ecologically healthy second- and third-growth forests regenerating after heavily mechanized clear-cutting. Canada is conducting a vast, reckless experiment.

The experiment is on shaky ground. Local shortages of wood are already occurring, yet industry spokespeople argue that because they are investing, through silviculture, in future forest regrowth, overcutting in the short term is justified. But foresters are questioning the reality of the alleged benefits of future silviculture, the so-called "allowable cut effect." British Columbia's Chief Forester, Larry Pederson, has said that "most current research indicates that while such [intensive forest management] practices improve the *quality* of timber within a forest stand, they have little effect on the actual *volume* of timber produced, in most cases."[19]

Yet it is precisely the volume that is consistently increased in the mathematical models for calculating annual allowable cut (AAC) rates across Canada. Underpinning the current rates of cut is the belief that pumping in silviculture investment in the

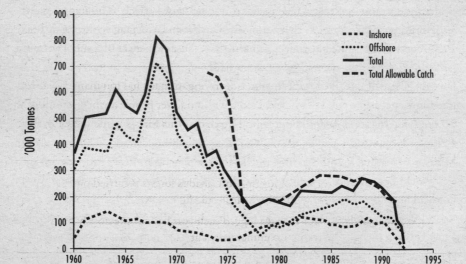

Annual Catch of Cod (1960-1995)

Annual Area of Timber Harvest (1920-1994)

future justifies overcutting in the short term. Meanwhile, the silviculture subsidies have ended, the rates of cut have not declined, and for the most part Canada is still working its way through the original forest.

Foresters know that the primary, virgin forest always contains more wood than the younger forest that will replace it. The reduction of volume in a second-growth forest and the impact on future cut rates is called "the fall-down effect." The impact is particularly significant in British Columbia, where commercial logging is moving through some of the tallest and largest trees on earth. The fall-down effect of a supply of only second-growth forest, when it hits, will hit hard.

Much in the state of Canada's forests is worrying. Canada has too many mills. Too much wood is being cut and too fast. And fewer and fewer people are being employed to do it. Canada is eroding the ecological diversity of its forests while reducing their

---

Approximately 90% of logging in Canada's forests is carried out through clear-cutting

Approximately 90% of the area logged each year has not previously been commercially cut

---

SOURCE: State of the Environment (SOE) Bulletin, No. 95-4, Environment Canada, Summer 1995

economic value to that of a pile of chips. And the wild creatures and rare plants of the forests have fewer and fewer places to call home.

Wood-supply analyses provide clear evidence that, even by the most optimistic interpretation of the facts, there is *no* margin for error. What should be of particular concern are those variables that are never taken into account as the industry and its government servants justify rates of over-cutting. Speculation about changes in future forest condition always leads to projections of enhanced productivity, never the reverse. Yet even the most confident True Believers in Forest Eugenics and High-Tech Growth cannot deny that the wood supply is alarmingly tight nearly everywhere.

These trends are disturbingly reminiscent of the cod fishery. Clear-cutting is the forestry equivalent of the large draggers, and as in the fishery, a reduced labor force exploits more of the resource. Another parallel is that as supplies of wood fiber have gone up through over-cutting, more and more mills have been established that rely on that fiber-flow, just as the fish processing plants increased in number when the catch went up. The political dynamic that stayed the hand of ministers of fisheries who should have reduced fishing quotas now maintains excessive logging levels. Wood must flow to mills, or jobs will be lost. Built-in overcapacity and entrenched self-serving stupidity risk destroying the forests.

2

Myths, Propaganda and Half-Truths

The Canadian forest industry in recent years has been alarmed by the discovery that people don't like or trust it. Public-opinion surveys indicate that whereas forty years ago the term "threats to forests" brought to mind fires and insect plagues, today the term is associated with the big forest companies.

And public disapproval of the industry was growing. In 1989, 33 percent of Canadians identified acid rain and pollution as the number-one threat to forests, with forest-industry mismanagement and over-cutting a close second at 31 percent. By 1991, concern about over-cutting had increased: 79 percent of Canadians believed that clear-cutting was a poor forest-management practice, and the forest industry itself was identified as the greatest threat to forests by 49 percent of those sampled, while acid rain and pollution were in second place at 18 percent.[20] And while only 25 percent of professional foresters agreed with the statement that "most old-growth forests should be protected," 86 percent of the public supported that view.

Similar polls were once conducted about the chemical industry in Canada. The Canadian Chemical Producers' Association was horrified to realize that most Canadians would be happy to see the whole lot go out of business. So they organized an industry-wide policy, which they advertised as "Responsible Care," and started moving the industry to higher standards of performance. While its record is far from perfect, the chemical industry does have a functioning public advisory committee and has improved its performance over the last ten years.

The forest industry, on the other hand, views its low public-approval rating as a communications problem. It has never accepted the idea that if 86 percent of the public think clear-cutting is wrong, use of the method should be reduced. The response to every complaint from environmental, conservation, and aboriginal groups is a slick new campaign by public-relations professionals. If the Canadian public thinks the forests are in trouble, then the appropriate response is to use the most persuasive means available to convince people that there is no problem: that clear-cuts are "temporary meadows"; that they mimic natural disturbance patterns and reflect the best ecology that money can buy.

The forest industry has turned to the world's largest and most successful public-relations firms. Burston-Marsteller, the PR giant called in to help Tylenol through the poison-caplets crisis and Union Carbide through Bhopal, devised a strategy that included persuading the public of the industry's environmental *bona fides*. For this purpose a neutral-sounding front was needed, and the industry created the B.C. Forest Alliance and placed pro-clear-cutting spokesmen, such as Jack Munro and Patrick Moore, both of whom were previously affiliated with labor and environmental organizations, at the forefront. Its two-million-dollar annual budget is nearly entirely funded by the forest industry.[21] New polling reflects that the PR campaign is working and Canadians believe the forest industry has improved its practices.

The British Columbia and federal governments have worked closely with industry to promote Canadian forest practices abroad. During the 1990s, it is estimated that the government–industry propaganda effort has totalled in excess of sixty-eight million dollars.[22]

In another effort to blunt environmental criticism, the industry has helped spawn groups that have the appearance of grassroots community organizations. Throughout the United States, such groups go by the name "Wise Use." In Canada, they are more likely to be called "Share" groups, as in "Share the Stein [Valley]."

Working with media experts, the industry has developed a series of messages. The key, from an industry point of view, is to neutralize the response to horrific visuals of clear-cuts. Convincing people that the evidence of their own eyes is not believable takes a lot of work. But the industry has one element of human nature strongly in its favor—most people would rather believe that everything is all right. It is deeply disturbing to hear that the ozone layer is thinning, that the climate is being dangerously disturbed, and that forests and the wildlife that depends on them are dwindling. Any convincing-sounding counter-argument will be readily accepted. Outrage takes energy, and most people have enough to worry about just to make their mortgage payments in the absence of job security.

Environmentalists tend to call such industry propaganda "myths." This is the wrong term. Myths generally embody some larger cosmic truth, which is conveyed to mere mortals through allegory. While they are not scientifically true, myths have more symbolic veracity than the fables industry concocts.

The problem with such messages is that the debate about forest practices never moves beyond polarized and entrenched positions. The hope of this book is that a meaningful debate can begin, and that some bottom-line issues can be resolved. We need to know how much the cut should be reduced to maintain a supply of wood for legitimate needs while preserving other forest values, such as fish and wildlife habitat. Many within the forest industry know perfectly well that there is a wood-supply crisis and that over-cutting must stop. Such individuals must get industry colleagues to stop the propaganda war and start talking honestly about a common ground for the future of Canada's forests. All parties with a stake in the economic and ecological future of Canada's forests need to exchange views—ideally, reasoned as well as impassioned ones. Getting to that sensible discussion will not be possible so long as industry and government put forward public-relations smokescreens or retreat into a state of denial.

The dynamics of denial and propaganda were in operation in the fishery on the East Coast. No one wanted to admit the truth, although it was plain to see in the poor catch rates of inshore fishers. Fisheries officials didn't want to admit that there were flaws in the mathematical models and biomass calculations, or that dragging the ocean floor with 1.5-ton steel doors might have an impact on marine habitat. No one (except the displaced workers) wanted to think about the fact that draggers were scooping up half of the total catch with only 10 percent of the workforce. Draggers were modern and efficient; small fishers were outmoded and inefficient—and, once they couldn't find any cod, they were deemed inept to boot. Myth-making and an advanced state of denial allowed the industry to wipe out the fishery.

Many authors have done a brilliant job of unmasking the forest industry's myths.[23] But, as so many of these myths are remade and repeated in forest debates and statements to the media, as if they had never been disproved, it is important to put the major ones to rest.

Myth 1: "Environmentalists are urban dwellers who don't understand forests. They don't like clear-cuts just because the aftermath is ugly."

Most of the forest activists in Canada are people living and working near forests. In fact, in contracting with the best forest researchers in Canada to assist with this book, the Sierra Club of Canada drew on expertise from a logging contractor, a logger, a forester, and people concerned about logging because they live with the consequences of bad logging practices, such as the loss of water supply as a result of poor road construction, eradication of valuable salmon runs, or contaminated crops from forest-spray drift.

The problem cannot be brushed aside as a mere matter of aesthetics. Of course, it is easier to convince people that damage has occurred when the damage is visible and ugly. The results of clear-cutting are more obvious than damage to the ocean floor. But the real problems are damage to biodiversity, loss of soil, and reduced ecological productivity. Ugly as clear-cuts may be, if a forest could re-establish itself and be left for the requisite time to develop all the varied characteristics of a natural forest, the issue would be quite different. Clear-cuts on a planned rotation of seventy to one hundred years do not allow a forest to replace itself. The evidence from clear-cuts across Canada is that regrowth is in lower-value species—more balsam fir in the East, more aspen in the Prairies.

In Newfoundland, for example, the relative proportion of black spruce has declined through clear-cut logging. Tracking the reduction of black spruce is difficult, as the province's forest service lumps species together and indicates densities by individual species only if the volume is above 25 percent. But regeneration surveys show a worrying decrease in black spruce after logging, reflecting the greater ability of balsam fir to regrow after a logging disturbance. "Regeneration failure is a problem on black spruce cut-over sites," reported a government survey. Less than 32 percent of logged-over black spruce areas were adequately recovering in black spruce.[24]

In Ontario, the original boreal forest was dominated by white and black spruce, jack pine, balsam fir, trembling aspen and white birch. In recent years, the effects of widespread clear-cutting are being felt. And, unlike the natural fire suppression regime, removing all the trees over vast areas through clear-cutting is leading to a massive species conversion across the landscape. A 1992 government-commissioned study that examined more than a thousand clear-cuts across Ontario's boreal found that softwoods were being replaced by lower-value small hardwoods. In fact, regenerating spruce had dropped by 77 percent, while the proportion of poplar and birch had increased by 216 percent![25]

Clear-cutting is simply the single most damaging way to log. Forests destroyed to the extent that new growth has a hard time taking hold, and where commercially valuable trees have not recovered from logging, are referred to as "NSR" (not satisfactorily restocked) lands, and they are generally priority areas for replanting. Nationally, in 1992, 2.5 million hectares were "officially" in this category, although adding in the "unofficial" NSR lands in B.C. brings the NSR lands for B.C. alone to three million hectares.[26] B.C.'s unofficial NSR lands remain excluded from federal totals through the simple expedient of redefining the criteria for NSR classifications.

The number of NSR areas is rising, because clear-cutting on a massive scale makes it increasingly unlikely that natural seed stock will reach usable soil. In comments that foreshadow the criticisms that would be made in the 1990s of clear-cut logging practices, Nova Scotia's 1958 inventory deplored the fact that

clearcutting . . . of medium aged, high density stands for pulpwood or small logs has effected a sudden and excessive exposure of the forest floor. The resultant drying from this exposure, and the scarcity of seed, has delayed natural reforestation of some lands for many years. Where seedlings have become established, the regeneration is frequently very light, and uneven under these circumstances.[27]

In a descriptive caption under a photo of a red spruce stand being clear-cut, the inventory report noted critically: "A thinning would have produced pulpwood and increased the diameter growth of those trees [remaining] . . . Also with maturity the remaining stand seed production would have ensured better chances of red spruce reproduction in the future."[28]

Such candid appraisals of the risks of clear-cutting have been purged from more recent government reports. Currently, clear-cutting is defended by both government and industry as an acceptable "silvicultural tool."

In 1975, 585,000 hectares of Canadian forest were considered NSR. By 1991, after over ten years of federal-provincial subsidies for tree planting, the area classified NSR was officially 2.8 million hectares.[29]

Myth 2: "Clear-cuts mimic nature."

This was the industry's first and cleverest defense of clear-cuts. Large-scale disturbances do happen naturally in forests. Of course, they don't happen on seventy-year rotations, and they don't do as much damage as clear-cutting. Fire disturbance patterns vary a great deal across Canadian ecosystems. They were never as prevalent in the Atlantic provinces as in the prairie ecoregions, and not at all a disturbance factor in the ancient coastal temperate rainforest. One provincial biologist suggested at a forest conference that the only natural event that comes close to doing as much damage as a clear-cut is a landslide.

The comparison between fire damage and clear-cut damage has been well developed by foresters and environmentalists who have studied both. The key differences are:

1. Fires do not leave behind a network of logging roads, landings and skid trails, creating a long-lasting risk of landslides. Logging roads themselves have been a significant cause of ecological degradation. As the Newfoundland Poole Royal Commission noted in 1980: "Bulldozing for access roads and wood landings causes deep mineral exposure on an estimated 10 percent of the area harvested, and compaction by stockpiling of wood and by heavy vehicular traffic affects an additional 26 percent or about 4,000 hectares per year."[30]

   It is also increasingly accepted that logging roads do substantial long-term damage to the ecosystem by opening the wilderness to hunters, anglers, and other traffic. It is a simple equation: roads destroy wilderness. If it's not roadless, it's not wilderness.

2. Fires usually do not consume every tree on a site. The more fire-resistant survive, creating stronger genetic characteristics.

3. Fires "may kill trees, but they leave the bodies on the site," says Herb Hammond, one of Canada's leading ecological foresters.[31] The diversity of structures left behind—fallen trees, standing snags—provide habitat for a range of species. The decomposing organic matter left behind rebuilds the soil. As Dr. Jerry Franklin has observed:

> The effects of clear-cutting are not ecologically similar to the effects of most natural disturbances, including wildfire. Levels of biological legacies are typically high following natural disturbances, leading to rapid redevelopment of compositionally, structurally and functionally complex ecosystems. Traditional approaches to clear-cutting purposely eliminate most of the structural and most of the compositional legacy in the interest of efficient wood production.[32]

The removal of all the trees over vast areas, through clear-cutting, is leading to a massive species conversion and simplification across the landscape.

4. Fires generally do not happen every fifty to eighty years over the same area.

5. Fires and other natural disturbances rarely do substantial damage to the soil. Clearcuts often do. The heavy mechanization of clear-cuts gouges the soil, often removes the top layer of organic material, exposes mineral soils, and compacts the soil beneath the heavy equipment. Ruts from the logging equipment increase erosion. And except in the case of extremely hot fires, fire disturbance generally does not destroy the subterranean mycorrhizal fungi. These fungi and other soil bacteria perform essential functions, deriving nutrients from the tree roots while giving the tree a vast network of threads, drawing water from a huge soil area. Thus, fungi and tree enjoy a perfect symbiotic relationship. Without the fungi, the soil is nutritionally and functionally impoverished. Clear-cuts destroy this fungal network. Erosion follows.

6. Fires do not revisit recently burned-out areas to extend the damage through new fires, as progressive clear-cuts do.

7. We cannot eliminate fires and choose to have clear-cuts instead. Climate change will make it increasingly difficult to suppress forest fire damage, and clear-cutting will not help. Is it in anyone's interest to practice resource management that can be defended only by comparison with a natural disaster?[33]

The Clayoquot Sound Scientific Panel summarized the ecological impacts of clear-cutting as follows:

1. Clear-cutting affects streamflow by significantly changing patterns of evapotran-spiration, snow accumulation, and snowmelt;

2. Clear-cutting leads to increased instability and soil erosion on steep slopes. This often results in increased sediment in streams, which degrades aquatic habitats, and creates long delays in re-establishing forest cover, with attendant losses in productivity;

3. Clear-cutting exposes organic soils (folisols) and other thin soils to sunlight and wind, resulting in desiccation [extreme dryness] and subsequent soil loss from steep rocky areas, fissured limestone and bouldery ground;

4. Clear-cutting removes all trees older than the length of the cutting cycle. Therefore, all plant and animal species that require old trees can no longer be sustained on that site;

5. Clear-cutting replaces naturally uneven-aged forests with even-aged forests, greatly reducing structural age-class diversity and often changing tree species composition;

6. Clear-cutting removes all living trees and standing dead trees, thereby removing both present and future sources of large, decaying trees. This removal affects many wildlife and fish species that require specific structural components of forests (e.g., snags, downed wood, woody debris in streams), as well as other organisms such as epiphytes and fungi;

7. The large tracts of young, even-aged forest that grow following clear-cutting have fewer gaps than natural, uneven-aged forests. These gaps are important to a variety of species;

8. Clear-cutting has damaged areas of cultural significance to Native peoples and has removed culturally modified trees.[34]

Natural disturbances do not create effects comparable to the damage of clear-cutting.

Myth 3: "Modern industrial forestry does not reduce biological diversity."

High-grading in the past culled only the most valuable species from the forests. With a perverse logic, which one must almost admire, the forest industry now vilifies high-grading. It is the bogeyman conjured up by defenders of egalitarian clear-cutting: everything must go.

But clear-cutting always leads to the loss of biological diversity; and under current industrial forest plans, every clear-cut will be logged again as early in its rotation as possible, which will simply heap degradation on degradation. As Canada cuts the last of its old-growth forests, ancient forest characteristics will be lost forever. Any logging regime that permits the wholesale destruction by clear-cutting of all old-growth forest with planned logging early in the next forest will inevitably have a negative impact on biodiversity. Certain species need old growth. Without it, they do not have a home. As Dr. Bill Freedman of Dalhousie University has put it: "Old-growth stands are never managed by foresters as renewable, natural ecosystems. Rather, old-growth forest is always 'mined' by harvesting, which along with silvicultural management converts the ecosystem to one of younger, second-growth character."[35]

Clear-cuts also remove the biodiversity you do not see—that which is underground. Northern temperate forests hold much biodiversity in a healthy web of life in the earth surrounding root systems of the life above. Plantations established after clear-cuts have significantly reduced soil biodiversity. For example, a healthy Douglas fir has between thirty and forty species of ectomycorrhizal fungi, compared to only three to five species on the Norway spruce found in Germany's intensively managed plantations.[36]

There are a number of variants in the pro-clear-cutting myth about biodiversity:

1. "Herbicides do not cause a loss of biodiversity."

    Herbicides kill trees and bushes. That is their purpose. Industry argues that just as many species end up on the site, and that herbiciding, which is used to kill weed species on recently clear-cut land, does not lead to species conversion. But herbiciding is part and parcel of the industrial forest intensive-management regime. "Weeds" are a symptom of clear-cutting. Herbicides are used only because clear-cutting has been so damaging that natural regeneration either needs "help" or has failed, and plantations need protection. But the so-called "weeds" are actually part of the healing process after disturbance. Some hardwood trees and bushes, such as alders, are nitrogen fixing, improving the fertility of the soil. They hold the soil against erosion and provide micro-climatic shelter to new growth. These benefits are removed by chemical defoliants.

While it is true that herbicide use does not *cause* extinctions, the model of industrial forestry, of which herbiciding is an ingredient, inevitably simplifies forest ecosystems with the goal of fiber production.

2. "Clear-cuts *increase* biodiversity."

This is a clever argument. What it alleges is that biodiversity is protected, because when you add up the species growing on a clear-cut site, you get big numbers. A post-clear-cut area may change from an apparent war zone to a riotous proliferation of wildflowers, weeds, and bushes. The area may actually have a higher number of species. But that does not mean that the original biodiversity has been enhanced, much less preserved. It is essential to understand the difference between counting species and protecting biological diversity. The *number* of species present may be high. But, if the *kinds* of species are fundamentally different, biodiversity has been affected even if the counting exercise produces a bigger number.

Research in New Brunswick found as many songbirds in a second- as in a first-growth forest, but the species differed. Those in the second-growth forest were the more common species that did not depend on the attributes of old-growth forest.[37] As Dr. Chris Pielou, a member of the Clayoquot Sound Scientific Panel, wrote: "Protecting common species is like saving old newspapers from a burning house, while leaving irreplaceable documents and the family photo albums behind . . . Common species will come back—their ability to make a quick comeback is what makes them common. But a much larger number of comparatively uncommon true forest species will take much longer to return, and a good many will probably never make it."[38]

3. "Clear-cutting and planting do not reduce genetic diversity."

There is evidence that plantation and second-growth forests lack the genetic variations within species of the natural forest. The most extreme cases would be those of large clear-cuts with subsequent planting of nursery-reared and genetically engineered seedlings. But research also suggests that even shelterwood and selection-cutting may have a negative impact on the genetic diversity of the trees themselves.[39]

Forest geneticist Roy Silen has noted that large-scale clear-cuts represent a risk to genetic diversity: "(O)ur native tree populations, which we seem to thoughtlessly waste, may be our prime resource when the world of the twenty-first century must once again return toward truly sustainable yields."[40]

4. "Clear-cuts are a temporary meadow."

Industry sources don't claim authorship of this pretty phrase; however, it is clearly trademarked by Patrick Moore, the Greenpeace founder who changed sides and has found his niche as the industry's most effective flack.[41] The tactical skill of an anti-seal-hunt campaigner has been let loose on a pro-clear-cutting campaign.

Dr. Chris Pielou focused many of her arguments on the euphemisms of Patrick Moore. In response to this one, she wrote: "A meadow is a level expanse of water-logged soil that floods in wet periods and supports a rich growth of moisture-loving plants, chiefly sedges and grasses. The conditions are so ideal for these plants that trees are crowded out. It's hard to believe that anybody who has ever strayed off a sidewalk could mistake a clearcut for a meadow."[42]

Myth 4: "Clear-cutting is a regeneration tool."

Clear-cutting is often defined as though it were actually a tree-growing system. For example, consider this common definition from the Canadian Council of Forest Ministers: "Clearcut: A method of regenerating an even-aged forest stand, in which new seedlings become established in fully exposed microenvironments after removal of most or all existing trees."[43] The definition could be taken from a dictionary of Newspeak, the propaganda language of George Orwell's *Nineteen Eighty-four*. In the Orwellian world, names often convey the opposite of what they seem to mean: the government censorship department is called the Bureau of Information; some animals are more equal than others. And clear-cutting is a tree-growing system.

No one would have invented clear-cutting if the goal was to grow a forest. Clear-cutting is an efficient method of logging vast areas quickly for short-term profit. Clear-cutting stresses the ecosystem beyond its natural capacity to maintain a forest. While trees can and will grow back, a forest, in all its enormous complexity, often cannot replace itself.

Industry flacks will argue that a forest is imperiled if left alone in the shade, without the liberating effect of a clear-cut. While it is true that some trees regenerate better in bright sunlight, others don't. Those that do, such as Douglas fir, are perfectly capable of regrowing in the patches of sunlight that strike a forest floor after a single tree has fallen.

Clear-cuts are necessary if the goal is even-aged stands. But even-aged stands are not ecologically desirable. They are more vulnerable to insects and disease, and lack the habitat opportunities that the mixed structures of a natural forest offer to a range of species.

However, even-aged stands are desirable from a forest-fiber point of view. Clear-cutting one stand of same-aged trees maintains fiber flow to the mill. Selection logging of a mixed-age stand, taking only those trees old enough for harvest, is more costly in terms of labor, but leaves an intact forest with ongoing value.

Myth 5: "If it greens up, it's fine."

This is a variant of the "temporary meadow" myth. The fact that something will grow back in Canadian forests after clear-cutting is a tribute to the resilience of the natural world. Trees may re-establish themselves naturally. Plantation trees may take root, and what was a scarred and charred ruin will likely be green again.

But the forest that pre-existed the clear-cut will not come back unless the area is given adequate time to re-establish itself before the next clear-cut logging. Second-growth forests have neither the ecological variety nor the economic value of first-growth forest. Canada is fortunate: its climate, hydrology, soil, and forest-species types are such that logged sites in most areas do not become moonscapes. But that is not an argument against concerns that the forest is impoverished, and biodiversity lost, by clear-cutting on a short rotation.

The resilience of the natural world, the ability to recover from outrageous assaults, is not a legitimate justification for continued damage. Imagine if violence against another were justified because the victim was strong, and could recover. Given therapy and counseling, many victims can regain their health and lead full, if somewhat diminished, lives after abuse. In other words, there is no need to stop the violence as long as we establish a program of intensive counseling. The silviculture equivalent of this argument is manifested as tree-planting programs.

Myth 6: "More than 12 percent (50 million hectares) of Canada's forests have been protected from harvesting by policy or legislation."

This myth has authorship. The statement is from *The State of Canada's Forests, 1995-1996*, published by the federal Department of Natural Resources, Canadian Forest Service. It is intended to suggest that Canada has reached the goal established by the World Wildlife Fund (WWF) and adopted by all provinces and the federal government, calling for the protection of *at least* 12 percent of the country's land base, in a network of representative protected areas.[44] The 12 percent figure was drawn from the 1987 Report of the World Commission on Environment and Development (the Brundtland Commission). As the 12 percent target became increasingly used as a ceiling instead of a floor, WWF emphasized that the goal was an ecologically viable system of representative protected areas by the year 2000. But the 12 percent target achieved such salience that the federal government wants to claim it has accomplished the goal.

In fact, far less than 12 percent of Canada's forest land is protected within parks. An accurate figure would be closer to 4 percent, and many provinces have less than 2 percent of their forest base in protected status. Manitoba still allows logging in some of its provincial parks. Ontario's old-growth white pine trees are said to be "protected," but fewer than one-third of 1 percent are currently within parks. British Columbia has made the most progress in protected areas, but protection has been skewed toward rock and ice. On average, 14 percent of the province's alpine and subalpine zones have been protected, but of the most valuable forest in the lower to mid-elevation zones, only 5 percent is in parks.[45] Particularly poorly represented in B.C.'s parks are the boreal white and black spruce, coastal Douglas fir, interior Douglas fir, ponderosa pine, sub-boreal pine spruce, and sub-boreal spruce zones.

The claim in numerous federal government publications that 12 percent of Canada's forest area is protected is designed to mislead. It is not actually a statement about protected areas. The 12 percent figure, so conveniently matching the WWF target, is based on adding together all the buffer zones along waterways, beauty strips along highways, deer yards, steep hillsides, and otherwise unlogged and inaccessible areas. Many of these buffer zones are suggested or mandated by provincial guidelines and regulations. It is not known whether these guidelines, regulations, and policies are actually observed. But if areas of true protected forest lands are added to the hodgepodge of leave strips, buffer zones, and deer yards, the total allegedly equals 12 percent of Canada's forests. Despite requests for the data leading to this claim, none has been produced. It is, at best, a back-of-an-envelope calculation.

Collections of thirty-meter buffer zones do not constitute viable ecosystems. They are not part of a protected-areas strategy of representative ecoregions. They are not connected by wildlife corridors. Indeed, most of these areas would be too small to support large species. The government's 12 percent claim is analogous to saying that city green space constitutes 12 percent of the downtown, based on adding up the areas of median strips between highway lanes. Children cannot play on the median strip, even if it is grassy. Biodiversity is not protected through the minimal restrictions placed on logging next to large streams or on very steep slopes.

Myth 7: "Clear-cutting is a carefully designed system used only in the appropriate ecological conditions."

This argument attempts to create the impression that the decision to clear-cut is always site-specific: that the stand age, species mix, and other factors of the particular ecosystem in question are always carefully considered. The big hole in this claim is that 90 percent of the forest logged in Canada every year is clear-cut. Given the diversity of Canada's forests, the claim that the choice to clear-cut is tailored to local conditions is absurd. Patrick Moore, the prominent defender of clear-cutting, has perfected this argument. But he confirmed, when pressed, that 90 percent clear-cutting was "about right" for all of Canada.[46]

Myth 8: "Clear-cutting is the only economical way to log."

This blanket answer to all objections, that there is no alternative to clear-cutting, is implicit in much industry propaganda. Government efforts to achieve more ecologically sustainable logging often focus on reducing the size of clear-cuts, in an attempt to calm the public outrage at clear-cuts visible from outer space. But simply reducing the size of clear-cuts can actually worsen ecological damage, through increasing fragmentation of wildlife habitat, and the requirement to build more roads to the smaller cutblocks. Of course, the use of the term "smaller" to describe clear-cuts of up to one hundred hectares is quite relative.

Proponents of clear-cuts have argued that any opening is a clear-cut, reducing anti-clear-cut arguments to an absurdity. Such semantic hair-splitting also obscures the alternatives. No environmental group has ever argued that no clearings, of any size, should be allowed in a forest. Their position is that the opposite extreme—indiscriminate reliance on clear-cutting—is unacceptable.

The alternatives to clear-cutting are many. In some ecosystems, shelterwood cutting, or even-aged forest management, could be an appropriate method. In the shelterwood system, two cuts are made; first a "regeneration cut," leaving young trees at intervals; and second a "harvest cut," made when the trees left after the regeneration cut are old enough for logging. Like clear-cutting, this method has the disadvantage of leaving trees of more or less the same age after the two cuts have been made.

In contrast, the selection logging method, or uneven-aged forest management system, more closely approximates a natural forest. Defined by ecological forester Herb Hammond, "Single stems in a single tree selection system or small groups of trees in a group selection system are cut at each entry, with careful regulation of crown closure, species composition, health and vigor of the remaining stand."[47] The selection system ensures that new trees will continually grow to replace those removed. As openings fill, new ones are logged. Thus, there will always be at least three different age classes, and the forest will remain available for logging on a sustainable basis.

While short-term logging costs may be higher, the forest maintains healthy growth, and generates higher economic benefits in the long term. And the logging itself is still profitable, even on an annual basis. In Oregon, Individual Tree Selection Management, Inc. (ITS), works with small landowners to ensure a steady cash flow from their woodlots. Years of using selection management have generated more than enough data to establish the system's profitability. On one Oregon woodlot of 172 hectares, thirty years of logging yielded an average annual profit, after costs, of $4,000(U.S.), and the standing volume of timber has more than tripled. The land was originally purchased for $17,250 (U.S.).[48] Similar success has been achieved by British Columbia forest operator Merv Wilkinson, by the Menominee Nation of Wisconsin, by Leonard Otis of Quebec and Donald George of Algonquin Provincial Park, to name a few. There is no particular magic to the notion that a standing forest will produce more wood than bare ground. A well-managed forest is the goose that lays the golden egg, but modern industrial forestry constitutes a golden goose massacre.

These alternative methods avoid the need for costly and environmentally destructive replanting efforts, herbicide treatments, rehabilitation of fish habitat and many other corrective measures after devastation by poor logging. Selection logging of smaller volumes over a longer time period can also reduce the need for a network of logging roads designed for heavy equipment and large loads.

The Clayoquot Sound Scientific Panel recommends a "variable retention silvicultural system." This is a selection method whose main focus is not maximum removal of fiber in the short term. Instead, its primary objective is to establish what elements of the forest must be left behind after logging.

"I cut for the forest, not for the trees," observed the head of the ITS forestry consulting, Scott Ferguson, in an article published in 1988. "Then I maximize the value of the product through marketing. Trees grow in groups, not in a grid pattern. I try to maximize what the group can do."[49]

But whether called "variable retention" or "selection system," to quote Herb Hammond, "it is not the words that matter, but the ecological impact on the forest."[50]

Myth 9: "Canada keeps its international commitments."

Canada has signed and ratified the United Nations Convention for the Protection of Biodiversity. This in itself is a significant achievement. The United States has signed the convention, but its ratification has been blocked by the anti-environmental forces that have been on the rise in the United States Congress since the Earth Summit in 1992. The difference between the two countries' actions may be that when the U.S. ratifies an international agreement, it is more likely to honor it.

A key commitment under the Biodiversity Convention is the protection of endangered species, but Canada still has no endangered species legislation. After years of campaigning, environmentalists were extremely pleased when former Environment Minister Sheila Copps committed the Liberal government to bringing in federal legislation. But the legislation finally tabled in the House of Commons in the fall of 1996 was flawed by the government's refusal to accept the responsibility to guarantee protection for all species in Canada threatened with extinction, no matter where they live. The law would have protected only those species considered "federal," leaving approximately 60 percent of Canada's species with no legal tools to halt extinctions. Provinces are free, of course, to pass their own legislation, but so far only four have done so. The endangered species bill was further weakened through a series of loopholes and exemptions. It died on the Order Paper in April, 1997. Canada has created a Biodiversity Strategy, but it is only a non-binding statement of intent, and does not have the force of law.

Similarly, Canada has a National Forest Strategy. But for all its good words, the only level of enforcement is the provincial governments. Even if Canada succeeds in its current effort to negotiate an international convention on the world's forests, the federal government will have no way to implement its policy. Jurisdiction over forests in Canada remains with the provinces. The federal government has only the power to beg.

Myth 10: "We need to keep clear-cutting to maintain employment."

This is the Big Lie. It is the old jobs-versus-environment argument, which falsely divides the workforce from the environmental movement. In fact, both groups should focus on their common enemy: an economic system that rewards reducing labor while encouraging the liquidation of natural capital.

There is something inherently perverse about the goals of modern economic activity. Industrial agribusiness, fisheries, manufacturing of all kinds, and, increasingly, even the service industries, are running their companies as if there were a significant shortage of people, and an abundant supply of energy, water, soil, fish, and trees. With ruthless determination, to become more efficient and more "competitive," companies have become increasingly resource-, capital- and energy-intensive. Labor has been drastically reduced per unit of production.

It is all too easy to attribute base motives to those causing such environmental devastation and human suffering, but, as Paul Hawken put it in *The Ecology of Commerce*,

CEOs of large corporations do not awaken each bright new day and ponder gleefully how they can rape and pillage the planet.[51] Nor are they particularly venal and rotten. In fact, on an individual basis, many forest-industry executives share the concerns expressed in this book. They can be thoughtful and concerned, just like the crowd at an environmental meeting. Why, then, does the environment suffer while jobs disappear? As Paul Hawken's brilliant insight has it, what we have here is "a design problem."

The reason that corporate logic has such unfortunate results is that the market and fiscal indicators by which businesses steer their course dictate the wrong direction. The taxation system makes corporations pay a hefty price for every employee, but not for the machine that replaces that person or for the gas that runs the machine. We tax things that in themselves are harmless or even beneficial, such as corporate profit and individual income, and accord tax holidays to activities we ought to discourage. If we had deliberately designed our economic system to ensure high unemployment and maximum ecological damage, we couldn't have done it better.

Of course, what we design we can redesign. A whole new field is opening up called "ecological tax reform." Advocates of redesigned tax policy even suggest we could remove all taxes on personal income and corporate profit to sweeten the pot as the tax burden is shifted to resources and energy. As tax expert Ernst Van Weizsacher of the German Wupertal Institute has said, "If we could increase the productivity of resources and energy in anything like the same way as we have increased the productivity of labor since the turn of the century—in other words twenty times—there would be a veritable revolution."[52]

It sounds like such a wonderful idea: the root causes of forest devastation and high unemployment could be removed through something as apparently easy as tax reform. However, anyone who has tried to convince any finance department bureaucrat of the value of changing anything knows that even minuscule changes to tax policy are hard won, and major change of the kind suggested here might take decades. Those advancing change, including any finance minister with the temerity to try, generally lose.

Over the last forty years Canada's forest industry has undergone substantial technological change, with significant implications for the workforce. It cannot be overstated that mechanization is the overriding cause of ecological devastation by the industry. It is the driving force behind the wood-supply crisis. It is also the major reason that Canada exports jobs along with its pulp.

The technological revolution in Canada's forests transformed logging. What was once a picturesque and dangerous trade performed by individual loggers, who hacked at the forests with cross-cut saws and axes and then hauled the wood out of the forests with horses and oxen, has become a model of space-age technological efficiency. Today, a logger is likely to be in an air-conditioned cab, listening to the tape player, monitoring the species in front of him through his on-board computer, and accessing satellite data.[53]

The first major shift occurred when the handsaw was replaced by the chainsaw. With the chainsaw came the skidder, essentially a modified tractor with a cable winch, or grapple, that was used to pile the logs. Bulldozers were brought in to create trails for skidders and grapple-yarders, with overzealous operators doing serious damage. Then came the forwarder, the trailer that could replace the horse and ox. By 1970, another wave of innovations hit the forest industry, with equipment that became increasingly complex and capable of performing several functions. The feller-buncher was introduced in this period. This is a machine capable of chopping down a tree, cutting it up into even lengths, delimbing it, and piling the logs neatly in an attached trailer. The feller-buncher was immediately popular, allowing a single operator to replace between twelve and fifteen workers. Of course, feller-bunchers can cut down only trees of a smaller diameter. The giant claws grasp the tree and, like some bionic lobster claw, snap it off as if it were a twig. The forest giants of British Columbia could not be felled with claws suited to the boreal. Loggers there still used chainsaws, but increasingly it was not men who mowed down Canada's forests, but machines.

When trees were delimbed at the stump, much of the organic material was left on site. This method was known as "tree-length logging." But in this period loggers also began a different approach, called "full-tree logging," in which the entire tree was taken to the roadside or the mill yard and delimbed there. This method avoided having to take delimbing equipment into the woods at all. The machines had a simpler time cutting the whole tree and delivering it somewhere else for delimbing and cutting into even lengths. As Jamie Swift observed in his classic book *Cut and Run*, "Under a full tree system, wood can be delivered to the mill untouched by human hands. Silviculture treatments could now include use of fertilizer to compensate for lost nutrients from logging. All of these developments were facilitated by the new machines. Limbs and other woody debris could be put through a chipper for use as biomass fuel . . . "[54]

By the 1980s, forest companies and contractors had newer and more devastating types of equipment. The trend was still toward bigger and better machinery. The feller-forwarder joined the feller-buncher and grapple-skidder.[55] Less and less organic material was left on the site. Due to the weight of the logging equipment, soil compaction became a problem. More permanent roads had to be built for the heavy equipment. More of the soil was lost to erosion, through poor road building for the machinery as well as from the giant ruts left by wheels as big as ten feet in diameter. Problems of lack of regeneration following logging increased. Where the poor forest practices of the past, such as high-grading, had involved lots of labor and few machines to accomplish one type of ecological damage, modern logging was devastating huge areas. No one could accuse mechanical harvesters of choosing only the best. They took everything.

Large mechanized harvesting was economical only if it was used for clear-cutting. Bringing in the largest heavy equipment for selection logging just doesn't work. For the really big logging machines, the ideal type of cut is a huge land area through which the feller-forwarders, feller-bunchers, and grapple-skidders can move with ruthless efficiency. Clear-cutting went from a small portion of total logging prior to 1940, to about 70 percent in 1970, to over 90 percent in the 1980s.[56]

As logging became increasingly capital-intensive, pressure increased to log more trees faster. With the use of headlights, logging crews could now work around the clock. With huge tires and greater mobility, logging became less susceptible to seasonal changes and weather.

Read advertisements for this new wave of forest equipment and realize how far Canada has come from the days of long-saws and axes, or even from chainsaws. The Timbco T415-B is hailed as "the best and most versatile feller-buncher available today! Built by loggers for loggers." Standard equipment includes the Caterpillar tractor undercarriage, track shoes like a tank, the Timbco 28-inch barsaw "with directional felling capabilities," as well as an air conditioner and heater. Optional equipment includes the full halogen-light package for night logging and the AM/FM cassette radio with headphones. The Thunderbird TMY-70 has 4 outriggers, 430 horsepower, 5-speed transmission and yarding capabilities of 823 meters. The DDC 5000 ads proclaim: "Delimb, debark and chip with one machine and one operator. Whether in the woods or in the yard . . ."

Individual contractors with hundreds of thousands of dollars' worth of bank loans hanging over their heads had to find ways to make the maximum dollar each month, just to break even.

At the same time, the number of jobs per unit of production tumbled. In New Brunswick the number of people employed in the forest industry dropped from 4,756 in 1966 to 2,057 by 1993.[57] Over the same period, logging increased. The same thing happened in Newfoundland. In 1925, for every 725,000 cubic meters cut, 8,000 Newfoundland loggers had jobs. By 1995, fewer than 1,500 loggers felled more than three million cubic meters.[58] The trend is the same across Canada.

As a measurement of employment per unit of production, jobs have been lost across Canada. It took 5 workers to produce 1,000 tons of wood pulp in 1971. By 1990, only 3.1 workers produced that same volume. In 1971, 2.3 workers were required to produce 1,000 cubic meters of dimensional lumber, the number dropping to 1.2 workers by 1990. And the number of people required to produce 1,000 tons of paper and paperboard fell from 10.9 workers to 7.4 over the same period.[59]

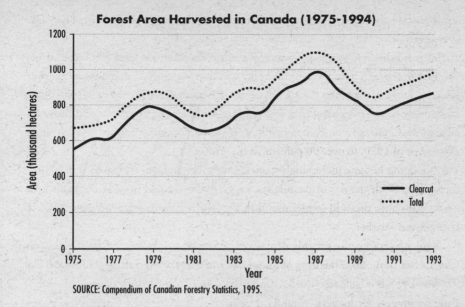

Forest Area Harvested in Canada (1975-1994)

SOURCE: Compendium of Canadian Forestry Statistics, 1995.

Many of these job losses have been offset by the increases in production. Canada is producing a much larger volume of wood products with fewer people. But even accounting for the larger volumes of wood logged, the number of jobs in the forest industry has been reduced in absolute terms by mechanization. Between 1971 and 1990, total employment in the manufacture of wood pulp decreased by over 17 percent, while production volume went up by 32 percent. Employment in the dimensional-lumber sector fell by 25 percent, while volume produced increased an astronomical 153 percent! And jobs in the manufacture of paper fell by 9 percent while production volume rose by 34 percent.[60]

In the words of the union of Pulp and Paper Workers of Canada, "If we keep cutting trees at current rates, our forests will disappear forever. Forest company methods, like clear-cut slashing and burning, are wiping out our forests . . . *Forest companies use technological change to make less people cut more trees faster*. Production goes up, while jobs are disappearing throughout the pulp and wood industries" (emphasis added).[61]

Jobs in the forest industry are typically subject to extreme fluctuations based on worldwide pulp supply, as well as recessions. The industry is used to wild cycles of highs and lows, in production, sales, and jobs. In 1970, more than 260,000 people were directly employed in the forest industry in Canada. Between 1970 and 1991, employment figures rose to a high of nearly 310,000 jobs in 1979, and fell to a low of 250,000 jobs by 1991.[62] The forest industry has been one of the major beneficiaries of Canada's unemployment-insurance schemes, laying off workers to save money in the short term

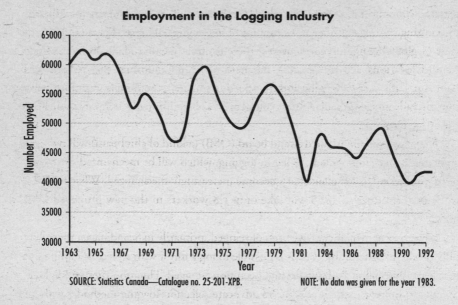

Employment in the Logging Industry

SOURCE: Statistics Canada—Catalogue no. 25-201-XPB.   NOTE: No data was given for the year 1983.

and rehiring as it suits them. This is yet another type of "subsidy" that irritates competitors—not to mention the new austerity forces in unemployment insurance.

The average percentage reductions hide big impacts in particular communities. For example, the Special Job Creation Commissioner for Port Alberni, British Columbia, relying on logging within Clayoquot Sound and adjacent areas, found that between 1980 and 1990, 2,200 forestry-direct jobs were lost in the district. Most job losses were from MacMillan Bloedel. By 1993, a further 590 jobs were lost in the Port Alberni area.[63] These losses were caused by mill closures as well as mechanization. Overall, in British Columbia, employment per 1,000 cubic meters dropped from 1.5 people in 1977 to 1.0 people in 1987. It has been estimated that since 1970, 22,000 forest industry jobs have been lost in B.C., primarily because of mechanization. Recently, the employment picture has improved, as it now takes 1.4 workers to produce 1,000 cubic meters of forest product on the coast, but still only 0.9 workers as a provincial average.[64]

Still, the national outlook for forest-related employment is bleak. An analysis by Price Waterhouse in 1994, examining employment prospects across all of Canada's pulp-and-paper sector, predicted that a further 15,000 to 20,000 people currently employed in pulp-and-paper mills across Canada would be unemployed by the year 2000.[65] These job losses come from problems within the mill industry itself.

The report identified three causes for the anticipated job losses: a failure to modernize mills, which makes them more susceptible to global competition; demand for recycled content in newsprint, for which Canadian mills are not prepared; and lastly, the coming shortage of fiber as we run out of never-logged forests. From the point of view of global competitiveness, even if there is more wood available in increasingly remote locations across Canada—northern British Columbia, the Yukon, and Labrador—the costs of logging and transporting smaller trees to mills start to equalize the price advantage Canadian forest companies have traditionally enjoyed from cheap stumpage rates.

The new boom in oriented strand board (OSB) (a kind of chipboard) will not generate much new employment, either in logging, which will be mechanized clear-cuts, or in production. OSB plants have become increasingly mechanized. What took 7.2 workers to produce in 1978 will take only 1.8 workers in the new proposed OSB mills.[66]

New types of machinery have been developed, primarily in Scandinavia, that allow fully mechanized selection cuts. It is possible to log a forest with a piece of equipment that leaves it looking as though it had been horse-logged. Flotation tires and lighter-weight equipment make it possible to advocate selection logging methods, without advocating hazardous working conditions.

Competitiveness is an interesting phenomenon. It has driven Canadian industry to significant increases in the productivity of each employee, by eliminating his or her co-workers and providing the most efficient machines ever invented for removing trees. It has encouraged downward pressure on regulations and on stumpage prices, and militated against protected areas or regulations to protect ecosystem values.

The competition has been a race for the bottom. Canada has been prepared to move heaven and earth to ship out more wood faster, with fewer people. The forest industry in Canada has become largely volume-driven and is quantity-based. But what would happen if Canada's competitive drive was harnessed in a race for the top? What if a quality-based industry could develop, focusing less on the volume logged and more on the value-added forest product—the violin instead of the roll of toilet paper.

The reality is that competition to produce the world's cheapest raw forest products is destroying jobs, impoverishing forest environments, and taking us to the brink of a wood-supply crisis.

Myth 11: "Clear-cutting is the best way to log if you have an entirely mechanized operation and government subsidies, and want a short-term profit."

Actually, this is not a myth. It is true.

3

Over-Cutting and How It Is Justified in Canada

Canada is over-cutting. The rates of cut are set to meet industry demands for fiber, and not to ensure that no more is cut than will regrow. Yet if you examine any government or industry publication, you will be convinced that a rigorous scientific process is being employed to ensure sustainability. In order to understand the state of Canada's forests, it is essential to penetrate the smoke and mirrors of modern "forest management."

Just as the management of the fisheries had a dizzying array of acronyms and complicated formulas, from total allowable catch (TAC) to estimates of spawning biomass, so too do the forest industry and its regulators. Once these concepts are examined and explained, the intimidating technical façade of professional competence crumbles. And it becomes clear that the little boy is right—the Emperor has no clothes.

Setting the allowable level of logging

The key to figuring out whether Canada's forests are sustainably managed is the supply of wood and the rate at which it is cut. This basic rule harks back to the early conservation movement of the 1890s: do not cut more wood in any year than will replace itself through growth.

Neither of these figures should be hard to discover, but in fact, Canada's estimates of how much wood is in the forest (the forest inventory) and how much is a sustainable rate of cut in any given year (the AAC—annual allowable cut) are quite subjective and open to interpretation and manipulation.

Inventory: Counting the trees

The public can be forgiven for assuming that basic facts about Canada's forests are known. Government documents report confidently about wood supply and categorize it as "available," "commercial" or "protected." While anyone can imagine the difficulties of counting masses of fish in the open ocean, trees are, after all, visible and do not move. Hence, logic suggests they should be easy to count accurately.

They are not. The problem is that Canada's forests cover such a vast area that the business of counting them is crude and the results unreliable. Overall, Canada's forest regulators have only a general idea of the nature and extent of the forest. As one knowledgeable writer and forest industry commentator, Ken Drushka, commented, the inventories are "more often than not . . . outdated, speculative, or just plain wrong."[67]

Here's how Canada's forest inventories are made. The basic information is from aerial photographs. The photographs are examined, trying to differentiate tree species. Estimates are made of what is really on the ground. Species that look alike, for instance, aspen and balsam poplar, will just be lumped together. Species occurring at low densities are often simply omitted.

The bird's-eye view doesn't even begin to give a picture of volumes on the ground. Canada's forests grow trees at widely varying rates, depending on soil, climate, hydrology, and the extent of damage done to the forest by disturbances, whether from insects, fire or logging. To determine how much can be cut, it is critical to know how fast the forest is growing, how much wood is in any given stand, and how the forest breaks down along age categories.

In order to come up with even general estimates of rates of growth, as well as to verify whether the species identified in aerial photos actually exist on the ground, provinces establish permanent sample plots (PSPs). These are revisited over the years to provide some benchmarks of how the forest is growing in local conditions. But maintaining PSPs is expensive. Some provinces have relatively good coverage, while others have only scanty access to the data from too few plots. Manitoba, for example, has one-third the permanent sample plots of the much smaller province of Nova Scotia.

But even data from those few areas which have received the personal attention of a forester can be wholly unreliable. Recently a number of studies have been conducted to assess the accuracy of foresters' assessments. Uniformly, these studies found significant rates of error.[68]

Information gathered by field crews is increasingly recognized in the forestry literature as a significant source of error. Major problems exist in estimating the height of trees, but data can even be unreliable when remeasurements are taken of the tree trunk diameter at the height of a man's chest. This measurement, called "DBH" or "diameter at breast height," is clearly the simplest and least open to interpretation. You just need to use a tape measure around the trunk of a tree. But errors of 5 to 15 percent have been reported for remeasurements of DBH.[69] A series of faulty estimates of tree age, size and height only compounds the lack of precision in estimating how much forest can sustainably be logged.[70]

Stand measurement errors are particularly disturbing as they tend to *overestimate* rates of growth and stand volume coming from younger forests and plantations.[71] Cutting more now based on a false sense of security of how much forest remains is highly risky. Yet inventory data, especially once codified and issued in impressive reams of statistics, are not treated with caution. As Ken Drushka remarked in his book, *Stumped*, ". . . so frequently have these [inventory and measurement] inadequacies been revealed that one can only marvel at the assurance with which politicians and bureaucrats quote the latest inventory data."[72]

While some provinces are marginally better than others at compiling data, the over-arching reality is that the data represent best guesses—not absolutes. Overall, Canada doesn't have much better science to figure out how much wood is available than to figure out how many fish were in the waters off Newfoundland.

Log now . . . pay later: Setting the rate of cut

Once government foresters decide on how much wood they think is there, they then estimate the "timber supply." The inventory is "netted down" to exclude areas that are "unloggable." The unloggable include barrens, lakes, areas that are too rocky or that are unavailable for economic reasons (trees too small or too far from any mill), as well as those areas protected in parks. There is an exception to every rule, of course, as some provinces allow logging in parks. In fact, clear-cutting was allowed in some provincial parks in Manitoba until 1997, when the government zoned its parks under a new act. However, logging continues in three parks.[73]

Once the amount of wood considered commercially available is determined, the province sets its allowable level of logging called the "annual allowable cut," "allowable annual cut" or simply the "AAC." It should be an estimate of what can be safely cut now so that nature can replace the loss from year to year.

The AAC is usually defined as it was in the *State of Canada's Forests Report* : "The amount of timber that is permitted to be cut annually from a specified area. The AAC is used to regulate the harvest level to ensure a long-term supply of timber."[74]

But it is hardly ecologically based. The AAC is influenced by a whole range of sleight-of-hand maneuvers. For example, any tree species in a Canadian forest not already slated for logging is considered "under-utilized." When new technologies to use these trees are developed, overnight what was a forest running out of commercially valuable species becomes an industry boom. Hardwood, of course, is considered "under-utilized" and now forms the basis of the bonanza for clear-cutting across Canada to feed oriented strand board mills.

Distant forests justify local over-cutting

Many provinces factor in totally inaccessible wood when they set the AAC, which is supposedly based on the available wood supply. Quebec and Ontario's AACs benefit enormously from remote northern forests, while Newfoundland's provincial inventory includes the over-cut forest of the Island of Newfoundland as well as the virtually unlogged forests of Labrador. The lumping together of the wood supply from these different forests and the corresponding calculation of an annual allowable cut based on the composite forest is quite misleading.

Voodoo forestry

There are other tricks to be played with the AAC. One easy way to allow more logging without increasing the number of trees is to change the age at which trees are logged. If the AAC has been calculated assuming that it will take ninety years before a new forest will be old enough to clear-cut, the simple expedient of reducing the harvest age to seventy will allow more logging now.

Dr. Chris Pielou, a British Columbia scientist, has warned of the impact of the rotation age chosen by government and industry. She ridiculed the concept of logging at maturity in what she calls "the maturity scam." Through this device, over-cutting is accelerated as a Douglas fir, which can live 750 years, is declared ready for logging at 60 to 80 years old.[75]

But the most outrageous way to justify over-cutting is the "log now, pay later" plan, the so-called "allowable cut effect."

Here's how it works. A forest company agrees to a range of measures called "intensive forest management"—tree planting, spraying herbicides and insecticides, and thinning the growing trees over time. Then it claims the right to cut more now, based on the speculative increase in growth later.

This approach was developed by large forest companies in the late 1970s and early 1980s. As C. Calvert Knudson, then president and CEO of MacMillan Bloedel, recalled, "(T)he way the annual allowable cut is calculated, as you harvest large old growth and second growth comes in, your annual allowable cut drops substantially in proportion to the reduction of the annual volume of fibre growth in the area, *unless you do something about it*" (emphasis added).[76]

What he did was actually *increase* the AAC at a time that it would otherwise have declined. "I knew," Knudson continued, "that unless we adopted a more intensive management program to offset the forecast decline in harvest we would wind up without enough timber for our mills. If you conduct an aggressive forest management program you can *accelerate your old growth harvest* in the knowledge that the growth of the next crop will be accelerated. In fact, you can even expand your annual allowable cut. . . . you offset the lack of standing inventory with rapid growth" (emphasis added).[77]

Over-cutting now, based on the belief that you can grow more trees faster later, is rolling the dice on the future outcome. The forest companies get credit for silviculture that is not yet even begun. Whether companies will actually reinvest in the forest is questionable; the industry record suggests silviculture only happens when government subsidizes it, and such subsidies are a thing of the past. Moreover, even if the companies did faithfully contribute the energy and chemical inputs called "intensive silviculture," *there is absolutely no proof the forest would grow better trees, faster.*

Tree planting has already been shown to be unreliable in boosting the "future forest." According to a federal Forest Service eleven-year review of silvicultural statistics:

An awareness that regeneration success rates based on stocking or density are inadequate to assess regeneration performance is developing in Canada: *mounting evidence casts doubt on the premise that yields of second growth stands will at least equal the yields of the natural stands they replace* (emphasis added).[78]

The companies are given credit as though it were proved that intensive silviculture was capable of pushing production to even higher levels in the second-growth forest than in the old-growth; yet plenty of evidence suggests it cannot equal the primary forest. As 90 percent of everything logged in Canada today is in previously unlogged areas, the reduced volume in second growth should be cause for concern.[79]

Moreover, there is no proof that the use of herbicides will speed growth. The theory is that humans can improve on natural succession: industry foresters argue that since pioneer hardwood species are the first to recover a site after logging, and since they shade the new softwood seedlings, they should be removed by herbicides as quickly as possible to boost the growth of the commercial species. Any company that employs this technique, it is further argued, should then be allowed to cut more trees faster. The practice is called "conifer release," as though little pin cherry and birch trees were holding the softwood seedlings hostage. In fact, herbicides can damage the new seedlings they are designed to liberate. The shade from alders and other early successional species protects the conifer seedlings from UV rays, while providing shelter from winds and storms. And, of course, the future forest is deprived of the positive ecological role provided by the hardwoods and bushes that give nutrients to the soil and help prevent erosion.

Most provinces calculate expectations for increased forest yields in "allowable cut effect" (ACE) accounts. Such accounts include future accelerated growth, supposedly to be gained through yet-to-be-performed intensive forest management, as if the putative future growth were already part of the standing inventory. As long ago as 1976 the Report of the British Columbia Royal Commission on Forestry, by resource economist Peter Pearse, described the allowable cut effect as ". . . so obviously perverse that the degree of acceptance of the system is surprising."[80] So confident is New Brunswick, for example, of future increased productivity—or so desperate is the industry for increased AAC now—that 35 percent of the province's cut is based on the hypothetical future forest. If the forest does not somehow grow 35 percent more on the same land in the future, then New Brunswick's current AAC is 35 percent too high.[81]

In the fall of 1996, the British Columbia government passed legislation that will allow forest companies to receive increases in their current AAC if they use "innovative practices" to increase future yields.

Voodoo forestry is complete. Every province is manipulating figures on the rate of growth to accommodate over-cutting now, in order to guarantee wood supply to mills. Meanwhile, it is not only the environmental community that worries that AACs are too high across Canada. A 1990 opinion survey of 4,500 Canadian professional foresters, conducted by the federal Forest Service, found that over 60 percent of them believed that the AAC in their province was probably or definitely too high. And more than three-quarters agreed with the statement, "There is a growing scarcity of timber in Canada today."[82]

Sustainable, until it's gone

Government regulators reassure the public. They urge the concerned citizen not to worry about sustainability if the AAC is too high or if it is exceeded. The key, they claim, is the "long run sustained yield" (LRSY)—sometimes called the "long term sustained yield" (LTSY) or "long-run harvest level" (LRHL). The bafflegab can be quite entertaining in expressing the differences between unsustainable cutting within an AAC and the long-range view. For example, one Forestry Canada publication claims that:

> The AAC is not necessarily equal to the long run sustained yield (LRSY) level, nor is it necessarily sustainable in the long run, although sustainability is usually a long-run objective.[83]

Or this priceless example from the Newfoundland timber supply analysis:

> Although the AAC is used synonymously with sustained yield, it does not
> imply a wood supply that can be harvested in perpetuity. Rather, the AAC
> concept refers to a level of harvest over the specified analysis period only. It
> makes no statement about the availability of wood beyond that period.[84]

In other words, forestry in Canada is sustainable until it's gone.

The LRSY can differ from the AAC and be explained away by government and industry as follows: As Canada moves through its old growth and converts the whole forest to what they like to describe as a "thrifty, productive young forest,"[85] there will be a reduction in the AAC.

This drive to force the natural forest into convenient rotational ages for the industry has its origins in the earliest days of forestry, as advocated by the University of Toronto's first Dean of Forestry, Bernard Fernow. The "proper" distribution of ages of the forest, with no over-preponderance of young trees and, equally, no over-supply of the very old, is essential if the forest industry is to have a steady, even flow of timber. Since the turn of the century it has been the goal of "sustained yield forest management" to produce a forest with age distribution to meet the model. Of course, the goal is not to have mixed ages within the same stand. That option has been eradicated by the widespread practice of clear-cutting. But over a patchwork of vast landscape, a province wants roughly equal amounts of young, nearly mature, mature, and old forests.

Some analysts have pointed out that creating this age mix of single-aged stands filling different age slots gives the government a strong incentive to have the full AAC cut in every year. "From the government's point of view, unused allocated cut . . . delays the conversion of old-growth forests to faster growing plantations."[86]

The old forest has large trees with high volumes of wood. A second-growth forest cannot supply those volumes. So the AAC for an area of old growth will have to drop when that same area comes back as second growth. This is called the "fall-down effect," and is a large part of recent reductions to some of British Columbia's AACs in certain TFLs. Government regulators claim that it is fine to have high AACs while the last of the old growth is mowed down. All of this will be sustainable on the basis of the LRSY as soon as the second growth comes in with lower AACs. Just what is supposed to happen to an industry operating at full tilt and dependent on levels of wood fiber that are no longer available does not enter into the sustainability equation.

4

Environmental Threats to Canada's Forests

What if future events compromise the health of our forests? Rates of logging are set based on optimistic assumptions; the possibility that future conditions may threaten or damage forest health is just not factored into the equation. But we have no way to know if the present rate of regrowth and survival will continue. Through widespread clear-cutting, Canada has reduced the biological capacity of the forest to respond to new stresses. As Canada's Ambassador for Environment, the Honourable John Fraser, found when reviewing West Coast fisheries policy, the resource is being "managed" up to the outer limits of what we think is there. Despite the fact that calculations of the annual allowable cut rest on faulty data and questionable assumptions, there is no margin for error.

We have known for many years that human-caused environmental stresses, such as airborne toxic chemicals and acid rain, reduce forest health. But those impacts are overshadowed by the coming disruptions of global climate change.

Forests: Lungs of the planet

Trees heal. Plants are air purifiers. Urban tree planting is suggested as a way to improve air quality in cities, while massive tree planting is urged as a solution to the greenhouse effect. Forests are part of the global carbon cycle, intimately connected to the planet's climate. They are, in the language of the international negotiations to forestall the most disastrous impacts of climate change, carbon "sinks." As a sink, forests sequester carbon from the atmosphere. The planet's boreal region is estimated to hold 90 million tons of carbon in its trunks, branches, and leaves, and a further 470 billion tons in its soils and decaying matter. Every single year, the boreal region absorbs roughly 0.4 to 0.6 billion tons of carbon from the atmosphere.[87] But humans are releasing far more carbon into the atmosphere than can be recovered by forest and ocean sinks. We are liberating millennia's worth of stored carbon. Locked away in plants when dinosaurs roamed the earth, the fossil fuels we are burning now are creating previously unknown climatic conditions.

In 1994, more than seven billion tons of carbon was released to the atmosphere from burning oil, coal, and gas, as well as from deforestation.[88] As human-induced massive releases of carbon dioxide to the atmosphere are the number-one cause of the "greenhouse effect" or climate change, the role of forests in reabsorbing tons of carbon is critical.

But just as forests are part of the regulating system for the giant engine of life called Planet Earth, so, too, are they vulnerable to the impact of air pollution. Ever since the maple diebacks of the mid-1980s, the health of Canada's forests has been linked to air pollution, in that instance to acid rain. The long-range transport of sulfur dioxide leads to acidification, not just of rain, but of fog and snow, and even to dry deposition of acid. The forests of New England and Quebec were the most affected, with serious crown dieback in the maple-syrup-producing forest in 1988. The relationship between acid rain and tree health is complex. One explanation for damage to forests from acidification suggested an indirect connection. Acidification increases the leaching of heavy metals from the soil. Research at the University of Toronto found that dying trees had high levels of soluble aluminum in their soil. The soil was also deficient in nutrients, with low levels of phosphorus and calcium. University of Toronto scientist Dr. Tom Hutchinson concluded that maple seedlings "do not like growing on the declining soil."[89] Other research in the Appalachian Mountain chain found damage to forests at high and low altitudes when trees were exposed to acid fog and high levels of ground-level ozone. Again, as in the Canadian research, toxic heavy metals such as aluminum were more available to plants, while nutrients, such as calcium and magnesium, had leached out of the soil.[90]

Fortunately, the health of the maple forest has consistently improved since the reduction of sulfur dioxide emissions by Canada and the United States. Between 1988 and 1993, the crown condition of sugar maples substantially improved.[91] But acid rain remains a threat and the air carries more than precursors of acid rain. Toxic chemicals are also carried by air, and cause stress to trees, impeding growth and imperiling forest health.[92]

So, too, does ground-level ozone, drifting from urban and industrial areas, reduce the health of forests. Some trees are more ozone-sensitive than others, but, in general, the impact of ground-level ozone on forests is negative.

Ironically, while ground-level ozone is a threat to both plants and animals, including humans, the stratospheric ozone is critical to protecting forests, and indeed all life on earth, from the sun's most harmful rays. Stratospheric ozone screens out most of the ultraviolet radiation that otherwise would make Planet Earth inhospitable for life. Increased ultraviolet radiation does affect the health and growth of the forest. In Canada's boreal, research on jack pine demonstrated a 25 percent loss of biomass from UV-B exposure, while white spruce and black spruce biomass dropped by about 50 percent.[93] Similar experiments found that loblolly pine seedlings grew 20 percent less when exposed to ultraviolet radiation.[94] While the ozone layer still requires more complete protection, substantial efforts have been made to eliminate ozone-depleting substances.

Much research points to the impacts of multiple stressors from different sources. A forest can and is hit with several environmental problems all at once. It is affected by ground-level ozone and the toxic chemicals deposited on its leaves, while it tries to cope with increased ultraviolet radiation and acid rain.

But, for all the stressing of Canada's forest by air pollution, the next wave of pollution-induced impacts to our forest environment will have unprecedented effects. Climate change threatens Canada's forests in ways we can only guess at.

"Climate change" is a term for "global warming" or the "greenhouse effect." It refers to the theory, now accepted by most scientists as fact, that releasing vast amounts of greenhouse gases into the atmosphere is likely to cause significant disruption in the global climate. The most significant greenhouse gas is carbon dioxide, and most of that is released when fossil fuels, such as oil, coal and gas, are burned. Current climate-modeling by the federal government's Canadian Forest Service and Environment Canada has attempted to extrapolate the impact on Canadian forests of the anticipated atmospheric doubling of carbon dioxide. The results are frightening. The boreal forest would be reduced to areas of northern Quebec and Labrador, with a small section in the Yukon and Northwest Territories. Nearly all of Saskatchewan and three-quarters of Manitoba would cease to be in a forest belt at all. Most of the Prairies would be grassland. Semi-arid sections of Canada would spread, and the tundra would shrink. The climate disruption would change much of the country where boreal forest now thrives into inhospitable conditions for the boreal. Meanwhile, climate would warm the North, creating the potential for expanded boreal toward the tundra. But, although the weather may shift, it will take centuries for soil quality to improve. The thin soils of the far north will not be able to support forests, even if the thermometer readings suggest they should. The stress created by changing temperatures, shifting rainfall patterns, drought where rain used to be abundant, increased rainfall in areas adapted to be dry, all point to a lengthy period of readjustment for Canada's forests. It is possible that, with time, forests will adapt to the new regime. After all, much of Canada's forest stands on areas once covered in ice. But such transitions usually move

Changes in Forest and Grassland Boundaries Resulting from a Typical Doubled-CO_2 Climate

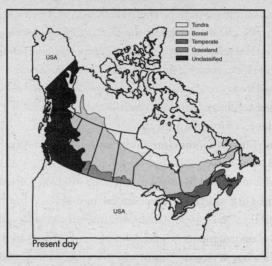

Present day

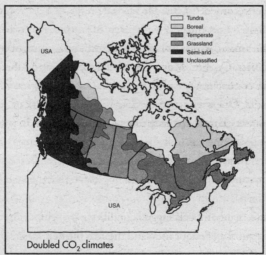

Doubled CO_2 climates

SOURCE: Rizza, SOE Report 95-2, Environment Canada, 1995.

at geological speed. These changes will happen too fast for the earth—and too fast for Canadian society.

The best way to ensure that climatic disruptions to Canada's forest are not devastating economically is to keep the forests healthy and resilient while significantly reducing our greenhouse gas emissions. But industrial forestry practices are subjecting natural systems to the maximum degree of stress now. Recovering from clear-cutting is a trauma that many areas of forest simply cannot cope with. In the collapse of the East Coast fishery, climatic stresses helped push an over-exploited ecosystem over the edge. Melting glaciers added frigid waters to the prevailing current, driving water temperatures down. So, too, does climate change threaten to make recovering forests slip into barrens. As one early research effort by Canadian Forest Service scientists concluded: "The rapid rate of climate change that is predicted to occur could also have a significant impact on the flowering, pollination, seed formation, germination, and competitive success of tree seedlings. This may result in the increased failure of regeneration and restocking done in harvested areas."[95]

But the stress visited upon the clear-cut forest will not come just from disordered weather patterns. One of the most significant impacts to the Canadian forest will be from increased risk of fire and insect assault. Recent years have already demonstrated the increased threat to Canada's forests posed by fires resulting from climate change. One study found that, since 1970, "natural" disturbances, such as insects and fire, have doubled in Canadian forests.[96] Since 1980, Canada experienced five of the seven worst forest-fire seasons in recorded history. In that time, Canada also had nine of the warmest years ever recorded.[97] Canada's second-worst year for forest fires was 1995, when, all told, 8,467 fires burned over seven million hectares of forest. The fires stretched from the Yukon, which lost over three million hectares of forest, through the Northwest Territories, Quebec, Manitoba, Saskatchewan, and Alberta.[98]

Of course, the connection between any particular forest fire and climate change is still only conjectural. One major confounding factor is the work of decades of fire suppression. Government efforts have been increasingly successful in reducing losses from fire, leaving large areas that naturally are part of a fire cycle ripe for the successional impacts of flame. As one of Canada's senior forest scientists explained, "In some cases, when stands are mature and overmature and not harvested, then forest fires will play a role in rejuvenation."[99]

Still, the climate-change models suggest conditions are being created that will increase the severity and frequency of major fires, and the area burned. Forest fires in recent years have already caused losses far in excess of the amount lost through logging. But AAC calculations and wood-supply analyses continue to be modeled as though forest fires will be held at low levels, and with no provision made for increased losses to fire.

The same is true for the risk of new insect migration into Canada's forests. Climate scientists and public-health experts are concerned that the shifting climate will allow new vector-borne diseases to migrate north. Malaria in the southern United States is a real risk. So, too, are forest insects new to Canada, creating yet another stress on an already overloaded forest.

Lastly, there are significant feedback loops by which the various impacts of climate change will themselves worsen climate-change disruption, leading to yet more damage to the forest. The most obvious of these is the massive release of carbon when Canada's forests go up in smoke. Due to increased fires, logging, and insect attack, Canadian forests have already shifted from being a net sink, holding carbon out of the atmosphere, to being a net *source* of greenhouse gases. Prior to 1970, Canada's forests sequestered 118 million tons of carbon per year. Recently, our forests are *contributing* 57 million tons of carbon to global warming. Making matters worse still, scientists in Germany have discovered that burning forests release a chemical which is a rapacious ozone depleter, methyl bromide. Plans for international action to protect the ozone layer will be inadequate if this new and ever-increasing source of greenhouse gases is not factored into the projections.[100]

In the face of mounting evidence of the threat to the forests from climate change and of the crucial role played by forests in holding carbon out of the atmosphere, Canada's forest industry has attempted to jump on the bandwagon. It has argued that replacing old-growth forests with young plantations will accelerate the take-up of carbon by our forests. The reality, unfortunately, is the contrary. While it is true that the rate at which young trees absorb carbon exceeds that of old forest giants, the young forest simply does not have anywhere near the biomass to replace the carbon-sequestration abilities of an old forest. Research published in *Science* concluded that logging and replanting an area will not "approach old-growth storage capacity for at least 200 years. Even when sequestration of carbon in wooden buildings is included in the models, timber harvest results in a net flux of CO_2 to the atmosphere."[101]

Furthermore, clear-cutting itself increases the release of carbon dioxide to the atmosphere. Exposed soil on clear-cut land may decompose more rapidly, thus releasing increased levels of carbon to the atmosphere.[102]

The forest industry participates in the "Voluntary Challenge Registry" (VCR), the federal government's primary approach to reducing carbon dioxide emissions. Not surprisingly, the voluntary approach has not driven Canada's carbon dioxide emissions down to meet announced targets. In fact, Canada's emissions of carbon dioxide are climbing. But regulations and meaningful policy changes are politically unpalatable, so forest industries are allowed to set voluntary goals. The pulp-and-paper industry claims credit for switching from fossil fuels to biomass fuels. So far, so good. However, they also claim that since they are managing the forest sustainably, the carbon released when such wood-based fuels are burned need not be included in the totals of carbon dioxide emissions. They provide no evidence that this is the case.[103]

Given the enormity of the threat posed by climate change, preserving old-growth forests as carbon sinks is arguably their highest value to the economy—and the future.

5

Environmental Threats from Canada's Forest Industry

Pollution from all over the industrialized world falls on Canada's forests, but Canadian industry itself is a significant source of toxic contamination. While most attention is focused on damage caused by logging, the forest industry is also a polluter in a more conventional sense. In the woods, the use of insecticides and herbicides is part and parcel of the intensive forest management used to justify over-cutting in the short term. Around the older mills, a witches' brew of chemicals has fouled the waters. Mills have traditionally been built along rivers as a means of providing ease of access to logs brought down in booms along watercourses, as a source of water for production processes, and as a place to dump the waste. Battles between the pulp-and-paper industry and its neighbors over the pollution of downstream water led to some of the earliest cases in Canadian environmental law. The case of Reed Paper's pollution of the White Dog and Grassy Narrows Reserves was recorded in one of Canada's first environmental exposés, *No Safe Place*, by journalist Warner Troyer.[104]

Pulp-and-paper pollution

Depending on the type of processing used, pulp mills produce a toxic brew in their effluent, which can have devastating impacts on the aquatic ecosystem as well as on other resource industries.

Overall, pulp mills use vast amounts of water and consume prodigious amounts of energy. In 1990, it was estimated that the pulp-and-paper industry was responsible for fully half of all the waste dumped in Canada's waters.[105] In fact, "one kraft mill discharges oxygen-demanding substances equal to a city with a population greater than 120,000 people."[106]

There are two primary types of pulp-and-paper manufacturing: chemical and mechanical. Making pulp and paper is basically a process of breaking down wood fibers. This can be done either by grinding the wood into pulp through a mechanical process, or by "cooking" it with a mix of chemicals to break down the lignin fibers. Sometimes the fibers need to be brightened for that extra-white sheet of paper, and that involves chemicals as well. Many pulp-and-paper operations use a mix of chemicals and mechanical processing.

Chemical pulps are stronger and brighter than mechanical pulps, as the chemical cooking removes the lignin fibers from the wood. On the other hand, mechanical pulping produces a larger volume of pulp for the wood used, so trees are more fully utilized.

Within the chemically produced pulp, there are two primary types of process: sulfate or kraft mills, and sulfite pulp. You can tell a kraft mill from miles away from the sulfurous odor. The major chemicals used in the kraft process are sodium hydroxide, the main cooking chemical, and sodium sulfide. The resulting paper is then often bleached with chlorine.

The sulfite pulp is generally produced without bleaching chemicals. The main cooking chemical for sulfite pulp is a bisulfite–sulfurous acid solution.

New types of processing use aspects of both chemical and mechanical pulping. The method developed by Repap is a bleached chemi-thermal mechanical pulp (BCTMP) mill. This process was developed to manufacture bleached pulp without the environmental hazards of chlorine bleaching.

For many years, Canadian mills built before 1971 were exempted from effluent controls on a range of polluting discharges; for everything from dioxins and furans to suspended solids and oxygen-depleting substances, pre-1971 mills were subject to guidelines only. Public concern began to focus on the widespread distribution of dioxins and furans in the environment in the mid-1980s. Dioxins are a large family of chemicals, related to the furans, both within a chemical group called "organochlorines." They are produced in the bleaching process whenever chlorine is used. Some members of the dioxin and furan family are unbelievably toxic. In fact, the most toxic human-made chemical is a dioxin isomer—2,3,7,8,-tetra-chlorodibenzo-para-dioxin (2,3,7,8-TCDD). Studies around the Great Lakes demonstrated unacceptable levels of dioxin in gulls' eggs. Reproductive failure and unusual birth defects were also on the rise.[107] In 1987, Greenpeace decided to test sediments and shellfish in the vicinity of mills in Howe Sound, British Columbia. The Greenpeace reports were sent to the federal government for comment prior to release to the media. It happened that, at the same time, Environment Canada had been running tests. While Greenpeace's sampling had detected some startling dioxin and furan contamination, some of the government testing showed even higher levels. The Greenpeace tests had the positive effect of moving the federal results up to the minister's desk much faster. It is an unhappy reality of large bureaucracies that no one wants to be the messenger who brings bad news. Greenpeace got the minister's attention. Former Environment Minister Tom McMillan made the decision to release the government's tests and begin work for the control of dioxins and furans from pulp mills.[108]

It took years to promulgate regulations under the Fisheries Act for improved controls on oxygen-demanding substances that imperiled fish, and, through the Canadian Environmental Protection Act, for controls on dioxins and furans. Before the federal government could bring forward new laws, the Howe Sound shellfish industry was closed because of the unacceptable levels of toxic contamination. Other shellfish closures near B.C. mills followed. British Columbia responded by bringing out its own effluent regulations in the spring of 1989. B.C. mills faced the toughest laws in Canada, with a requirement for no more than 1.5 kilograms of total organochlorines (dioxins and furans) per ton of pulp produced. At the time, mills were releasing an average of four to eight kilograms of organochlorines per ton of pulp.[109] Industry howls of protest could be heard all the way to Sweden, where chlorine bleaching had already been banned.

In 1988 the federal government assessed the effectiveness of guidelines to control mill pollution. What it discovered was not really a surprise. Effluent from Stora Kopparberg, the Swedish pulp-and-paper giant in Nova Scotia, for example, had so consistently failed toxicity testing that Environment Canada officials told the local press that they no longer bothered to run tests, knowing that Stora would fail. With only guidelines, instead of regulations, they could do nothing about it.[110] Stora's president, Tom Hall, did not strike an apologetic chord when it was revealed that his mill was one of the two worst polluters in Atlantic Canada. "There are no government regulations enforcing the company to do so [limit effluent]," he said. "We are not in non-compliance."[111]

The internal review of 1988 confirmed that, of the 122 pulp mills in Canada at the time, 83 were violating the pollution-control guidelines.[112]

Finally, in 1992, the federal government announced its new regulations. Even after years of consultation, the regulation did not demand immediate compliance. It set a deadline of the end of 1993 for the reduction of dioxins and furans to non-measurable levels from kraft mills.[113] These controls applied for the first time to mills built prior to 1971, the mills most likely to be polluting because of the older technologies in use. They would require reduction of dioxins and furans, but not total elimination. Government regulators claimed the target levels would avoid toxicity in fish.

But new science continues to emerge about the risks of organochlorines and a larger group of chemicals known as "endocrine disrupters." Endocrine-disrupting chemicals actually mimic the human hormones released through our endocrine system, such as estrogen and testosterone.[114] Studies on fish downstream from pulp mills have revealed that, even at very low levels, and even in mills that do not use chlorine, endocrine-disrupting chemicals are having a weird and widespread impact on wildlife. A review in 1996 of the fish in Alberta's northern rivers, for instance, found increases in abnormalities like tumors, lesions, deformities, and parasites downstream from the pulp mills. The study also found significantly lower sex hormones in the burbot within 100 kilometers downstream, while both burbot and longnose suckers had significant-ly higher levels of sexual immaturity compared with fish upstream from the mill.[115] The impact on all forms of wildlife and humans from endocrine-disrupting chemi-cals remains controversial, but clearly points to health effects ranging from sterility to reproductive difficulties, birth defects, and cancers.[116]

The reaction from the pulp-and-paper industry to the announcement that mill effluent would be regulated was to swing into action and immediately issue calls for an extension. Ultimately, the federal government agreed to give pulp mills until the end of 1995 to put in place the required pollution-control technology. Mills across the coun-try claimed that the pollution controls would drive them out of business. Some mills managed to get financial assistance as well as time extensions before complying. Nevertheless, between 1988 and 1993, the amount of dioxins and furans in kraft-pulp-mill effluent decreased by 98.4 percent.[117] As of 1993, of the 145 pulp mills in Canada, forty-six were still using bleach to whiten their pulp in the kraft process. Mills are continuing to look for substitutes for bleach, and some are moving toward "closed-loop" systems. This is clearly the way of the future, involving the recovery of useful byproducts traditionally discharged into the environment as waste. Discharges of other effluent, from all types of mills, also fell in the last decade, due to the regulations under the Fisheries Act. Total suspended solids (TSS) and oxygen-demanding substances, measured as levels of biochemical oxygen demand (BOD), also fell, down 7.9 percent and 6.8 percent, respectively, between 1983 and 1993.

Meanwhile, the oriented strand board industry is introducing a whole new group of toxic chemicals into the forest industry. When Louisiana-Pacific decided to open a mill in Manitoba, there were no regulations dealing with its emissions. The company volunteered to comply with standards that prevail in the United States after public concern about its poor pollution record began to make headlines.[118] Canadian juris-dictions have yet to catch up with the volume of waste that can be expected from the burgeoning OSB industry. Manufacture of OSB involves phenol, formaldehyde, and, sometimes, methyl isocyanate. Not only does the manufacture raise new pollution issues, but use of OSB as a building material creates concerns for indoor air quality.

While much remains to be done to reduce forest-industry pollution, the lessons of the early 1990s are instructive. The use of voluntary guidelines for two decades resulted in the discharge of millions of tons of pollution into Canada's waterways. When caught with triple the acceptable levels of pollution, most corporate CEOs would have responded as did Stora president Tom Hall: "We're not in non-compliance."

Voluntary measures just don't work. Regulations and enforcement do. But as we enter the last years of this millennium, all the political trends and budgetary pressures run counter to strong regulation. In fact, Canada's only response to the threat of global climate change has been a voluntary program. Devolution of powers threatens to remove the Fisheries Act as an effective tool for environmental protection. Recent slashing of budgets for enforcement at both the federal and the provincial levels, and the substantial reduction of Forest Department staffs in Alberta and Ontario, suggest another set of worrying national trends.

Pesticides: Deliberately spreading toxics over the ecosystem

Chemical pesticides are the only chemicals in use in industrial society that can be treated as hazardous waste in one context and deliberately dispersed over the ecosystem in another. Their introduction to modern forestry is a fairly recent phenomenon. The province that led the way, adopting pesticide spraying as an annual rite of spring, was New Brunswick.

The only province to have experienced anything like the controversy spraying created in New Brunswick was Nova Scotia, the recipient of budworm overflow from New Brunswick's permanent epidemic. Battles over use of herbicides and insecticides have flared up in Newfoundland, Quebec, and British Columbia, but they lacked the epic quality of Nova Scotia's Spray Wars (related in greater detail in the Nova Scotia chapter of this book), in which local environmentalists clashed with Stora Kopparberg over a period of nearly a decade. Initially, the environmental and community groups were successful in blocking the planned aerial spraying of all forested parts of Cape Breton Island with insecticides. Once the insect outbreak had collapsed, Stora, joined by the province's other large pulp mills, embarked on a herbicide spray program to kill "competing" vegetation and deciduous trees. That conflict led to a protracted court battle in which small communities and environmentalists suffered a punishing loss.

Animosity between local environmentalists and the Nova Scotia and New Brunswick pulp companies is as fierce as anywhere in the country. Environmentalists are often personally attacked by the company representatives, ridiculed, and threatened in the press with lawsuits that are never filed.

Industry and government propaganda proclaims that public participation and consultation are now an accepted part of doing business. Unfortunately, the facts are otherwise. In the summer of 1996, local men, women and children staged a peaceful protest on an airstrip in the Cape Breton Highlands, opposing the planned spraying of the bacterial insecticide Bacillus thurigiensis (Bt). In a story from the "wonders of science" archives, chemical companies have been able to transform Bt from the virtually harmless bacterium championed by Rachel Carson as an alternative to chemicals to something far from benign. Bt has been chemically re-engineered so that it can be sprayed with toxic substances, encapsulated to last far longer in the environment. It is no longer, in its commercial formulations, to be used without caution.

The protesters had hoped they would be given a chance to voice their opposition in a democratic way at formal public hearings, but they were frustrated by the refusal of the Nova Scotia government to hold so much as a public meeting before aerial spraying of their local water supplies was to begin. The picnic protest on the Highlands was met by armed Department of Natural Resources staff. It was a bad day for democracy in Nova Scotia.

Pesticides, pulp mills and politics

The bulk of this book addresses the vast ecological damage of logging, but across Canada, too little attention is paid to the direct polluting impact of the forest industry. In assessing the real cost of society's addiction to wasteful paper consumption, every part of the process has to be factored in—from clear-cutting and herbicide spraying of plantations to pulp mill effluent and oriented strand board off-gassing in homes. There is no such thing as cheap paper.

6

The U.S. Appetite for
Canada's Forests

Since the early 1990s, a number of factors have combined to help Canadian exports of forest products reach new levels—low stumpage rates, increased post-recession demand, and a lower Canadian dollar. In 1991, after several bad years, the total value of Canada's forest exports was $20.6 billion. By 1994, this figure had climbed to a new all-time high of $32.4 billion—an increase of 57 percent in three years! But even before the increases, Canada was the world's largest exporter of forest products, most of which, by a large margin, are headed for U.S. markets.[119] Of all of the imported softwood lumber in the U.S., nearly 100 percent comes from Canada, while 93 percent of all U.S. imports of wood pulp come from Canadian clear-cuts.[120] Canada's share of imported U.S. newsprint has declined from a high some thirty years ago of nearly 70 percent to a current level of 56 percent of all U.S. newsprint imports. Part of this decline is attributable to legislation in a number of U.S. states requiring newsprint to have recycled-paper content.

After the United States, the next-largest importer of Canadian forest products is Europe. Canada also exports significant amounts of forest products to Latin America and Japan.

But it is the trading relationship with the United States that registers on the political Richter scale. For one thing, while the United States is Canada's largest market, it is also Canada's toughest competitor—and our trading relationship is a two-way street. Canada imports certain U.S. forest products. The trade flows reinforce the reality that Canada is selling itself short in value-added and higher-value forest products. While Canada ships raw lumber and pulp to the United States, it imports higher-priced U.S. structural lumber, such as large-dimension Douglas fir, hemlock, and other high-value products. Canada exports far more pulp and newsprint than higher-value paper products. Canada's ratio of pulp-and-paper exports is two to one in terms of low to high value. This is the opposite of the forest products export ratio of Sweden and other northern countries.[121]

The United States has been reducing Canada's share of the global marketplace in several forest-product areas, and increasing the proportion of imports from Europe and the Pacific Rim. But over the same number of years, Canada has maintained and increased its market share within the United States—all of which led to the biggest ongoing trade battle between the two nations: the softwood-lumber dispute.

The softwood-lumber dispute (And, by the way, of course our exports are subsidized ...)

One of the most significant trade irritants between Canada and the United States over the last two decades has been over Canadian lumber gobbling up an ever-larger share of the U.S. market. For Canadians unfamiliar with the forest industry, the crisis over "shakes and shingles" in the mid-1980s seemed too arcane to generate much interest. Besides, it sounded like some sort of nasty disease.

For people in the forest industry in both Canada and the United States, the softwood-lumber dispute was about economic survival. But for all the time taken up by trade negotiations, the one aspect of the forestry trade disputes that didn't even rate a mention was the environmental impact of Canadian subsidies.

The trade dispute erupted in 1986, as Canadian lumber exports began to make significant inroads into the U.S. market. These gains were seen to be at the expense of U.S. forest companies, particularly in the western states. From 1975 to 1985, Canadian exports expanded their share of the market from 18.7 percent of U.S. softwood consumption to nearly double that, at 33.2 percent.[122]

U.S. industry representatives lobbied hard in Washington. They claimed that Canadian imports violated fair-trade rules through the low stumpage rates for Canadian wood. Low charges for government-owned wood seemed to them to be an unfair subsidy. And in terms of trade rules, if one country is unfairly subsidizing its exports, then countervailing duties are the appropriate response to level the famous playing field. As well, U.S. trade reviews noted the high level of subsidies to build mills and roads.

Canadians reacted with rage to news of a preliminary duty placed on Canadian exports by the United States in October 1986. This was U.S. protectionism at its worst. The former CEO of Noranda Forest, Adam Zimmerman, recalled that "a portion of the American lumber industry and a fair number of American politicians indulged in acts of outrageous protectionism, bolstered by highly spurious arguments and the selective use of dubious 'facts' and figures."[123]

It seemed that the bigger, more powerful trading partner was slamming poor old

Canada again. Canadians could be forgiven for assuming that Uncle Sam was in the wrong. For the most part, media commentators in Canada never actually examined what stumpage rates were in Canada. In 1986, stumpage in the U.S. northwest came to $130 per thousand board feet of timber. In the same year, stumpage in B.C.'s forests came to $18 per thousand board feet.[124] The conflict was particularly focused on B.C. lumber, which was so much a part of Canadian export success, but the stumpage rates from all across Canada were also at bargain-basement levels. Canadian costs for access to publicly owned trees were roughly one-half to one-third of what they were in comparable forest types south of the border.

Industry countered that labor costs in Canada were higher, that trees were farther from mills, and that, over all, they had a hard time making a buck. Canadian industry pointed out that the U.S. lumber industry was the author of its own misfortune by valuing timber through an auctioning system that locked them into excessive lumber prices.[125]

The imposition of the preliminary duty set the stage for desperate bargaining leading up to the deadline for a negotiated settlement at the end of December 1986. What the Canadian negotiators managed to do was better for Canadian forests and the environment than had previously been the case. It was also better for Canada. But you never would have known it from the abuse hurled at Pat Carney, the Trade Minister who signed the deal. The negotiated Memorandum of Understanding (MOU) converted a duty imposed by the United States, with funds paid into the United States, into a 15 percent duty collected in Canada, to be used for forest management in Canada. In exchange, the United States agreed not to pursue its case against Canada. Within the year, the 15 percent Canadian duty was converted into an equivalent increase in the value of provincial stumpage collected. Thus, the increased stumpage more closely approximated market value and—potentially—reduced the over-exploitation of Canada's forests. By 1987, the percentage of the U.S. softwood market occupied by Canada began to slip toward the pre-1975 norms.

The federal government collected a 15 percent lumber-export tax, with revenues targeted in British Columbia for forest worker retraining and replanting. In 1987, the Socred B.C. Minister of Forests of the day redirected the approximately $375 million in the silviculture fund to reduce the deficit. B.C.'s senior ranking federal cabinet member at the time, Pat Carney, denounced the state of the province's forests in the House of Commons: "Every British Columbia Member of Parliament knows that our forests are a silvicultural slum."[126]

A further $500 million was in fact spent on silviculture as part of the federal/provincial Forest Resource Development Agreements (FRDAs).

Subsidies to the industry come in many forms. Across the country, cheap power is

FOREST INDUSTRY: MAJOR EXPORT MARKETS (1994)

	United States	European Union	Japan	Others
Newfoundland & Labrador	35%	33%		21%
Prince Edward Island	99%			
Nova Scotia	54%	26%		
New Brunswick	71%	12%	9%	
Quebec	84%	9%		
Ontario	96%			
Manitoba	93%			
Saskatchewan	46%	23%	15%	
Alberta	43%		26%	
British Columbia	55%	11%	23%	
Yukon				
Northwest Territories				
CANADA (Total)	70%	9%	12%	9%

FOREST PRODUCTS—EXPORT (1994)

Province	Softwood lumber	Wood pulp	News-print	Other paper & paper board	Wrapping paper	Wafer-board
Newfoundland & Labrador			100%			
Prince Edward Island	44%					
Nova Scotia		43%	44%			
New Brunswick			21%	25%		
Quebec	18%		35%	19%		
Ontario	22%		22%	22%		
Manitoba	34%				29%	
Saskatchewan	10%	59%		16%		
Alberta	13%	61%				12%
British Columbia	54%	25%	8%			
Yukon	3.5%					
Northwest Territories	13%					

SOURCE: *The State of Canada's Forests 1995-1996*, Canadian Forest Service, Natural Resources Canada, 1996. Note tables do not always add up to 100%. Numbers taken directly from government sources.

a common indirect subsidy to the energy-intensive pulp-and-paper business. In Newfoundland, for example, hydroelectric rights are thrown in free along with the lease, and elsewhere, power rates are subsidized. The Crown hydroelectric corporation B.C. Hydro provides power to the forest industry at giveaway rates, often less than the cost of production.[127]

Traditionally, trees have also been given away. For many years, British Columbia's stumpage rate was so low that even when B.C. produced a volume of timber equal to that of the rest of the provinces combined, the stumpage collected did not even offset the cost of running the Forest Service. As recently as the early 1980s, the average stumpage rate to a large B.C. forest company was less than $2 per cubic meter. In 1995, the average provincial stumpage rate on Crown timber was $26.46 per cubic meter. As of 1992–1993, Ministry of Forest revenues, at long last, actually exceeded costs. At the same time, of course, the government was making more investments in the forests.

But Canadian industry was deeply unhappy about the "voluntary" Canadian imposition of a 15 percent increase in the costs of production for export. By 1991, the Canadian share of the U.S. softwood market had fallen to under 27 percent. Under industry pressure, the Canadian government decided to terminate its 1986 MOU. The U.S. Trade Representative responded swiftly with a temporary duty on Canadian softwood, pending completion of an investigation by the U.S. Commerce Department. But Canadian share of the U.S. market began to climb. By 1995, the Canadian market share had surpassed its mid-1980s high of 33 percent and had reached just over 36 percent of the U.S. market.[128] Meanwhile, the U.S. lumber industry claimed that Canadian subsidies were responsible not only for their loss of market share, but for downward pressures on U.S. lumber prices.

To resolve the 1995 trading impasse, Canada once again negotiated an export duty, but this one was more complex. In exchange, the U.S. government promised not to launch any more trade complaints against Canadian softwood exports for five years.[129] In the words of former Trade Minister Art Eggleton, the agreement will buy "five years of peace."[130] The Canadian government is to police the amount of lumber and the timing of shipments. Exports are allowed on a duty-free basis within a certain quota. No more than 14.7 billion board feet of duty-free exports can be shipped to the United States from British Columbia, Alberta, Ontario, and Quebec in any year. Furthermore, to avoid Canadian lumber flooding the U.S. market, the government has to ensure that no more than 28.5 percent of that annual allotment is exported in any quarter.[131] The new agreements have actually increased the "flooding" of U.S. markets. As soon as a new quarter arrives, Canadian forest industries rush to ship into the United States in order to avoid risking an export duty if total shipments exceed the allowed limits.

What no one has ever asked is how the trade war has affected the forest environment in Canada and the United States. Admittedly, trade relationships and the environmental content of trade are an immensely complex subject, but it is undeniable that the undervaluing of environmental resources, like energy, water, or forests, leads to waste and environmental damage. Free trade agreements, from the original Canada–U.S. Free Trade Agreement to NAFTA to the global free-for-all competitive market policed by the World Trade Organization, put downward pressures on the environment. They do so because current economic indicators fail to value anything not currently traded in the marketplace. Pure air, fresh water, the pine marten, children's health, or our great-great-grandchildren's existence cannot be bought and sold—and, hence, are without value. Globalization of trade could lead to improved standards, *if* the full value of resources was included in the equation.

Internalizing the environmental costs of logging and the environmental and economic benefits of a standing forest will lead to higher prices for forest products. Thus, the impact of Canadian subsidies in the early 1990s has been harm to the environment in both countries. Canada's low stumpage rates led to lower prices, not only in Canada, but in the United States as well, with downward competition-driven pressure on the forest environment. Perhaps if environmental groups on both sides of the border could cooperate, it might be possible to inject an ecological assessment of trade flows and subsidies when the question blows up again, as it will, in the year 2000.

7

Deregulation, Industry Self-Regulation and the Certification Scam

Even in the time it has taken to research and write this book, Canada's forest regulation has taken an enormous step backward. The current political hype favoring industry self-regulation, particularly prevalent in Ontario and Alberta, threatens to slacken already sloppy logging practices.

Budgetary pressure has resulted in two very different approaches. Some provinces, such as Alberta and Ontario, have taken the view that drastically reducing forest service staff is an acceptable way to decrease governmental deficits. These provincial governments appear to have complete confidence in the forest industry's ability to police its own operations, gather its own data, and report on the sustainability of its forest operations to a much smaller group of provincial forest bureaucrats. Other provinces are recognizing the need to increase the revenues received from forest companies benefiting from long-term, low-cost tenure over Canada's forests. British Columbia has been aggressive in requiring higher payment for its wood, to the point that the revenues are actually enough to fund forest and stream rehabilitation programs, as well as covering the costs of the Forest Department for the first time. Saskatchewan is also in the process of negotiating increases for access to Crown land.

Budget cuts, particularly where they result in less silviculture, should translate into automatic decreases in the annual allowable cut (AAC) around the country. The whole house of cards of increased AACs justified by future rates of intensive silviculture should come tumbling down as lack of government subsidies translates into less silviculture. While this reality of reduced silviculture expenditures is evident everywhere, nowhere has it led to fundamental rethinking of the exaggerated rates of cut. This could be because no one ever really believed that tree planting, chemicals, road building, and thinning would actually produce more wood. Taking away the pretense matters little if the whole approach is accepted, on an insider basis, as a scam. Without the greenwash of intensive silviculture, there should be substantial reductions to the annual allowable cuts, at least back to those levels which, by the government's own modeling exercises, were totally dependent on a successful future scenario of growing more trees, faster. But in Nova Scotia, even when 70 percent of the silviculture targets were not met, the AAC based on that crucial silviculture investment remained unchanged.[132]

As budget cuts lead increasingly to voluntary measures and industry self-regulation, the climate is ripe for a new method of assuring that forest practices are sustainable—voluntary eco-labeling, or certification. In fact, the Ontario Forest Sustainability Act actually references a forest-certification scheme currently under development as an aspect of forest regulation.

Certification

Pressure to develop forest certification has come from a number of trends. As noted, budget cuts and the lack of political will to impose regulation have increased interest in voluntary approaches, not just in forestry, but in all areas of Canadian environmental policy. Pollution regulation, for example, is threatened as companies make the pitch that "regulations don't work." Industries like to argue that they respond better to carrots than to sticks. But historical evidence for these claims is scant. Certainly the record on pulp-and-paper effluent in Canada makes an excellent case for "command and control." Without regulations, tons of toxic effluent would still be entering Canada's waterways, while voluntary guidelines would be ignored.

Coupled with the overriding pressure to devolve federal responsibilities to the provinces, reduced regulatory "burdens" have become an extremely popular political rallying cry. As Ontario's former Minister of Environment, Brenda Elliott, put it recently when explaining why she did not believe in further efforts to reduce health threats from smog, "We were elected to get government out of your face."[133]

In addition, another factor has heavily influenced the push for voluntary certification schemes in the forest industry. Given the serious threats to trade in Canadian forest products resulting from bad publicity—media reports of poor logging practices and widespread clear-cutting—the forest industry wants a way to circumvent consumer boycotts. Environmental campaigns in Europe and the United States have already succeeded in drying up markets for some Canadian forest companies. German newspapers and California telephone books are just two of the end-products for which non-Clayoquot Sound pulp was demanded. Recent Cree campaigns in Europe have extended the notoriety and potential green-market impact of Canadian forest practices. Clear-cutting Canada's forests increasingly creates an economic threat to the industry's markets.

The response from industry has been to fund a major process under the direction of the Canadian Standards Association (CSA). The CSA is a national standards-writing body which has, for over seventy-five years, been responsible for developing technical standards for everything from toasters to televisions. The CSA is, in turn, linked to the international standards-setting body, the International Standards Organization (ISO). With over a million dollars in funding from the forest industry, the CSA began what was advertised as a multi-stakeholder consensus-based process to develop standards for certifying sustainable forest management.

The difference between setting safety standards for toasters and sustainability standards for forestry should have given CSA pause. It more or less stumbled into an area for which they had no professional competence and less political sensitivity. But, based on what had seemed a successful formula for standards of consistent quality, the ISO 9000 series, the CSA approached the quagmire of forest certification with misplaced confidence.

Early in the process, the CSA managed to alienate most of the environmental and aboriginal communities.[134] But it persevered, and developed a systems-based approach similar to the ISO 9000 approach. The ISO 9000 series allowed companies certification for adopting a management system rather than for any particular outcome. While it was readily endorsed by industry, critics pointed out that, under ISO 9000, if you make a lousy widget, you could be quality-certified as long as your widget is consistently lousy.

Internationally, the ISO was also turning its attention to environmental standards. The CSA not only was developing a certification scheme for Canada, but also hoped to present it to the ISO as a model for forest certification around the world.

Like the ISO 9000 approach, the CSA sustainable-forest certification would accredit companies committed to a management system.[135] Actual forest products would not be labeled. Instead, the corporation doing the logging would receive certification for the adoption of a systems-based process. In each instance, the forest company would develop its system with reference to a set of criteria endorsed by the Canadian forest ministers, through the federal and provincial Canadian Council of Forest Ministers (CCFM), as well as to the recommendations received from the public through a company-led consultation effort.[136] It would remain the exclusive decision of the company forest manager to develop the recommendations for sustainable forest management. If he or she decided that goals of preserving biodiversity were best met through clear-cutting and herbiciding, then those practices would be part of the Sustainable Forest Management System, certified by the CSA. CSA boosters like to point out that the system is a mixture of systems- and performance-based approaches. Once the forest management system is in place and CSA-certified, there would be independent audits every few years to ensure that the certification terms were being met. This is a growth industry for independent audit firms. Price Waterhouse, the people who reliably tallied the votes for Miss America, are currently hiring forest technicians in order to conduct assessments across Canada. But the auditors will be assessing only whether the company did what it said it would do in its plans. Hypothetically, if a CSA certification was based on clear-cuts, and the company subsequently shifted to an ecosystem-based approach, they could lose the Sustainable Forest Management Certification.

As the CSA process started to generate public debate about forest eco-labeling, another approach to forest certification was receiving increased attention in Canada. The Forest Stewardship Council (FSC) was started internationally by the World Wildlife Fund and other environmental groups in 1993. Despite the key role played by environmental groups, the council was always structured to include corporate and economic interests as well as aboriginal and other social concerns. The FSC used many of the same words as the CSA, but had a completely different approach. The FSC certifies products from a specific forest area, based on the ecological acceptability of practices on the ground. The FSC certifies the certifier, who is then allowed to use the FSC name to attest that practices in a particular area meet FSC international standards. It is a performance-based, rather than systems-based, approach. The FSC met with early success through the strong participation of a group of retailers in Britain. Many of Britain's largest stores, including the do-it-yourself home-supply stores, committed to using only FSC-certified wood by the year 2000. The market for FSC products was immediately guaranteed, at four billion pounds a year. But finding enough certified wood to meet this market demand could prove difficult.

The FSC process has taken off in Canada. On the ground, ecosystem-specific indicators to match the vague international principles of the FSC are under development for British Columbia, Ontario and in Atlantic Canada for the Acadian forest region. At every stage, the FSC process involves the environmental, aboriginal, economic, and social sectors. Large industrial forest companies, such as Al-Pac and MacMillan Bloedel, are also at the table, participating as observers. If the FSC becomes the only route to large markets, smart forest companies don't want to be left outside looking in.

It may well be confusing for the consuming public, both in Canada and in the United States and Europe, when Canadian products are available under two different certification schemes. While it is still possible that the CSA and the FSC in Canada will find some route to coordinated or complementary application, the risk is that the larger industrial companies will embrace CSA certification, while wood products from the smaller and more ecologically minded forest operators will carry the FSC logo.

A further complicating factor is the possibility that voluntary eco-labeling will be restricted through decisions at the World Trade Organization (WTO). The WTO is the most recently created international powerhouse. Depending on the ongoing erosion of the influence of the United Nations, it is quite likely that the WTO will become the most powerful organization in the world. The WTO was created to provide an organizational home for the General Agreement on Tariffs and Trade (GATT). The GATT rules are the most extensive codification of the laws of trade liberalization and globalization. They have been called a Bill of Rights for Transnational Corporations. Based in Geneva, the WTO has been examining whether certain environmental measures constitute unlawful barriers to the free flow of goods. The issue of whether voluntary eco-labeling violates the GATT has been the subject of much discussion within the WTO Trade and Environment Committee. The idea that labeling produce as "certified organic," or forest products as "sustainably harvested," could violate international trade agreements would certainly surprise most citizens. But governments have expressed frustration in international fora over their inability to control consumer boycotts. Pressures from non-legislated political actions threaten the essence of GATT rules. The most recent round of GATT negotiations, the Uruguay Round, included an Agreement on Technical Barriers to Trade. This agreement actually dealt with voluntary certification schemes. The member governments have committed to use "their best endeavors" to ensure that such voluntary labeling is "WTO-compatible" and adheres to principles developed by the ISO.[137] Thus, the ISO has the inside track to WTO acceptability. It remains possible that the ISO, which has received recognition from the GATT, may ultimately be recognized as the only legitimate source of voluntary eco-labeling standards. Should this occur, then even voluntary consumer efforts to obtain environmentally sustainable forest products will be undermined.

Although certification schemes may be attractive to the forest companies as a way to forestall regulation, their primary benefit to the industry is in securing export markets. Trade in Canadian forest products is bound to be under increasing pressure from environmental campaigns, as wood shortages force the logging of increasingly remote and valuable wilderness. As well, Canadian forest exports are nearly always in conflict with competitors. As years of trade disputes with the United States should have taught Canadian business by now, the Americans will do everything possible to protect domestic loggers from Canadian subsidies.

II

WHAT WAS ONCE A
LAND OF TREES...

Introduction to Part II

Four centuries ago, when Europeans first set foot on Canada's shores, forests spanned its entire huge territory. Since then the forest has been substantially diminished through settlement, agriculture, urbanization, and industrial expansion; not only the size of Canada's forest, but also its biological characteristics have been altered. Species have been lost; forest ecosystems have been impoverished; what was complex and magnificent has been reduced to something far less diverse.

The process of change has been slow in human terms, but extremely rapid in geological, or even biological, ones. Forests are constantly shifting, never static. In the language of forest ecologists, "succession" is the advance of forest; "disturbance" reverses the movement toward a climax state. In the absence of major human disturbances, the forest composition, age, and structure rolled and shifted over time. What several human generations can do to a forest may fall within the span of life of a single long-lived tree. It is in understanding the pace of human interference with the forest and the pattern of historical settlement that we can comprehend why forest disputes are so intense in British Columbia, whereas environmentalists in Atlantic Canada are more likely to be concerned about controlling logging practices than about stopping logging.

Simply put, other than fragments of original stands found along steep ravines and along valley bottoms, there is almost nothing of Atlantic Canada's pristine pre-contact forest left to save. Where New Brunswick environmentalists battled to preserve the roughly five thousand hectares of the province's largest remaining unlogged forest in the Christmas Mountains, British Columbia activists struggle to protect intact watersheds of 250,000 hectares. Most of the forests of the Atlantic provinces have seen hundreds of years of logging, whereas virtually all of the temperate old-growth forest of coastal British Columbia is being logged for the first time.

When the economic exploitation of the forests is tracked from east to west, a consistent pattern emerges. Not only in biological terms, but in strictly economic ones, we wipe out our most valuable species, and then move on to the ones we considered worthless at the first cut. In the fishery, we moved down the food chain as we wiped out more valuable species, but the time frame has been briefer. Newfoundlanders recall the days of giant cod, redfish, American plaice and haddock, even as they listen to promotion efforts highlighting the potential in harvesting sea urchins now that the fish are gone. But the changes wrought on the forests cannot be experienced by the human observer. No one currently alive in Atlantic Canada ever actually participated in the building of the great tall ships. Those trees now live only in our imagination.

To know what we once had and what we've lost, we would need to ask a tree.

8

Atlantic Provinces

NEWFOUNDLAND

The forests of Newfoundland are a study in contrasts. The province boasts a large expanse of never-logged forest in Labrador, while the island of Newfoundland has been subject to logging since 1550. It has now been so heavily logged that it is the first province to report officially that it is running out of wood.[1]

Newfoundland was also the first place in Canada to experience extinctions. The aboriginal people of Newfoundland, the Beothuk, were the only First Nation in

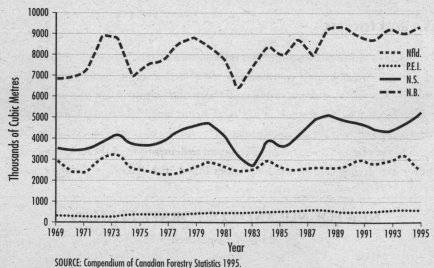

Provincial Comparison of Harvested Roundwood – Atlantic

SOURCE: Compendium of Canadian Forestry Statistics 1995.

Canada to be totally annihilated by the onslaught of Europeans. The great auk, a flightless bird of the sea bird rookeries off Newfoundland's coast, was exterminated for its eggs, feathers and flesh.[2] Gone also are the Newfoundland wolf and the Labrador duck. And Newfoundland was the first place in Canada to convert forest land into permanent barrens. Some areas, particularly on the Avalon Peninsula, have never regenerated after logging. This is a relatively rare phenomenon in Canada, although not unknown. For example, the Magdalen Islands in Quebec have been deforested through logging. And large areas of Newfoundland's forests have been replaced with kalmia heaths or barrens. Kalmia (*Kalmia angustifolia*), commonly called "sheep laurel," currently covers 25 percent of eastern Newfoundland, with most of that considered to be post-logging "unnatural" kalmia, replacing the boreal forest.[3] The few trees still found on these windswept heaths are of the stunted variety referred to as "krummholz" from the German words for "crooked wood."

This litany of extinctions is not meant to suggest that there is any particular anti-conservation animus within the heart of Newfoundlanders. But it was the place where European exploitation of Canada began in the 1500s, and the settlers have had a lot more time to damage their surroundings.

As one of Newfoundland's many Royal Commissions on Forestry reported in 1955:

> One of the outstanding traits of the Anglo-Saxon race has always been its disregard of forests, both direct and indirect. The progress of the settlement of North America has been a story of forest destruction, wanton devastation by fire and heedless exploitation with no thought of the morrow.[4]

Fish and forests

What strikes a visitor to Newfoundland is the intimate connection between its people and the sea. Small fishing communities cling to the rocky shore like tenacious barnacles. The fishery was everything to the heart and culture of this province.

Even forestry in Newfoundland was ruled by the sea. The forests within five kilometers (three miles) of the coast were reserved for the use of fishing communities. Trees were used for wharves, docks, boat building and settlements. Even the bark was used to lay over the drying fish on the long tables called "fish flakes" in the days before

---

NEWFOUNDLAND CORPORATE PLAYERS

Abitibi-Consolidated
Kruger

---

refrigeration. This common-property approach to the coastal forests led to some serious overharvesting in areas where population pressures were high.[5] Even so, the so-called three-mile-limit lands were judged to have a desirable amount of the quality spruce and fir required by the industry. In 1979, the three-mile-limit was abolished.

Meanwhile, the granting of large leases and outright land giveaways over Newfoundland's forests rivals anything anywhere in the world.

Giving away Newfoundland's forests

The first big company to benefit from a large land grant was the Reid Newfoundland Company in 1897. Reid had built the cross-province railroad and was granted ownership of vast areas of the island's forest in exchange. Reid was given more than 150 lots across the province, some as large as 259 square kilometers. Over the years, the company sold its forested land to the first pulp-mill builders in the province, Bowater and Price.[6]

In 1905, the first large timber lease was approved by the province's legislature. It granted the Anglo-Newfoundland Development Company a ninety-nine-year lease for 5,180 square kilometers (52 million hectares). The lease conveyed not only rights to

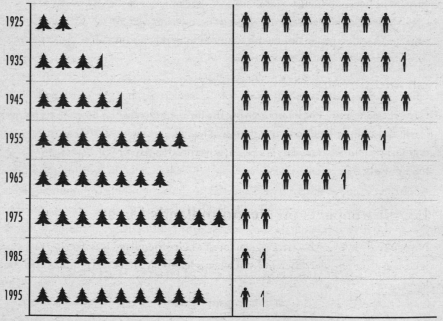

Newfoundland: Logging and Jobs

Pulpwood Cut (× 100,000 cords)   Loggers Employed (× 1000 people)

SOURCE: Forest Alliance.

timber, but water and mineral rights as well. The inalienable private right to build dams and use hydropower was also granted. All of this was for the astonishingly low compensation of $2 per square mile (2.6 km^2) per year (or less than a third of a cent an acre), with a royalty of fifty cents per thousand board feet of lumber produced.[7] Pulpwood was subject to neither stumpage nor royalties based on production. With such extremely attractive arrangements, a newsprint mill was built in Grand Falls by 1909, where it remains in production to this day.

Between 1875 and 1946 another form of contractual arrangement between the province and its forest companies was developed. Under these timber licenses, exclusive rights to minerals, water and timber were granted for an area of over eighteen million acres (7.3 million hectares). The same terms applied as in the 1905 timber-lease arrangements—minimal royalty charges for lumber, less than a third of a penny an acre in "rent," and no stumpage at all for pulp; and all conveyed for a ninety-nine-year period.

Even more remarkable is that the terms of the lease and licenses still apply! The two companies currently operating Newfoundland's three pulp mills enjoy all the favorable terms of the 1905 lease. Kruger operates the pulp mill in Corner Brook, obtaining 90 percent of its electricity free of charge from its own hydroelectric facility as part of its leased water rights. It can even sell its surplus power back to the provincial utility! It is now proposing an extension of its hydroelectric dam capacity—with impacts into the watershed of Gros Morne National Park. Kruger is also exempt from most forms of taxation.

Newfoundland is the only province with zero stumpage for trees from its licensed lands.[8] Even the rent has not increased to reflect inflation. Current charges amount to 77 cents per square kilometer ($2/square mile).

Sawmill owners and independent pulpwood producers cutting on unalienated Crown land, that is, Crown land not within a timber lease, pay stumpage, although the fee is still quite low.[9] The habit of giving the large multinationals generous terms, long leases and a bigger break on costs than smaller local operators ever see is also part of a national pattern. It seems that Canadian governments just cannot do enough for large foreign-owned forest companies.

Logging impacts on Newfoundland's forest

No one really knows what the original forest of Newfoundland was like, but one thing is certain—it was quite different from what is left today after several hundred years of logging.

Newfoundland and Labrador constitute the farthest eastern regions of the Canadian boreal. While black spruce and balsam fir currently predominate, there would have been greater species diversity in the primeval forest. A mid-1800s account of touring the Bay of Islands area related: "One feature of this locality, and of the whole Bay of Islands, is the predominance and luxuriance of deciduous timber. Birch, Beech, Poplar, and Ash in many places quite take the place of the Spruce and Fir, and lofty Pines over top of the other trees."[10]

According to historical data, white pine probably made up 7 to 10 percent of Newfoundland's coniferous forest. These trees likely were "over top," as the pine are recorded at heights of more than seventy feet (21 m). The balsam fir and spruce would have been just fine crowning under the pines, both because fir and spruce are shade-tolerant species and because the white pine would have been scattered throughout the forest.

The "lofty pines" are a thing of the past. Between 1875 and 1925, it is estimated that six million board feet of white pine were logged and processed *every year* in Newfoundland. Astonishing production levels in pine were achieved more than a hundred years ago, with 11.4 million board feet produced by fifty-five mills in 1884, and a staggering 45.2 million board feet in 1910 by a prodigious 347 mills.[11]

Very little remains of the "pine-clad hills" that are celebrated in Newfoundland's provincial song. One of the last reserves, the Serpentine Valley, previously slated for protected area status, was recently opened up to mineral and hydrocarbon exploration.

Other disturbances have shifted the natural forest balance. By the 1930s, the province began an active program of fire suppression, which had the effect of maintaining certain species and shifting regeneration patterns. As well, various non-native species have had their impact on the forest. The introduction of snowshoe hare and moose, neither indigenous to the island, caused a shift in the forest understory, as these browsers have different eating habits than the native caribou. So too have non-native diseases posed threats to the forest. The white pine blister rust made its way to Newfoundland from England, worsening the pine's chances of survival.

Historically, Newfoundland logging required very few roads. In the winter months, tractors or horses would pull logs over the snow to wait on the frozen ice of a nearby river for spring. A network of railroads was also used. While driving logs down rivers was not environmentally appropriate, the type of damage shifted when Newfoundland began using the line skidder, a logging machine that could work year round. Damage to the soil and the surrounding ecosystem was certainly increased by the shift from river and rail to road. Logging roads erode soil.[12] It is increasingly accepted that logging roads do substantial long-term damage to the ecosystem, not only because of the immediate damage but also from the opening of wilderness to hunters, anglers and other traffic.

While Newfoundland's boreal remains primarily a spruce/fir forest, within that composition the relative proportion of black spruce has declined through clear-cut logging. Tracking the reduction of black spruce is difficult, as the province's forest service lumps these together and indicates densities only for species with volumes exceeding 25 percent. But regeneration surveys show a worrying decrease in black spruce after logging, reflecting the greater ability of balsam fir to regrow after a logging disturbance. "Regeneration failure is a problem on black spruce cut-over sites," reported a government survey. Only 31.9 percent of logged-over black spruce areas were adequately recovering in black spruce.[13]

NSR (not satisfactorily restocked) lands, where commercially valuable trees have not regrown after logging, are generally priority areas for replanting. Nationally, 2.5 million hectares are in this category.[14] Currently, Newfoundland has a particularly high percentage in NSR lands—22 percent of its logged Crown lands.[15]

Within this degraded forest ecosystem, wildlife is diminished as well. The logging pressures of recent years have all but eliminated old-growth forest on the Island of Newfoundland: of all the remaining forest, only 5 percent is in old growth. The fur-bearing forest mammal the pine marten, which depends on old-growth forest for habitat, was added to the national endangered-species list in 1996, in the most critical category for species in peril. There are fewer than three hundred individual animals of this Newfoundland species left.

The pine marten's survival is affected in virtually every province as old-growth forest is removed and replaced with younger, "more productive" forest. As wood-supply shortfalls loom, the rotations between harvests become shorter. Long before the fertile stage at which the forest is richly layered with dead standing trees ("snags"), decaying logs, and old living members of the plant world, loggers arrive and remove everything, eliminating the cavities in the old-growth forest that are essential to the marten. Windfalls in old-growth forest are particularly important in providing shelter and food in deep-snow conditions. Unfortunately, Newfoundland's forests are logged by clear-cutting only. The marten, it seems, will go the way of the Newfoundland wolf and the great auk.[16]

The province has adopted the Endangered Spaces target, but since only a very small proportion of its forest is within protected areas, the promise of protection is an empty one.

While forest management guidelines have been established to minimize logging damage to the endangered pine marten habitat, these "suggestions" have not been heeded by the large pulp-and-paper companies. In fact, of the very few places considered as possible sites for protection of marten habitat, many are now slated for logging.[17] The clear-cut logging of critical habitat of a species on the national endangered-species list by Corner Brook Pulp and Paper (a division of Kruger) has provoked no reaction from the federal or the provincial governments. At the time of this writing, there is no endangered-species legislation in force, in Newfoundland or Canada.[18]

NEWFOUNDLAND	(1995)
Forest Land in million hectares	22.5
Stocked Harvested Crown Land in hectares	255,000
Area Logged in hectares	19,731
Volume Logged in million cubic meters	2.2
Annual Allowable Cut in million cubic meters	3.0

SOURCE: Natural Resources Canada, Canadian Forest Service, *The State of Canada's Forests, 1996-1997* (Ottawa, 1997). These are federal government summaries, based on provincial government data. The figures are not necessarily accurate.

Current timber shortages have also led to logging in critical salmon habitat previously considered off limits. Many watersheds, especially in western Newfoundland, such as the Upper Humber, Main River and Robinson's River, are being logged near sensitive spawning grounds for Atlantic salmon. Forest-dwelling species are also in decline, including the brown bat and the muskrat.

Unfortunately, provincial forest departments tend to focus exclusively on the issue of supplying timber to the mills. There has been little research about terrestrial biodiversity in Newfoundland, which is clearly threatened, but even the threat to the wood supply appears likely to be ignored until it is too late. The excruciatingly slow process of convincing several levels of government that an essential resource is being exploited to extinction seems fated to be played out again, just as it was with the troubled cod fishery.

When does Newfoundland run out of wood?

The provincial inventory includes the over-cut forest of the island of Newfoundland as well as the virtually unlogged forests of Labrador. The lumping together of the wood supply from these different forests, separated by a brief ocean crossing, and the corresponding calculation of an AAC (annual allowable cut) based on the composite forest can be quite misleading. In reviewing the current wood-supply crisis in Newfoundland, it is important to keep the Labrador situation separate from that on the Island.

Including the forests of Labrador in the AAC figure creates a comforting illusion of surplus. In fact, Labrador's forests have always been commercially undesirable. They are physically remote. An early 1980s estimate put the cost of Labrador pulpwood delivered to the island's pulp mills at $102.60 a cord, with local wood at $47.19 a cord, and wood from Prince Edward Island, far more distant but with better marine transportation links, at $64.02 a cord.[19] Moreover, the trees of Labrador have traditionally been described as a lichen forest, of very small conifers, growing very slowly. Only the desperate could see them as a likely wood supply.

Thus, while the national forest database reports that the province has 22.5 million hectares of forest land,[20] the relevant information is the 5 million hectares considered forest on the island of Newfoundland. Of that 5 million hectares only 57 percent, or 2.8 million hectares, is considered productive.[21] It is from this land base that three pulp mills, 1,800 small sawmills and untold numbers of firewood gatherers have removed far more wood than the ecosystem can spare.

The three pulp mills on the island of Newfoundland are unable, at this moment and well into the future, to find adequate wood supply within the companies' enormous leases, or even with the addition of the rest of the island's forest. The dire shortages on the island of Newfoundland are compelling Abitibi-Price to plan the clear-cutting of remote northern Labrador.

The forest companies control the majority of the productive forest on insular Newfoundland—63 percent or 1.77 million hectares.[22] The land controlled by Kruger and Abitibi, through a patchwork of large licenses, smaller leases and industrial freehold, is the province's most productive forest. The 35 percent of unalienated Crown land is generally found in the coastal regions, where forests do not achieve the volumes of more protected inland areas.

As late as 1980, it was believed that the huge areas controlled by the mills would never be fully exploited. In that year, John Gray, author of one of the few books on Newfoundland's forests, *The Trees Behind the Shore*, wrote:

> The zero stumpage charges on pulpwood and the token charges on lumber produced created problems . . . With virtually no revenue from the forest, the government had little incentive to engage in forest management, as the financial benefits would go to the companies. On the other hand, there is little incentive for the companies to engage in forest management, since they already have a sufficient or excess timber supply.[23]

Yet by 1992 the Newfoundland government was struggling to come to terms with an immediate wood shortage. For the first time, the province undertook a twenty-year forestry-planning exercise, reviewing the inventory and re-examining the assumptions that went into the AAC. The central reality was alarming: the requirements of the mills and other local users outstripped what was available. Even increasing the AAC by crediting future speculative growth based on intensive silviculture did not erase shortfalls on insular Newfoundland. According to the most recent provincial Forest Development Plan, demand for wood on the island is 27 percent above supply.[24]

In fact, even that dire news probably underestimated the extent of the shortages. The figure was based on requirements of the three pulp-and-paper mills, sawmills, fuel wood for industrial chips and the cutting of domestic firewood on Crown lands. Newfoundland's forests are the only ones in Canada where logging pressure for domestic firewood is actually a significant factor. Fuel wood and firewood logging combined come to an estimated 964,000 cubic meters a year, far less than the two-million-plus cubic meters required for pulp, but still a substantial amount.[25] This fuel-wood figure includes wood chips used to heat hospitals and other industrial fuel uses, but a large component is firewood for private homes. The Poole Royal Commission estimated that there is probably an equivalent amount of firewood cut from Crown land without permits, unreported. Even the national park at Gros Morne is not off limits to legal domestic fuel-wood logging.

There is no doubt that Abitibi-Price woodlands have the biggest problem. The Kruger company, which now operates what was the Bowater pulp mill, totally dominating the city of Corner Brook, claims a small surplus within its license. It continues to benefit from the 1905 lease conditions, giving it free of charge 90 percent of all its energy requirements from its own hydroelectric station, while also being exempt from most forms of taxation.

Abitibi-Price, on the other hand, with mills in Grand Falls and Stephenville, has only 64 percent of its total wood requirements, and is looking to purchase more wood from the unalienated Crown land. But those lands are already in a worse shortage position than Abitibi. Based on reported users, the Crown lands have a 38 percent deficit of demand above supply.[26]

How did the island so overexploit its forests that it can now maintain its mills only through off-island imports?

Part of the problem may stem from overgenerous terms, even by Newfoundland standards, for the sale of the Stephenville mill to Abitibi. Abitibi already owned the province's oldest mill, at Grand Falls, built in 1909. In 1978 it opened negotiations with the province to purchase a second mill in Stephenville: the Labrador linerboard mill. The deal, like all timber licenses in Newfoundland, included exclusive logging rights, as well as all mineral and water rights. The terms of the lease suggest that, despite a requirement to manage the lands on a "sustained yield basis," it is Abitibi-Price's exclusive prerogative to decide how much it will over-cut.[27]

The only concession to the twentieth century was the inclusion of stumpage rates for pulp, on a scale from 85 cents to $3 per cubic meter.[28] But the company is entitled to rebates for any silviculture operations on its leased land approved by the province. The government is also committed to assisting in the building of primary roads and bridges.

The problem seems to have been that no one checked the timber supply before guaranteeing Abitibi over one million cubic meters a year from the forests. The story goes that, the day after concluding the agreement to sell the Labrador linerboard mill and its timber lease to Abitibi-Price, the government called in its foresters and told them to find the wood to keep the mill going for twenty years. While such colorful rumors are hard to prove, the story fits. The 1970 Royal Commission, one of four commissions and task forces that have reported between 1955 and 1973, expressed concern that, with a possible new mill at Stephenville, the wood supply should be carefully re-examined. In particular, it pointed to potential weaknesses in the inventory and growth data.[29]

There were good reasons to be concerned. Unfortunately, the problems with the inventory persist. In calculating the amount of wood on the island, unwarranted assumptions were made throughout. Even the confirmation of wood shortages in the *20 Year Forestry Development Plan 1990–2009*, was based on wildly optimistic premises. For instance, the inventory analysis predicted the volume of a fifty-five-year-old stand of regenerated forest, after one thinning, at an unrealistic 300 cubic meters per hectare. The volume in particularly productive natural forests is actually 190–210 cubic meters per hectare.[30] The future wood supply was also based on the assumption that damage by fire and insects will never be above "salvageable levels." A wood-supply analysis that assumes 100 percent effectiveness in its fire-suppression and insecticide program is assuming the impossible.

More magical attributes were implicit in the wood-supply analysis. The working rule on regrowth was that "there was no regeneration time lag for any regenerating stand."[31] This assumption requires the forest to recover from clear-cutting with almost miraculous speed. But in fact, Newfoundland has a particularly high percentage in NSR (not satisfactorily restocked) lands—22 percent of its logged Crown lands.[32]

Another working assumption, to improve the overall bright picture, was that 90 percent of the best forest would be available for harvest. As bulldozers for road building and skid trails have been calculated to take out 10 percent of the land base in Newfoundland logging operations, this assumption leaves absolutely no room for buffer zones around streams, nor for any other impediment to total clear-cutting.[33]

Still, despite these and other unrealistically optimistic assumptions, the Newfoundland forest service admits it is in a wood-supply crisis. Logging pressure has increased dramatically in the last forty years. In 1955 approximately 1.6 million cubic meters were logged.[34] Now the annual allowable cut is twice as high, at 3 million cubic meters. In fact, the rate of cut has actually increased since the province determined it was in a deficit situation. Kruger's plant at Corner Brook retooled in January 1996 in order to increase the output from one paper machine.

In the most recent of the government's forest development plans, still in draft, it is acknowledged that:

Demand, defined as desire for timber, currently exceeds supply by 27% for the Island (industry and Crown lands). Actual timber consumption, controlled through limiting the allocation, is estimated at 12% greater than the 1995 AAC.[35]

Meanwhile, Abitibi-Price has set its sights on the forests of Labrador. With a notional AAC of 600,000 cubic meters, an adequate state of desperation exists to plan for clear-cut logging of even the marginal forests edging up to the tree line.

The Innu struggle in Labrador

As Newfoundland's forests are exhausted, the greedy have turned their eyes to the tiny northern trees of Labrador. Abitibi-Price has plans to clear-cut Labrador forest land that lies within the land claim of the Innu Nation.

In Labrador, which is politically part of Newfoundland but geographically an extension of Quebec, two First Nations live—the more southerly Innu, and, toward the Arctic, the Inuit. The Innu have been occupiers of Nitassinan, "our land" in the Innu language, for at least two thousand years. It is one of the last large roadless areas on earth.

The Innu people are dependent on the huge caribou herds that thunder across the rugged wilderness like a pulsating river of fur and hooves. The Innu also hunt geese and fish the clear streams. But all of that is under assault from an intimidating invasion of military and industrial developments.

The Innu have been subjected to low-flying fighter-bomber training from the former U.S. army base at Goose Bay. Every year, fifteen thousand ear-shattering low flights take place in training exercises for the British, Dutch, German, French, Italian and Belgian bomber forces. Innu protests, arrests on airstrips, and complaints that the flights are ruining their traditional life in the bush have been to no avail.

Now Labrador is the site of one of the richest mineral-deposit finds in history, and governments are doing whatever is necessary to abridge the proper environmental hearing process so the riches of Voisey's Bay can move from the ground into bank accounts around the world.

In an atmosphere of rampant resource extraction and violation of the traditional rights of the aboriginal people of Newfoundland, the Innu asked Herb Hammond, a nationally respected ecological forester from British Columbia, to assess the wood supply in Labrador and Abitibi-Price's logging plans. His report confirmed that clear-cut logging was completely inappropriate for the fragile and slow-growing forest of Labrador. The forests of Labrador are at the far northern reaches of the boreal. Essentially a lichen forest of small trees on fragile soils, it would never be considered commercially viable if not for the desperation engendered by wood shortages to the south. Moreover, Abitibi-Price's logging plans were for heavily mechanized, low-labor clear-cutting. Hammond doubted that, once clear-cut, such a forest would be capable of recovery at all. The Innu have in the past blockaded clear-cutting near Goose Bay. They demanded an environmental assessment and resolution of their land claims before Abitibi-Price is given the go-ahead.

In December 1993, the provincial Environment Minister registered the proposed logging plans for one-third of what Abitibi-Price ultimately plans to log in Labrador for a "mini-assessment." The process is to develop an "adaptive management" strategy, which the Innu and island environmentalists believe will be too little too late once clear-cutting is approved. In April 1995, members of the Innu Nation asked the Environmental Assessment Committee's chair why a full environmental-assessment process, including a complete environmental impact statement (EIS), had not been required. The chair replied, "If an EIS had been required, it would have been exempted by cabinet. With the pressure from Interwood and Labrador Forest Resources [two industrial logging firms planning to set up operations in Nitassinan], we had to try a new approach or end up with nothing."[36]

In response, Innu Nation Environmental Advisor Larry Innes pointed out: "In resilient and contextually-limited situations, adaptive management may be a useful approach. But Nitassinan forests are neither. There is very little room for 'error' in a fragile, climate limited forest, and it is the Innu who will have to live with the mistakes. The proposed management plan contains no provisions which would suggest that adaptive management is anything other than 'business as usual': it outlines an aggressive road building program and slates 500,000 cubic meters for cutting in the first five years of the plan. At this rate, by the time Forestry 'adapts,' there will be nothing left to 'manage.'"[37]

With an inadequate wood supply on the island, current forest plans are dependent on opening up Labrador. The Innu continue to block the logging of the remote northern forests of Labrador.

Public relations versus wood shortages

In the face of the forest crisis in Newfoundland, politicians maintain that the situation is under control. A February 1, 1996, news release from the Premier's office expressed buoyant optimism. Newly elected Premier Brian Tobin announced $41.7 million in new silviculture investments, primarily from federal and provincial government sources. Although the release conceded that the estimated wood-supply deficit would hold at 25 percent (500,000 cubic meters per year) for the next ten to fifteen years, the announcement created the impression that pumping new money into the forests would somehow avert the crisis.

"The $41.7 million worth of initiatives announced here today will significantly address the major issue facing the forest sector which is the availability and security of short-term wood supplies," said Premier Tobin. "Today's announcements will secure current jobs in the forest industry and create new ones in the process, which is exactly what the new Liberal Government is all about."

Previous federal-provincial silviculture investments had not prevented a wood-supply crisis. In fact, between 1974 and 1992, $180 million had been spent in Newfoundland through the federal-provincial Forest Development Agreements—a direct subsidy to an industry that was, for the most part, not even paying stumpage.[38] These figures do not include loans made available from another federal pocket, the Atlantic Canada Opportunities Agency (ACOA), for assistance to companies wanting to buy feller-bunchers to reduce the workforce.

No amount of press releases and silviculture subsidies can create forests. The threats to jobs and "security of short-term wood supply" are from over-cutting, building too many mills, and using logging methods that create large areas where nothing grows back. So long as industry and government use terms like "the wood supply is tight," when they mean "we've run out of wood for our mills"; so long as they excuse present over-cutting on the false premise of increased growth through future intensive silviculture, Newfoundland is destined to be a land of no fish and no forests.

NOVA SCOTIA

Nova Scotia is a province of gentle pastoral valleys, breathtaking ocean views and forests that are a pale reflection of their former glory. Its forests were part of the Acadian forest ecoregion, encompassing the original forests of Nova Scotia, Prince Edward Island and New Brunswick. Agricultural land clearing coupled with the impact of imported browsing deer led to massive species conversion, while centuries of high-grading (taking the most valuable and preferred trees) led to a steady erosion in the quality of the forest. In much of Nova Scotia, one would be hard pressed to distinguish the spruce-fir softwood forests from those of the boreal.

The first trees felled by Europeans were used to construct the fort at Port Royal in 1605. Early settlers described a forest where hemlock, white pine and northern hardwood predominated; elms, oak and ash were common in the deciduous forest.

According to historical accounts, the northern plateau of Cape Breton was boreal forest, spruce and fir, while along the lowlands, coastal areas and river valleys a luxuriant mixed-wood forest provided timber for shipbuilding and masts. By the early 1700s,

NOVA SCOTIA	(1994)
Forest Land in million hectares	3.9
Stocked Harvested Crown Land in hectares	170,000 (1995)
Area Logged in hectares	49,968
Volume Logged in million cubic meters	5.2
Annual Allowable Cut in million cubic meters	5.3

SOURCE: Natural Resources Canada, Canadian Forest Service, *The State of Canada's Forests, 1996-1997* (Ottawa, 1997). These are federal government summaries, based on provincial government data. The figures are not necessarily accurate.

sawmills in Cape Breton were supplying timbers for the construction of the walled city of Louisbourg, built with no expense spared by King Louis XVI. Logging and the clearing of land for settlement and agriculture were removing the highest-quality species from within the forest.

Nova Scotia was the first province to take a scientific interest in estimating the amount of timber available in its territory. An inventory was undertaken in 1801 by Titus Smith, who was known as Nova Scotia's "first scientific naturalist."[1] His work, which is chiefly a description of the forests, would hardly be called an inventory by today's standards.

"Forests grow and are grown to be cut to furnish valuable material to man." So wrote Bernard Fernow in 1909. The Lumberman's Association of Western Nova Scotia had persuaded the government to undertake "a forest reconnaissance of the Province."[2] To do so, the province recruited, for the munificent sum of two thousand dollars, one from among North America's new league of professional foresters. Bernard Fernow, trained in Germany, had come to North America in 1876; like Gifford Pinchot, he was an advocate of "sustained yield forestry." Although he argued for the preservation of natural forests as a crucial aspect of water conservation, he had a utilitarian view of forest resources, believing that their "influence, climatic and hydraulic, is by no means destroyed or checked by a well-conducted, systematic forestry which utilizes ripe

NOVA SCOTIA CORPORATE PLAYERS

Stora Forest Industries
Kimberly-Clark (Harmac set to purchase)
Bowater Mersey
MacTara

timber, taking care for its immediate regeneration for the continuity of the forest as well as the timber supply."[3]

By 1907, Fernow had become the first dean of the newly established school of forestry at the University of Toronto. He trained virtually all of Canada's early foresters. He was one of the first foresters to believe that old growth was an obstacle to sustained yield, and his legacy remains a powerful force. Fernow realized that the pattern of land ownership in Nova Scotia would make it extremely difficult for the government to influence forest policy. Nova Scotia was an anomaly in the development of forest-land tenure across Canada. In an exception to the rule that Canadian forests are primarily publicly owned as Crown land, Nova Scotia sold off large parts of its public forest land to private companies. By the turn of the century, only 600,000 hectares of Crown forest remained—and it was considered of poor quality and relatively inaccessible.

Turn-of-the-century Nova Scotia politicians looked longingly to New Brunswick, where a lease system covering large tracts of Crown land had been providing forest revenue since the late 1800s. Despite the small amount of remaining Crown land, Nova Scotia changed its Lease Act in 1899 in an attempt to make the most of its public forest resources. The new legislation allowed for the lease of Crown land for twenty-year periods, for a rental fee of sixteen cents per hectare. No stumpage fees were included, and logging was limited to trees at least twenty-five centimeters in diameter.[4]

When Fernow came to survey the forests of Nova Scotia, he was hoping that Nova Scotia's experience would persuade the government of Ontario to begin its own forest inventory, with Fernow at the helm.[5] Fernow's work, while it was broad in intention, zeroed in on key issues of forest degradation: "each year sees changes from virgin into culled, from culled into stripped, from stripped into burnt forest or into new young growth . . ."[6] A decade later, in 1922, the process of species conversion by logging was documented by the provincial entomologist, Dr. J.D. Tothill:

> There has been a great increase of balsam fir in our eastern forests in the past century and especially in the latter part of it. The big pines were the first to go from the forest, and the gaps were filled by spruce and fir, whose seed trees were undisturbed. Then the market demanded spruce and the big spruce were cut, leaving the large fir trees to reproduce. Thus there has gradually resulted a greatly increased percentage of fir in our softwood stands.[7]

At around the same time, the government initiated a review of the impact of the 1899 changes to the Lease Act. Nova Scotia's Chief Forester reviewed the situation and found that, despite the giveaway terms of the lease, leaseholders were generally ignoring the rules against logging immature trees, and that the rent collected was "ridiculously small." In fact, the revenue from Christmas-tree sales in some years surpassed the total rent collected for leasing the Crown forests.[8]

The largest single area of Crown land, the "Big Lease," was on Cape Breton Island. Fernow identified the fir of Cape Breton as ideal for the pulp-and-paper industry in his 1909–10 survey, and the province began the search for a pulp mill. The Big Lease proved to be a gold mine for speculators, some of whom gained more in commissions from buying and reselling the lease than the province earned in rent. After one such speculative trade, in 1917, the original "purchaser" walked away with over a million dollars in profits, and the Oxford Paper Company of New England ended up with the lease.

Portions of the highlands of Cape Breton were logged for the Oxford mill in Rumford, Maine. At the height of the logging in the 1920s, nearly one thousand men were working in the Cape Breton woods, using long saws and axes, and horses to pull logs to the road. The highlands provided nearly half of all the softwood used by the Maine mill, boosting its production. While Oxford held on to the Big Lease in Cape Breton, it also bought forest land throughout Nova Scotia and New Brunswick, as well as a controlling interest in a pulp mill in Fairville, New Brunswick, and the Crown lands that went with it.

Nova Scotia: Where multinationals rule

Early in its history, Nova Scotia sold most of its Crown forest land to private timber interests, and by 1926, the rest of its forests were in the hands of foreign and out-of-province pulp companies. Nova Scotia's Chief Forester, Otto Schierbeck, commented on "the alarming rate at which American pulp and paper producers are buying Nova Scotia freehold land for the export of pulpwood. Over 810,000 hectares of the best timberlands in the Province are in the hands of American pulp and paper companies who have no manufacturing plans in the Province and are only concerned with the export of pulpwood."[9]

As well, a major British firm moved into Nova Scotia. In 1928, the Mersey Paper Company built a pulp mill in Liverpool, Nova Scotia, supplying all of its pulp from lands leased from the Crown on generous stumpage of one dollar per cord as well as promised low power rates. The province began a program of expanding its Crown-land base in the 1930s, trying to rectify the loss of so much forest to large private landowners. At the same time, it negotiated the buy-back of one-third of the Big Lease, the last large chunk of Crown forest land, for the creation of Cape Breton Highlands National Park in 1940, with compensation to the U.S.-based Oxford Paper of nearly

$400,000. But the provincial government grew increasingly unhappy with the bulk of Crown forest lands being tied up by Oxford, which, since closing its small operation in Cape Breton in 1931, had done almost no logging on the lease.

In the mid-1950s, the Conservative government of Robert Stanfield took over a province with a depressed economy. The steel-and-coal industry of Cape Breton was on the ropes, and no pulp mill was yet in place to log the Big Lease. Stanfield's government set its sights on attracting a major Swedish pulp-and-paper company, Stora Kopparberg, to Nova Scotia. To do that, they needed more forest. Since the buy-back effort of the 1930s began, the province had increased Crown-owned forest to nearly one-quarter of the province. But, so long as Oxford Paper Company had the Big Lease, there would not be enough uncommitted forest to attract Stora. Oxford's speculative exploitation of the Cape Breton forests paid off when the provincial government bought Oxford out at rates far above what it had received seventeen years earlier in the park settlement. With seventeen fewer years on the lease, the value of the ownership interest should have gone down, but Oxford received more than twice per acre what they had in 1940, for a total buyout of nearly four million dollars!

Selling out Nova Scotia's forests

Once free of Oxford, the province set about wooing Stora Kopparberg. Stora is the oldest firm in the world, with articles of incorporation dating back to the year 1288. Stora had discussed the Big Lease with the previous provincial government, and Stanfield's government was prepared to offer nearly anything to get it to locate in Nova Scotia.

What they offered was a 405,000-hectare lease over the Crown-owned forest of Cape Breton Island, and the eastern mainland counties of Guysborough, Pictou and Antigonish, coupled with low electricity rates, grants in lieu of taxes, and cut-rate stumpage. In fact, Stora's lease guaranteed stumpage at one dollar per cord—the same rate Mersey had secured thirty years earlier. Research by L.A. Sandberg, published in his book *Trouble in the Woods*, confirmed that Stora would have been willing to pay three times as much if the province had negotiated instead of begged. The province also gave Stora the building site for a mill at the Strait of Canso and paid for the survey work. For all this, Stora did not even commit to building a mill until July 1959, when the firm officially took over its negotiated instrument for doing business in Nova Scotia—Nova Scotia Pulp, a wholly owned subsidiary of Stora.

Attracting Stora to Nova Scotia coincided with the province's first serious effort at an inventory. Between 1953 and 1957, the province undertook a series of aerial photographs of the forests. Data derived from the analysis of these photos and from ground cruising of sample plots were compiled and released in 1958.

The 1958 inventory quoted Fernow's view of the province's forests: "It is now largely in poor condition, and is being annually further deteriorated by abuse and injudicious use, because those owning it are mostly not concerned in its future, or do not realize its potentialities."[10]

The report noted that "Fernow's remarks of 1910 are no less apt in 1958. The forest conditions have deteriorated considerably since, making the 'conservative' and 'recuperative measures' even more imperative now."[11] The 1958 survey found that the proportion of balsam fir had increased, while species prevalent in the 1800s, such as ash and oak, had all but disappeared. The amount of overmature fir forest was a cause for concern, as it provided ideal conditions for the spruce budworm. The inventory also took note that immature forests had been logged, contributing to regeneration problems.

The forestry advice from the 1958 inventory conflicted with the province's political ambitions toward pulp. The inventory was concerned with maintaining the sawlog industry, which had been the mainstay of the provincial forest industry since shipbuilding had ended. It warned that the province was already over-cutting its forests:

> One immediate corrective measure for the present overcutting is a reduction
> in production. It is clear that any such reduction must be applied primarily to
> the sawmill industry. In order that the present inventory be maintained a
> reduction of about fifty percent in saw log harvest is required. If this is not
> accomplished, the growing stock will be reduced in size to material which will
> bring about a pulpwood economy, exclusively. . . . If the pulp industry
> expanded on the basis of the total inventory of pulpwood resources, there
> could be no future sawlog industry.[12]

This was to be the last government report that predicted shortages and recommended less logging. In the new era of industrial forests, the prescription for shortages was to be more intensive management and increased logging.

The political preference for large multinational pulp-and-paper companies over small, locally based sawmills was conspicuous. Pressure from the new corporate clients, Stora and Scott, undermined the province's own foresters, who were advocating long-rotation sawlog forestry. Pulp was soon to rule the roost. As the head of the Halifax Power and Pulp Company put it in 1961, "We see that the forests of Nova Scotia, in general, are destined to become pulpwood producing forests . . ."[13]

Beating the forests to a pulp

By 1962, the production of pulpwood overtook the sawmill industry, beginning the process of closing down small mills and expanding the pulpwood forests.

The sawmill industry had traditionally provided jobs throughout the province. Small family-owned businesses, such as the Prest Brothers Mill in the Musquodoboit River Valley, sold quality hardwood and softwood lumber to markets in the United States, the Caribbean and abroad, as well as providing for local building.

The shift to pulp was brought about by more than market pressure. It was legislated. In 1965, some of the best forests of mainland Nova Scotia were turned over to Scott Paper, based in Philadelphia, through the Scott Maritime Pulp Agreement Act. Under this legislation, Scott was given a lease for 100,000 hectares of the best forest and standing timber in the province. To sweeten the pot, Scott was given a five-year income-tax holiday and a twenty-year tax break on all land owned or leased by the company as well as on its new mill site in Pictou County. The government also kicked in a five-million-dollar donation to Scott's new operation. Scott opened a bleached-kraft pulp-and-paper mill at Abercrombie Point, midway along the mainland's north shore, dumping toxic waste into a Mi'kmaq reserve. As a further concession, Scott's waste-treatment facility was owned and run by the provincial Department of the Environment, all the while dumping twenty-five million U.S. gallons of effluent every day into Boat Harbour.

Murray Prest, owner of the Prest Brothers Mill and active spokesperson for the sawmill industry, rues the day Scott Paper came to Nova Scotia. "We were kind of having a love affair with industry at any cost," recalls Prest. "That's when we started looking for whatever we could give away to business to buy industry. The forest was one of those things."[14]

Concurrent with the Scott Act was legislative "reform" of the forest management legislation. The Stanfield government repealed the Small Tree Act which had banned the logging of immature trees. In its stead, the government brought in the Forest Practices Improvement Act. While the new act was a forward-looking piece of legislation, it was not proclaimed for more than ten years, during which time, in the absence of any law, the field was wide open for clear-cutting small trees. Murray Prest described the results of the Scott Act and the repeal of the Small Tree Act as a "full-scale blitzkrieg—twenty years of the most destructive methods of forest harvesting in Nova Scotia's history."[15]

For Murray Prest and many sawmill owners like him, the shift to clear-cutting to feed the pulp mills spelled the end of an era. Quality trees were lost. Regeneration was compromised, and businesses like his, once prosperous and sustainable, went under.

The provincial government, against the advice of its forestry professionals, embarked on a deliberate program of forest degradation. By design, the forests, already degraded, were to be converted from a source of multiple ecological and economic values, from sawlogs *and* pulp, into virtually exclusive pulp production.

Pulp-and-paper domination

By the early 1970s three major pulp-and-paper companies were established in Nova Scotia—all of them foreign-owned. The largest pulp-and-paper operation, Sweden's Stora, managed to purchase freehold more than twenty thousand hectares of forest land, supplementing the large lease of Crown land. The next largest was Scott Paper, based in the United States. The largest forest landowner in the province, it owned 520,000 hectares, over one million acres, outright, and held leases on more than one hundred thousand hectares. Kimberly-Clark now owns Scott's mill and forest lands and, at this writing, is expected to sell to Harmac, expanding its primarily B.C. operations. A U.S.-based firm, Bowaters, runs the mill originally built by Mersey in Liverpool. Bowaters, which is 49 percent controlled by the *Washington Post*, owns its whole wood-supply area, over three hundred thousand hectares in the western part of the province.

As well, the Irving Company, of New Brunswick, has been buying Nova Scotia's forests as a cushion against predicted wood-supply shortages in its home province. No one actually knows how much land Irving owns in Nova Scotia, but, in one sale alone, the company bought over 42,000 hectares in Cumberland County, close to the New Brunswick border. Cumberland County is one of the last places in the province where logging had not completed multiple cut-over cycles in the last several hundred years. Irving's clear-cuts on an 80,000-hectare woodlot in Yarmouth County threaten a neighboring Carmelite religious retreat. Nuns and monks have pressed Irving to halt road building, and end thunderous night-time logging. Two smaller pulp-and-paper companies, Canexel Hardboard of East River and Minas Basin at Hantsport, have large undisclosed holdings.

Meanwhile, a sawmilling operation in Musquodoboit, MacTara, has become a significant drain on wood supply, with an appetite for one hundred million board feet a year, purchased from Crown and private lands in the province. The previously little-known operation began to achieve industry dominance when it added a new log line in late 1996, becoming the largest sawmill in the province.

Power struggles and politics

The stranglehold on both supply of pulp logs and production of pulp and paper in Nova Scotia has had a significant political impact. Even though the large corporate interests own over 22 percent of the province's forests, and control another 27 percent through Crown leases, nearly half of the forests of Nova Scotia are in the hands of small private woodlot owners, each holding four hundred hectares or less. From the 1960s on, there have been intense political struggles in Nova Scotia to allow these thirty thousand woodlot owners and pulp producers to establish collective-bargaining rights against the big companies.

The price paid by mills in Nova Scotia for wood cut on private land and hauled to the roadside has historically—and notoriously—been substantially less than that paid for similar wood in New Brunswick or Maine.

Most woodlot owners were juggling several types of activities to make a living for their families. Cutting pulp off the family woodlot and selling it to the mill was only one source of income; farming and fishing, or other seasonal employment, were others. This pattern of logging—a little bit every year—had the advantage of producing healthy forests. In contrast to some of the Crown lands, the private woodlots had a greater age mix and species diversity. But the work was difficult and, at the prices being paid by the large mills, woodlot owners figured that either they were donating their labor to the pulp mills, or they were being paid for their time and giving their wood away. There was no way to make a profit cutting and hauling wood to the roadside for $10–12 per cubic meter. In fact, the mills realized that even with the bargain-basement stumpage prices, it was still cheaper to buy wood from private woodlot owners than to log it from land owned or leased by the company—but only so long as the private woodlot owners did not have any bargaining power.[16]

In the 1970s, when the Nova Scotia Woodlot Owners and Operators Association (NSWOOA) was finally certified as a bargaining agent by a legislated Pulpwood Marketing Board, Stora played hardball. First it simply refused to bargain. Then it challenged the whole process in the Nova Scotia courts. The judicial system of Nova Scotia has always been kind to Stora. Nova Scotia board members in the shell company, Nova Scotia Pulp, have always been drawn from the ranks of one of Halifax's oldest and most conservative law firms—McInnis, Cooper and Robertson. There never has been a shortage of legal tricks of the trade in Stora's strategic arsenal. After tying the small producers up in court over several years, the Nova Scotia Supreme Court decision was issued in June 1975. Stora won and the court quashed the certification of the NSWOOA over procedural errors of the Pulpwood Marketing Board. The enabling legislation had to be reworked, and the movement for collective-bargaining rights was set back by years.[17]

But the ecological impacts of the sharply contrasting types of forest management on large industrial and small private lands have also played a major role in Nova Scotia's forest politics. As the Crown land on the Cape Breton highlands became increasingly dominated by the spruce budworm's favorite food, balsam fir, and the fir became older and (in forester's language) "decadent"—conditions were ripe for a major budworm outbreak in the mid-1970s. The private small woodlots, in contrast, held sufficient sources of supply to meet shortfalls should the budworm outbreak cause significant mortality in the highland softwood. But for Stora, the costs of becoming dependent on small woodlot owners were too high. In 1976, as the budworm outbreak reached epidemic proportions, Stora demanded that the province undertake, at taxpayers' expense, an aerial insecticide spray program over forty thousand hectares of Cape Breton Island. Initially, the Department of Lands and Forests recommended against a spray program. It noted that New Brunswick had been spraying annually since 1952, and still had a budworm outbreak. Nova Scotia had not sprayed in the early 1950s at the point of the last outbreak and the epidemic had died out of natural causes. The provincial entomologist in the 1950s had prophesied this outcome when he recommended against toxic chemicals, saying they would be "a vain attempt to offset a natural trend."[18]

Spray wars

The provincial cabinet, under pressure from Stora, overruled the Department of Lands and Forests and approved a spray program with the organophosphate insecticide fenitrothion, which has since been banned. And thus one of the great forest debates of Nova Scotia was sparked. Grassroots opposition to the spray mobilized throughout rural Cape Breton. News reports publicized research in Halifax linking the spray in New Brunswick with children's deaths from a rare disease, Reye's syndrome. Within months of approving the spray program, cabinet reversed its decision on the advice of the Minister of Health.

The following year, with higher budworm-population counts, Stora pulled out the big guns. Its president and CEO, Erik Sunbladt, flew in from Sweden to issue an ultimatum: either Nova Scotia agreed to a much larger spray program, covering all of Cape Breton Island, both Crown and private lands, or the company would close its mill within five years and put two thousand people out of work. Mr. Sunbladt told the local television news: "Nova Scotia is sick. It must take the medicine."[19]

In fact, the costs of the spray program would have exceeded the value of the annual harvest from the Cape Breton forest, but Stora wanted to maintain its control over its source of supply. Stora issued a massive report, arguing that, without spraying, half of its wood supply on Crown lands would be lost. It claimed that the remaining wood would not provide more than a five-year supply, thus justifying the threat to close the mill by 1981. But independent assessments, even using the company's worst estimates of softwood mortality, reported that there would be adequate wood supplies from

Crown and private land for at least forty years, with no provision for growth. Stora was never able to explain the five-year shutdown calculation as anything but job blackmail.

The campaign against the spray made local woodlot owners and executives of the Woodlot Owners' Association into active environmentalists. (It was my personal introduction to fighting forest companies.) A loose coalition of beekeepers, woodlot owners, schoolteachers and local concerned citizens formed, calling themselves Cape Breton Landowners Against the Spray. In all, the battle was restaged every year until the outbreak collapsed of natural causes, as predicted, in 1981. The Liberal government of Premier Gerry Regan and Lands and Forests Minister Vince MacLean held firm, despite mountains of propaganda and personal invective directed at them by Stora, with the full support of Scott and Bowaters. The budworm issue was a landmark in Nova Scotia, being the first time that a major pulp-and-paper company had not extracted exactly what it wanted from the government. It was also the last time.

The empire strikes back

When, against all odds, the environmentalists won the budworm spray wars, I came to think of the experience as "Star Wars" and the next brutal contest, which we lost, as "The Empire Strikes Back."

In the next provincial election, all three major political parties had a firm "no spray" position. But when the Conservative government of Premier John Buchanan had its first taste of Stora pressure, it turned out their position had a loophole. They never said they would not allow *herbicide* spraying. With a new program of government subsidies in 1982, Stora, Scott and Bowaters had received permits to spray vast areas—nearly one hundred different locations, ranging in size from several hectares to several thousand. The spraying was to be from the air, with 2,4-D and 2,4,5-T, the phenoxy herbicide mixture known as "Agent Orange." The announcement of the spray permits came without warning or prior public discussion, the day after the provincial legislature broke for the 1982 summer recess.

Already banned in Sweden, the United States and the Canadian provinces of Saskatchewan, Quebec and Ontario, 2,4,5-T had never before been used on Nova Scotia's forests. The rationale for its use was that following clear-cutting, the small herbaceous shrubs, the "pioneer" species of pin cherry and birch, were competing with coniferous growth. Over-cutting softwoods now could be approved by the Forest Department, as long as "intensive" silviculture methods offered the possibility of accelerated growth in the future. And the companies would receive reimbursement through the federal-provincial subsidy program. Once again, the pulp companies in Nova Scotia were demonstrating political muscle.

The Mi'kmaq Nation was one of the first to become actively opposed to the planned defoliation. Their reserve at Whycocomagh was just below a spray site on Skye Mountain, which was also the source of the community's drinking water. Chief Ryan Googoo led a dawn protest of men, women and children up the mountain, where they uprooted seedlings planted by Stora, the planned beneficiaries of the toxic spray. As publicity mounted, the cabinet announced that the spray permits were canceled.

Within a month, however, notices appeared in newspapers across the province that herbicide spraying was to take place with 2,4-D and 2,4,5-T. Having phoned the Nova Scotia Department of the Environment every day to ensure that no new applications for spray permits had been received, I was convinced that any herbicide spraying by the big three pulp companies must be illegal. When I phoned the usually friendly information officer with whom I had spoken every day for over a month, he put me through to the Deputy Minister of Environment. Mr. E.L.L. Rowe explained that the permits had never been canceled. "The Minister may have said the permits were canceled, but what he meant was, they were *varied*."

In fact, the permits had merely been altered from approved aerial spraying to approved ground spraying. Same chemicals, same spray sites, only now spraying was to begin within the week. With no time and fewer options, communities throughout Cape Breton and eastern Nova Scotia opted to seek a court injunction. In what became known as the "Herbicide Case," seventeen plaintiffs, their families, and local support groups saw nearly two years of their lives vacuumed up in a brutal court battle. Stora's lawyers resorted to every procedural obstacle imaginable to force the plaintiffs into bankruptcy before the trial could begin. In one round of threats of sending the sheriff around to collect on a collateral bill of costs, from an effort to stop spraying on the Scott Paper lands, my family lost eighty acres. In all, the plaintiffs, Cape Breton activists and their families, were able to raise nearly a quarter of a million dollars for their own legal costs. As the well-known activist June Callwood commented at the time, "It was a David and Goliath struggle, only this time Goliath had the sling shot."[20]

The injunction, granted on an emergency basis in August 1982, prevented any spraying on Stora's holdings in Cape Breton and most of what it had planned to spray on the mainland. We ran the legal marathon of appeals against our injunction, court orders for costs, and a month-long trial, in which the company successfully argued that we be denied access to a jury. After hearing from dozens of expert witnesses, following the second season during which our injunction held off the spraying, Mr. Justice Merlin Nunn, in his first major trial, ruled that the chemicals were safe. He went so far as to find, as a matter of fact, that 2,4,-D and 2,4,5-T had not caused any ill effects in Vietnam, and that dioxin had been of no lasting harm in Sevesco, Italy.

And then he ruled that the plaintiffs owed Stora for all of their court costs. While Stora's press-relations people speculated that the plaintiffs owed over a million dollars, nerves were frayed, spirits flagged, and ultimately the plaintiffs accepted an out-of-court settlement rather than take the issue to appeal.

Ironically, it turned out that Stora could not spray 2,4,5-T even after Judge Nunn ruled that it was safe. The U.S. Environmental Protection Agency and the herbicide's manufacturer, Dow Chemical, agreed to allow no more old stock of the banned 2,4,5,-T to be exported. Meanwhile, Stora had sold the Agent Orange it planned to spray on Nova Scotia. It was sprayed in New Brunswick instead.

Stora continues to benefit from government largesse. It has made the Nova Scotia government pay, again and again, for its decision in the mid-1970s to allow the budworm outbreak to run its natural course. Although at the time Stora threatened to close the mill by 1981 if the provincial government did not conduct a spray program, the company has expanded operations since that time. It gained government subsidies for the salvaging of budworm-killed wood. The provincial government put ten million dollars into a new on-site electrical generator running on wood waste. It received extensions so that new federal pollution standards would not have to be met during an economic downturn, even though Stora had reported profits of one and a half billion dollars between 1983 and 1993.

And in another grandstand play in 1993, Stora threatened to close the mill in light of new pollution laws coupled with the recession. Responding to the threat, the government provided a $15.4-million loan, and Stora's workforce accepted pay cuts amounting to one and a half million dollars, with the company committing to no new increases. The cited rationale was Stora's reported losses in the early 1990s. Yet a close reading of Stora's financial statement for 1993 suggests a different picture. The main purchaser of Stora's Nova Scotia pulp was another arm of the Swedish conglomerate, Stora Feldmuhle. Stora reported the market rate for pulp as averaging $430(U.S.) per ton for bleached long-fiber pulp. But the company's annual report indicates the Nova Scotia mill was selling its bleached long-fiber pulp for approximately $330(U.S.) per ton.[21] By discounting sales of pulp, Stora would have been able to transfer as much as seventeen million dollars (Can.) in revenues to other divisions within the company. While Nova Scotia workers and wood suppliers took significant pay cuts, Stora CEOs and directors rewarded themselves with a 10 percent increase in salaries and bonuses.

In December 1995, Stora announced a major expansion in order to produce a more finished paper product suitable for magazines, integrated with its existing newsprint and pulp lines.[22] This is the same company that claimed there was an inadequate wood supply to see it through 1981 without massive chemical spraying.

But accountability is unknown in forest management. Other than the chemical insecticide-spray program the company demanded, Nova Scotia pulp companies have always gotten whatever they wanted from a compliant provincial government.

Industrial forestry and loss of species

Over centuries, previously common and valuable long-lived tree species have been mined out of Nova Scotia's forest. With them have gone the woodland caribou and the timber wolf.

Environmentalists of the 1990s must be grateful for the foresight of the government in 1940 in setting aside part of the Big Lease as Cape Breton Highlands National Park. Of course, Oxford Paper of Maine received a windfall in compensation for its forest lease on the highlands, but one of the largest intact old-growth Acadian forests anywhere in the province was spared logging when the national park was created. But it is by no means the only Acadian old-growth forest remaining.

Significant Acadian forest in a pristine state can still be found on the steep slopes, as well as north of the park, and in pockets throughout the province. Currently, the government of Nova Scotia is actively pursuing its protected-areas strategy. With so little Crown land available, and with a tight wood supply, the areas set for protection are relatively small. In 1995, the province set aside thirty-one candidate sites for protected status. In December 1996, the Nova Scotia cabinet subsequently withdrew one significant area on the Cape Breton Highlands, Jim Campbell's Barrens, to make room for a possible gold mine. The Barrens contains old-growth forest, and local activists have identified five rare plants, including the pharmaceutically valuable Eastern Canada yew. Thanks to widespread public outcry, new premier Russell McLellan returned the area to protected status in October 1997.

There is still inadequate protection for forest biodiversity, as witnessed by the brouhaha over clear-cutting the hardwood forests for export. Hardwood is being shipped, both processed and unprocessed, to the United States, Germany, Great Britain, the Middle East and Sweden. When Stora, with a mill and cutting rights throughout eastern Nova Scotia, clear-cut an area of Acadian hardwood forest in the Keppoch Highlands of Cape Breton in 1990, a raging controversy ensued. Local environmentalists claimed the area had been predominantly birch and maple, some as much as 170 years old. The clear-cut hardwood was shipped to Sweden for Stora to pulp there. Stora's initial response was to deny that the area had been a hardwood forest. Television news crews toured the site with foresters and environmentalists who pointed out the hardwood stumps and branches. Stora admitted the clear-cut had some hardwood, but maintained it had to be logged, due to the dead softwood component. Stora president Tom Hall ridiculed the environmentalists' claims, insisting that only an "infinitesimal" amount of maple had been shipped to Sweden.[23] A campaign was launched to set aside the remaining original Acadian forest in the six-thousand-hectare watershed of Trout River on the Keppoch Plateau. Meanwhile, the provincial Department of Lands and Forests representative, Ed Bailey, defended the continuing conversion of the forest from hardwood to softwood: "A lot of softwoods were killed by the budworm and we had to have replanting to restore the forest . . . The industry we have here utilizes softwood species. If we are not able to supply these, the industry will fold."[24]

One of Cape Breton's leading forest activists, Charlie Restino, put it differently: "They're trading in Rolls-Royces and Cadillacs for Volkswagens and Chevrolets."[25]

When does Nova Scotia run out of wood?

Nova Scotia has probably the most intensively harvested forest in Canada. With only 1.3 percent of Canada's productive forest land base, Nova Scotia forests produce nearly twice that—2.4 percent—of total roundwood (a term for logs and pulp) for Canada.[26] In addition, an unreported amount of Nova Scotian forests is exported to New Brunswick and Maine by private woodlot owners.

A government Forest Management Strategy paper produced in 1994 recognized the historic damage done to the province's forests:

> The practice of removing the best and largest trees (high-grading) over centuries has reduced the physical and genetic quality of our forests. Natural events such as wildfires, insect infestations, hurricanes, land clearing and abandonment in many instances created overmature stands. Over forty percent of Nova Scotia's forests are more than sixty years old.[27]

Thus, despite the budworm's silvicultural efforts at removing the older forest, in 1990 an oversupply of old trees presented a coming wood-supply problem, as insufficient stock of mature and young trees remained to log once the old forest died or was logged.

The Royal Commission on Forestry public hearings in the early 1980s examined a range of options for the future of Nova Scotia's forests. It found that, at predicted rates of logging, by 2025, the demand for wood would exceed supply by 44 percent and the annual allowable cut would drop by 33 percent.

The commission then examined the "basic silviculture" option, but found the supply of wood would still fall short of demand by 28 percent by 1994, and by 36 percent by 2025.

Last, the commission looked at an "intensive management" option. This approach involved a full array of silviculture treatments over Crown and private lands: thinning, planting, herbiciding, and use of faster-growing seedlings, called "plus trees." Backlogged NSR areas, after years of neglect, would receive special attention to reclaim them as viable productive forest. Under this option, the coming shortage was re-engineered into a *doubling* of wood supply.

It will likely strike those uninitiated in the mumbo-jumbo of forest regulation as silvicultural alchemy that a province facing shortages should be treated as one on the verge of doubling supply. This is how it was done.

In determining the annual allowable cut, Nova Scotia has, in recent years, relied on a simulation model called "SAWS" (Strategic Analysis of Wood Supply). Every province has its own system of projecting wood supply, each using a different modeling approach. The only thing they seem to have in common is clever acronyms: while Nova Scotia SAWS, British Columbia foresters listened to the sound of MUSYC (Multiple-Use Sustained-Yield Calculation). The SAWS model is applicable only to even-aged management. Moreover, it essentially treats all the forest as though it were softwood, without differentiating between softwood species. Hardwood is dealt with through an adjustment to the overall softwood assumption. Like all computer models, everything in the result is determined by the initial assumptions. Recent forest reviews have cast doubt on the accuracy and reliability of the SAWS model. Because so much is aggregated in terms of species, growth projections are unreliable. Also, the model is based on an assumption that all the wood in the province is 100 percent available. This is a questionable approach in a province with nearly 70 percent of the forest in private hands. Moreover, the way the SAWS model was used received criticism: "These models are really nothing more than accounting tools to keep track of user defined scenarios of future management interventions and harvest levels. . . . The reasonableness of the analysis does not depend so much on the model itself, but rather in how the model is used."[28] Or, in the vernacular, "garbage in, garbage out."

Once the SAWS model was adjusted to allow for the desired level of "garbage," it was possible to project a doubling of the wood supply. All the industry needed was a compliant bureaucracy and a pile of dubious assumptions. It also needed government subsidies.

The goal of doubling the wood supply by 2025 was adopted during the peak years of federal-provincial silvicultural subsidy agreements. Between 1977 and 1993, a total of $416.4 million was spent in Nova Scotia's forests. Government funds reimbursed landowners and the pulp companies for road building, chemical spraying, silviculture, and fire and insect protection. Much of this subsidy was paid to privately owned small woodlots.

The land-ownership patterns in Nova Scotia have had a major impact on Nova Scotia's efforts to stabilize its wood supply. With nearly 70 percent of the forest privately owned, and most of that in small woodlots, implementing industrial intensive forest management across the province has been a major government preoccupation since the mid-1970s. Small woodlot owners are responsible for 59 percent of the wood supplied to mills, with 29 percent coming from industry-owned forests and 12 percent from Crown land.[29] In the wake of the budworm outbreak, the province created funding to assist independent wood co-operatives, known as "group or joint ventures." The idea was to combine small woodlots into units sufficiently large so that management plans could be drawn up. Landowners would be reimbursed for building logging roads, planting seedlings, herbiciding, and thinning their forests.

The government paid for a great deal of environmental damage. Poorly built roads ruined stream quality, and defoliation spraying was done in areas where even by industry standards there was no excuse for it. But the intensive silviculture option was fulfilling its primary objective: justifying over-cutting, premised on speculative future growth. In 1988, the area harvested was 42,000 hectares, with a 3.5-million-cubic-meter demand for wood to the mills.[30] By 1994, that figure had increased to 49,968 hectares, and the total volume logged to 5.2 million cubic meters.[31]

Various audits of performance under federal-provincial silviculture agreements should have given the supercharged industrial forest modelers cause for concern. In 1987, an evaluation of one round of spending concluded:

> The problems created by the existing age distribution are evident from the small area in younger stands; *in twenty years there will be insufficient mature forest available to meet the needs of the forest products industry*. The age distribution problem stems from the lack of adequate forest management over the last fifty years. . . .
>
> Low density stocking, less than 60 percent stocking on over 53 percent of the forest land, is also a serious problem . . . Some of this land lacks natural regeneration, and some has sparsely stocked, poor quality, older forest. The net result is a large area of non-commercial forest.
>
> Taken together, the consequences of these problems are a *serious deficit in the volume of harvestable wood relative to current levels of use beginning in about twenty years* (emphasis added).[32]

In March 1995, another consulting firm was hired to assess the success of a further round of subsidies. The goal for spending up to 1995 was to achieve an immediate increase in the AAC to 3.75 million cubic meters for softwood and 1.5 million cubic meters for hardwood, working toward the ultimate goal of a combined hardwood and softwood annual allowable cut of 7.3 million cubic meters by 2025.

The audit report found that the target had not been met at either end of the equation. First, the AAC was an over-cut, going 5 percent above allowable levels. This was possible because, although Nova Scotia includes private lands in the AAC, it cannot regulate the cut on those lands. The cut may well have been more than 5 percent above the AAC, as private forest landowners had been lured by sky-high pulp prices in the mid-1990s into clear-cutting entire woodlots. Contractors sought out economically desperate landowners, particularly in forest-rich Cumberland County close to the New Brunswick border, with offers of $30,000 to clear-cut a standard family woodlot. The wood generally was trucked to New Brunswick, or through to Maine. Wood-supply shortages in New Brunswick will only worsen the devastation of Nova Scotia's forests. But even as pulp prices plummet, over-cutting of small private woodlots appears to be continuing, with no regulation or monitoring.[33]

Moreover, private woodlot owners are also over-cutting preferred species, even when those trees are too young for harvest. As the province has an abundance of old trees and needs to keep young growth intact for coming shortages, this is a disturbing trend.[34]

Second, the targets were not met because the levels of silviculture upon which the AAC was calculated were not met. The silviculture effort faltered on two promised goals—there was less planting and less thinning of trees prior to their commercially valuable state. On the other hand, there was overharvesting by thinning in merchantable stands. The failure to meet planting targets was primarily due to a drop in subsidies. Of course, the targets were hardly scientific. Overall, the program encouraged widespread clear-cutting.

The auditors flunked the province: "The market demand study . . . concludes that from 1994 to at least 1999, *the demand for softwood will exceed the AAC.* . . . We conclude that the Agreement has not met the AAC's objectives specified in CAFD 2 due to a combination of lower than expected budget approvals (and, therefore, underachieved silvicultural treatment targets) and harvests that exceeded the AAC in the latter part of the 1991-1995 period"[35] (emphasis added).

The consultants expressed concern that, even with subsidies, small-landowner participation was lagging. Small woodlot owners are being asked to turn their forests into fiber farms for the pulp-and-paper industry. Some object. For instance, the audit report noted that the Mi'kmaq participants found the subsidy program incompatible with their own land-use priorities:

The Mi'kmaq participants . . . did not believe that the overall management plan allowed for multiple uses of their land. They wanted to conduct multiple species plantings, but these were not supported by the Agreement . . . we concluded that the *Mi'kmaq Bands were less committed to the goal of total growth than they were to the development of a broad species forest base*"[36] (emphasis added).

In other words, the Mi'kmaq did not want to sacrifice biological diversity in the drive to produce more pulp.

"Add her up, folks."

The wood-supply crisis in Nova Scotia is becoming sufficiently obvious that industry voices are being heard for the first time raising concerns. As cited earlier in this book, the head of the Forest Group Ventures Association of Nova Scotia, John Roblee, told a legislative committee, "Add her up, folks. We don't have the data of what is leaving the province by rail, by truck and by boat. It's going on 24 hours a day . . . It's just clear-cutting."[37]

Nova Scotia's AAC is still being set as though wood supply were increasing due to the intensive silviculture model. Despite reports from the province's own auditors that silvicultural targets have not been met, the over-cutting continues. Unbelievably, Nova Scotia is welcoming yet another mill. The Sheet Harbour Hardwood Chip project promises to ship 250,000 tonnes of hardwood chips every year to Mitsubishi's operations in Japan.

Government statistics for what was logged in 1994 are for over 5 million cubic meters, making 1994 a record-setting year for volume logged in Nova Scotia.[38] The AAC for softwood of 3.75 million cubic meters had been significantly exceeded, and despite the fact that Nova Scotia's AAC is designed for a five-year periodic average, logging rates have not declined in order to compensate for the over-cutting.

Nova Scotia has created an extremely dicey wood-supply situation. By choosing maximum industrial silviculture options, it has allowed increased levels of harvest even as a wood-supply shortage looms. Everything is based on the accuracy of the models and on achieving the level of required silviculture. Of course, even if the intensive silviculture is performed, the expected levels of forest productivity remain entirely speculative. But the reality should be discouraging, even to the architects of the "forests on steroids" model.

For one thing, federal government subsidies are over. The era of money for planting and thinning and spraying from the federal government is no more, but the whole increased AAC is based on such investments. In their absence one would expect the Nova Scotia government to revise its goals.

But in fact, when past targets have been missed, the AAC just went up anyway. Between 1982 and 1989, eighty-eight million dollars of taxpayers' funds was spent in silviculture. Despite finding that less than 70 percent of the required silviculture treatments had actually been performed in that period, the government kept increasing the AAC. The forest department merely recalculated, and decided these essential treatments were not needed after all.[39]

Given that history, it is likely that the goal of doubling the wood supply by 2025, however unrealistic it was even in 1986 with millions of dollars in subsidies, will remain on the books, allowing over-cutting to continue until the house of cards comes tumbling down, taking Nova Scotia's forests and mills with it.

NEW BRUNSWICK

NEW BRUNSWICK	(1995)
Forest Land in million hectares	6.1
Stocked Harvested Crown Land in hectares	425,000
Area Logged in hectares	98,000
Volume Logged in million cubic meters	10.0
Annual Allowable Cut in million cubic meters	11.2

SOURCE: Natural Resources Canada, Canadian Forest Service, *The State of Canada's Forests, 1996-1997* (Ottawa, 1997). These are federal government summaries, based on provincial government data. The figures are not necessarily accurate.

New Brunswick's forests are still described as predominantly of the Acadian forest type, and classed as a single ecoregion along with the forests of Nova Scotia and Prince Edward Island. These forests were unique in the world.

The original forests of New Brunswick were described in 1847 in a report for *Simmonds Colonial Magazine*. The author, M.H. Perley, an early timber surveyor, was overwhelmed by the great diversity of deciduous species—"tall, durable oaks," butternut trees "plentiful and abundant" along the Saint John River Valley, five different species of maple and three of beech. As for softwood, Perley recorded, "In New Brunswick, hemlock forms a large proportion of the evergreen forests," reaching heights of eighty feet (21 m).[1]

As early as 1849, leaders of the Mi'kmaq people made a heartbreaking appeal to the New Brunswick House of Assembly:

In old times, our wigwams stood in pleasant places along the river sides. These are now all taken away from us; and we are told to go away. Upon our old camping grounds you have built towns, and the graves of our fathers are broken up by the ploughs and the barrow. Even the Ash and the Maple are growing scarce. The lands you have given us are ruined or taken away.[2]

The Acadian forest of towering hardwoods and strong white pine, hemlock, and black and red spruce was substantially diminished. In fact, the last complete inventory for the province, completed in 1986, placed the percentage of hemlock at about 1 percent of the total softwood.[3] Anyone hoping to see the magnificent stands of old-growth hemlock need not waste time searching the province's hinterlands. One of the best remaining examples can be found in Odell Park in the provincial capital, Fredericton.

No other province in Canada has so completely brought its forests into full industrial production. For modern industrial foresters in New Brunswick, it is a source of considerable pride that the province's forests are all accessible by a network of logging roads—fifty thousand kilometers of logging roads on Crown land alone. No forested area is farther than one hundred kilometers from a mill.[4] True wilderness in New Brunswick, outside of parks, is rarer than a non-Irving gas station. Of all of New Brunswick's forests, only 1.2 percent of the land base is within a provincial or national park.[5] And those forests outside national parks are entirely spoken for. As Max Cater, head of the New Brunswick Forest Products Association, put it, "Every tree has a company's name on it, and a destination."[6]

How New Brunswick's forests came to be a fiber farm

The social and economic factors that have led to the colonization of New Brunswick by its pulp-and-paper industry go back to the earliest days of the province's history. Since the 1800s, the province allowed large tracts of its forests to be controlled by a few large sawmill owners. Profits from the forest washed through the province until the large trees of the highest value were gone. The high-grading process allowed the faster-growing and commercially undesirable balsam fir to become predominant, increasing

---

NEW BRUNSWICK CORPORATE PLAYERS

Irving Pulp & Paper Limited
Fraser Inc.
NBIP Forest Products Inc.
Repap
Abitibi-Consolidated

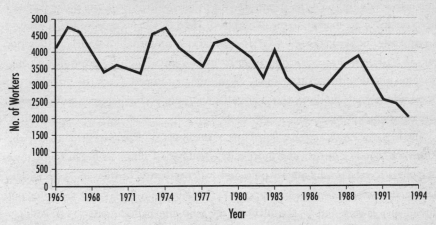

New Brunswick Forest Jobs

from its original proportion of the forest. The common species in the original boreal-like and Acadian forests of New Brunswick were the red and white spruce, with black spruce on poorly drained soils and in higher elevations.

By the 1920s, the sawmill kings of the nineteenth century were losing their political foothold. The Great Depression sharply reduced sawmilling profits. But the decline began earlier. What had been a 46 percent share of total provincial revenue in 1920 dropped to 22 percent by 1922.[7] The first pulp mill in the province was built in 1915 by Bathurst Lumber. Where the sawmill industry was experiencing more difficulty finding quality logs, the forest was virtually perfect for the pulp-and-paper industry, for which fast-growing small trees are ideal. Both the government and the banks set policies that favored the rise of pulp mills. After the Depression the banks were unwilling to risk loans to the sawmill industry. And the government seemed eager to grant generous leases to large pulp-and-paper companies.

By 1930, the two largest pulp companies, Fraser Company and International Paper, had been granted long-term leases, on very attractive tax and royalty terms, for over 70 percent of the province's Crown land. Six years later, the pulp companies also owned 36 percent of the province's privately held forest land.[8] What high-quality trees still existed were now increasingly hard for the sawmill industry to access. Cutting for the sawmills became restricted to smaller private lands, with over-cutting the result.[9]

Controlling vast areas of the province, the pulp mills developed an economic stranglehold on New Brunswick that exists to this day. For the small private woodlot owner or pulp cutter, economic leverage was hard to find. Moreover, the pulp-and-paper industry has a pattern of internal boom-and-bust cycles. The international price of pulp and newsprint is subject to wide fluctuations. When the economic conditions were bad for the industry as a whole, it was the small private landowners who suffered the most. Not only could the large pulp-and-paper companies dictate prices through their control of the market, in the period from 1948 to 1954 they were actually meeting regularly and setting prices to be paid the farmers and woodlot owners in Ontario, Quebec and New Brunswick. The price-fixing was uncovered in a government commission, but it didn't matter much. Without guaranteed access to markets, the independent small producers were bound to comply with whatever conditions the pulp companies dictated.[10]

By the early 1960s, in the wake of one of the cycles of depressed demand and low prices, the woodlot owners and independent pulpwood suppliers began to organize themselves to take on the mighty pulp-and-paper industry. In what looked like class warfare, the woodlot owners' associations pointed out that the province was losing not only quality sawlogs but also farmland to the pulp-and-paper industry. The Acadian Federation of Northern New Brunswick argued that the people of New Brunswick would not "tolerate the existence of a private industry which enriches itself at the expense of tar paper shacks, wasted minds and bodies, impoverished, badly educated children, despairing fathers, despondent mothers and ruined communities."[11]

It was not until the 1970s that pulpwood marketing boards were finally created. They allowed for region-by-region negotiation among the large mills, the sawmill owners and the small producers. But they still lacked the power to set prices or to dictate what proportion of wood should come from private woodlots. It was not until 1982 and the massive reforms of the Crown Lands and Forests Act that the marketing boards were given teeth. The new legislation established the overriding directive that the industry's primary source of fiber must be the private woodlots. This concession to the economic interests of the private woodlot owners was more than balanced by a sweeping shift in Crown leases, consolidating all Crown land in ten licenses to be held by pulp mills and sawmills. The pulp mills themselves were given the responsibility for managing the forests within their leases to ensure supply, not only for themselves, but for the roughly one hundred smaller sawmills still operating in the province. Nevertheless, industry objected to the new power of the marketing boards.

In the wake of the recession in the early 1990s, the provincial government brought in amendments to the Crown Lands and Forests Act, known as the "Pulp and Paper Rescue Plan." The 1992 amendments, among such provisions as deferred stumpage, abolished many of the marketing boards' powers.[12] The private woodlot owners lost their legislated position as primary suppliers, although the pulp companies were urged to continue to buy from them.[13] But no one controls the level of production on private lands.[14]

New Brunswick's war on the budworm

For decades, the provincial government seemed to define its role in forest policy as doing the bidding of large industry. In 1952, the New Brunswick forests were hit with a serious infestation of spruce budworm. This indigenous forest pest is perfectly suited to balsam fir. The appearance of the fir's tender buds in springtime is exquisitely timed to the emergence of the budworm larvae. While always present at low levels, the spruce budworm has reached epidemic proportions every forty years or so, for thousands of years. But the logging patterns of the last 150 years had, as if by design, created vast expanses of the budworm's favorite food.

New Brunswick had been warned of the risks it faced by allowing the forest to go to fir. In the 1920s, during a previous period of high budworm infestation, entomologist Dr. J.D. Tothill wrote:

> In the primeval forest bequeathed by our forefathers there were no important outbreaks of insects because Nature had established a natural balance that prevented any one insect becoming too abundant. There were no pure stands of fir . . . on a large scale, there were great numbers of insectivorous birds, and insect parasites were uniformly distributed and destroyed vast quantities of spruce budworm . . . For a century we have been working in direct opposition to Nature and in the course of our ordinary lumbering methods have finally succeeded in destroying this delicately adjusted balance.[15]

From what he observed, Tothill recommended that the province begin an immediate silvicultural program to "budworm-proof" the forest. He urged that more hardwood be present, with more trees in mixed-age stands. While the original forest had always included a large portion of spruce, it was generally the less budworm-susceptible red spruce. Logging was increasing the proportions of balsam fir. Unless the natural species mix was restored, he argued, the next budworm epidemic would come sooner and with greater severity.[16]

Rather than heed the warnings, the pulp-and-paper industry went about converting the forest to spruce and fir. When faced with the serious budworm outbreak Tothill had predicted, the provincial government did not address the root cause of the problem, the unnaturally high proportion of fir. Rather, the province armed itself to fight the symptoms. New Brunswick declared war on the spruce budworm.

In order to fight the budworm outbreak the province began a massive insecticide-spray program, at public expense. It began in 1952 as a one-hundred-thousand-hectare spray program with DDT, with the stated objective of eradicating the budworm. The following year, the spray program was extended to an area four times as large. It created an artificial state of permanent epidemic. Rather than collapsing from natural causes within four to five years, as would normally have occurred, the outbreak lasted for more than forty years. The insecticide had the unintended effect of knocking out the budworm's natural predators, birds and other parasitic insects, while maintaining the food supply, thus preventing conditions for natural collapse. While significant short-term mortality in balsam fir was averted, the province experienced continual losses to budworm for over forty years.

In the course of the war against budworm, the government and the industry jointly created a spraying air force, Forest Protection Ltd., bought it a squadron of Second World War Grumman Avenger bombers, and supplied it with millions of liters of chemicals. Rachel Carson related the early years of the spray program in *Silent Spring*, with a chapter on the Miramichi called "Rivers of Death." From DDT to phosphamidon to fenitrothion, the chemical arsenal the province used against budworm has since been banned. Songbird mortality was huge. Depending on the chemical, the province lost its fish or its birds or both. Blueberry growers had to be compensated for crops that failed because pollinating bees had been eradicated by spray drift. The province lost a court case launched by local residents after spray-drift had affected their health. In order to avoid that problem in the future the government changed the law to allow insecticide spraying over private property, with or without the landowners' consent, through the right of eminent domain. In several painful years, 1976–1978, the insecticide's emulsifier was linked to a cluster of children's deaths from the rare disease Reye's syndrome.[17]

The Minister of Natural Resources at the time, Roland Boudreau, said: "I don't like to see people dying. This is one of those things I wouldn't really like to see. But, at the same time, knowing the forest as it is, my decision will have to be with the forest and the future of New Brunswick."[18]

By 1994, the budworm outbreak began to decline. Use of a biological alternative, Bt, had allowed natural predators to rebound from the effects of chemical spraying. In the early 1990s, fenitrothion was deemed "environmentally unacceptable" by the federal Environment Department. In 1995, the federal government announced that fenitrothion would be banned, phasing out the chemical by 1998.[19] While the provincial government stopped spraying it, Irving continued to use fenitrothion on its privately held lands.[20]

By the time the government stopped its annual chemical dousing of the province in 1994, in total over thirty-nine million hectares of forest had been sprayed since 1952—the equivalent of spraying the entire forested land base of the province nearly seven times over![21]

Nothing has ever been allowed to interfere with the business of making pulp and paper, whether it was deteriorating air quality or the pulp-and-paper effluent turning Reversing Falls in Saint John from a tourist attraction into a sewer. In describing the pulp-and-paper empire that is New Brunswick, it is hard to avoid the word "feudal."

Impact on forest biodiversity

The dominant view of forests from the New Brunswick government and its industry is that the forest is like a garden. It grows a crop. The crop must be tended, sprayed, thinned and harvested. The industry can walk the visitor through vast stands of plantations. Irving was the first company to engage in extensive tree planting. It actually calls itself "The Tree Growing Company" and boasts of planting nearly four hundred million seedlings in the last thirty years.

But the New Brunswick vision of the forest is a dark one indeed if you value a forest for anything other than fiber production. Current logging plans ensure that no significant stands of old growth will ever occur again. In fact, in some species, even middle-growth classes will never be reached. Every stick is to be harvested on a rotation of forty to sixty years.

It is clear that the pattern of human exploitation of the New Brunswick forest has fundamentally altered the richness of its ecosystems—from both the biological and the economic point of view. For example, a single unprocessed bird's-eye maple can command between five and ten thousand dollars in today's marketplace. This tree, which is a sugar maple, has a genetic defect that creates a unique pattern in its grain. Conversion of the forest has reduced its abundance, while those few trees that remain are likely ending up in pulp or veneer mills.[22] The same would hold true for other high-value fine furniture woods. They are increasingly rare.

As logging has impoverished the forest, shifting composition of both species mix and age classes, New Brunswick has also lost plant and animal species. The big predators, cougar and wolf, have all but disappeared from the province's forests, with the Canada lynx on the provincial endangered-species list. Woodland caribou was extirpated in the 1930s. Species relying on old dead trees for cavity habitat, food and shelter are also disappearing. The pine marten and the fisher are in decline. Woodpeckers and other old-growth-dependent birds may be in trouble. No one really knows of the impact on amphibians and reptiles due to logging, as the research has not been undertaken.[23]

The life of streams has been affected. Poor road construction and running equipment through streams will, of course, cause serious loss of fish habitat. But even "acceptable" clear-cuts have a damaging impact on watersheds. Studies in New

Brunswick show significant decreases in brook trout and invertebrates in clear-cut watersheds.[24] General studies in the Maritimes show that although songbirds will live in a post-clear-cut forest, they are not the same species as those found in the original forest. Once abundant in the mature hardwood forest, the least flycatcher, hermit thrush, ovenbird, red-eyed vireo, a number of warbler species and others were totally absent from the clear-cut forest five years after harvest. Trees and shrubs were creating new habitat and a completely new set of species moved in.[25] Simple counting or wandering around with an untrained eye to look for birds might lead to the false conclusion that all was well.

Biodiversity is inevitably lost when old growth is removed. While this holds true for almost all of Canada's forests, the situation in New Brunswick is particularly troubling because of the total absence of adequate old-growth forest in protected areas.

In recent years the government has become more sensitive to its critics. The vast majority of New Brunswick's forestry production is destined for export, mostly to the United States. *National Geographic* magazine is published on glossy paper that was once fir and spruce in Northumberland County, while pulp from Fraser's Edmundston mill goes to phone books in Europe, and poplar and white birch in the Saint John River Valley become photographic paper for Kodak and Fuji.[26]

Concern for markets, coupled with strong citizen action and public pressure within New Brunswick, has resulted in the formulation of new rules to protect non-timber values. Since the late 1980s, clear-cut size has been restricted to one hundred hectares. Since 1992 the forest management plans for Crown land, now drawn up every five years, must include protection for certain commercially valuable wildlife, with deer yards in place. Buffer zones along streams are now mandatory, as is a requirement for 10 percent of the softwood to be maintained as mature coniferous forest habitat (MCFH).[27] The requirements for MCFH have been designed to accommodate twenty-nine species known to require older coniferous habitat. The pine marten has been used as the umbrella species, as the impacts on the province's timber supply of requiring habitat for other mature-conifer-dependent species were not known.[28] No effort has been made to protect species dependent on deciduous or mixed-growth forest habitats.

The deer-yard areas are, of course, to ensure the proliferation of a valuable game species. The white-tailed deer increased in numbers as the indigenous woodland caribou disappeared. Generally, deer can do well in clear-cuts, which increase the area for browse. But large clear-cuts make it difficult for deer in winter months. They dislike venturing out into large openings at any time, and given the network of roads that bring hunters into all parts of the province, this instinct must be preserved. In winter, clear-cuts accumulate much deeper snow than does a forest. The obvious fact that the forest canopy intercepts a lot of snow has implications for the soil hydrology and climatic conditions year round. But with the immediate object of maintaining deer populations, the licenses require the maintenance of winter deer yards with areas of standing forest near the clear-cuts. The areas set aside as winter deer yards often overlap with the 10 percent requirement for mature-conifer habitat, but the total acreage is totted up as though these requirements were cumulative.[29]

The industry points to these commitments, and the reduced annual allowable cut (AAC) to allow for them, and claims to have done enough to protect non-timber values.

Initially, the New Brunswick government had committed itself to the Endangered Spaces campaign. The campaign goal is a network of parks and protected areas, interpreted as comprising a minimum of 12 percent of Canada's land base in representative ecosystems. Environmentalists in New Brunswick identified a number of key areas where it would still be possible to protect areas of old growth. Steep ravines along the Fundy coast of the Point Wolfe, Goose, and Big and Little Salmon rivers are good candidate areas for finding inaccessible old growth. Seven hundred hectares of the Point Wolfe River watershed were protected, but protection of other areas has slowed to a standstill. The most controversial protected-area proposal was the Christmas Mountains.

The Christmas Mountains are in the north-central part of the province, so called as each mountain is named for one of Santa's reindeer. As Donner and Blitzen were clear-cut, protesters began to organize. There was a wintry blockade by students from Mount Allison University and Université de Moncton in November 1994. Their claim that the Christmas Mountains were New Brunswick's last remaining tract of old-growth wilderness was ridiculed by the industry, which argued the area had been logged in the past. In fact, parts of it probably had. But the province's Department of Natural Resources confirmed that the Christmas Mountains contained some significant never-logged areas, spared because of elevation, as well as steeper slopes and inaccessibility.

In the midst of the debate in 1994, a devastating wind storm occurred. Huge amounts of timber were blown down, primarily adjacent to clear-cuts and logging roads. The government and industry immediately began plans for a salvage operation. The Christmas Mountains are within the Crown license held by Repap for two Miramichi pulp mills and a sawmill. Any area with 50 percent or more of blowdown could be harvested. All of Repap's operations for two years were shifted to the salvage operation. For the men who performed it, the salvage was an act of heroism, logging in nearly impossible conditions. For conservationists, it sealed the fate of the Mountains. The salvage resulted in extensive clear-cutting, interrupted by patchy areas of partial blowdown. The remaining forests adjacent to the Christmas Mountains are still a conservation goal for local groups as well as for the Sierra Club and World Wildlife Fund. The best hope for a large, intact area for protection is likely the neighboring Nalaisk and Serpentine Mountains.

But the government has reneged on its commitment to the Endangered Spaces campaign. The province has no plans to create new large parks for protection of old-growth or other ecosystems. It argues that the winter deer yards, mature conifer habitat, and buffer zones around streams should satisfy "protected areas" requirements. The problem is that none of the required deer yards or mature conifer stands is a permanent plot. They cannot possibly be considered large tracts of protected forest, as they are found in small strips along rivers and small areas within Crown licenses. Neither are the deer yards or mature conifer areas actually off limits to logging. Selection cuts are still encouraged to avoid any further drop in the AAC. As long as there is close to 10 percent in mature forest within any forest license at any given time, the guideline is satisfied.[30] The mature-forest requirement does not protect true old growth. It merely lengthens the rotation period in some cut blocks. One year's protected area is next year's clear-cut. And there is no effort to ensure wildlife corridors so that the displaced mature-forest-dependent species can find a new home.

"We're building non-fiber values into our Crown lands, which we've never had before," said the Minister of Natural Resources and Energy, Alan Graham. "We're going to get our protected areas from moving mature conifer forest."[31]

Not since Birnam wood removed to Dunsinane in *Macbeth* has so much depended on a mobile forest. (And that, too, was an illusion.)

New Brunswick's wood supply: When will it run out of wood?

Once we examine the management of New Brunswick's forests for fiber production, it becomes clear why the province will not create parks. "We're running out of timber," said one New Brunswicker who ought to know.

The statement was not from a wide-eyed environmentalist or an alarmist from the Federation of Woodlot Owners. It was from Minister Alan Graham in the fall of 1995.[32]

Since the early 1970s, there has been concern that New Brunswick was running out of wood. The efforts to revise the Crown license systems in 1982 through a substantial overhaul of forest legislation, the Crown Lands Forest Act, was largely in response to supply concerns. The Deputy Minister for Forests of that day, Dr. Gordon Baskerville, recalled, "There was pretty severe denial among most people about the seriousness of the problem. . . . All of the computer forestry models forecast a problem. None of them showed a sustainable harvest forty or fifty years in the future."[33]

In response to the coming supply crunch, 483 parcels of Crown land were consolidated into ten. The prerequisite for a lease was simple. You had to own a mill. As a result, there are currently six pulp-and-paper conglomerates and two sawmills controlling half of New Brunswick's forests through leases. All of its Crown land is controlled by the pulp and sawmill companies, as is the case in Nova Scotia. New Brunswick has a higher-than-average level of private land ownership. Of the remaining half of the provincial forests in private hands, 21 percent is classified "industrial freehold," that is, the industry owns that too. Another 30 percent of forest is in smaller, privately owned woodlots.

The AAC has decreased only slightly in anticipation of the potential shortfall. The AAC set in 1992 was 18 percent lower than the AAC in 1987, largely to accommodate new guidelines for deer yards and mature habitat.[34] But while the AAC has fallen, the rate of cut has not. In fact, it has gone up. In 1993, New Brunswick cut 8.8 million cubic meters from a total AAC of 10.9 million cubic meters. By 1994, the rate of cut increased to 10 million cubic meters.[35] In 1996, the rate of cut exceeded the AAC. Since 1960, New Brunswick's annual harvest has doubled.[36]

New Brunswick's AAC is 35 percent too high on the basis of natural rates of growth. Only one with blind faith in the benefits of intensive silviculture and voodoo forestry could imagine that level to be sustainable. And even then, the rate could be considered sustainable only if ecological values and biodiversity were excluded. Nevertheless, even by industry and government estimates, the current timber supply in softwood is fully utilized. There is no margin for error.

Everything depends on the absolute accuracy of the inventory, the reliability of computer models, and the wonders of modern industrial forestry. No variables are permitted. No new budworm outbreaks or fires or reductions in tree growth resulting from climate change or air pollution are allowed—and certainly, no new parks.

The inventory is the first problem. It was last completed in 1986 and, in contrast to those conducted in other provinces, it was fairly thorough. The entire inventory was entered into geographic information system (GIS) software. Soon thereafter the accuracy of the 1986 inventory was called into question. In the 1992 Crown license granted to the Irving Company for the Queens–Charlotte County areas, the Forest Management Plan noted a number of problems. In particular, Irving found "a large discrepancy between what was assumed to be available for harvest according to our wood supply model; and what our foresters (and their reconnaissance) think is operationally available."[37]

Revising the inventory became an ongoing effort in 1992, with the goal of a completed inventory by 2002, to be compiled by 2004. It is currently anticipated that every ten years the province will have a complete picture of its forests. However, even with the newer inventory information, the confidence level is placed at only 80 percent, and many species are still merely lumped together. Furthermore, the inventory relies on the private companies to report the status of industrial freehold lands. In the meantime, there is no question that AAC levels, with no margin for error in the inventory, are being allocated before the inventory is complete.

What the current inventory shows is that the softwood supply is, optimistically, "tight" or, realistically, falling far below demand. The age classes of the standing softwood are unevenly distributed. Much wood is in older age classes; although one has to bear in mind that an eighty-year-old balsam fir is considered, in foresters' language, "overmature" or "decadent." There are also a lot of trees in the younger age classes. What is in short supply are the trees that should be ready for harvest twenty to thirty years from now.

To avoid the anticipated shortfall, New Brunswick is trying to defy time and nature; first, by believing younger trees can grow faster, and second, by hoping old trees will not die. The AAC not only expands to take advantage of potential future growth through intensive silviculture, but also stretches out the life span of old trees to cover the coming shortfall in wood supply.

Having converted the province to short-lived low-quality species, it is not surprising that companies are concerned that the predicted yields from these older stands may not hold up. The stands will likely die before the pulp companies get to them.[38]

J.D. Irving Ltd. addresses the risk directly in its Forest Management Plan: "Since the 1982 photography, we have noticed an almost complete mortality of the remaining balsam fir component on the License as well as a significant and accelerating spruce deterioration. . . . It may indicate that our natural unmanaged stand yields may be somewhat optimistic."[39] But the problems do not end there. Inventory information suggests that the individual tree size will continue to decline. The sawlog industry has already adapted its equipment to handle smaller logs, as the anticipated "harvested piece size," or log, is going to get much smaller quite quickly. Some sawmills have already retooled to handle smaller logs. Maintaining a forest where high-quality logs became a priority has not been suggested. This is again reminiscent of the collapse of the cod fishery. As the large cod disappeared off Newfoundland, fish plants brought in new equipment to process increasingly small fish. As an ecosystem warning sign, it was ignored.

Other bad news comes from the small private woodlots, comprising 30 percent of the forest land base. For the first time in the province's history, over-cutting these smaller private forests has become a serious problem. Traditionally, a family farmer with a woodlot treated the forest like money in the bank. He would fell a certain amount of his forest every year, and, depending on quality, sell the wood to the sawmills or pulp mills. The stewardship of private lands was always something that formed an ideal for conservationists. The best species diversity and age mix tended to occur on these gentle valley lands. But several factors have conspired to change that picture. First, after depressed global pulp prices in the early 1990s, the price shot through the roof.

Second, the workforce on Crown lands has been reduced. Many of these independent contractors have purchased expensive mechanized harvesters that can cost hundreds of thousands of dollars, and need to find somewhere to clear-cut to generate income to pay the interest on loans for their mortgaged machines. The increasing mechanization of logging inevitably leads to greater clear-cuts, as machines like feller-forwarders and feller-bunchers are good for nothing else.[40] These pressures, coupled with high unemployment and favorable federal tax treatment of clearing forest land, have led to a new phenomenon in the Maritime private woodlot—"the liquidation cut." It is the next step in the industrialization of the forest: extending the liquidation clear-cut from Crown to private land.

Contractors have literally gone door to door in New Brunswick asking owners of one-hundred-hectare woodlots if they would consider clear-cutting the entire area for a quick profit. It is encouraging that, according to the president of the New Brunswick Federation of Woodlot Owners, Peter deMarsh, contractors have to approach several dozen landowners before they find one ready to liquidate a forest.[41] But, in the absence of the power of marketing boards to regulate the harvest, a power abolished in 1992, there has been no way for the province to regulate or even monitor the rate of cut. Some of the harvest is being shipped to Maine and is unreported. For purposes of the AAC, the government estimates the unreported softwood export at three hundred thousand cubic meters a year, but notes that it could easily be much higher.[42] Even as pulp prices have tumbled in the late 1990s, the pressures to liquidate family woodlots remain high.

In May 1996, the province announced plans to levy higher property taxes against landowners who clear-cut more than 10 percent of their woodlots in any given year. But some observers fear that this will do little to deter out-of-province landowners, and that unpaid taxes will simply lead to more land in the hands of the Crown for the benefit of the large forest corporations.[43] The province's motivation in acting to discourage liquidation cuts is clear. It is not a concern based on the ecological unacceptability of clear-cutting. Ninety percent of New Brunswick's logging on Crown lands is by clear-cutting. The driving motivation to restrict liquidation cuts on private lands is that, with an impending shortage of softwood, the last thing the New Brunswick-based mills want to see is wholesale cutting for export. Every stick of wood in the province will be needed if mills are not to start closing for lack of supply in the next fifteen to twenty years.

Liquidating capital

Meanwhile, the "under-utilized" hardwoods in the province are feeling increasing logging pressure. Pulp mills are adapting processes to make use of intolerant hardwood species, such as poplar and birch. New Brunswick also has expanded its forest industrial sector to include its oriented strand board (OSB). The newest OSB mill opened with His Royal Highness Prince Charles flipping the switch in April 1996. The opening of an OSB mill should be seen as a neon sign over an ecosystem: "Going-out-of-Business Sale! Everything Must Go!"

An OSB mill does not take trees to make forest products, in the sense that first shipbuilding, and then sawmills, and then, at a lower level, the pulp mills do. It actually takes trees to make flakes. The flakes are then "oriented," or lined up perpendicular to each other. Add glue, press, and—voila! You've got oriented strand board, or chipboard, for use in construction. Given the processing method, it is fairly obvious why OSB mills are on the increase. Literally any small tree, particularly small hardwood, can be flaked and converted to chipboard.

The laudatory story in the Saint John *Telegraph-Journal*, heralding the plant's opening at a once-bankrupt Miramichi pulp, and then waferboard, mill, noted: "As big trees and old-growth forests get harder to find in North America, OSB is becoming a cheaper, more popular construction material. It is expected to outpace plywood as North America's building panel of choice by the turn of the century."[44]

Combined with other industrial expansions to take advantage of "under-utilized" hardwood, the annual allowable cut for hardwood is expected to go up by 1.6 million cubic meters by the year 2000.[45] Meanwhile, the government regulators admit they have no idea how much wood is exported from private land, or how much is cut for firewood by local residents. Timber-supply analysts are already predicting that if traditional uses for hardwood continue as increased industrial demand for it builds, the demand for hardwood will soon outpace supply.[46]

Again, as in the fishery, the "under-utilized" species may soon be overexploited in a rash effort to maintain economic activity despite a dwindling resource. As fishers in Newfoundland say, "Species go from under-utilized to extinct."[47]

The inventory is inaccurate, and no margin for error has been allowed. These realities, plus the fact that old trees are not likely to extend their life span to accommodate industry harvesting plans, spell a shortage of softwood by the year 2015. Meanwhile, the New Brunswick courts have confirmed that the Mi'kmaq have rights to log Crown lands. The hope for the forests is that First Nations' rights will be used to advance sustainability.

New Brunswick is a vast fiber farm, crisscrossed by a network of logging roads and colonized by industrial interests, with every tree spoken for in the effort to assure a sustained supply of wood to the mills. Claims by the forest industry that they are preserving non-timber values begin to sound very hollow as it becomes apparent that even timber values are being recklessly used up.

PRINCE EDWARD ISLAND

PRINCE EDWARD ISLAND	(1995)
Forest Land in million hectares	0.29
Stocked Harvested Crown Land in hectares	19,700
Area Logged in hectares	3,131
Volume Logged in million cubic meters	0.4
Annual Allowable Cut in million cubic meters	0.5

SOURCE: Natural Resources Canada, Canadian Forest Service, *The State of Canada's Forests, 1996-1997* (Ottawa, 1997). These are federal government summaries, based on provincial government data. The figures are not necessarily accurate.

Prince Edward Island and its forests are unique in Canada. Almost none of the generalities about forests in other provinces apply here. The Island has no pulp mills, and no AAC is set; more than 90 percent of the Island is in private hands; there are no large-scale leases. But in one respect it is no different from any other province in Canada: the forest has been substantially degraded by centuries of human exploitation.

This little jewel of green in the Atlantic, with the Northumberland Strait separating it from the mainland, is Canada's smallest province. With a population of 135,000 and a land base of only half a million hectares, Prince Edward Island is smaller than any number of parks found across the country.[1] Most Canadians would be surprised to hear that Prince Edward Island even has a forest industry. But prior to European contact, the Island was 98 percent forested in the species and composition typical of the original Acadian forest ecosystem. As in its neighboring provinces, Nova Scotia and New Brunswick, the character of the forest has been wholly altered. Shipbuilding and sawmills took the best wood in the nineteenth century, but it was the clearing of land for agriculture that removed most of the original forest. By the early 1900s, only 20 percent of the Island remained forested as the industrious settlers established the pastoral and well-manicured landscape made famous by Lucy Maud Montgomery in *Anne of Green Gables*.

Following the Second World War, Islanders left the farms in droves. Abandoned fields came back in forest cover, but as in New Brunswick and Nova Scotia, they regenerated in the early successional species. In P.E.I. this led to a predominance of

PRINCE EDWARD ISLAND CORPORATE PLAYERS
No pulp mills
Small sawmills

white spruce, with a small component of hardwoods—white birch, gray birch, poplars, red maple and pin cherry.

Although nearly half of the Island is now classed as forest land, none of it is the original forest. There is no area of productive forest land that has not been cut at least once, *including* land within national and provincial parks.

Having discussed the impact on biodiversity of the cutting down of the original Acadian forest in other provinces, it is not necessary to dwell on that same impact in P.E.I. But the list of species that have become extinct in Prince Edward Island is longer than that of its neighbors. The lynx, black bear, pine marten, fisher, river otter, moose and other forest dwellers disappeared from Prince Edward Island long ago. Certain songbirds likely have been affected by the clear-cuts, but no specific studies have been done.

Of particular concern to Prince Edward Island ecologists is the disappearance of the rare indigenous forest trees and shrubs. The few remnants containing rare species such as ironwood, witch hazel and hobblebush have insufficient protection. In 1995, 95 percent of the province's known remaining stock of witch hazel was cleared by a work crew *within* one of the province's dedicated "Natural Areas."[2]

Despite Prince Edward Island's small role in the Canadian forest industry, it does have logging, clear-cutting and mills. The Island exports to pulp mills and sawmills, and logging also supplies Island sawmills. Lately, some hardwood shipments have gone to Maine as the market for hardwood in pulp-and-paper increases. All told, in 1995 the Island logged 188,000 cubic meters for the pulp mills of neighboring provinces, 230,000 cubic meters for sawmills on the Island, and 190,000 cubic meters for domestic fuelwood, with smaller amounts for fuel chips and exported sawlogs.[3] Since almost all of this happens on private land, there is no set allowable cut and no legislated sustained yield. There is a weak provincial Forest Management Act, with little enforcement. However, recently the government instituted a Forest Renewal Fund, with two dollars from every cord of wood sold being placed in a fund for silviculture.[4]

As small as the Island's forest industry is, it is still overexploiting the degraded forest that remains. While unable to regulate harvest levels, the province's Forestry Branch does attempt to monitor them. Harvest rates jumped between 1994 and 1995, with increased logging of softwoods. In a January 1996 press release, the department warned that cutting levels of white spruce, mostly found in abandoned fields, was unsustainable. They reported, "this softwood resource will be gone in 10 to 15 years."[5]

Meanwhile, the traditional threats to the Island's forests continue in the form of agricultural expansion. The price of potatoes has been high in recent years, encouraging the clearing of land for potato farming. As well, the provincial agriculture branch actively promotes the conversion of marginal forest land to blueberry production.

The saga of forest plantations of blueberries should become a classic Canadian tale of battling subsidies. Through the 1980s, there was a federal provincial subsidy program called the "Forest Regional Development Agreements" (FRDAs). In Prince Edward Island, the FRDAs led to a number of intensive forest-management practices for the first time. Logging roads, herbiciding, thinning and planting were all subsidized on private land. The landowners, in turn, were contracted to maintain any plantations on their land for ten years, or be forced to compensate the province for the forest improvement.

The FRDAs dried up after fiscal year 1993–1994. And along came the Agriculture Department with subsidies to convert woodland to blueberries. It turned out that many of the best sites for blueberries were the previously subsidized forest plantations. They were accessible by road and easily cleared with a brush mower. So down came some of the six- to ten-year-old trees. Thus far, a few landowners who have failed to maintain their plantations have been sent bills by the forest service, but no blueberry growers have been charged.

Logging pressures on Prince Edward Island are likely to increase substantially due to the oncoming shortages in its neighboring provinces, combined with increased accessibility to mills now that the Confederation Bridge to the mainland is complete. In the absence of regulations on clear-cutting private lands, the Island will suffer even more drastic shortages than those projected on the basis of current levels of cut.

The dream of restoration of Acadian forests

Like Camelot, there was one brief shining moment when it seemed something magical might happen in Prince Edward Island's forests. It was the mid-1970s, when Dr. Stephen Manley became the director of the P.E.I. Forestry Branch. With a doctorate from the Yale School of Forestry, Dr. Manley had a vision of the future forest. He set about to recreate the original Acadian forest—to plant, not the species immediately required by the pulp-and-paper industry, but the original native species: white pine, red oak, eastern hemlock, white ash, yellow birch, butternut, and beech. Many of these species are long-lived, representing the climax stage of the Acadian forest, some living up to four hundred years. Repeated clearings and conversions to lower-value species had almost entirely removed them from the Island landscape. Early successional species of white spruce, white birch and red maple had grown in dominance from an original 10 percent of the forest to approximately 90 percent today.

For many Maritimers, the notion that their forests had once harbored large and valuable species, fine-furniture wood, and nut-bearing trees was a revelation. Dr. Manley's vision was featured in media across Canada, with a cover story in *Harrowsmith* magazine. He argued not solely from an ecological viewpoint, but from an economic one as well. The forests of the Maritime provinces, he said, should yield fifty to eighty cubic meters to the hectare, while our current "bastardized" forest provides only fifteen cubic meters to the hectare.

"We have literally reduced by orders of magnitude the capacity of the landscape to produce a lot of valuable material," Manley explained.[6]

He created a wonderful dream. Instead of allowing current economic pressures to steadily degrade the forest, why not restore the ecological wealth of the original forest for future generations? And, if there was anywhere in Canada where such a dream could be realized, it was Prince Edward Island.

Sadly, it was too bold a dream for the modern world. By 1979, the provincial government decided to shift its forest policy toward the production of softwood for pulpwood and sawlogs. Dr. Manley left the provincial government.

As he later said, somewhat ruefully, "I don't think anyone wants to take the chance on having vision . . . vision takes a long time."[7]

But the dream had taken root. Local environmentalists continue to work toward the restoration of the forest. The Environmental Coalition of Prince Edward Island has converted what had been planned as a historic preservation of a 175-year-old house and homestead into an Acadian-forest rehabilitation project.

The Macphail Homestead now boasts not only historic house tours, but a major Acadian-forest restoration project in the Macphail Woods. After conducting a biological inventory of the forests on the fifty-seven hectare property, the local environmentalists collected seeds from thirty-five representative species for the Macphail nursery. They have been successful, using cuttings and seed stock, in growing thousands of seedlings of such original species as red oak, white ash, beaked hazelnut, basswood, ironwood, yellow birch and butternut. They have also worked to preserve the rare shrub species and other woodland plants. The nursery is now providing seedlings, not only within the Macphail Woods, but to schoolyards and other properties across the province. They have helped individuals and communities set up small nurseries to cultivate native trees and shrubs. Biodiversity within the site is carefully monitored, particularly in the area of neotropical migratory songbirds that are declining in eastern North America.

The focus of Island environmentalists on restoring the forest that once blanketed 98 percent of the province is inspiring. We need a similar vision for the rest of Canada. In the face of the vast forest conversions to lower-value species that are occurring across Canada, the enthusiasm for working to achieve ecosystem health a hundred years hence suggests more than a quixotic dream. As Stephen Manley said, "Vision takes a long time."

9

Quebec

Alberta may claim to be the Canadian cultural equivalent of Texas, but geographically, Quebec has them beaten hands down. In terms of land mass, Quebec is approximately twice the size of Texas; it is Canada's largest province, with an enormous territory of 1.5 million square kilometers (154 million hectares).[1] Northwestern Quebec embraces the entire east coast of Hudson Bay, while its smaller relative, James Bay, juts toward Quebec's population centers. Still, the urban dwellers of Montreal are as remote from the source of Quebec's massive hydroelectric facilities as New Yorkers are from Newfoundland.

Quebec's forests cover eighty-four million hectares, about half of the province. The taiga, or far northern forest, which reaches up to the tree line, is typified by open forests and bog. Farther south is the Quebec portion of the transcontinental boreal forest ecoregion. The boreal within the province extends from the shore of southern James Bay all the way east to the Atlantic coast—the Gaspé to the south and the Labrador border to the north. The boreal of Quebec is predominantly a dense black spruce forest, interspersed with balsam fir and jack pine. Along the river valleys farther south is the mixed-wood Great Lakes–St. Lawrence ecoregion. Within Quebec, this ecoregion is luxuriantly covered in the sugar maples that provide Quebec with a high-quality edible forest product.

Historically, European settlers established themselves in the rich river valleys of southern Quebec—the St. Lawrence, the Ottawa and the St. Maurice. And it was in these valleys of Great Lakes–St. Lawrence forest that the mining of white pine began in the 1700s. The pattern found in the Maritime provinces was repeated here. One

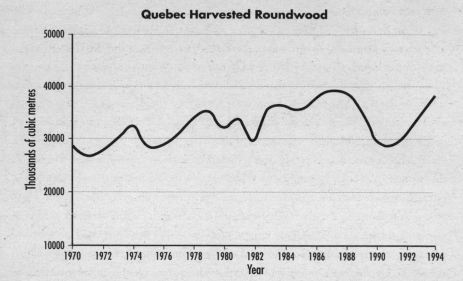

Quebec Harvested Roundwood

SOURCE: Compendium of Canadian Forestry Statistics 1995.

Quebec observer reported in 1808 the logging of pine trees that were 120 feet (37 m) long and 4 feet (1 m) in diameter.[2] These giant pines were first logged out for the British Navy. By the 1800s the prime use had shifted to sawmills and lumber. Quebec brought in its first forest regulations in 1849 and began to benefit from some revenue from stumpage fees—despite the minimal amount charged.[3] Early in the 1900s, the economic forest power shifted to the pulp-and-paper industry, as Quebec became a major exporter of pulp to the United States and Great Britain.[4]

For centuries, Quebec's forests have been heavily exploited, so much so that it is estimated that south of the forty-ninth parallel, a mere 10 percent of the forest remains untouched by human intervention.[5] Traditionally, large timber companies logged Quebec's largely Crown-owned forests, covering 85 percent of the productive forest area through twenty-year procurement contracts and large "evergreen" forest concessions.

While the Crown owns almost all of Quebec's forests, small woodlot owners are by far the most productive forest workers in the Quebec scene. Even though they hold only 12 percent of the forest, they produce 22.8 percent of the total volume of wood produced annually in the province.[6] Private owners are also the backbone of the province's lucrative maple-syrup industry. Of the over $150 million in annual sales of Canadian maple syrup, most is from the maple forests of Quebec.[7] The forest has been threatened by environmental stress, acid rain and airborne toxic chemicals, resulting in a frightening crown dieback in the late 1980s. The private woodlot owners worked with environmental groups in pressuring the United States to reduce its sulfur-dioxide emissions. In the last eight years, since the agreements to reduce SO_2 emissions from coal-burning plants and smelters in the seven eastern provinces and the United States, the health of Quebec's maples has steadily improved. While controversy still persists about the relative role of spring thaws and airborne pollutants in causing that particular maple die-back, scientists are continuing to amass evidence of the ongoing damage to forests caused by the combined stresses of increased UV exposure, ground-level ozone, acid rain and climate change.

Quebec boasts a highly productive forest co-operative sector—businesses in which the workers are both the employees and the owners. Some of these worker co-operatives own their own sawmills, as well as running logging operations. They account for about 8 percent of the sawmill production and five million cubic meters of wood logged annually.[8] They have argued that the smaller worker-owned co-ops have a better forest-stewardship record than the large corporate interests.

As the Quebec forests were mowed down, the province experienced local supply shortages, and the Quebec sawlog industry became an importer of wood. With fewer and fewer high-value trees available, Quebec mills were forced to look to Maine for a source of supply. By the early 1980s, two-thirds of Maine's sawlog spruce-fir lumber and half of its softwood lumber was exported to hungry mills north of the border. As U.S. forest critic, Mitch Lansky, noted:

> The main reasons large landowners give to explain why they export sawlogs to Canada are that the markets are handy. . . . *The Quebec mills lack a local sustainable supply and are willing to pay far more than the Maine mills.* Researchers have cited other reasons why the Canadian mills can afford the higher prices: the Quebec mills have the advantage of better exchange rates, experienced managers, cheap power, government-sponsored training, state-of-the-art equipment, export assistance, cheap Canadian wood (but shipped in from a distance), lower rates for workers' compensation, and subsidies for new mills or mill expansion (emphasis added).[9]

In the early 1970s, the Quebec government realized that it was not benefiting from the overly generous terms given to the large companies. There had been widespread and careless "cut and run" logging, with precious little silviculture investment to offset it.[10] Future wood supply began to look doubtful, especially after a spruce budworm outbreak in the mid-1980s that affected large areas of eastern Quebec. At taxpayers' expense, in 1976, the province conducted an aerial insecticide-spray program over 4.5 million hectares of forest.[11] While public opposition focused on the widespread

QUEBEC	(1995)
Forest Land in million hectares	83.9
Stocked Harvested Crown Land in hectares	4,051,000
Area Logged in hectares	357,443
Volume Logged in million cubic meters	39.5
Annual Allowable Cut in million cubic meters	57.8

SOURCE: Natural Resources Canada, Canadian Forest Service, *The State of Canada's Forests, 1996-1997* (Ottawa, 1997). These are federal government summaries, based on provincial government data. The figures are not necessarily accurate.

deleterious effects of dumping poison on the forest, the makers of forest policy were more concerned about reform of the tenure system.[12]

The province's large industrial players, of course, wanted no change at all. But a serious recession in the mid-1970s created an opening for a political review of the whole forest-management system for the province.[13] At the same time, the health of the forests was in doubt. As one forestry official said, "Quebec's forests are in such a pitiful state, we are facing shortages in many regions."[14]

The government blamed the impending wood shortages not on fundamental flaws in the industrial forest model, but on their antiquated tenure system. As a first step toward change, initially by policy in 1985, and subsequently by legislation in April 1987, all existing timber tenures were extinguished, with the promise that tenure-holders could either obtain compensation or be entitled to an agreement under the new system.[15] In anticipation of the new system, many large-scale pulp-and-paper firms bought out smaller sawmills. This gave them greater access to supply, as well as

QUEBEC CORPORATE PLAYERS

Abitibi-Consolidated*
Kruger
Donahue Inc.
Domtar
Repap
Avenor
Alliance Uniforêt
Cascades
Noranda–Maclaren
Cartons St. Laurent
Daishowa
Canadian Pacific Forest Products

*recent merger of Abitibi-Price and Stone-Consolidated

more effective vertical integration. The pulp mill could send good-quality roundwood to its own sawmills, while using the wood chips, a byproduct of the sawmills, as raw material for the pulp mill. There were so many buyouts in the mid-1980s that currently 60 percent of the province's sawmill production is owned by the pulp-and-paper industry.[16]

The pulp-and-paper mills received another boost in the lead-up to tenure reorganization. Massive federal-provincial subsidies poured into the pulp-and-paper sector for mill modernization in Quebec. Between 1983 and 1996, federal support came to over $456 million, with funding matched by the province.[17] These subsidies were, of course, additional to the subsidized lower power rates provided by the Crown-owned company, Hydro-Québec, until 1988. In that year, Hydro-Québec began to raise rates, prompting industry lawsuits against the government. Now the mills were about to be granted long-term tenure on virtually all of the province's forests.

By 1987, all the forested land in the province—the entire committed annual allowable cut (AAC)—had been consolidated into a series of contract agreements, established by the new Quebec Forest Act, passed in 1986. Called "CAAFs" (for "Contrats d'approvisionnement et d'aménagement forestier," or Timber Supply and Forest Management Agreements [TSFMAs]), the contracts tied up all of the productive forest base in twenty-five-year leases, with five-year renewal terms.

About ten major pulp-and-paper companies and fifteen independent mills control virtually all the CAAFs; about two hundred contracts allocate the only AAC for the province. In 1996, five pulp-and-paper companies controlled 80 percent of production; the companies are mostly Canadian-based, with Daishowa of Japan being the only completely foreign-controlled company. In February 1997, Chicago-based Stone-Consolidated merged with Quebec-based Abitibi-Price. Abitibi-Price already had four Quebec paper mills, churning out some of what ends up covered with "all the news that's fit to print" in the *New York Times*. But it also has operations in Georgia and Alabama.[18] The new conglomerate, tentatively titled Abitibi-Consolidated, will be the world's largest newsprint manufacturer.[19] The other Canadian companies are also international. Kruger has three pulp mills in Quebec as well as mills in the United States and Britain, and ownership interests in tissue mills in Venezuela, Colombia and Italy.[20] Other major industry players are Donahue Inc., with 1996 sales of $1.6 billion from operations in Quebec, Ontario and B.C.,[21] Repap, Avenor, Alliance Uniforest, Cascades, Maclaren, Cartons St. Laurent and Domtar. Domtar, while not a Crown corporation, is 45 percent owned by the Quebec government. In the first two quarters of 1995, Domtar posted record sales of $717 million. But recently, profits have fallen.

The system is criticized by various groups within Quebec, including the Grand Council of the Cree, for the government's conflict of interest, being both "shareholder in industry and protector of the forest." Quebec has long dabbled in government investments in logging operations.[22] In the post-recession period, the government bought out failing mills to protect jobs in remote areas. Its first forest Crown corporation, Rexfor, was established in the late 1950s. But the largest pulp-and-paper companies are privately held.

The CAAFs prohibit the processing of Quebec wood outside the province and compel contract holders to conduct sufficient silviculture to regenerate logged-over areas. CAAF holders are to abide by a new set of management guidelines, which include public consultation on management plans and incorporating respect for wildlife habitats, other non-timber values, and recreational areas. The Minister of Forests is empowered to terminate any CAAF for non-compliance, without compensation.[23] The Quebec government proclaimed its new legislation as a remedy to past forest practices and the legacy of clear-cutting, depleted ecosystems, diminished soil and water quality: "With this act, Quebec enters a new forestry era, in which public forests will not only be more productive (based on long-term sustained yield), but also more versatile, permanent and better protected, for the greatest benefit of industrialists and outdoor recreation enthusiasts."[24]

While the provincial government prides itself on the CAAF system as a great step forward in sustainable development, many environmental groups were appalled that the province had gone the route of long-term licenses—committing the best lands to huge forest companies. Indigenous peoples throughout Quebec have always opposed large-scale industrial forestry as they are only too familiar with its impacts on their traditional lands. They were outraged that the government had committed virtually the entire productive forest for the long term, without consultation with the traditional occupiers of the forest.

Another view was expressed by respected Quebec ecologist Jules Dufour:

> The new silvicultural system is a veritable windfall for the forest industry which will benefit from minimal cutting rights, disguised development subsidies, and exemption from paying the cost of restarting production in previously non-regenerated areas . . . The new system will contribute to the development of industrial silviculture, transforming the forest into a plantation consisting solely of species that are desirable from a commercial viewpoint.[25]

Another Quebec commentator, D. Vanier, in an article in French titled "A Gift for the Forest Industry," wrote: "Whether it is called 'forest concession' or 'timber supply and forest management agreement,' nothing has changed. Industry will continue to dominate forest use."[26]

The CAAF system gave control of Quebec's forests to centralized corporate powers, under contracts that will run for decades.

First Nations of Quebec defend the forest

The Algonquin of Barriere Lake, a small indigenous community two hundred kilometers north of Ottawa, have taken *Our Common Future*, the report of the Brundtland Commission (the United Nations World Commission on Environment and Development) as their inspiration and guiding document in efforts to reverse the tide of industrial domination of the landscape. They have a reserve located within the La Vérendrye Wildlife Reserve. It sounds perfect—a First Nations community surrounded by a wildlife reserve, with aboriginal rights of hunting, trapping and fishing intact. But unfortunately, nothing in Quebec law says a wildlife reserve cannot be logged.

When half of the land area of the wildlife park had been clear-cut, and after much of the area around their community had been treated with toxic herbicides, the community decided to take a stand. Blockades were erected along logging roads, and a long siege began. The Algonquins' intention was always clear. They did not want all logging stopped, but they wanted the principles of "sustainable development," as laid out in the Brundtland Report, instituted on their lands.

Chief Jean Maurice Matchewan took a copy of *Our Common Future* to government officials, asking them to incorporate its principles into any further logging of their reserve. Nothing changed. Clear-cutting, herbiciding and destructive road-building continued. After the blockades, the forest contractor obtained an injunction, and arrests were made by the Quebec provincial police. The SQ (Sûreté de Québec) have a reputation for shooting first and asking questions later. Even though Chief Matchewan's arrest was being filmed by a National Film Board crew, he was physically man-handled, thrown against a truck, and treated like a violent criminal, all the while urging his people to practice Gandhian non-violence.[27]

When the case came to trial, their lawyer urged them to advance land claims as a defense. To that point, the community had not seen the conflict as an ownership issue; for them, it was a question of the future of the land: the ecological sustainability of logging practices. It was about traplines being destroyed and traditional hunting and fishing areas devastated. It was about the rights of local communities to have a voice in decisions that affect them. That was what had drawn them to the Brundtland Report, which specifically recommended that indigenous people and other traditional communities have a "decisive voice in the decisions about resource use in their area."[28]

But acting for ecological sustainability is not an accepted defense to charges of violating an injunction, so the defense was based on a land claim. In general, the Quebec government has been unyielding, even dismissive, in relations with its First Nations communities. The Cree opposition to the dams at James Bay in the early 1970s had taught them about political confrontation. That conflict had pitted a government that believed it had an absolute right to every drop of water flowing to James Bay against an aboriginal people who refused to accept the inundation of their traditional lands by enormous reservoirs.

Part of the problem for indigenous peoples was the historic jurisdiction of the federal government. In a country defined as a bilingual society of French and English founding nations, the federal system ensured that—because they were not French—aboriginal peoples in Quebec received public education in English. They could speak their own languages, and English as a second language, but very few indigenous peoples of Quebec could speak French. In a political climate of separatism, nothing is more sensitive than the survival of a distinct Québécois culture. Language is a political powder keg. Moreover, the province's First Nations communities were seen as sympathetic to federal jurisdiction within Quebec.

The height of Quebec–First Nations conflicts occurred in the summer of 1990 in a Quebec town called Oka. Sûreté de Québec forces had attempted to storm a Mohawk barricade erected to preserve the old-growth pine forest near their reserve. The threat was not from logging in this case, but from a golf course. One police officer died in the cross-fire. The press reported that the Mohawk were viewed locally as "Anglos with feathers."

It was, to put it mildly, not an auspicious time for the Algonquin to negotiate with the provincial government. But on August 22, 1991, they accomplished something truly remarkable—an unprecedented agreement between the provincial and federal governments and the Algonquin of Barriere Lake. The "Trilateral Agreement" called for sustainable development of the lands in the traditional territories of the Algonquin. All told, it covered more than ten thousand square kilometers. The goal of the plan was to develop an integrated resource management plan, reconciling traditional indigenous concerns for wildlife, medicinal-plant collection, spiritual values and the preservation of the forest itself.[29]

As an immediate measure, the Algonquin were to identify "sensitive zones," areas likely to receive special treatment once the plan was completed; these zones would be given interim protection. The identification of sensitive zones was a community effort, with elders assisting younger community members in locating spiritual sites, hunters helping to delineate crucial moose habitat, and contracted ecologists and foresters helping to defend the highest principles for ecologically sustainable practice in the short term.

However, this remarkably peaceful solution to years of blockades was jeopardized on a nearly daily basis. The key difficulties were that neither the logging contractor nor the largest wood purchaser in the area, Domtar, was a party to the agreement, and that—although the entire Quebec government was bound by the document—it had been negotiated and signed by the Indian Affairs Minister only. The Forest Minister and the ground-level forest service bureaucracy were largely hostile to the effort, and allowed the new rules to be broken time after time. One branch of government would guarantee to the community that critical, sensitive habitat was under interim protection, and within days, the area would be logged. Provincial forest service employees would shrug their shoulders and admit that the contractor still had valid cutting rights for the whole area and they didn't know how to stop him.[30] The Algonquin began posting community members as observers around all sensitive zones. They rushed to scene after scene of logging, but there was little they could do but lodge complaints and issue reports.

Meanwhile, the five-year process of developing the integrated resource management plan for ten thousand square kilometers was also under way. The Algonquin set about mapping the entire territory, drawing on traditional knowledge and providing detailed overlays of the biological diversity and historical uses of the area, in far greater depth than any university team could have hoped to achieve. The Algonquin did not shun technology; they had the entire database entered into a GIS (Geographic Information System) that community members were being trained to use. The mapping exercise led to many fascinating exchanges between the forest service staff, who had done many maps and logging plans, and the Algonquin, whose maps conveyed a completely different picture of the landscape. In one memorable exchange, the forest service representative on a planning committee was heard to say, "But this map can't be right. Why would anyone put a graveyard next to a highway?"

Forestry industry forces gained the upper hand in Barriere Lake when the whole community was destabilized through internal factional disputes. In January 1996, the former federal Minister of Indian and Northern Affairs, the Hon. Ron Irwin, stepped in and appointed an interim band council. The next few months saw the closing of the school, suspension of basic services to the community, and the derailment of the Trilateral Agreement. Chief Matchewan and his supporters smelled a rat. It seemed that legal advice proffered to the anti-Matchewan faction had come from a Winnipeg lawyer who, coincidentally, also represented Domtar.

In early 1997, after nearly a year of rule by the interim council, the Algonquin defenders of the forest returned to the blockades, concerned that clear-cut logging was compromising the integrity of the future resource management plan.[31] In the spring of 1997, the Minister of Indian Affairs relented and appointed another interim band council that was satisfactory to the majority of the community. The Trilateral Agreement now has a renewed chance of demonstrating leadership to the rest of Canada.

As prime forest land in southern Quebec is degraded, logging pressure is increasing in the remote areas to the north. Having successfully dealt a knockout punch to the planned massive Great Whale hydroelectric project on Hudson Bay, the Grand Chief of the Grand Council of the Cree, Matthew Coon-Come, is now taking on the forest industry. Massive clear-cutting is taking place on traditional Cree lands, so far distant from population centers that they are invisible to the Quebec public and the media.

The rate of logging has increased substantially in the area the Cree call "Eeyou Astchee" (Our Land). In 1974, the total amount of forested land in Cree traditional territory was 24,000 square kilometers. By 1994, the "Contrats d'approvisionnement et d'aménagement forestier" (CAAFs) covered an area more than twice as large— 52,000 square kilometers. The CAAFs, each for a renewable period of twenty-five years, are held by seven non-Native companies, supplying twenty-eight different mills. The Cree have identified significant differences between the CAAFs on their territory and others in the rest of Quebec. The average CAAF in the rest of Quebec is 1,600 square kilometers, while the average area in Eeyou Astchee is more than twice that, at 3,471 square kilometers. One lease alone, to Barrette Chapais, covers an area of 17,000 square kilometers, or an area 4,000 square kilometers larger than the state of Connecticut. The wood from that lease feeds the largest sawmill in Quebec, also owned by Barrette Chapais. Although the mill is in the heart of Cree territory, not one of the 400 to 450 people employed there is Cree.

The Cree estimate that since 1975 over five thousand square kilometers of their lands have been clear-cut. Huge volumes of primarily softwood for sawmills and pulp mills are logged annually. In 1995, more than five million cubic meters of wood were taken from Cree lands.[32] The Cree have connected the increased rate of cutting and road-building with the drastic decline in moose numbers throughout their lands. Moose form an important part of the Cree diet, and hunting the moose is an integral part of their culture. In 1985 the moose population was estimated at 1,200. After increased logging and road construction in this most affected area, there are now fewer than 400 animals. The Cree are in court trying to protect the moose from unsustainable levels of hunting and poaching, which have come with the easy access provided by the hundreds of kilometers of logging roads built in recent years. Logging itself has led to loss of stream quality. Downed trees across streams make canoe travel impossible. Clear-cuts destroy habitat for fur-bearing mammals.

The Cree are taking their case to the world, just as they did to halt the devastation of their lands by flooding for hydroelectric power. They have toured Europe and asked for market pressure to force Quebec's forestry companies into more ecologically appropriate methods of logging. In a book prepared to enlist public support, *Crees and Trees*, they make the following plea:

Preserving the integrity of the boreal forest environment is imperative not only for the economic needs of our people, but also for the survival of our culture. It is not just a question of too many trees being cut by the forest industry but rather an issue of cultural survival and fundamental human rights. That is why the destructive practices of the forest products industry and the policies of Quebec's government must change.[33]

The state of Quebec's forests

Decades of poor logging practices have diminished and degraded the forest ecosystems of Quebec. It is difficult to know the extent of protected forest areas within Quebec. With only 3.7 percent of Quebec's land base having any protected status, the amount which represents forested ecosystems is far lower.[34] But federal and provincial estimates of protected forest areas differ for Quebec. The 1991 federal *State of Canada's Forests* report estimated total forested protected areas as 610,000 hectares, or less than 1 percent of Quebec's forests. But included as a note to the federal report was the recognition that Quebec claims a higher level of protection—1.3 million hectares, or less than 2 percent of the forest base.[35]

Many of Quebec's forested ecoregions have lost diversity, through selection logging of valuable species going back to the 1700s, and more recently through species transitions following clear-cuts. Quebec is one of four Canadian provinces with legislation to protect endangered species. It has identified seventy forest-plant species that may have to be designated threatened or vulnerable under the province's act. The pressures of logging and settlement have also led to population declines in the eastern cougar, while the woodland caribou and the wolverine are listed as endangered on both the federal and the provincial lists.[36]

As the wood-supply problem worsens in southern Quebec, logging roads are being pushed further into the north, opening up, and ending, the wilderness. The pressures on wildlife populations needing a large range, such as the wolf, will increase from the wilderness fragmentation created by logging roads. The roads also mean that hunters will now have access to areas where moose and caribou previously lived undisturbed.

Ecological forest reform

Quebec's response to environmentalists' criticism of its logging practices has—in some ways—been progressive.

Quebec is the only province with a commitment, contained in its 1994 Forest

Protection Strategy, to total elimination of chemical herbicide and insecticide use by the year 2001. In the early 1980s, Quebec was one of the first provinces to ban the use of the phenoxy herbicide 2,4,5-T at a time when the Canadian government still registered it for use. While the New Brunswick and Nova Scotia forests were slated for spraying with the same herbicides used in "Agent Orange," Quebec's position was a sharp contrast.[37] Quebec has also, in response to public opposition to toxic chemical spraying against budworm, instituted a "no chemical insecticides" approach. While budworm spraying continued, Quebec approved only the biological insecticide Bt. Although there are also problems with Bt use, Quebec is nevertheless progressive in having outlawed such toxic chemicals as fenitrothion (when it was still federally registered), carbaryl and matacil.

The Quebec Forest Protection Strategy guards vulnerable forest lands, threatened ecosystems such as wetlands, and forests on thin soils or steep slopes. The reforms of 1994 also brought in improved public-consultation mechanisms.[38]

But, more remarkable, the strategy claims that it will eliminate clear-cut logging. As clear-cutting has been the method of choice for about 90 percent of Quebec's harvesting, the commitment, if genuine, would amount to a radical shift in the direction of sustainability.

A policy to no clear-cutting would force the pulp-and-paper industry and its contractors to rethink their current commitment to mechanization over labor. In 1990, 69 percent of the logging on Crown lands was entirely mechanized, and 84 percent of it was whole-tree logging, wherein the tree is taken, branches and all, from the stump up, and hauled to the roadside and delimbed there.[39] These methods all require large machinery.

The Algonquin of Barriere Lake quickly became familiar with the various euphemistic phrases used by the forest companies: clear-cutting and its new and improved successors "cutting with regeneration and soil protection," "regeneration cut," "improved cutting," and "shelterwood cutting." For the most part, these methods, particularly cutting with regeneration and soil protection, and regeneration cut, are nothing more than repackaged clear-cuts. Cutting with regeneration and soil protection, for instance, still involves the complete clearing of all trees from sites as large as 150 hectares. The only innovation to make the practice "careful" is that the logging equipment is required to reuse the same route leaving as it used coming in to log an area, thus reducing some of the impact on the soil and on existing regeneration. The ecological differences were minimal. The Cree describe the new logging as "new names, old policies." In their territory they have found that, "in reality, these reduced clear-cuts are made adjacent to one another with thin tree buffers so that over time these clear-cuts add up to massive deforestation."[40]

Clear-cutting is still the dominant method of logging in Quebec, but the percentage of areas logged by other means is rising under the new strategy.

Wood supply

Quebec's wood supply is still huge, with the province allowing logging of less than 1 percent of available wood supply each year. With a published AAC of over 56 million cubic meters and annual logging of 39.5 million cubic meters,[41] comparisons with Newfoundland or New Brunswick could lead to the conclusion that, while Quebec forest practice is damaging environmentally, the industry itself is not at risk of supply shortfalls.

But the appearance of plenty is illusory. The sawlog industry is already importing logs from the United States as local forests are so depleted that the industry could not survive without the imports. The pulp-and-paper industry is also experiencing regional shortages, as the wood closest to the mills is logged out. Of Quebec's productive forest lands, it is estimated that over 180,000 square kilometers are inaccessible. Yet with its usual creative sleight of hand, the government includes the wood volume in those areas as part of the AAC. As pressure builds for new logging roads to open up remote areas, the individual tree size will decline. Trees growing farther north just naturally grow smaller. In fact, many of the new mill developments in Cree territory are specifically designed to handle the small trees found in the northern fringes of the commercial boreal forest. The industry will be paying more to truck smaller trees over greater distances. The volume on the ground is likely to fail to meet the estimates in provincial inventories, and climatic conditions will make regeneration more difficult.

Local supply shortages are expected throughout southern Quebec.[42] The forests are overexploited and degraded, and regeneration after clear-cuts is often difficult or unsatisfactory.

One encouraging sign that could lead to reduced pressure on the forests is the move to recycle paper. Driven by consumer demands, primarily from U.S. customers, a number of Quebec mills are installing de-inking facilities in order to process newspapers into paper. Some states have legislated a required recycled content. For instance, by the year 2000, 40 percent of paper used in New York must be recycled.[43] Abitibi is installing a $20-million de-inking facility at its Alma plant, while Kruger's board mill produces 100 percent recycled-content linerboard as well as other products.

Unlike mills in more remote parts of Canada, the Quebec mills are close enough to the urban forests of New York to make processing recycled paper an immediately viable proposition. Having clear-cut Quebec to run off the *New York Times*, Quebec mills may be able to turn the tables by harvesting the mountains of used newspapers from New York. In fact, Kruger has established a facility in Albany, New York, as a "harvesting" operation for the curbside collections in upper New York State, eventually planning to purchase used newsprint from as far away as Boston and Baltimore. Abitibi-Price, prior to its huge merger with Stone-Consolidated, was pursuing a different strategy, locating its new recycled-content mills in the United States, and putting a far larger investment into mills south of the border than in Quebec.

Recycled paper *should* reduce logging pressure, but there is no indication yet that it is doing so. In 1993, Quebec reduced its AAC for softwood slightly, while increasing the AAC for hardwood.[44] Between 1993 and 1995, the actual harvest rate increased from 32.3 million cubic meters to 39.5 million cubic meters.[45] As in other provinces, Quebec's AAC is set on the basis of the potential future growth that will result from silviculture. By relying on the allowable cut effect, the AAC level is in excess of a sustainable yield based on natural growth rates.

Between 1986 and 1995, when the subsidies were in place, Quebec replanted 2.1 billion trees on public and private lands. Between 1992 and 1996, subsidies for private lands alone came to $136 million.[46] However, in 1990, the government announced its preference for natural regeneration. Since then, the federal subsidies for replanting have ended. The companies still receive a 40 percent rebate on stumpage fees for silviculture performed on harvested lands; in 1994–95, this amount came to $58.4 million. But it did not lead to the intensive silviculture efforts of the FRDA agreements.

While natural regeneration is clearly preferable to plantations, with attendant herbicide use and regeneration problems, the success rate of natural regeneration is improved when logging methods do not ravage the site, as clear-cutting does. Natural regeneration should be allowed to take place, as the term implies, *naturally*. It is completely consistent with Quebec's current phase-out of herbicides to get out of planting and to allow the forest recover from logging in the normal successional fashion of a natural, preindustrial forest. But the AAC calculations should then follow suit and remove the voodoo projections of impossible gains from intensive silviculture. The pro-industry bias makes this unlikely.

Quebec's wood-supply information remains harder to access than that of other provinces. Political posturing has led to Quebec's absence from many of the national forest-review processes. For example, Quebec contributed no data to the complete national timber-supply survey conducted by the federal forest service.[47]

Recently, Quebec has made serious efforts to reverse its historic undervaluing of the forest resource. The Quebec government has significantly increased its stumpage fees. In 1997 stumpage jumped 40 percent. All told, Quebec is expected to collect

$335 million in stumpage fees in 1997, three times as much as it did in 1992–93.[48]

The industry has responded with calls to reduce the stumpage fees, echoing complaints increasingly heard from British Columbia mills. Donahue CEO Michel Desbiens warned shareholders at their annual meeting that "the lumber industry is at risk."[49] The Quebec Lumber Manufacturing Association chimed in, urging government not to weaken the industry. As Canadian provincial governments finally begin to realize the importance of reasonable fees for the logging of publicly owned forests, industry can be expected to fight back. This is especially predictable given the cyclical nature of forest product markets, which will inevitably move to lower prices and economic downturns for Canadian mills. Whenever global commodity prices fall, environmental and sustainable forest policies will be blamed for lowering corporate profits.

It is clear that significant sectors of Quebec's industry have already exceeded the supply of merchantable timber and are now relying on imports. The pulp-and-paper sector faces increasing costs as it expands operations farther north into Cree territory. A review of the accuracy of inventory information and the AAC is urgently needed if Quebec is not to jeopardize its entire forest industry through over-cutting.

10

Ontario

Ontario is Canada's most populous province, with 90 percent of its ten-million-plus residents in communities in its southern reaches, in and around the Great Lakes. Torontonians, stuck in bumper-to-bumper traffic on Highway 401, like to believe that just outside the stretches of Metro there is a vast expanse of wilderness, all the way to Hudson Bay. But as someone's teddy bear once said, "If you go down to the woods today, you're in for a big surprise."[1]

Ontario is huge—110 million hectares of land and water. It encompasses four distinct forest ecoregions, covering 58 million hectares of the province[2]—the far northern boreal, described by provincial forest officials as the "Hudson Bay Lowlands," the boreal, the Great Lakes–St. Lawrence forests shared with Quebec, and the most threatened of all Canada's forests, the southern deciduous or Carolinian forest.

The Hudson Bay Lowlands, or northern boreal, is too remote for its forests to have been of much interest as a commercial logging prospect until now, but every other forest ecosystem has been significantly altered by post-settlement exploitation. Recent developments north of the fiftieth parallel suggest that even these remote areas of low-density, small-tree forests may be opened up to logging.[3]

The Carolinian forest ecoregion is reduced to a tiny fragment of its original cover. This most southerly of Canada's forest ecoregions is amazingly rich in biological diversity, sheltering 2,200 different herbs, 70 tree species, over 400 different types of bird, and other mammals, reptiles and amphibians unique in Canada.[4] But the area of Carolinian forest has been reduced to less than 10 percent of its pre-settlement range. In some municipalities, forest cover is only 3 percent of the land base.[5] Most of the deforestation that occurred was due to land clearing for agriculture and settlement. As a result, over 40 percent of Canada's listed rare, threatened and endangered species are found in this small area.[6]

The other two major forest ecoregions are the sites of Ontario's booming forest industry. Wood from the more productive southern boreal and the Great Lakes–St. Lawrence forest currently supplies more than a hundred pulp mills, sawmills and other forest product operations. Historically, the areas that have been logged—some having a two-hundred-year history of commercial exploitation—are within these ecoregions. The result has been a steady decline in high-value species and a transition to new, early successional, lower-quality trees.

The mining of the Great Lakes–St. Lawrence forests

As European settlers established themselves, the pattern of logging experienced in the Atlantic provinces repeated itself in Ontario. The forest was immense, forbidding and unfriendly. As one early settler wrote, the forest of Kent County, Ontario, was "so thick with overhanging foliage that it not only shut out the sunshine, but almost the daylight."[7]

Logging spread to the west, to the Great Lakes–St. Lawrence ecosystem of Ontario and Quebec, where vast areas of the forest were removed for human settlement, agriculture and lumbering. Settlers had the first choice of high-value timber. Prior to European settlement, the forest covered 90 percent of the land base. Now it has been reduced to 30 percent in Ontario, and logging and clearing have replaced fire as the major disturbance factor.[8]

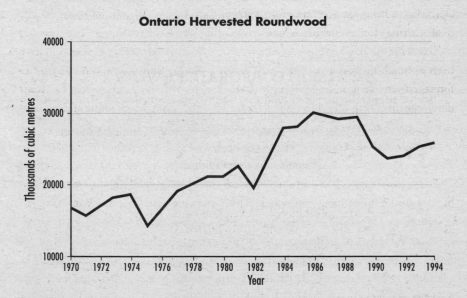

Ontario Harvested Roundwood

SOURCE: Compendium of Canadian Forestry Statistics 1995.

ONTARIO	(1995)
Forest Land in million hectares	58.0
Stocked Harvested Crown Land in hectares	3,174,000
Area Logged in hectares	211,660
Volume Logged in million cubic meters	24.6
Annual Allowable Cut in million hectares	0.4 (MAD)*

*MAD—Maximum Allowable Depletion due to all disturbances

SOURCE: Natural Resources Canada, Canadian Forest Service, *The State of Canada's Forests, 1996-1997* (Ottawa, 1997). These are federal government summaries, based on provincial government data. The figures are not necessarily accurate.

The forests of this ecoregion boasted sixty different tree species. Dominant ones included red and white pine, red and white oak, eastern white cedar, hemlock, black spruce, sugar maple, basswood, aspen, and white and yellow birch. The original forest was 30 to 40 percent old-growth pine.[9] So dominant was the white pine that it became Ontario's provincial tree. The same pressures to supply the British Navy that launched the forest industry in the Maritimes led to the mining of the Southern Ontario and Quebec Great Lakes–St. Lawrence forests as well. Huge pine trees from the Ottawa Valley disappeared onto the high seas. In Barrie, Ontario, logged red pine was recorded at sixty meters in height and eight meters around.[10] Currently, less than 3 percent of the Great Lakes–St. Lawrence forest is red or white pine, and much less than that is old growth.[11] Even so, the tiny remnants of old-growth pine in Ontario represent 95 percent of that ecosystem for Canada, and 60 percent of what remains worldwide.[12]

ONTARIO CORPORATE PLAYERS

Buchanan—Dubreuil Forest Products, Great West Timber, Mackenzie Forest Products, Northern Wood Preserves, Atikokan

Westons—E.B. Eddy Forest Products, (Nairn Centre, Timmins, Espanola), Elk Lake Planning

Noranda–Norboard Industries

Kimberly-Clark

Avenor

Macmillan Bloedel—Chapleau Forest Products

Abitibi-Consolidated

Tembec–Malette Inc., Malette-United, Spruce Falls

Domtar (Red Rock, Cornwall)

QUONO Corporation

Rainy River Forest Products

By 1835, most of the watershed of the lower Ottawa Valley had been denuded of its valuable pine, and the timber barons moved on to its upper reaches. Once the entire twelve million hectares of the Ottawa Valley were scoured, substantial timber interests moved westward, felling the tallest, straightest and most valuable trees. Through the watersheds of the Trent and Lake Simcoe, the Kawarthas and Muskoka, logging virtually eradicated the pine. Timber barons such as E.B. Eddy, J.R. Booth and F.H. Bronson employed thousands of people, built their own railways and began the steady process of industrial control over public forests. The province began to grant "timber limits" to the companies, guaranteeing access in exchange for a token license fee and duty on the wood actually cut.

In the late nineteenth century, an industry sprang up in hemlock bark, which was used in leather tanning; ultimately, over-cutting succeeded in reducing hemlock to a regionally rare species. In 1868, a government inquiry was launched to address the threat. The commission was doubly concerned when it discovered that much of the hemlock bark was being exported to U.S. tanneries, thus threatening not only Canada's hemlock, but Canadian tannery jobs as well. The inquiry concluded that an export duty should be placed on hemlock bark, "with a view to checking the wholesale destruction of our forests now going on."[13] No export duty was levied, and the hemlock-bark trade continued unabated.

By midcentury, the prime use of forests had shifted to sawmills and lumber. The forest was being fundamentally altered. White and red pine were disappearing; sawmills had sprung up to use the shorter timbers. But no one seemed to notice. The Ottawa Valley was described in the 1850s as having "timber enough here to supply the world for thousands of years."[14]

And so it would have seemed. The forest appeared unending, its riches just there for the taking.

"We are recklessly destroying the timber of Canada . . ."

That even one person wondered when we would run out of wood, and that that person was Canada's first prime minister, is quite remarkable. It was not some government commission that alerted Sir John A. Macdonald to a threat to the future of the forest. It was the view from his window. Both his home and his office were perched on the banks of the Ottawa River, which in those days was the liquid highway down which tons of timber were sent. In 1871, he wrote to a friend: "The sight of immense masses of timber passing my windows every morning constantly suggests to my mind the absolute necessity there is for looking into the future of this great trade."

The forests of the Ottawa Valley were literally disappearing before his eyes. "We are recklessly destroying the timber of Canada, and there is scarcely a possibility of replacing it. The quantity of timber reaching Quebec is annually decreasing, and the fires in the woods are periodically destroying many millions of money."

Unlike the observer who thought that the Ottawa Valley alone had enough timber for thousands of years, Sir John A. was worried. "What is to become of the Ottawa region generally, after the timber is cutaway, one cannot foresee."[15]

Dr. Bernard Fernow, the first Dean of Forestry at the University of Toronto, was also disturbed by the rapacious pace of logging in Ontario. Between 1867 and 1913, he estimated, Ontario had logged an astronomical twenty-five billion board feet of white pine. "As yet," he wrote, "the forests are viewed solely as a source of current revenue, not as capital, and the rights of people and of posterity are sacrificed."[16]

Impacts on biodiversity

The eradication of old-growth pine has had a profound effect on the Great Lakes–St. Lawrence ecoregion of Ontario and Quebec. Only 1 percent remains of the white pine forests that once blanketed almost half of the region. And of that 1 percent, less than one-third is within protected areas. Not only old growth, but even young trees are rare; regardless of the age, pine is a disappearing species in Ontario's forests, as a result of decades of a deliberate policy of liquidation, and the forest itself is degraded through the removal of such a key species.

Like a domino effect, degradation moves through the ecosystem. Without old-growth pine, wildlife dependent upon it for habitat or food are driven out, and other plant and animal species dependent on that wildlife vanish with them. Of course, this forest is not a moonscape. *Something* will grow back to replace the species that logging has depleted, and as these early successional species move in, their compatible fauna move with them. The entire forest composition is altered. And while one makes no subjective value judgments—that one type of fern, for instance, is "better" than another—there is no question that global biodiversity is diminished when a particular ecosystem, rare or unique in the world, is vastly reduced or disappears.

Old-growth white pine is necessary to many of the inhabitants of the forest. Female black bears prefer leaving their cubs near old white pine, so the cubs can more easily escape predators by climbing the ridged bark of the tree.[17] Black bears will even use dead trees for hibernation. The pileated woodpecker prefers old-growth pine, making large cavities in its search for food. The cavity left behind may then be used for nesting by a saw-whet owl, or, if near a wetland, by a wood duck.[18]

Old-growth pine forests are often the preferred habitat for the lynx, pine marten, three-toed woodpecker, and white-winged cross-bill. Both ospreys and bald eagles prefer old-growth pine for their treetop nests. Even when old white pines comprise less than 1 percent of the forest's larger trees, 77 percent of the osprey nests and 80 percent of the bald eagle nests are found in these few old pine trees.[19]

In addition to loss of biodiversity in both landscape and species, the genetic diversity of the trees themselves is reduced. Old-growth pine forests lose between 25 and 80 percent of their genetic variability, even after partial logging.[20] In contrast to logging, a forest fire would leave behind the mature, fire-resistant trees, allowing them to reproduce before succumbing to old age, thus maintaining natural genetic variability.

The boreal

The most productive boreal forest has also been exploited at an ever-increasing rate. The original forest of this region was dominated by white and black spruce, jack pine, balsam fir, trembling aspen and white birch. It was not subject to heavy commercial logging until the 1940s, when the white pine of the more southerly ecoregions was gone; but then logging pressure began in earnest.

In recent years, the effects of widespread clear-cutting are being felt. Although efforts to suppress natural fires have had an effect on forest age composition in certain areas, clear-cutting is having a more significant impact. Unlike the reversible disturbances caused by the natural fire regime, removing all the trees over vast areas through clear-cutting is leading to sweeping species conversion, right across the landscape. A 1992 government-commissioned study found that post-clear-cutting regenerating spruce dropped by 77 percent, while the proportion of lower-value hardwoods had increased by over 200 percent![21] On a province-wide basis, the proportion of spruce within the forest composition has dropped substantially, from an original 21 percent of the forest to only 4 percent today.[22]

The "green rush" for Ontario's northern boreal continues today. The area being logged quadrupled between the 1940s and the 1980s. In the 1940s, 2,000 square kilometers a decade were logged. Forty years later, the figure was 8,000 square kilometers.[23] Not surprisingly, it is the most productive areas that have been logged first. The boreal has varying topographic features, some very poorly drained, others quite rocky and unproductive. It is the geological features of outwash plains and eskers that support the most productive forests. Since 1940, virtually all of Ontario's forests on outwash plains and 70 percent of those on eskers have been logged at least once.[24]

In 1994 the provincial NDP government gave permission for the cut to increase by up to 50 percent. Eighteen months later, new mills have increased the total annual harvest rate by about 12 percent. In 1990, the actual amount of wood cut was twenty million cubic meters; by 1995 it was over twenty-four million cubic meters.

The steady erosion of old-growth habitat in the boreal has had an impact on bio-diversity. The woodland caribou is threatened, through loss of its preferred old-growth habitat, and many other species of mammals and birds face an uncertain future, with the steady loss of older pine and mixed-wood conifer forests in the boreal.

Biodiversity and protected areas

Forest biodiversity is eroded throughout all Ontario's forested ecoregions, through fragmentation of wilderness. Obviously, human settlements in southern Ontario are significant disturbances, amounting to permanent deforestation. But throughout the remote forested hinterlands, strips as narrow as hydro corridors and roads can render the wilderness unusable for wildlife. "A band of about four hundred meters on either side of the route is effectively lost," according to research to determine the impact of roads and other corridors on normal forest functions.[25]

The presence and use of logging roads leads to permanent disturbance. Not only are the roads themselves damaging to the ecosystem, particularly if they are poorly built, but access to previously remote areas increases hunting and can stress wildlife. A study in the forest management area around Temagami found that moose populations were significantly lower within two miles of logging roads, whether or not the forest had been logged.[26] A more recent study confirmed the earlier results, finding serious declines in moose populations over a larger area.[27]

As Ontario loses biodiversity through logging, it has set aside areas within provincial and national parks. A total of just over six million hectares of Ontario is protected within provincial parks, although not all of this represents forested ecosystems. In fact, one park—Polar Bear Provincial Park—occupies fully half of the protected area, and it has no merchantable timber. Some significant anomalies remain: Algonquin Provincial Park, for example, was created to provide for ongoing logging. So despite its ecological significance within the Great Lakes–St. Lawrence ecoregion, nearly 80 percent of it is still logged. Some of the most significant old-growth-pine ecosystems are still subjected to logging.

Key ecosystems remain underrepresented in Ontario's network of protected areas. According to the World Wildlife Fund, sixty of Ontario's sixty-five ecological regions lack a completed protected-areas system.[28]

The battle for Temagami

The flashpoint for old-growth pine is the fate of Temagami, near North Bay. The Temagami forests have been the subject of a long campaign for wilderness protection and for the rights of the Teme-augama Anishnabai, the traditional owners and occupiers of the forest. The Teme-augama Anishnabai call their ancestral homeland "N'Daki Menan." It is a vast territory of more than ten thousand square kilometers. N'Daki Menan stretches from just north of the northern reaches of Georgian Bay, almost to the height of land dividing the Arctic and the Great Lakes watershed. In 1877, Chief Tonene of N'Daki Menan traveled south to Lake Nipissing to stop activities by lumber companies in Teme-augama Anishnabai territory. His nation had never signed the 1850 Robinson–Huron treaty, Chief Tonene told the Indian agent, and the lumber companies had no right to log in N'Daki Menan in the absence of a signed treaty.

Nearly one hundred years later, in 1973, Chief Gary Potts filed "cautions" under the provincial land titles act to stop incursions by forest companies and the Ontario government. In 1978, the provincial government, having failed to have the cautions removed, brought an action in the Supreme Court of Canada against the Teme-augama Anishnabai. Eighteen years later, the highest court in the land held that the Teme-augama Anishnabai had had an aboriginal right, but that it had been lost through adherence to the Robinson–Huron treaty—which they had never signed. The court did find, however, that the government owed a responsibility, a fiduciary duty, to the First Nation. Negotiations began in 1990 to resolve the outstanding obligations to the Teme-augama Anishnabai, but the talks broke down under the former provincial government and have not been resumed.

Since the turn of the century, the Temagami district has been a tourism destination for urban dwellers. It has been logged for at least as long. Tourism and logging do not always mix, and conflicts between the forestry companies and tourists have occurred since the beginning of the twentieth century. Lumbermen worried that careless canoeists would start fires in commercial timber, while tourists complained that the water was brown from use as a floating-log highway.[29]

The history of recent battles over Temagami began in the 1980s. Decades of logging had degraded the Temagami forests and reduced the old-growth pine. Nevertheless, in 1983 the government proposed significant increases in the cutting rates for the Temagami district. The government, having what they called an "oversupply" of overmature spruce and jack pine, required a substantial increase in logging to meet market demand as well as to maintain the desired age classes in the forest. As a result, the softwood harvest was to shoot up by nearly 200 percent by the year 2000—from 93,000 net merchantable cubic meters to 255,000. Logging of hardwood species, such as poplar, was to increase even more drastically—from 24,000 to 125,000 cubic meters.[30]

But even before the huge logging increases had been announced, a forest-management analysis by C.A. Benson, a Lakehead University forestry professor, had argued that cutting rates were already too high, and that the Ministry of Natural Resources (MNR) calculations had been based on "a low intensity provincial ground survey."[31] As is the case across Canada, the methodology of forest mensuration is notoriously unreliable. In this case, Benson alleged, it had led to unjustifiably high estimates of the volume per hectare. Moreover, the MNR had underestimated the age at which pine became "overmature," a mistake that, once again, had the impact of increasing the cut. It was, in the view of Temagami experts Bruce Hodgins and Jamie Benidickson, "overly optimistic and outdated in its views on natural regeneration without fire and was determining the size of the allowable cut to suit the perceived needs of the local industry rather than considering the ecological reality."[32]

To provide access to the forest for increased logging, an extension of the Red Squirrel forest access road was proposed, which would link the existing Red Squirrel Road off one highway with an existing network of the Liskeard Lumber Road, *and* with another provincial highway. The effect would be to cut a through route across the heart of the Temagami wilderness. The forest industry would gain access to huge amounts of timber. Mills in one part of the district would gain access to timber in other areas, increasing logging pressure and threatening a newly created park, the Lady Evelyn-Smoothwater Wilderness and the recreational paradise provided by a large system of interconnected canoe routes around and through the wilderness park. The corridor for the Red Squirrel Road was quickly approved—before any of the legal requirements for public review and planning were fulfilled.

Opposition to the extended logging road was intense. The Teme-augama Anishnabai continued to demand recognition of their authority over the area. They maintained that the road construction was an infringement on their lands, their rights and their jurisdiction. Conservation, cottager and recreational groups demanded a full public hearing on the road construction, maintaining that the approval process had been illegal. When a public hearing was denied, they launched a court challenge against the road construction.

As work crews began to extend Red Squirrel Road, they were met with blockades. Hundreds of people were arrested in blockades that ran continuously from September 17 to December 19, 1989, including the New Democratic Party leader Bob Rae. The protests ended only after the Ministry of Natural Resources informed Chief Potts that road construction was completed. Protesters left the blockades, while provincial bureaucrats completed the necessary paperwork to allow an extension of road construction until June of the following year.

Once Mr. Rae became premier, hopes were high for permanent protection of the site. Instead, the government began a plethora of consultation processes with some interim protection attached. A multi-stakeholder local committee, the Comprehensive Planning Council, was created, a memorandum of understanding was signed to begin treaty negotiations, and the local mill was bought out by the provincial government, and shut down. But no permanent protection was afforded the area, nor was the issue of the rights of the Teme-augama Anishnabai resolved. In June 1996, the Progressive Conservative government of Mike Harris, elected one year earlier, rejected a compromise package of protection measures recommended by the Comprehensive Planning Council. The court lifted the legal caution and the government opened the land for mineral staking. Logging continues for a host of mills, some hundreds of kilometers away. The reality is that logging in Temagami never stopped.[33]

Threatened forests

In the days of the NDP government, the conservation community expected that Premier Rae would act to slow logging pressures and protect threatened forest areas. The Ontario government had signed on to the commitment of the Endangered Spaces campaign of the World Wildlife Fund to protect a network of ecologically representative wild areas. But instead of slowing the rate of clear-cutting, the provincial government *increased* the AAC. Discouraged environmentalists received some good news in the last hours of the Rae government, when a major expansion of the Wabakimi Provincial Park in the northwestern part of the province was announced. This boreal wilderness is key habitat for the woodland caribou. As logging fragments and destroys the species' favored old-growth habitat, the additional 900,000 hectares of protection afforded by the park expansion was essential. However, the full establishment and regulation of the park were left to the future government.

Another forest that is prime for protected-area status is the Algoma Highlands. Located northeast of Sault Ste. Marie, on Lake Superior, the Algoma Highlands wilderness covers approximately twelve hundred square kilometers. Its wild beauty inspired Canada's best-known wilderness painters, the Group of Seven, seventy-five years ago. Only six thousand hectares of the Algoma forest have been protected. Known as "Ranger North," this forest boasts an extremely rare combination of old-growth white pine and yellow birch. But logging is encroaching on the Algoma Highlands. Already the protected forest of Ranger North is virtually ringed by clear-cuts. The current logging and road-building plans approved by the MNR will further fragment the remaining wilderness. In response to public pressure and environmental-group campaigning, the government agreed to conduct a full environmental assessment of the Timber Management Plan for the Algoma Highlands. Although the process is ongoing at this writing, environmentalists are not expecting much protection for key ecological forest values. By its terms of reference, the environmental assessment considered the impact of logging only on remote tourism, setting up a tension between tourism and timbering, while ignoring other environmental and social concerns.[34]

Ontario's forests: Management regimes and sustainability

In the last decade, as logging increased, so too did the production of studies, commissions, environmental assessments and audits of the province's forests. It could be argued that the province's pulp-and-paper industry had to boost production just to provide enough paper for all the studies.

The forests of Ontario cover fifty-eight million hectares out of the province's eighty-nine-million-hectare land base. Of the forested land, 88 percent is Crown land, managed by the province. Eleven percent is in private hands, and a mere 1 percent is federal.[35] For forest management purposes, the Ontario MNR excludes the far northern boreal, also known as the Hudson Bay Lowlands, and concentrates on the productive forest occupying the lower two-thirds of the province, excluding the Carolinian forests. It is from within this area that the AAC is derived and to which all forest management decisions relate.

The inventory of the productive forest lands of Ontario was developed in the 1940s, and the province is currently in its third cycle of inventory.[36] Aerial photographs, with some ground sampling, were used to develop and update the information. Since 1986, some of the data have been entered into the Geographic Information System (GIS), but fewer than one-fifth of the province's management units have been entirely mapped using GIS. The lower two-thirds of the province are all that the inventory covered. Of this area, forty-six million hectares was classified as forest—both productive and unproductive, with seven million hectares excluded as non-forest.[37] Eighty percent of the logging in these areas takes place on Crown land.[38]

Almost from the beginning the reliability of the inventory was assailed. No one questioned its general accuracy as a broad-brush estimate, but its use to generate volume figures and to set logging rates was widely viewed as unwise. In 1974, an internal study by the provincial government concluded that the inventory was significantly overestimating the amount of available wood. In fact, the inventory had exaggerated volume by as much as one-third.[39]

A similar finding was made by an independent audit conducted ten years later by Dr. Gordon Baskerville, the Deputy Minister of Forests for New Brunswick at the time. He noted that the inventory had never been designed for the use to which it was now put, but simply to "provide an average representation of an area in the order of two hundred thousand hectares." It was not intended to predict volume within a single stand of two hundred hectares.[40]

Relying on a shaky inventory, the wood-supply picture is further muddied through use of an "acceleration factor" in calculating the annual allowable cut. In order to equalize the age classes within the forest, the MNR compares the average age of the existing forest with that of an ideal "normalized" forest, as described by Bernard Fernow. (That "normal" forest is still much sought after by foresters across Canada.) In such a forest there is an equal area within each age class. Where forests have been heavily logged and poorly regenerated there is a lack of young forest. The process of accelerating the AAC is to hasten removal of older trees to make room in the underrepresented young age classes. That is, trees are cut down in order to allow trees to grow. That, at least, is the theory. Several independent government reports and audits have drawn attention to the fact that use of the acceleration factor, coupled with poor regeneration of forests after clear-cutting, will lead to wood-supply shortages.[41]

Ontario has its own language and set of acronyms for calculating each year's allowable cut. The forest planners use a concept called maximum allowable depletion or "MAD." The MAD concept is used "to identify the area available for depletion from all sources (harvest, fire, insects, disease, management reserves and others)."[42] Within that area a planned harvest volume is derived, with the actual harvest usually somewhat lower. In recent years the MAD model has been supplemented with more sophisticated computer models—the Strategic Forest Management Model, to allow different strategies to accommodate different goals; and the Ontario Timber Demand Model, to anticipate through an econometric model what timber products the industry will need. The federal government's national forest database uses MAD as equivalent to what other provinces call an AAC.

The cut in Ontario has been slowly, but steadily, increasing. As noted above, in 1994 the Rae government gave permission for the cut to increase by up to 50 percent. Eighteen months later, the new mills had increased the total annual harvest rate by about 12 percent. In 1990, the actual amount of forest logged was 20 million cubic meters; by 1995 it was 24.6 million cubic meters.

The area of Ontario Crown land under long-term license to forest companies has increased dramatically. In 1985, 58 percent of Ontario's Crown land was licensed to the industry. By 1993, this figure had increased to 70 percent.[43] The rest of the forest was licensed as well, but on more short-term arrangements. The new Conservative government has committed to having all Crown land forests transferred to industry control through "Sustainable Forest Licenses" similar to Forest Management Agreements (FMA) by April 1, 1998.[44]

In exchange for exclusive rights to log Crown forests, the companies were obliged to reforest (with seed and seedlings provided free by the government), maintain logging roads and pay a stumpage fee. Of course, there are subsidies to offset some of the road-building costs, as well as a stumpage rebate for silviculture.[45] As in every province, the stumpage is far lower than that south of the border, in the United States. Ontario's stumpage rates in 1990 were $7 per cubic meter for softwood, and between $1.20 and $5.75 per cubic meter for hardwood.[46] The average annual stumpage revenue between 1990 and 1992 in Ontario came to a total of sixty-seven million dollars. Meanwhile, the total provincial expenditures in forest management came to an amount nearly four times the stumpage revenue.[47]

Reforms to the stumpage system were initiated by the NDP government. The new approach is a market-based stumpage system. The stumpage is calculated in three separate charges: a base stumpage, a residual stumpage, and a forest-renewal charge. The new base rate for fiscal 1995–96 was set at $1.25 per cubic meter for all species. The forest-renewal charge varies, depending on the kind of tree harvested and the anticipated costs of regeneration.[48] The last element of the stumpage is more complicated. It is tied to the average market price for a particular forest product. Whenever it appears that the industry has received a profit in excess of production costs and beyond a reasonable rate of return, the government will take a 29 percent share of the increased profit as "residual stumpage."[49] When the profits reach the "windfall" level, the province's share drops to 10 percent.

Out of this new stumpage system, both the base stumpage and the residual charge are applied to the province's consolidated revenue fund; only the forest-renewal component of stumpage collected will be placed in a Forest Renewal Trust Fund.

While potentially raising revenue from stumpage, the Conservative government of Premier Mike Harris is reducing the costs of running the province's forestry department. In April 1996, the government announced an astonishing 45 percent decrease in MNR staff.[50] Forest regulation will be significantly curtailed. The Temagami District Office, for instance, is closing, just as logging conflicts are increasing in one of Ontario's most significant forest wilderness areas.[51]

With deep cuts in the Ontario Ministry of Natural Resources, it is possible the gap between what the province spends on forest management and what it receives in stumpage may begin to narrow. But the costs in damage to the ecosystem from increasingly unregulated logging can only be imagined.

Even at the previous level of staffing and enforcement, violations of logging guidelines were rampant. In the past, many documented cases of non-compliance and non-enforcement have been cited, but dismissed by governments as unfortunate exceptions to the general rule.[52] The thought of the forest industry policing its own clear-cuts does not inspire confidence.

Meanwhile, environmentalists are keenly watching the provincial government offices in Queen's Park for signs of undoing requirements for forest management left by previous governments.

The legal trails of the Class Environmental Assessment of Ontario's Forests and the new Crown Forest Sustainability Act are tortuous, but understanding them is essential to understanding the current and future management of Ontario's forests.

The Class Environmental Assessment and the Crown Forest Sustainability Act

The Class Environmental Assessment (EA) of timber management in Ontario was the hearing to end all hearings. The process for examining the environmental impacts of timber management in Ontario remains a classic case of how *not* to involve the public in decision making. The hearings themselves took four and a half years. It was more than a full year before the Ontario Ministry of Natural Resources had entered its case in evidence. After 70,000 pages of recorded transcripts and 2,300 exhibits presented by more than 500 witnesses, it took a further year and a half for the board to render its decision. As a "class" environmental assessment, it dealt not with ecosystem-specific cases, but rather with the whole class of forest planning and decision processes. Many were frustrated that the mandate for the board excluded land-use decisions and the formulation of the vision for the future forest.

In April 1994, the Environmental Assessment Board issued its 561-page decision. In large measure, it rejected the case put forward by environmental groups, dismissing calls for alternative management approaches as impractical or untested. The board further found that "land-use guidelines are only guidelines . . . not binding land-use decisions."[53] But it did promulgate a new series of legally binding requirements for forest operations. Among the 115 requirements were the creation of citizen advisory committees at the local level, the development of a strategy for the conservation of old-growth forests, and research on the environmental impacts of logging.[54]

More than three years later, the province still has not implemented a comprehensive old-growth strategy created after a two-and-a-half-year public process, costing more than a million dollars. The unimplemented old-growth strategy enjoys broad public support and is based on a sound scientific foundation. Citizen committees have been created, but their role is one of passive adviser. Despite an initial assessment that "a guiding force in the Board's ruling was the public's right to be a partner in the decision-making processes that affect Crown forest resources,"[55] thus far the committees have not resulted in a meaningful public role in decision making.

While ignoring key ecological aspects of the Class EA ruling, government claimed to be responding through the passage of new forestry legislation, the Crown Forest Sustainability Act (CFSA). The new act shifts the object of timber management from providing a continuous supply of timber to the economy to providing "for the sustainability of Crown forests."[56] "Sustainability" is defined as "long-term forest health." But, before concluding that ecological principles reign, check the definition of "forest health": "The condition of the forest ecosystem that sustains the ecosystem's complexity *while providing for the needs of the people of Ontario*" (emphasis added). Thus the legal requirement for timber production remains at the heart of the new act.

Under the new act, Forest Management Agreements (FMAs) will become Sustainable Forestry Licences (SFLs), and the government has rewritten its timber manuals into a new Forest Management Planning Manual. Non-timber values, such as biodiversity, are supposed to be weighed in making management decisions. Most environmental groups in Ontario have been disappointed with the new act, finding it unnecessarily vague and discretionary. Their concerns were heightened when the government transferred responsibility for the Act's implementation to the forest industry.

Taking pages out of the Newt Gingrich "Contract with America," Mike Harris campaigned on a slogan proclaiming a "Common Sense Revolution." While reducing environmental protection was not part of the platform, it has been the result. The Harris government rushed through substantial deregulation over public lands through its "omnibus bill." In 1996, this collection of amendments to dozens of provincial laws overhauled the Public Lands Act and the Mining Act, reducing requirements for permits for road-building and other activities on public land. The government's ongoing Red Tape Review targets regulations to protect the environment.

The whole thrust of the Harris government is in the direction of the unfettered exploitation, by industry, of Ontario's natural resources. Its Forest Management Business Plan will ensure that *all* Crown land is contracted out in Sustainable Forest Licences. The entire forty-six million hectares of productive forest Crown land will be controlled and managed by the forest industry for the first time in the province's history.

In another Orwellian turn of phrase, the Harris government announced its "Lands for Life" land-use planning process in early April 1997. The purpose of the consultation process, involving round-tables composed of residents from forest regions, will be to identify areas to be reserved from industry control. "Lands for Life" is effectively part of the transfer of Ontario's publicly held forest to corporate control. Huge regions—the Great Lakes–St. Lawrence, east boreal and west boreal—will be examined to determine which forest lands should be protected. Tourism values will also be identified, while a simultaneous process will determine the forest management for forests outside protected areas. The entire process is to be completed by December 1999.[57]

Ontario's forests are losing critical ecosystems, and industry is about to become its own policeman. By the spring of 1998, nearly all the responsibility for the control of logging in Ontario's forests will be handed over to industry. Internal reports by government and industry are quite clear on the direction things are going, anticipating increased self-regulation by forest companies and intensified logging, while public policy is discarded in the name of fiscal restraint.

The invisible hand of corporate control

Ontario's vast forest industry appears at first glance to have a large number of companies, with far less centralization of corporate control than other provinces. But scratch the surface and discover that of an estimated five hundred sawmills, the largest fifty account for more than 90 percent of lumber production.[58] In 1991, more than a quarter of the provincial total of roundwood production was harvested by just two companies.[59]

Large pulp-and-paper mills fit the pattern of the industry across Canada. Major players include Avenor, Abitibi-Consolidated, Kimberly-Clark, Domtar, Tembec and E.B. Eddy. E.B. Eddy expanded in 1995 with the purchase of two other mills, entailing management responsibilities for over four and a half million hectares of forest within both the Ontario boreal and the Great Lakes–St. Lawrence ecoregions.[60] E.B. Eddy's operations make it one of the largest companies in both the sawmilling and pulp-and-paper sectors. Its purchase of forest products from threatened wilderness in Temagami and Algonquin Provincial Park has made E.B. Eddy and its related companies a target for protests.

A fairly anonymous corporate player exerts significant power and control over large areas of Ontario forest. Most Canadians, even those who consider themselves knowledgeable about the forest industry, have never heard of industry giant Ken Buchanan.

Buchanan is the ultimate self-made man. In the early 1960s his pig and potato farm was destroyed by fire. From the ashes, Buchanan set out in a new direction—a logging and hauling company. Over the next twenty-five years, the Buchanan Brothers grew steadily, through ambitious acquisitions. Buying mills in Thunder Bay, Hudson, Marathon, Sapawe and Dubreuilville, Buchanan Brothers, now the Buchanan Group of Companies (BGC), is arguably the largest independent sawmiller east of the Rockies. Of the five largest sawmills in Ontario, three are owned by BGC. The company is the second-largest logger in Ontario, just behind Canadian Forest Products. The BGC and Canadian Forest Products' combined harvest is at least 25 percent of the total provincial harvest of industrial roundwood.[61] Buchanan is able to exert considerable influence throughout northwestern Ontario as his forest operations supply wood not only to BGC mills, but also to seven of the region's nine pulp-and-paper mills. As a result, the Buchanan companies can act in a monopolistic fashion, able to determine who gets what wood from the forests within its leases.

Buying up weak mills, Buchanan has often been seen as exerting "job blackmail" to gain concessions from unions and government. In the words of one senior pulp-and-paper executive, "Buchanan uses the implied threat of mill closures to pressure provincial officials into granting him timber licences. Jobs in Buchanan's mills are crucial to the area's economy, especially in smaller sawmill communities like Hudson and Atikokan."[62]

Apparently, Buchanan continues to get his way despite a track record of violations of environmental, health, worker safety and forest operations standards. The company has had long battles with the Workers' Compensation Board, fought to delay pulp-and-paper effluent controls, and has an appalling number of logging violations. In fact, between 1986 and 1991, BGC received 31 percent of *all* infraction penalties and 33 percent of all warning letters issued by the Ontario Ministry of Natural Resources in the north-central region.

BGC is logging in the Lac Seul Forest, which provides critical habitat to the endangered woodland caribou. While current logging has allowed key habitat to remain intact, a government review of the company's forest management agreement observed, "conflicts between wildlife management objectives and forest operations may occur in future years as the wood supply in the forest changes and areas of present caribou habitat become alluring for sawlog production."[63]

There is no question that quality sawlogs in Ontario are in short supply. Given BGC's track record over the years, steps should be taken now to ensure that critical habitat is not at the mercy of the company's logging plans.

Ontario's wood supply: When will the province run out of wood?

There is a general consensus that Ontario is running out of quality softwood, particularly for sawlogs, and that absolute shortages will appear within twenty to thirty years. Government publications have speculated about how to increase silviculture investment as "a remedy for wood shortages in the 2020-2040 period."[64] Senior industry representatives have described the "reality" of "long-term wood supply . . . decreasing; quality . . . decreasing."[65] A review for the Ministry of Natural Resources concluded in 1992 that "Ontario's softwood sawtimber harvest has been held above sustainable levels in the past, and will have to be reduced in the coming decades as sawlog inventories are depleted."[66] In 1994, the Minister of Natural Resources referred to current localized "acute shortages of good softwood logs" in Northern Ontario and went on to predict "a wood-supply shortage or a scarcity of certain types of fiber within the next twenty years."[67]

What is happening to Ontario's softwood supplies is no secret. In 1970 about 70 percent of everything that was logged was clear-cut. Today, the figure is 91 percent.[68] Massive clear-cutting leads to species conversion on a large scale in the boreal, from spruce to small hardwoods. The softwood that remains is predominantly in older age classes. One exception within the boreal is logging of jack pine, which can be regenerated in jack pine plantations. Species conversion also occurs in the Great Lakes–St. Lawrence forest. Thus, Ontario is bound to run into softwood shortages. As the first forest is logged off, the second-growth trees lack the volume of the first. Thus the quality of individual sawlogs is decreasing as logs keep getting smaller. The end of the sawlog industry is in sight, although government publications announce the news in muted tones: "Supply of suitable timber products from Ontario's forests will limit expansion in this sector, which can expect a contraction after the turn of the century,"[69] and "softwood supplies will tighten throughout the province and mitigative measures will be needed to overcome this deficit."[70]

Nevertheless, pick up any industry journal and read optimistic projections for growth. In the same article with the statements quoted above appears the good news: "All sectors of Ontario's forest products industry, other than the lumber sector, are forecast to experience growth over the next fifty years."[71]

The growth in the forest industry is predicted through shifts to what was previously considered worthless. The small hardwoods, poplar and birch, are being targeted for massive expansion through oriented strand board (OSB) and fiberboard mills. In 1995, the government committed an additional 2.3 million cubic meters a year in hardwood logging. That amounted to a 10-percent increase in the annual harvest, without any opportunity for public comment.[72]

The government's econometric models forecast a tripling of the hardwood harvest by the year 2020. So as softwood harvests in the boreal go down, hardwood will go up. With industry and government both eager to get into the OSB business, Ontario now leads the country in new forest-industry investments, spending eight hundred million dollars in 1994 and one billion dollars in 1995.[73]

The bulk of these investments is for the production of oriented strand board (OSB) and medium-density fiberboard (MDF). Like OSB, MDF is made with wood fibers and glue, all pressed together in an attempt to imitate real wood. Seven new or converted OSB and MDF mills in central and Northern Ontario have already been approved—and given new wood allocations.[74]

Of course, it looks as if the "under-utilized" hardwood is already being over-allocated. The *Logging and Sawmilling Journal*, of all places, reports that, "according to

[Martin] Kaiser (Policy Manager for the Ontario Forest Products Association) . . . the [poplar] inventory was not particularly accurate. Now there is a question of whether or not the amount of poplar the government says is there actually exists. *There is concern in some quarters that the government may have over-committed the hardwood supply*" (emphasis added).[75]

The article also quotes Mr. Kaiser as saying, "From the standpoint of using the productive land base, [the Ministry of Natural Resources] is trying to get every last stick of wood out there into the mills."[76]

Another government publication is blunt on the subject of hardwood supply. Referring to the vast northeast forest planning region, the report notes: "The demand for hardwood fiber in this region will exceed supply within twenty years."[77]

Ironically, public efforts at ensuring forest sustainability are falling off now, just when they are needed most. At a public consultation in June 1996, the Deputy Minister of Natural Resources, Ron Vrancart, indicated that the department would seek to avoid the requirements for sustainable-forest practices imposed by the Environmental Assessment Board. The reason offered for seeking an exemption from the Class Environmental Assessment requirements was that government cutbacks had diminished ministry staff, leaving no one to implement the changes.

Ontario will be experiencing shortages of softwood within twenty years. Forest-dependent communities will suffer, with the probability of mill closures. The pulp mill sector is also at overcapacity and will likely close mills as well. The new OSB and MDF investments are likely to cause shortages of poplar and birch.

In the absence of environmental assessment, public review or accurate inventories, the province of Ontario is promising away its previously uncommercial poplar and birch. These low-value hardwoods have increased in abundance because of clear-cutting. What will regenerate, once the poplar and birch are gone? Is sustainable-forest management always to be defined as finding new economic uses for the species that come in once the previous forest has been destroyed?

The question is not rhetorical. In fact, that self-defeating definition is the only way Canadian forest practices over the last two centuries can possibly be viewed as sustainable.

11

Prairies

MANITOBA

A vast province, Manitoba encompasses such a huge and varied chunk of the planet that the polar bear and the prairie burrowing owl are both residents. The frigid waters of Hudson Bay force the tree line farther south than in neighboring Saskatchewan. While all the forests of the province are classed as "boreal," there are substantial differences both in species composition and ecology between the various sub-categories of the Manitoba woodlands.

Manitoba's farthest northern forests are not considered commercially viable. They are in the transition zone to tundra and are wholly excluded from the forest inventory. The commercial forest consists of very small trees growing in adverse conditions. The Precambrian boreal is a forest clinging to existence on thin soils, acidic bogs along the northern end of productive forest. The soils of the Precambrian shield were sheared off by glaciers thousands of years ago. The work of millennia in rebuilding soils through the actions of mosses and lichens allows coniferous trees to survive, but they grow slowly—spindly and small. The boreal plain forests farther south are also dominated by conifers—black spruce and jack pine.

The vast dark green northern forest gives way, closer to the prairie, to the mixed-wood boreal, a transition-zone forest leading into the original tall grass prairie. The mixed-wood boreal of Manitoba covers the lower part of the province in a predominantly deciduous forest of aspen and poplar.

European settlement left these forests largely untouched well into the twentieth century. Early settlers cleared land for agriculture, but the vast forests of the province were economically unattractive to the huge commercial interests that were busy removing the best trees from the east and from coastal British Columbia. The primary forest

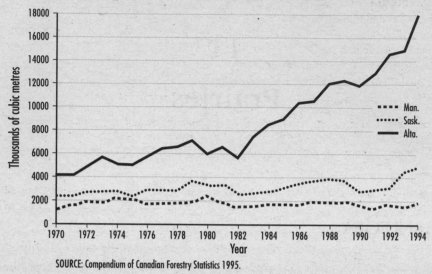

Provincial Comparison of Harvested Roundwood – Prairies

SOURCE: Compendium of Canadian Forestry Statistics 1995.

users were the aboriginal peoples, Ojibway, Cree and, farther north, the Dene. The First Nations communities relied on the forest for fuel, sustenance and shelter. The forest mammals were traditionally harvested for clothing and food, while the waters of the forest provided fish. Although the first white man traveled through what is now Manitoba in 1690, the forests were little disturbed by human intervention until the first large-scale paper mill was built in 1925 in the southeast corner of the province at Pine Falls.

Manitoba: Scandals, politics, and pulp

Manitoba's colorful approach to giving away its forests spans three decades—from building the mill at The Pas in the early 1960s, to doubling the rate of cut to accommodate Louisiana-Pacific in the 1990s.

The history of the mill at The Pas—the scandal that erupted when the public found out the extent of taxpayers' funds pumped into the mill, with subsequent deals and subsidies to keep the mill in production—warrants a book of its own.

The whole mess goes back to the Conservative government of Duff Roblin, which came to power in Manitoba in 1957. The province searched for years for an entrepreneur willing to open a pulp mill at The Pas, midway to the province's northern border. The project was not an easy sell. The province's own feasibility studies estimated the

MANITOBA	(1995)
Forest Land in million hectares	26.3
Stocked Harvested Crown Land in hectares	220,000
Area Logged in hectares	14,176
Volume Logged in million cubic meters	1.9
Annual Allowable Cut in million cubic meters	9.7

SOURCE: Natural Resources Canada, Canadian Forest Service, *The State of Canada's Forests, 1996-1997* (Ottawa, 1997). These are federal government summaries, based on provincial government data. The figures are not necessarily accurate.

surrounding forests to have "timber . . . spread out over a large area, generally of small diameter and young growth. Over 80 percent of the timber volume is less than 10 inches in diameter."[1]

To sweeten the deal, the province decided to offer substantially reduced stumpage rates; cut-rate hydropower to be held at lower-than-normal costs for a long term; fire protection and other costs to be covered by the government; and, of course, access to a long-term lease on a vast chunk of territory, as much as fifteen thousand square kilometers. Even this proved insufficient for the innovative and shrewd businessman who ultimately opened the Churchill Forest Industries complex at The Pas. By the time Dr. Kasser was done, the province had paid the entire cost of building the privately owned mill, nearly one hundred million dollars. Not only that, the developer had managed to get twenty-four million dollars in provincial funds into Swiss bank accounts.[2]

Once elected, the New Democratic Party government of Premier Ed Schreyer ordered a full commission of inquiry into the tangled web of the mill at The Pas. Three years and two million dollars later, the commission concluded its work, and in 1973 the province took over the Churchill Forest Industries mill to be run as a Crown corporation, called "MANFOR."

Under the MANFOR regime, the mill complex was never a winning proposition. In good years it broke even. And no one wanted to know about the bad years. The media tagline for the MANFOR mill became "the troubled mill at The Pas," and, in

MANITOBA CORPORATE PLAYERS

Repap Manitoba Inc.
Pine Falls Paper Company
Louisiana-Pacific Canada Ltd.

the late 1980s, the new Conservative government of Gary Filmon began looking for ways to get the public mill back into private hands.

It is ironic that the MANFOR complex actually began to make a profit in early 1989, just months before the closing of a sweetheart deal that rivaled the original development.[3] In secret negotiations, the province of Manitoba was wooing Repap to take over the mill. The Montreal-based company is one of the few remaining forest giants to reverberate with the name of only one man. Just as in New Brunswick, J.D. Irving *is* Irving Pulp and Paper, so George Petty is Repap. From fairly humble beginnings, Repap ("paper" spelled backward) had by 1989 become one of North America's leading producers of coated printing paper.[4] Now the province of Manitoba was intent on getting Repap to take over the MANFOR operations at The Pas.

By March 1989, the province had confirmed its decision to sell the company to Repap, but still the text of the agreement was kept secret. No public hearings or reviews were held while Manitoba negotiated the deal that would give Repap long-term leases covering a fifth of the province—an area of nearly eleven million hectares, equivalent to 110,074 square kilometers![5] As George Petty bragged, "It's probably the largest single remaining under-utilized softwood resource in Canada and probably the world for that matter, if you exclude the Soviet Union."[6]

Pressure from citizens' and environmental groups was mounting. What publicly owned resources and businesses were being traded away behind closed doors? When the agreement was made public in May 1989, it was not because the government had acceded to public demands to know what was going on, but because a group of Manitoba Cree were familiar with the secretive ways of government. The Manitoba Keewatinowi Okimakanak (MKO), an organization that represents twenty-five Northern Cree bands, obtained a copy of the text of the agreement from New York, where, by law, it had been filed with the U.S. Securities and Exchange Commission.[7] Once MKO saw the agreement, it realized nothing in it would protect their treaty rights over the same territory.

Both the mill under Churchill Forest and later MANFOR had had the legal right to log within a forest area nearly as large as that leased to Repap. But Repap planned to *triple* the rate of logging within the area. Repap also committed to one billion dollars in new investments—building a new bleached-pulp mill at The Pas as well as a wood-chipping facility at Swan River, nearly one hundred kilometers due south of The Pas. The community of Swan River was owed something, in political terms. While the provincial government had been negotiating with Repap, the municipal leaders of Swan River had successfully interested another company in building a chipboard plant in their town. The only problem was that the province had secretly negotiated away the wood needed for the Swan River venture to Repap. The

 FRONTIER FORESTS UNDER LOW OR NO THREAT: large, intact natural forest ecosystems that are relatively undisturbed and large enough to maintain all of their biodiversity

FRONTIER FORESTS UNDER MEDIUM OR HIGH THREAT: ongoing or planned human activities (e.g. logging, agricultural clearing, mining) will, if continued, significantly degrade these frontiers.

NON-FRONTIER FORESTS: secondary forest, plantations, degraded forest, and patches of primary forest not meeting this study's criteria as frontier.

FRONTIER FORESTS UNASSESSED FOR THREAT: insufficient information prevented evaluating the threat level of these frontiers.

Projection: Lambert Azimuthal. Basemap data from ArcWorld. Assistance in data preparation, mapping, and analysis provided by 🌐 World Wildlife Fund & 🌐 World Conservation Monitoring Co Data sources (i.) Forest cover data provided by World Conservation Monitoring Centre. (ii.) Frontier forest data derived through expert assessment and from other sources.

WORLD RESOURCES INSTITUTE   FOREST FRONTIERS INITIATIVE

Threatened frontier forests of North America

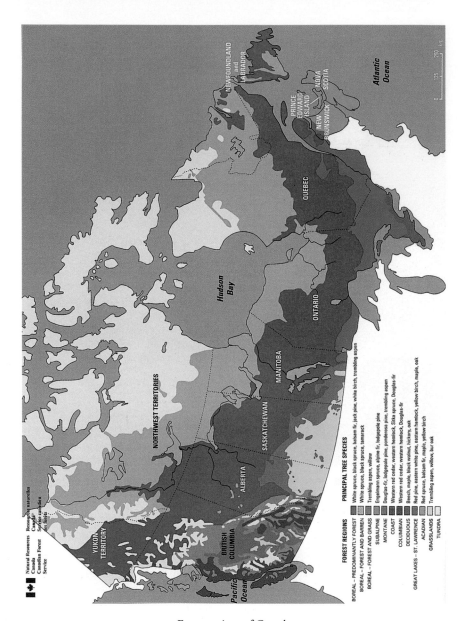

Forest regions of Canada

RARE, UNIQUE AND THREATENED
A thin green band of coastal temperate rainforest lies on the west coast of North America. Such rainforests cover just one fifth of one percent of the earth's land area. The ancient temperate rainforest that blankets British Columbia's coastal valleys represents almost one quarter of all that is left in the world.

HOW MUCH IS GONE?

LOGGED 53.1%

PRISTINE PROTECTED 5.8%

PRISTINE UNPROTECTED 41.1%

Remaining Ancient Forest

Mountain Hemlock, High Elevation Forest

Bog, Muskeg, Scrub, Open Canopy Forest

Logged Areas, Immature Forest, Urban

Bare Ground, Snow, Ice

ALASKA

Massett

Prince Rupert

Kitimat

Skidegate

HAIDA GWAII

Hecate Strait

BRITISH COLUMBIA

PRINCESS ROYAL ISLAND

Klemtu

Bella Bella

Bella Coola

Rivers Inlet

Pacific Ocean

Port Hardy

VANCOUVER ISLAND

Clayoquot Sound

Nanaimo

Vancouver

Juan de Fuca Strait

Victoria

USA

Ancient forests at risk

Standing living and dead trees after a fire in a boreal forest.

Aspen forest in fall, Riding Mountain National Park.

"Old-growth pine, such as these giants, once covered 50-60 percent of the Great Lakes-St. Lawrence ecosystem. Now they make up less than three percent—and the giants are gone. ..."

"We are recklessly destroying the timber of Canada, and there is scarcely a possibility of replacing it." Sir John A. Macdonald

This was once an Acadian forest.

Gary Schneider

In Prince Edward Island, rare forest species, such as hobblebush, have insufficient protection.

Benny Malone

The endangered Newfoundland pine marten is dependent
on old-growth forest for food and shelter.

Acadian forest on Cape Breton Island

Acadian forest

These old-growth pines stand in the less than 1 percent that remains of old-growth red and white pine in North America (Temagami, Obabika Triangle: The Three Sisters).

Are we trucking away our future?   Mechanization

Big Crow old growth—Temagami

An aerial view of road networks and clear-cuts in Temagami, Ontario

Feller-buncher—"replacing a bunch of fellas."

The largest single-line bleached kraft pulp mill in the world (Al-Pac mill, Alberta)

Boreal forest, Whiteshell Provincial Park, Manitoba

Great grey owl, Duck Mountain Provincial Park, Manitoba

Fire-driven boreal ecosystem

Mule deer, southern Saskatchewan

Sunpine clear-cut near Rocky Mountain House

Coal River watershed
clear-cut, Yukon

Winter clear-cuts in Alberta

Datlamen Watershed in
Haida, British Columbia

Mount Paxton, near
Kyoquot, Vancouver
Island, September 1997

Ingram Mooto, British
Columbia

Mike Pierce's horse logging operation on Vancouver Island— second growth

Selective logging operation on Vancouver Island— second growth

province also committed a further ninety million dollars on roads for Repap's use.

No environmental hearing took place to examine the impact of tripling the rate of cut. One unnamed official was quoted in the provincial press as saying, "No comprehensive ecological studies were made when MANFOR came into being in 1966 and none have been done since."[8]

The commercial softwood forest was close to wholly committed to pulp mills with the giant Repap agreement in 1989, and the trend toward rapid industrialization of Manitoba's forests increased in subsequent years under new forest agreements.

The OSB boom

New technology in the manufacture of chipboard was creating increased interest in Manitoba's mixed-wood boreal forest at just the point that the Conservative government of Gary Filmon was looking for ways to expand the provincial forest industry. Hardwoods in the province had been considered "under-utilized," and that rationalization was soon to form the basis for clear-cutting of aspen throughout the southwestern portions of Manitoba's boreal. The tiny aspen tree was suddenly commercially viable as raw material for oriented strand board (OSB). A 1989 symposium in Minnesota concluded that

> Canada has five times as much aspen as the United States . . . [which] is widely dispersed from Ontario to British Columbia. . . . The last few years are proving that this increase in aspen utilization, particularly in western Canada, far exceeded our expectations. *What was considered a weed species before 1972 is now described as a champion species or the Queen of the North* (emphasis added).[9]

Suddenly, the Manitoba commercial forest expanded. Since estimates of what is commercially available are always premised on known technology, the emergence of a technology that prized, not lumber, but wood flakes, substantially increased the volume of forest the government considered "available." The aspen forests of the mixed boreal could be used to lure a multinational giant to the province. Meanwhile, the Repap deal was proving disappointing, particularly for Swan River. A downturn in pulp prices through the end of the 1980s and early 1990s significantly reduced Repap's financial position. By 1995 Repap had not met the promised commitment of a one-billion-dollar investment in the province. It had not built a new plant for bleached pulp at The Pas, nor had it proceeded with the wood-chipping plant at Swan River.

Enter Louisiana-Pacific—the giant pulp-and-paper firm that had once been part of Georgia Pacific. Louisiana-Pacific already had Canadian plants—a mill producing oriented strand board in Dawson Creek, British Columbia, and a small fiber gypsum plant in Nova Scotia. The OSB industry was expanding everywhere. The price of OSB had more than doubled since 1990. Analysts did not believe the market was yet saturated. And Manitoba was about to make an offer they could not refuse.

Prior to any public hearings, Manitoba offered Louisiana-Pacific a long-term lease to log 900,000 cubic meters of hardwood a year from its mixed-wood aspen forests. The province sets stumpage rates substantially lower than most provincial governments, and well below U.S. rates. The Manitoba rate would come to $1.17 per cubic meter, while the current Ontario rate for comparable wood for OSB use is $6 per cubic meter.[10] With planned rates of logging, Louisiana-Pacific would be producing $180 million worth of OSB annually, while paying stumpage rates totalling only one million dollars.[11] In return, Louisiana-Pacific would build an $80-million OSB plant near Swan River. The Forest Management Licence (FML) area of some 5,863 square kilometers includes cutting rights to parts of Duck Mountain Provincial Park and the last remaining stands of old-growth hardwoods in the province. Almost half of the Duck Mountain Provincial Park is open to logging, after the recent review of all Manitoba parks. Logging was also committed up to the very boundary of Riding Mountain National Park. Compounding problems of unprecedented clear-cutting of the aspen forests is the fact that 40 percent of Louisiana-Pacific's AAC is to come from private land. Forest regulations for public land do not apply on private land.

To accomplish all this, the province had to renegotiate the Repap deal, as Repap's exclusive logging rights to 20 percent of the province included areas now needed by Louisiana-Pacific. Fortunately for the province, it had some bargaining power. Repap was behind on its commitments. And it did not plan to log hardwood anyway. The Repap deal was re-announced in November 1995. Louisiana-Pacific got the hardwood, Repap got comparable rights over the same areas in order to log softwood. Repap reorganized its promised investment. Any plans for Repap to build in Swan River could now be safely scrapped as Louisiana-Pacific would be building near there. And Repap committed to building a $250-million bleached chemithermal mechanical pulp (BCTMP) mill at The Pas. The BCTMP mill had been developed by Repap to manufacture bleached pulp without the environmental hazards of chlorine use. The plant also had the "advantage" that it, too, could utilize small hardwood species like poplar.

The province got out of its promised ninety-million-dollar commitment for road-building for Repap, and it got Repap to pay twenty million dollars for its outstanding preferred shares.[12] The long-term viability of the Repap mill at The Pas is in question.

Repap's financial fortunes from coast to coast were substantially reduced when the shareholders of Avenor turned down a proposed purchase of Repap assets in early 1997.[13] Repap is heavily indebted, and flirting with going under.

The First Nations of Manitoba were alarmed by the government forest leases. With 40 percent of the province tied up under binding logging contracts, indigenous peoples in Manitoba escalated their organized opposition to logging. The Manitoba Keewatinowi Okimakanak (MKO) filed a statement of claim in federal court in July 1995, asking for a court review of the Louisiana-Pacific deal with Manitoba and potential abrogation of First Nations' rights. The Grand Chief of the Assembly of Manitoba Chiefs, Phil Fontaine (now elected Chief of the National Assembly of First Nations), asked for federal intervention in a full environmental assessment of the increase in clear-cutting that was authorized to accommodate Louisiana-Pacific. The federal Minister of the Environment refused to conduct an environmental assessment. The MKO and Swampy Cree Tribal Council, representing several Cree bands, have filed a request for judicial review of the minister's refusal.

Local communities are turning to direct action. In April 1996, the Mathias Colomb First Nation blockaded a railroad car, preventing Repap from unloading road-building equipment. The projected road would have opened up First Nations' traditional lands to logging, despite the fact that both the federal and the provincial government acknowledged that the First Nations of Manitoba have outstanding treaty entitlements to the land. In order to protect treaty land entitlement areas where the community had made land selections, the men, women and children of the small community of Pukatawagan, 710 kilometers north of Winnipeg, blocked the railcars. Even after Repap had obtained a court injunction ordering them to suspend the blockade, the community remained adamant: the blockade continued, in defiance of the injunction. The local RCMP Superintendent, George Watt, decided to take a cautious approach. Through an unlikely twist of fate, Watt was a veteran of forest blockades at Clayoquot Sound in British Columbia, where nearly one thousand people were arrested, and of blockades by the Lubicon Cree in Alberta against logging by the Japanese multinational Daishowa. No arrests were made. Having initially insisted that failure to remove the roadblock would result in a two-month shutdown at the mill, throwing 150 people out of work, Repap relented and removed the contested equipment from the area.[14]

Environmentalists also worried about Louisiana-Pacific's arrival in the Manitoba woods. The company has a terrible reputation for pollution offenses in the U.S. In fact, it had recently been levied the largest pollution-related fine in United States history—$11.1 million (U.S) for toxic air emissions from one of its OSB plants.[15] Its then CEO, Harry Merlo, had been quoted as saying, "We need everything that's out there . . . We log to infinity. Because we need it all. It's ours. It's out there, and we need it all. Now."[16]

While Manitoba promised to submit the Louisiana-Pacific OSB mill to provincial environmental assessment, environmentalists and First Nations vigorously opposed the government's decision to split the assessment. On a fast track to accommodate Louisiana-Pacific's building plans, the government first assessed the mill itself, and concluded that the toxic effluents of the Louisiana-Pacific mill were within environmental standards, and that they would not be subject to the same level of regulation in Manitoba as in the United States. In response to public outrage, just before the conclusion of the environmental assessment hearings, Louisiana-Pacific agreed to install the same pollution-abatement technology required by the more stringent laws in the United States.

Once the mill was approved and under construction, the company's plans to log 900,000 cubic meters per year of hardwood—or about four million trees per year—were subjected to a separate environmental review. The exercise had a sense of futility. The agreement signed with Louisiana-Pacific had already confirmed that the mill was to receive the 900,000 cubic meters of hardwood a year, and the mill was being built to those specifications. The agreement further confirmed that, should the province decide to reduce the wood supply to the mill, it would either pay Louisiana-Pacific substantial moneys in compensation or find sources elsewhere at no greater cost to the company. It was no surprise to anyone that the logging plans received provincial approval.

Prior to any public review, Manitoba doubled the level of permissible hardwood logging in Louisiana-Pacific's license.[17]

In announcing the Repap and Louisiana-Pacific deals, the Industry, Trade and Tourism Minister, the Hon. James Downey, claimed, "Our forestry sector, *which operates under the principles of sustainable development*, now has two strong companies producing four products, so these jobs will be less vulnerable to the ups and downs of the marketplace. This is great news for the people of northern Manitoba and for the Manitoba economy" (emphasis added).[18]

Are Manitoba's forest policies sustainable?

Manitoba stands out as a province deep in sustainable-development rhetoric, if not practice. For instance, when Premier Gary Filmon joined Prime Minister Brian Mulroney in announcing the International Institute for Sustainable Development, based in Winnipeg, he enthused that the provincial capital would be to sustainable development what Vienna is to opera. Now that vast sections of the province have been allocated to just three companies, the province has an excellent opportunity to prove that the principles of sustainable development do indeed guide its forest policy.

Manitoba's first serious attempt at maintaining a forest inventory began in 1963, when the Churchill Forest Industries complex was under development at The Pas. As in all provincial inventories, the basic assessments were made from aerial photographs, with some ground "cruising" to determine if estimates from the air corresponded to what was actually in the forest. But while no provincial inventory is without significant inaccuracies, Manitoba's system lags behind that of other provinces. The province did not establish permanent sample plots to assess changes over time until 1979.[19] Thus the database for average rates of growth is extremely limited. Growth data are only available since 1979, and only for mature timber and two density classes.

The inventory itself was also limited in area. The province surveyed only those areas believed to be valuable to the forest industry; thus inventories of the southwestern part of the province began only in 1986–87. The Manitoba Department of Natural Resources, Forestry Branch, acknowledges that its current information is accurate only to within plus or minus 27.9 percent. As a research goal, the Branch hopes to reduce the margin of error for any particular Forest Management Unit (FMU) to below 20 percent.[20]

Manitoba has one of the worst records in the country for protected areas. Parks established prior to 1986 were open to various resource extraction activities, including clear-cutting. Parks established during the 1990s have been off limits to forestry and mining. A recent review of the older parks resulted in a concept found only in Manitoba—"protected zones" within parks, with prohibitions on forestry and other activities. Forestry operations continue in portions of the Grassy River, Whiteshell, Nopoming, Clearwater Lake and Duck Mountain parks. Nopoming Provincial Park, representing a unique convergence of forest ecosystems, has been heavily clear-cut and was the site of protests. Half of Duck Mountain Provincial Park is still being logged. A significant proportion of Louisiana-Pacific's wood flakes will come from the aspen forests of the park. Moreover, Louisiana-Pacific's license gives the company cutting rights along the northern and western boundaries of Riding Mountain National Park. This permission violates the United Nations Convention for the Protection of Biodiversity, which specifically requires a transition zone as a buffer between protected areas and industrial activity. Requests for a federal environmental assessment of the impact of clear-cutting on the national park have been rejected.

Using a flawed information base, the Forest Branch has set rising annual allowable cut rates over the years. It may seem unlikely, but apparently as the number of industries increases, so does the number of trees! This alchemy is not all that difficult to explain, although it is far more difficult to defend.

Manitoba estimates that 14.8 million hectares, or 43 percent of the forested land of the province, is "productive forest."[21] The vast majority of this land base—94 percent—is Crown land, publicly owned, and managed by the province. Most of it is open and available to logging. Manitoba began the practice of long-term leases only in fairly recent times.

The first such license was included in a "Forest Management License Agreement" (FMLA), which was not issued until 1989, when it was granted to Repap for the famous mill at The Pas. Everything derives from the FMLA. It is the Agreement that establishes access to fiber. The FMLA guarantees the Forest Management License, defines the area to be logged, sets stumpage rates and stipulates the agreed-upon volume to be cut; all of this is based on the current AAC calculations, and negotiations for the FMLA are done in private. The public process that follows, including any environmental assessment, cannot change anything about the FMLA. It is impossible in Manitoba to change any of the FMLA contents . . . or results.

The first mill in the province, the Pine Falls mill, was established in 1925. The wood for its first lease came from a local First Nations reserve, as well as from large tracts of land running north of the Winnipeg River. The viability of the mill was enhanced by cheap power from the hydroelectric dams upstream. Under the management of the Spanish River Pulp and Paper Company, the mill was producing 258 tons of paper a day by 1929. Eventually, Abitibi Price took it over and operated it from the 1930s until 1944, when it was sold to the employees. At the time of sale, the mill was still using some of its original 1920s equipment. The new Pine Falls Paper Company was given an FMLA and a thirty-million-dollar provincial loan guarantee—and the local community presented a Browning Citori Grand Lightning shotgun to the new CEO.[22]

A separate FMLA has been negotiated with Louisiana-Pacific, with more in the works. Terms vary from license to license, but in general, Manitoba demands very little from licensees. The government remains responsible for collecting the data to develop the annual allowable cut (AAC), seedlings are provided to the industry at no cost, and the forest companies are not required to return the forest to healthy regeneration. In most other provinces, the industry is held financially responsible until the forest has reached a so-called free to grow state after logging. Manitoba not only does not require this of its licensees, but caps the industry costs for reforestation.[23]

In any event, Manitoba has shown a total lack of appreciation for the importance of regenerating the forest that existed before logging. While its official policy document on sustainable forestry practices maintains that "reforestation shall maintain the natural species diversity found within the forest ecosystem," the agreement with L-P orients planting around "site suitable species as good as, *or better than* the present forest" (emphasis added).[24]

Between the three large FMLAs, 40 percent of the productive forest AAC is locked up. In addition, another set of smaller forest companies buys timber quotas and other short-term agreements for forest access. All told, Manitoba can boast that its rate of cut is far below its AAC. The AAC for 1997 is 9.7 million cubic meters.[25] The actual amount logged in 1993–94 was 1.8 million cubic meters. Now that Louisiana-Pacific has been logging for two years, adding its allocation of 900,000 cubic meters, the amount logged is 2.7 million cubic meters. Logging pressures are likely to increase as both Repap and the Pine Falls Paper Company are currently negotiating increased allocations. Repap's expansion is 1.5 million cubic meters for its paper mill and 1.1 million cubic meters for its sawmill. The province's twenty-year plan forecasts a rate of cut more than three times the current level at 8.27 million cubic meters.[26]

This picture can be a bit misleading, as some areas of Manitoba's forest are substantially more attractive to industry than others. The primary reason is access. The forest regions with the largest AACs, for example, are inaccessible. The Pine Falls Paper Company is applying for government approval for an environmental license for an all-weather road along the east side of Lake Winnipeg, which will open up vast tracts of roadless wilderness. The company wants access to more northern forest within existing AACs in order to build a 1,200-ton-per-day paper mill.[27] The licensing process for this road is being done incrementally, with no assessment of the cumulative environmental impacts.

Even at existing rates of logging, many forest species are already at risk. The woodland caribou west of the Ontario border has now been listed as a vulnerable species by the Committee on the Status of Endangered Wildlife in Canada (COSEWIC). New roads and radically increased clear-cutting will only make matters worse. Repap's annual plan has nearly seven hundred kilometers of both winter and all-weather roading.[28] The woodland caribou is endemic to all three forest license areas. Its habitat on both sides of the Ontario-Manitoba border is under assault. The great grey owl, the grey fox, the wolverine and the cougar, black bear and elk are also already suffering the effects of logging.[29]

The forest regions with the highest rate of cut, described by the Forest Branch as the Mountain, Highrock, Interlake and Saskatchewan River regions, are virtually totally committed to long-term logging. In fact, these regions are all at over 97 percent of their softwood AAC. While many forest companies are not utilizing the AAC to the full extent permitted, in terms of available timber supply, Manitoba is arguably short of softwood. As early as 1986, "The First 5-Year Review of Manitoba's Forest Royalty System" concluded that local industry was already approaching total utilization of available softwood.[30] A major government-sponsored report concluded in 1995: "Given current AACs, regional allocations of coniferous timber are tight, particularly after allowances are made for Crown timber that is considered inaccessible."[31]

The hardwood, of course, is considered "under-utilized" and now forms the basis of the bonanza for clear-cutting aspen through the southern portions of Manitoba's mixed boreal. As a deal with Louisiana-Pacific came into focus, Manitoba quite neatly doubled the hardwood AAC in the area of L-P's license. The allocation for hardwood logging in the Mountain Forest Region surrounding Swan River went from 578,290 cubic meters to 1,372,510 cubic meters. As L-P had stated its intention to log 900,000 cubic meters a year, it would not have been possible to lure the OSB development to the province with the original hardwood AAC. The government defended its decision as being premised on the technological innovation of OSB. Where previously only forest stands capable of producing more than 40 cubic meters to the hectare had been included in the AAC, now all hardwood was included, with a mere 10 percent reduction for decay.[32]

A provincial biologist who criticized the ease with which this conversion was computed was quickly fired. Dan Soprovich had been with the Department of Natural Resources for fifteen years. Having sat through the environmental review hearings, he realized that the government's guarantee of a 900,000-cubic-meter AAC to Louisiana-Pacific was based on a very fundamental misconception. In setting levels to meet L-P's requirements, the government was assuming that all hardwoods were interchangeable. But in the hearings, L-P representatives made it clear that they would need 80 percent aspen and only 20 percent birch or balsam poplar. Dan Soprovich became convinced that this would inevitably lead to "drastically over-harvesting the aspen."[33]

As a wildlife biologist, Soprovich knew that aspen forests are essential habitat for neotropical migratory songbirds. A wide array of birds migrate annually, wintering in South America and returning to Canada in summer. The hardwood forests of southern Manitoba are key habitat for many of them, from hummingbirds to warblers. These forests had never been subject to widespread clear-cutting, and no one seemed to be looking at the biodiversity implications of L-P's plans. Even the federal scientists from the Canadian Wildlife Service expressed concern that Louisiana-Pacific's logging plans could prove disastrous for biodiversity. In testimony before the environmental hearing, they urged L-P to avoid logging the aspen altogether in the key migratory months of June and July, and sharply criticized "the lack of baseline data, which includes . . . breeding bird surveys, community and habitat work."[34] They urged L-P to undertake this essential work prior to logging. When they discovered that L-P planned to "selectively log" even in the buffer zone areas around streams, federal wildlife scientists and federal fisheries biologists lodged an official objection.

But only Dan Soprovich was fired. Following his presentation to the hearings, he received a letter of dismissal, citing his public criticism of the L-P logging plans. He told the media, "I have absolutely no regrets. I honestly believe I did the right thing."[35]

The Manitoba District Office of the federal forest service also objected to the province's calculation of the AAC for Louisiana-Pacific. The director was caustic about the approach the province's Forestry Branch had used. For one thing, as Dan Soprovich had noted, the Forestry Branch treated one type of hardwood as interchangeable with another. In a strongly worded letter, Jim Ball wrote, "Lumping aspen and balsam poplar together will obfuscate 'forest inventory' now and into the future . . . how will one know whether balsam poplar is being overcut or undercut? Combining two species in one height/diameter equation is really pretty sloppy forest mensuration."[36]

One reason for Mr. Ball's concern was that balsam poplar and aspen respond very differently to logging. Balsam poplar will do better in wet soils and its regeneration improves with mineral disturbance. The opposite is true for aspen. It thrives in drier sites and does not regenerate well after soil disturbance. Thus, treating them as the same is ecologically flawed. But given L-P's desire to log 80 percent aspen, it is also economically flawed and environmentally disastrous.

Mr. Ball noted, in a document presented during the environmental assessment hearings, that the proportion of balsam poplar had been "trivialized" to 2 percent of the total volume. In fact, numerous studies had shown the average balsam poplar densities in Manitoba to be at least 10 percent of total hardwood. Mr. Ball speculated that perhaps the sample plots had been chosen on drier sites, creating a bias in the data in favor of aspen and against accurate reporting of balsam poplar.[37] The implications of this were indeed significant. It meant that the entire forest inventory for L-P's FMLA was premised on a super-abundance of aspen, 98 percent of all hardwood. Mr. Ball concluded that "data showing 98 percent aspen for an area the size of FML3 are seriously flawed."[38] But if there was less aspen, then the AAC could be out of whack. Over-cutting of aspen would be unavoidable if L-P was to meet the production targets guaranteed by its agreement with the province.

He also took issue with the magical doubling of wood supply. The remarkably low "cull" rate of 10 percent, the estimate of wood unavailable due to decay, was not justified in the view of the federal forest service. Mr. Ball asked, "How was the [Forest Resource Inventory] massaged to double the hardwood AAC? The magnitude of the AAC increase . . . is provocative . . . [and] requires explanation beyond an unstated increase in utilization standards for OSB using smaller diameter trees . . ."[39] It is likely that the province also exaggerated the AAC by underestimating the amount of decay and "cull" that should be excluded from the anticipated volume per hectare.

Clearly, testimony from the federal forest service would have been of use to the environmental hearing on Louisiana-Pacific's wood supply. But Mr. Ball did not testify. The morning he was to appear, he was instructed to stay away.[40]

Prognosis

With the AAC increases, and both the Repap and PFPC licenses up for renewal, Manitoba is poised for an assault on its forest without historical precedent. The committed volumes for softwood and hardwood resources are arguably already unsustainable, and new mills continue to be contemplated. What is certain is that the inventory is faulty and the AAC is designed to meet industry demand, rather than ecological carrying capacity.

The Manitoba government continues to act as a co-sponsor of industrial forest expansion. The process of negotiating in private and presenting "fait accompli" deals to the public virtually eliminates meaningful public participation. The province has ignored the advice of its environmental commission, both that logging in parks be reviewed and that logging be stopped in Nopoming Provincial Park. New protected areas throughout Manitoba's boreal forests are essential for the future.

Underscoring all of the problems is the consistent undervaluing of the forest. Manitoba subsidizes industrial expansion through cheap stumpage, road construction, incentives and tax expenditures. Even if the forest amounted to a pile of sticks, Manitoba is undervaluing that resource. But a forest is much more than a source of raw material for mills. The value of the Manitoba forest lies in its ecological services, providing clean air, water, and a cushion in global climate change. The forest has immeasurable value as the habitat of a wide range of creatures whose interrelationships are, as yet, little understood. Moreover, the Manitoba government consistently ignores the value of the forests to First Nations and their treaty entitlements to use the forest.

Repap may be "paper" spelled backward. But, in a real sense, Manitoba has forest issues backward.

SASKATCHEWAN

Ask the average Canadian to describe Saskatchewan, and forests are not likely to come to mind. Vast, undulating fields of grain, open prairie skies and unending horizons are the hallmark images of this prairie province. Yet forests cover more than half of the province and as logging has intensified, so too have controversies and conflicts. It is Saskatchewan that holds the national record for the longest-running forest blockade—one and a half years of camping by First Nations people on a remote logging road near Canoe Lake.

SASKATCHEWAN	(1995)
Forest Land in million hectares	28.8
Stocked Harvested Crown Land in hectares	123,000
Area Logged in hectares	21,907
Volume Logged in million cubic meters	4.2
Annual Allowable Cut in million cubic meters	7.6

SOURCE: Natural Resources Canada, Canadian Forest Service, *The State of Canada's Forests, 1996-1997* (Ottawa, 1997). These are federal government summaries, based on provincial government data. The figures are not necessarily accurate.

There is little of the original forest left in central and eastern Saskatchewan. Old-timers can still recall the days of huge trees, but such specimens are no longer easy to find.

Prior to European settlement, the forests of Saskatchewan were home to nomadic aboriginal peoples. The forests provided for their needs in a wide variety of ways—from berries and game to teepee poles and firewood, even to the use of the core of dead wood as a soft and absorbent material for diapering babies. But European contact changed the forest even as it colonized and oppressed the aboriginal residents of what was to become Saskatchewan. By 1774 the first trading post had been established, and the trapping of fur-bearing animals drastically increased. For the first time, the land was asked to do more than provide for the needs of the people. It was to create wealth for the Hudson's Bay Company.

Once the white pine was gone from the eastern forests, the market turned to the white spruce, a prominent part of its southern boreal ecoregion, growing along the valleys and near lakes. It grew well with the other prevalent deciduous species, willow and alder.[1] With a strong demand for white spruce, the predictable high-grading followed, and the provincial government introduced logging quotas in response.[2]

The province's first sawmill opened in Prince Albert in the winter of 1878. Other large mills followed, but as local timber resources were exhausted, the larger facilities

SASKATCHEWAN CORPORATE PLAYERS

Mistik Management (NorSask & Millar Western)
Weyerhaeuser
Saskfor-MacMillan
L and M
Clearwater

closed. By 1920 smaller, portable sawmills were in operation. In 1931, the province firmly established its control over the forests by passing its Forest Act. The object of the legislation was to ensure the perpetual growth of timber on lands reserved as provincial forests. Yet after the Depression, pressure on the forest increased again, with over-cutting of white spruce and jack pine. There was no effective forest regulation, no inventory, no annual allowable cut (AAC), no fees or stumpage.

Nearly all of Saskatchewan's forests—88 percent—are Crown land, and management of this publicly held resource left a lot to be desired. As the public became increasingly alarmed about disappearing forests, the government appointed the Royal Commission on the Forest Resources and Industries of Saskatchewan in 1945. Its recommendations set the stage for a modern, regulated forestry. It took nine years to complete the first inventory, but by the mid-1950s, Saskatchewan's forest service was trying to reduce the logging of white spruce, while setting AAC levels for the commercial forest. As the best sawlogs had already been removed through high-grading, the government began to look to pulp and paper, as well as to new sawmill technologies capable of utilizing smaller trees. In the mid-1970s, seven new sawmills had been established, and pulp mills had arrived.[3]

The industry went into a brief decline in the 1980s and early 1990s. Due to the effects of decades of over-cutting combined with the impact of a severe forest fire, which destroyed a ten-year supply of timber, one mill was forced to close in 1990 for lack of wood.[4] But while the steadily increasing level of exploitation took a slight dip in those years, the overwhelming trend was to increased logging. In the 1990s, Saskatchewan's forests are three times more heavily logged than thirty years earlier.[5]

Prairie aspen and multinationals

While most Canadians would hardly identify Saskatchewan as a logging province, in recent years large multinationals like MacMillan Bloedel and Weyerhaeuser have expanded production in the aspen forests of this prairie province.

MacMillan Bloedel, one of the largest forestry companies in Canada (with $3.9 billion in sales in 1994), was the first industry giant in the forests of Saskatchewan. Back in 1965, it bought a waferboard plant in the town of Hudson Bay, a community virtually on the Manitoba border and far south of its marine namesake. They expanded it and ultimately converted production to oriented strand board. In corporate promotions for new OSB plants, MacMillan Bloedel claims its Saskatchewan plant "was the base from which the multi-billion dollar commodity OSB industry has grown."[6]

Weyerhaeuser is also active in Saskatchewan. Based in Tacoma, Washington, it is one of North America's largest forest-product companies. In 1986 it purchased the province's first pulp mill, at Prince Albert, which had originally opened in 1969, as well as a chemical plant in Saskatoon, a sawmill, and their related woodlands in Big River, in the mid-regions of the province. Weyerhaeuser substantially expanded the facilities, constructing a 200,000-ton-per-year paper mill adjacent to the older pulp mill.[7]

But while other privately owned corporations are also active in Saskatchewan's forest industry, this heartland of the CCF and the wellspring of social-democratic politics has, not surprisingly, an unusually large number of government-owned industry players.

The first was the Saskatchewan Forest Products Corporation (Saskfor), a Crown corporation established in 1949. It has been involved in a range of forest products over the years—from railroad ties to fence posts and pulpwood. In 1973, it built the province's only plywood mill, at Carrot River. But there is a recent trend in Saskatchewan to cobbled-together ownership schemes, including an alliance of Saskfor and MacMillan Bloedel, Saskfor-MacMillan, which was created to bring in a new OSB plant on the Saskatchewan/Manitoba border. While MacBlo's existing plant requires 316,000 cubic meters of wood annually, its new mill would require an additional 860,000 cubic meters in a district already supporting the Saskfor sawmill, the plywood plant and thirty smaller sawmills. Logging would be in the same ecoregion, supplying the Louisiana-Pacific OSB plant on the Manitoba side of the border. Despite repeated attempts by First Nations and environmentalists to initiate a federal review, the notion of looking at the *cumulative* impacts of logging the same ecoregion on two sides of an interprovincial border seems to be beyond any government. In September 1996, then federal Minister of Environment, Sergio Marchi, refused to undertake an environmental assessment of the OSB logging boom along the Saskatchewan-Manitoba border.

Protectors of Mother Earth

In Saskatchewan, the green rush for the boreal has led to more blockades and protests. In the Hudson Bay area in the east of the province, and in Meadow Lake to the west, there has been substantial and rapid expansion of the forest industry. The Meadow Lake blockade was organized by indigenous residents around Canoe Lake, calling themselves "the Protectors of Mother Earth." The irony is that the company they were blockading, NorSask, was partially owned by the Meadow Lake Tribal Council.

The NorSask sawmill in western Saskatchewan has a complicated ownership structure: 40 percent is owned by a corporation representing the workers (Techfor Sask), 40 percent owned by the Meadow Lake Tribal Council, and the remaining 20 percent by Millar Western, an Alberta-based pulp-and-paper company. The Meadow Lake pulp mill is 49 percent owned by a government investment corporation, which has no management role in the mill, and 51 percent controlled by various holding companies related to the only private corporation in the structure—Millar Western. The financing of the new Meadow Lake pulp mill, arranged through an agreement in 1990, suggests a rather friendly brand of socialism. The government put up $60 million in direct investment, and a further $186 million in loans, under terms that call for repayment only after the company makes a net profit. Millar Western bought its 51 percent share—in a $360-million, zero-effluent aspen pulp mill—for $10.2 million. Meanwhile, the forest-management operations for NorSask's sawmill and the Meadow Lake pulp mill are looked after by a company called MISTIK Management, owned jointly by Millar Western Pulp and NorSask.[8]

To attract greater levels of investment and increased production, the Saskatchewan government has been making favorable arrangements for long-term tenure through Forest Management Licence Agreements (FMLAs). The newer agreements have ranged from 100,000 to in excess of two million cubic meters per year![9] In all, nearly eight million hectares of provincial forest are committed under FMLAs. As is the norm in other provinces, holders of FMLAs must be owners of forest-products processing facilities. Industries operating in Saskatchewan get the benefit of very low stumpage fees. In 1996, Weyerhaeuser, for example, paid a total of $1.85 per cubic meter of hardwood logged and $5.81 for softwood. MacMillan Bloedel, with a much older agreement, paid only $0.31 per cubic meter, while paying an additional $3 per square mile in "ground rent." And the MISTIK Management group, covering NorSask and Meadow Lake Millar Western interests, pays a single rate of $3 per cubic meter regardless of the species.[10]

The trouble with the NorSask FMLA for the Meadow Lake area began almost the minute the agreement was signed. In 1988, the government conveyed an FMLA to the MISTIK Management group to provide raw material for NorSask's sawmill and the Millar Western pulp mill, granting rights for a twenty-year period to over 3.3 million hectares of forest—with an annual allowable cut (AAC) of over two million cubic meters of combined hardwood and softwood per year.[11] Approval and financial support were given to Millar Western to build and operate the pulp mill—before the completion of an environmental-impact statement on the wood supply. The same approach—approvals first, environmental-impact study later—is being followed for the building of a new oriented strand board plant in the Hudson Bay area.

Following protests by Cree and Métis residents in the Meadow Lake area and provincial environmentalists, the Environment Minister conceded that the twenty-year management plan did need an environmental assessment. But MISTIK was given six years—until 1994—to prepare the plan and environmental assessment, and in the event, the plan was not available for public review until August 1996. In the meantime, logging had been under way for years under the authority of the FMLA. The Protectors of Mother Earth (POME) pointed out that, by the time the assessment is complete, over 60,000 hectares of their traditional lands will have been clear-cut.

The situation got more confusing when it turned out that the indigenous community of Green Lake had actually been owners of a sawmill, which the government, mistakenly believing it was Crown-owned, had conveyed to NorSask. The conveyance of the sawmill had to be reversed, as the Crown had had no title to convey. Of course, the value of the sawmill went from $84,000 when NorSask "bought" it two years earlier, to $445,000 in compensation to NorSask when it turned out it could not properly be conveyed. As well, the FMLA included the traditional lands of the Cree and Métis people. Meanwhile, both POME and the Green Lake community alleged that cutting took place without prior legal authority, and that the mill had been operating without the required license under the Clean Air Act.

Underlying this whole mess was a morass of conflict of interest. The government was part owner of several entities that it was required to review and consider for approval. Anything more than a rubber-stamp response would have been a shock.

In May 1992, as allegations of illegalities swirled around the government, the indigenous men, women and children of the communities around Canoe Lake, dissenting from the pro-clear-cut views of the management of the Meadow Lake Tribal Council, set up their blockade. Community divisions ran deep, with the Meadow Lake Tribal Council pointing to the 80 percent unemployment rate on the reserve and the need for development to save the lives of dispirited communities. The leadership had become convinced that their economic interests lay in industrial development. Once the NorSask sawmill and the Meadow Lake pulp mill were up and running, the Tribal Council entered into discussions with Atomic Energy of Canada Ltd. about becoming a high-level nuclear-waste repository, dissociating themselves entirely from the protesters, whom they termed lazy community members, addicted to welfare.[12]

Led by the Elders, the protesters included local Cree and Métis people committed to the defense of Mother Earth. On June 30, 1992, the RCMP decided that an injunction should be enforced. As one of the POME leaders put it, there was "an onslaught of close to one hundred uniformed RCMP, a SWAT team with heavy weapons, shields and dogs."[13] The unarmed POME protesters refused to budge, so the Mounties moved to the clear-cut to allow NorSask contractors to remove logs felled before the blockade had been erected. When Elders sat on the logs, they were arrested and taken away. In all, thirty people, including Elders and pregnant women, were charged with intimidation—a charge subsequently amended to "obstruction," and eventually stayed.

The next day, Canada Day, the protesters, who had been charged and released, returned to the encampment by the logging road at Wiggins Bay and continued the

blockade. By the fall, as the weather grew colder, they began to consider more permanent structures and some source of heat to help them over what looked likely to be the
long haul. In late October, the Minister of Resources, Eldon Lautermilch, sent in the
RCMP for the second time. Asked by the news media if it was not hypocritical to
enforce laws against the protesters when so many outstanding questions remained
about the granting of the FMLA and the operations of the pulp mill, the Minister
replied, "I can't just pick and choose the laws which I'll enforce."[14]

There were good reasons for the Protectors of Mother Earth to oppose the rapid
expansion of industrial forestry in their territory. Many indigenous people in
Saskatchewan are dependent on the forest, returning to the bush to escape the grim
social problems of the reserves, to hunt and fish and trap. Others make their living
from the non-timber resources of the forest. There is a $5-million-a-year industry in
wild rice in the Saskatchewan forest, and a smaller but growing business selling wild
berries, fresh, and also made into jams and jellies. Still others are seasonal mushroom
pickers; about 4,500 kilograms of mushrooms are collected from Saskatchewan's forests
every year, amounting to $100,000 in sales.

More traditional forest occupations bring benefits to the provincial economy, with
tens of millions of dollars in revenue from commercial fishing, outfitting, big game
hunting and trapping. Meanwhile, camping and tourism are estimated to have an economic impact of $891 million per year in the province.[15]

But it is the loss of economically less quantifiable values that strikes at the heart of
biodiversity—the forest margin habitats gone with clear-cutting, the loss of hardwood
habitat for neotropical migratory songbirds, and the vanishing of old-growth forest
habitat. As one ecologist observed:

> Boreal forests do not have the popular appeal of rainforests, and they contain
> no high profile endangered species. However, in Saskatchewan terms, forests
> such as these are rich ecosystems . . .[16]

The recent boom in hardwood logging for oriented strand board mills poses a serious
threat to the biodiversity of the mixed-wood boreal. Saskatchewan's forests are being
transformed, with hardwood on a rotation schedule of clear-cuts every seventy years,
and softwoods every ninety. The characteristics of old growth will disappear. The
Saskatchewan government has estimated that, of the rare plants of the province,
29 percent are found in the commercial forest region.[17]

The drastic increase in logging, with three new FMLAs granted since 1986, has led
to a renewed push for logging roads into previously untouched areas. As of 1987, there
were 42,000 kilometers of logging roads, which cumulatively removed 65,874 hectares

of the forest land base. The impact of roads on forest biodiversity is significant and lasts well past the initial logging.

As logging increases, it is critical that adequate representative ecosystem areas are given protected status. Less than 1 percent of Saskatchewan's land base has strictly protected status, although a further 5 percent is protected, with some tourism, fishing and hunting allowed.[18]

Inadequate protection of the forested ecosystems of the province is still a problem. There are other non-forest-industry threats to Saskatchewan's forests. In the southern regions, deforestation occurs as forested lands are converted to agriculture, while in the far northern forests, widespread uranium mining threatens ecosystems for miles around.

Legislative reform

In 1996, Saskatchewan was the scene of battles between the industry and reformers who want to create a new sustainable-forest policy. Big surprise: the industry won.

The provincial government had introduced a new Forest Act to remedy weaknesses in its forest regulations. The draft act, by doubling stumpage fees, would have generated far more revenue for the province, which could have helped with the costs of an accurate inventory and seedling nurseries for reforestation. Where the province currently receives $3.5 million for all its major mills and clear-cut forests, under the new law the government would have received $7 million. As well, individual companies would be hit with new fees to cover silviculture, firefighting and insecticides.[19]

Looking at the new costs, industry went ballistic. Ray Cariou of NorSask complained that, "They're just making the situation in the north untenable. Jobs that would be created in the north would be cancelled."[20] Weyerhaeuser announced that it had been contemplating plans to double the size of its pulp-and-paper mill in Prince Albert as well as its sawmill in Big River. All told, the company claimed that the new law could kill one billion dollars' worth of expansion. Steve Smith, Weyerhaeuser's vice-president, said, "This is not what we would consider fertile ground for growth and investment."[21] And Saskfor-MacMillan CEO John Robillard began to express doubts about restarting its postponed Hudson Bay oriented strand board project: "We couldn't survive as a company, with all the down-loading of government and the doubling of stumpage."[22]

Interestingly, no one in the Saskatchewan media compared the costs with what the companies are now paying in other provinces, much less what is paid south of the border. Even doubled, the Saskatchewan stumpage rate would only equal Ontario's hardwood stumpage. Inadequate inventories don't trouble the industry. As long as it can get virtually free wood, subsidized mills, and lax environmental enforcement, the industry will stay in business—until it runs out of wood.

The industry's relentless lobbying paid off. Between the first and second reading of the legislation, it was substantially weakened. Stumpage fees were not raised—that was left to future negotiation, and the industry will not have to finance insect, fire and disease protection. The industry also succeeded in protecting the favorable terms it enjoys under lease agreements. And any changes to the FMLA will have to go through the legislature, instead of the proposed, more accessible route of a change by regulation.[23]

Does Saskatchewan have enough forest to feed the new mills?

Of Saskatchewan's 28.8 million hectares of forest, half are classified as commercial.[24] It is from this area that the AAC is calculated, even though the forest leases are primarily the eight million hectares in the mid- to southern zones of the provincial forests.

Ever since Saskatchewan's first provincial inventory was completed there have been concerns about its reliability. But recently the doubts about the inventory have become even more pronounced. Cutbacks have forced the government forest service to abandon rudimentary ground checks and permanent plot sampling, and the quality of the aerial photography, used as the basis for the inventory, has been compromised.

Saskatchewan's 1993 *State of the Resource Report* provides a surprisingly candid and blunt appraisal of the inventory and its limitations. The inventory was criticized for "out-of-date" information and low-quality aerial photography (photographers were hired on "short annual contracts, based on selection criteria stressing the lowest bids"), widely varying standards of accuracy and detail from one part of the forest to another, weaknesses in the stand classification system and the existence of areas where "inventory coverage is lacking." All in all, the inventory was summarized as having "weak areas, inefficiencies, and . . . some serious deficiencies brought about by recent cutbacks. The shortcomings will become more critical if the forest resource management is expanded."[25]

Forest exploitation *is* being expanded and intensified. Huge areas are being committed, in the absence of either environmental assessment or an accurate inventory. The province's confidence in proceeding has no doubt been bolstered by an Annual Allowable Cut figure of over 7 million cubic meters, and a current logging rate of 4.2 million cubic meters.[26]

The 7 million cubic meters includes the estimated volume from vast areas that are currently uneconomical and inaccessible. Those are also precisely the areas identified in the *State of the Resource* critique as having "received less economic attention . . . because of smaller timber values and lack of accessibility." The inventory for such areas "took on more general standards and contained less detail."[27]

There is no doubt that areas in the mid- to southern reaches of the boreal and aspen parkland, referred to by the forest service as the "Commercial Zone," are being over-cut.[28] As in other provinces across the country, as the softwood becomes over-cut and supplies dwindle, the government and industry look to the "under-utilized" hardwood. Of course, the birds and animals that live in those forests utilize them quite nicely. But, for industry purposes, the aspen and mixed-wood boreal represent only an opportunity for expansion at a time when industry would otherwise be forced to reduce logging operations.

The five largest forest industries in the province all use both softwood and hard-wood in their mills. In fact, logging rates for hardwood are catching up with softwood. In 1992, 2 million cubic meters of softwood were logged, as well as 1.4 million cubic meters of hardwood. But the new and proposed mills are moving more toward hard-wood. The new pulp mill at Meadow Lake, part of the MISTIK management group, runs entirely on hardwood—825,000 cubic meters annually. And further large increases in hardwood use will come from the wood-flakes-and-glue business called oriented strand board.

As more hardwood is logged, some forest operations have shifted from taking only the softwood and leaving the mixed wood behind, to one-hundred-percent clear-cutting—removing all the trees of all species from the site.[29] About 80 percent of the logging in Saskatchewan is by clear-cutting, and the forest service is actively promoting increased reliance on clear-cuts, claiming that there are problems with regeneration success after selective cutting.[30]

There has to be a saturation point for oriented strand board. With the recent addi-tion of twelve new OSB plants, Canada will have a total of twenty-five. The quick increase in supply led to a glut in the market between 1995 and 1996. Prices fell from $300(U.S.) for one thousand square feet, in September 1995, to $190(U.S.) in February 1996. The CEO of Saskfor-MacMillan, John Robillard, announced that con-struction of the new Hudson Bay OSB mill would be postponed by one year.[31]

The "Green gold rush" has hit Saskatchewan. While the numbers for timber supply may look healthy, the reality is far different. The best forest areas are already substan-tially over-cut. The reserves are currently unavailable, and their inventories inexact and unreliable. By caving in to industry, the government lost its chance to establish more sustainable practices.

As every province overbuilds its processing capacity, as every province over-cuts, all the elements of an ecosystem disaster are in place. In the words of former World Bank economist Herman Daly, "There is something fundamentally wrong in treating the Earth as if it were a business in liquidation."[32]

ALBERTA

ALBERTA	(1995)
Forest Land in million hectares	38.2
Stocked Harvested Crown Land in hectares	506,000
Area Logged in hectares	44,371
Volume Logged in million cubic meters	20.3
Annual Allowable Cut in million cubic meters	22.1

SOURCE: Natural Resources Canada, Canadian Forest Service, *The State of Canada's Forests, 1996-1997* (Ottawa, 1997). These are federal government summaries, based on provincial government data. The figures are not necessarily accurate.

Canada's Texas, Alberta is oil and cattle country, where business barons are heroes, and the annual Calgary Stampede rodeo is the most identifiable cultural icon.

But Alberta also has a long tradition of eco-tourism (if you can call Victorian travelers relaxing in the hot springs at Banff "eco-tourism"). The first National Park in Canada was established in Banff, Alberta, in 1886. The Rocky Mountains provide a rich habitat for a wealth of biological diversity. A second Rockies National Park followed in Jasper. And countless other areas of Alberta's complex landscape, from flat prairie to mountainous peaks to forests and unique habitats like the Whaleback, are magnificent ecological treasures and essential parts of another Alberta identity. But the Alberta business ethic is a threat to them all.

The Wood Buffalo National Park, for example, is designated a World Heritage Site by the United Nations, yet it took a court case to stop its despoliation by logging. Subjected to clear-cut logging since the end of the Second World War, the park has been stripped of virtually all its old-growth boreal.[1] Hotels and ski resorts, sprawling developments, golf courses and highways are hemming in the wildlife in Banff, while open-pit coal mining has been approved bordering Jasper, threatening critical ecosystems even within Canada's most strict protection designation.

Unlike the eastern provinces, Alberta did not experience early surges in logging followed by a gradual transition to the kind of full-throttle exploitation endured by, for example, New Brunswick. Alberta has a forest history all its own; a very short history, with exploitation of the forest moving into high gear only in the last decade. The Alberta "green rush" for the forests provides an alarming illustration of Herman Daly's "business

ALBERTA CORPORATE PLAYERS
Mitsubishi-Honshu: Al-Pac
Daishowa-Marubeni
Sunpine Forest Products
Canadian Forest Products
Millar Western
Weyerhaeuser
Weldwood of Canada Ltd.
Alberta Newsprint Company

in liquidation" analogy. Huge areas of the province have been offered up to transnationals. Large investors, primarily from Japan and the United States, are moving in on Alberta's boreal. It's the last big land grab. The boreal forest, auctioned off at the lowest prices anywhere; Premier Ralph Klein, receiver in bankruptcy, says, "Everything must go."

The forests

Alberta's fire history created forests that were even-aged and dominated by few species. Currently, the government estimates that 47.4 percent of the forest is composed of pure coniferous stands and 32.8 percent of pure deciduous trees, representing the impacts of fire and succession.[2] Fire typically removed the climax species of white spruce, and replaced it with the invading pioneer species, like aspen, rebuilding after the catastrophic impact of the flames. In the Alberta foothills, the pattern was slightly different, with lodgepole pine moving in after fire destroyed that zone's climax forest of black spruce, white spruce, and alpine fir.

Into this naturally driven engine of change, death and rebirth came the first settlers. As townsites sprang up in the late nineteenth century, large sawmills began to provide for Calgary, Edmonton, Red Deer and Crowsnest Pass. But the forest did not inspire huge levels of trade, as it had in the east (and to the west, where British Columbia's timber trade was burgeoning in the mid-1800s). Alberta's forest industry primarily served local needs until the first plywood mill was built in 1953. Located in Grande Prairie, the mill utilized only hardwood species. A few years later, a pulp mill followed in Hinton, northwest of Edmonton. By 1970, the forest industry was cutting over four million cubic meters a year to feed its mills.[3]

Forests for sale

In the mid-1980s, the Alberta government adopted a deliberate industrial forest strategy. Unlike most Canadian provinces, where land-use decisions were constrained by existing industrial tenures, Alberta was still in a position to decide where logging could go, where oil and gas would be allowed, and where tourism would be encouraged.[4]

With the goal of diversification of the provincial economy, federal and provincial governments provided research and development funding to adapt Japanese technology to the pulping of aspen. As aspen dominated much of Alberta's post-fire successional ecosystem, technological innovation could provide a commercial value to a previously "worthless" tree. Once the technology had been perfected, Alberta's Forest Minister hit the road, hoping to lure Japanese- and U.S.-based corporations to northern Alberta.[5] With 87 percent of the forest in Crown land controlled by the provincial government, Alberta could promise investors huge tracts of forest, low stumpage rates and a cookie jar of other subsidies.

As an industrial strategy it has been a smashing success. Between 1986, when the venture was launched, and 1994, over $3.7 billion in new investments had been made in Alberta's forest industry—moving forests up to the rank of the province's fourth-largest business, after oil and gas, agriculture, and tourism.[6] In fact, the bulk of the aggressive marketing and landing of new mill commitments was packed into the breathtakingly short space of eighteen months, between September 1987 and March 1989. By the time Forest Minister Leroy Fjordbotten was through with the marketing blitz of the century, Alberta and the federal government had committed a billion dollars in loans and subsidies and thousands of square kilometers of forest to the industry, in seven new and two renegotiated Forest Management Agreements (FMAs), each with a twenty-year renewable license.[7]

Alberta's big forest giveaway covered 136,120 square kilometers, or roughly one-fifth of the province. The FMAs required the companies to do any road-building not specifically subsidized through other agreements, but left the province responsible for all fire and insect protection. The FMA holder also committed to being financially responsible for the regeneration of the site. But the subsidy that keeps on coming is the cheap stumpage rate. Subsequent to the first round of negotiations, Alberta doubled its stumpage, which was embarrassingly low, even by Alberta standards of corporate charity. Softwood stumpage for pulp mills ranged from $1.50 to $2.50 per cubic meter, dropping as low as $0.25 per cubic meter for aspen.

But even with the doubling of stumpage, and with nearly five billion dollars invested in new mills, Alberta collected only $66 million a year, and spent over $110 million on running the forest service and fulfilling its obligations to provide fire and insect protection to the FMA holders.[8] For all its devotion to commercial goals, not only did the province not negotiate to make money on its new forestry industrial base, it arranged to lose money and export jobs.

In exchange, Alberta had nailed down Mitsubishi, Honshu Paper and Daishowa-Marubeni of Japan, as well as increased investments from existing mills, for a total of two new bleached-kraft pulp mills, expansion of two existing bleached-kraft mills, two new chemical thermal mechanical pulp (CTMP) mills, one new oriented strand board mill, and several new or expanded sawmills. Mitsubishi and Honshu Paper formed one partnership, called Alberta Pacific, or Al-Pac. Its mill on the Athabasca River was highly controversial. The Athabasca is a major tributary to the enormous Mackenzie River Basin, which covers 570,000 square kilometers of Canada's North. In 1990, a joint federal-provincial environmental assessment pointed to existing high levels of dioxin and furans in the Athabasca, raising concerns for the safety of fish for human consumption downstream in the Northwest Territories. The sheer size of the mill and the cumulative impact of so many mills led the panel to recommend that it not proceed.

In response, Alberta convened its own "independent" assessment of the scientific data, angering many who felt the environmental assessment process was being undermined. Meanwhile, Al-Pac suddenly realized that its corporate interests might actually coincide with a higher environmental standard. It revised its proposal, reducing organochlorine emissions by a factor of five. The province issued the approval and the mill went into production.[9]

It is the largest single-line bleached kraft pulp mill in the world, but all the secondary paper processing is done elsewhere. The economics of changing cheap Alberta wood into expensive Japanese paper go something like this: The stumpage rates charged by Alberta when it first negotiated the deal would total $90 for a stand of sixteen aspen trees, fifty feet tall. Once converted into pulp, they would fetch $590. After finishing and paper processing in Japan, the end-product is worth $1,250.[10]

The Daishowa mill benefited from generous provincial government assistance, and also received a federal subsidy from the Western Diversification Office for road-building to the mill. However, neither government gave much thought to the rights of local First Nations residents of the area: Daishowa's Forest Management Agreement covered much of the traditional lands of the Lubicon Cree.

The Lubicon had already been subjected to serial abuses from the combined impacts of oil-and-gas development and logging. Within a two-year period in the early 1980s, more than four hundred oilwells were drilled within a twenty-four-kilometer radius of the Lubicon village of Little Buffalo. UNOCAL, a California-based oil and gas company, recently built a sour gas battery plant within five kilometers of the same community. Sour gas is exactly what it sounds like, with the rotten-egg smell of hydrogen-sulfide emissions posing health problems for the Lubicon.

The health of the Lubicon is also compromised by logging. As traditional sources of food in the bush become unavailable, they are forced to rely on store-bought food. The rates of diabetes have soared, as have suicides, still-births and other social problems. What was once a healthy, self-sustaining community has been devastated. Currently, 95 percent of the population is on welfare, and 35 percent have health problems ranging from tuberculosis to respiratory problems and cancer—at rates that exceed the national average.[11]

When the Lubicon Cree discovered that the giant forest deals with Japanese multinationals had taken place in their traditional territory, they mounted blockades and appeals across Canada and around the world for help. A "Boycott Daishowa" campaign followed, featuring consumer boycotts causing some of Daishowa's customers, like Pizza Pizza, to switch suppliers. Daishowa initially tried intimidation, suing a number of young people in Toronto, known as "Friends of the Lubicon," for their estimated millions in business losses.

The Japanese investors used intimidation to good effect in silencing an Albertan critic. John McInnis, Associate Director of the University of Alberta Environmental Resource Studies Center, attended a conference in Japan and spoke critically of the giant giveaway of Alberta's forests to Mitsubishi, Honshu Paper and Daishowa-Marubeni. Shortly after he returned to Canada, his job at the University of Alberta was gone. Something had been said to the university about a promised multimillion-dollar commitment to research that could be in jeopardy under the circumstances. John McInnis's lawsuit against Al-Pac, Daishowa and three of their managers for unlawful interference with his contract is still before the courts. In 1996, he was countersued by a senior Al-Pac executive for more than $300,000.[12]

Daishowa modified logging and began to deal more directly with the Lubicon, instituting a temporary moratorium on logging Lubicon land. But Japanese investors complained that when the government was courting them, no mention was made of disputed land titles with Alberta's indigenous peoples. In fact, many of the FMAs, negotiated without consultation with Alberta First Nations, are for unceded traditional lands. The Grand Chief of Treaty 8, Johnson Seewepegaham, has stated his position that the FMAs are inconsistent with existing First Nations' rights pursuant to treaty entitlements.[13]

A Cree elder spoke eloquently of what these developments mean to his people:

This you must know: this land, these forests and waters, are not just resources to be harvested and managed. They were given to us to take care of and treat with respect, the way our grandfathers have always done. We are responsible for taking care of Mother Earth because she takes care of us. These pulp mills will take those things away from them. The land won't be the same after they take away the trees. This destruction weighs heavily on us, like a war. You don't need a war to destroy a native person. Just take away the bush, just take away the trees. That will destroy us. The money will be all that is left.[14]

Still, the current Conservative government of Premier Ralph Klein, like that of his predecessor, Don Getty, remains unwilling to address issues of First Nations' rights and resolution of land claims. What is more curious is that the federal government, with a constitutional obligation to protect First Nations' rights, has been willing not only to turn a blind eye to the Alberta development boom on First Nations' land, but even to subsidize it through the regional development fund, the Western Diversification Office.

The Lubicon Cree are still embroiled in a battle with Daishowa. While not logging on Lubicon land, Daishowa is purchasing wood from those lands, logged by others. A recent court decision has finally overturned previous rulings and found that the Daishowa boycott interferes with the company's rights. An injunction against the Friends of the Lubicon boycott was awarded by the Ontario Divisional Court.

The large expansion in the production capacity in Alberta's forests led to a drastic increase in clear-cut logging. Twenty years before, Alberta was cutting about four million cubic meters of wood a year. By 1995 that amount had increased five-fold, to over twenty million cubic meters logged.[15] And there is no sign that the development boom has stopped. New mills and new developments are being aggressively promoted. A huge complex for producing coated fine paper is being proposed for Grande Prairie. It would be a two-phase project, requiring a total of 500,000 cubic meters of softwood every year, and 300,000 cubic meters of hardwood. But after all the Forest Management Agreements and long-term leases issued in the last ten years, many people, even within the industry, are wondering if there is enough wood to go around.

How much wood is available in the Green Rush?

Alberta has invested heavily in the technology to pulp aspen, and laid the groundwork for a massive marketing campaign for the world's forest companies to consume Alberta's forests. One would be entitled to assume that the province had also conducted a careful inventory of its forest to determine how much wood was available. One would be wrong.

The forest inventory in place when Alberta dished out eleven FMAs, covering a fifth of the province, was completed using aerial photographs taken between 1970 and 1982. Unlike other provinces' efforts to continuously update the inventory with permanent plot sampling and new photography, Alberta's updates consist of removing areas of inventory known to have been devastated by fire or logging.[16] Relying on photos creates real problems in differentiating between hardwood species, such as aspen and balsam poplar. Moreover, while such a rough cut at the inventory stage provides guidance as to the broad generalities of forest age and composition, it is notoriously unreliable as a basis for making specific assessments of volume.

Before 1966, record keeping was spotty. No one really knows for sure what areas were cut in the past, and so their regeneration success is hard to judge. Meanwhile, with the recent surge in clear-cut logging, it is likely that 95 percent of what is being logged has never been logged before.

Alberta has established only about a thousand permanent sample plots and has done little to verify the actual state of the forest on the ground. In 1991, the forest service itself called on the government to provide the necessary funds to establish another three thousand permanent sample plots, so that the work of verifying estimates based on aerial photography could begin.[17] But no such increases were made. In fact, the budget has continually been reduced.

From this doubtful inventory, the province estimated its allowable annual cut (AAC). The government's own view is that "the approach used to determine the AACs must be flexible and sensitive to a wide range of users . . . the selected AAC was a management decision and not strictly a calculation."[18] There is a remarkable degree of candor in the Al-Pac Forest Management Plan as to what factors directed the level of permissible cutting. "The proposed annual allowable cut (AAC) on the deciduous land base was *calculated based on the mill requirements*, plus an eleven percent allowance for stand structure, fire losses and local timber permits, less the volume of deciduous wood that is expected from the coniferous land base" (emphasis added).[19]

Alberta adopted an intensive forest management regime in the early 1970s, and like the other provinces it uses the allowable-cut effect to authorize more logging in the short term, based on speculative future growth as a result of promised silvicultural treatments.[20] In short, every effort has been made to exaggerate the wood supply.

Alberta has already run into problems in overestimating the forest. In a general overview of the most recent inventory, an expert review panel on forest management in Alberta concluded: "In at least one volume sampling region, the stand volumes associated with the . . . inventory types appears to be too high by as much as thirty percent."[21] The FMA for the Alberta Newsprint Company, producing a partly recycled newsprint, and holding one of the province's smaller FMAs for half a million cubic meters a year, also overestimated the available wood by as much as 30 percent. Leaked briefing notes from the forest service in April 1993 argued that the AAC for the FMA should be reduced by the same amount.[22]

Another problem emerged when the province was courting Procter & Gamble to come to the Manning area. Having offered the company an area with a 675,000-cubic-meter AAC, the forest service discovered that, in reality, the wood supply was nowhere near that volume. Chief Forester Ken Higginbotham was quoted as saying, "The timber supplies are very young and there is virtually no timber that is harvestable at present."[23] Fortunately for the province, it was in the rare position of not having executed the FMA in advance. Procter & Gamble backed out, and the AAC was reduced to 300,000 cubic meters. In the case of Al-Pac, the timber inventories were done *after* the FMAs were signed.

Part of the reason for Alberta's casual attitude toward its wood supply is that its bureaucrats suffered from the same misconception as the early loggers of the Ottawa Valley, a century before: they believed that Alberta enjoyed virtually inexhaustible timber resources. Back in 1970, when total logging came to 4.143 million cubic meters, the annual allowable cut was set at 26 million cubic meters. The wood supply had a healthy margin for error.

But the margin is shrinking. Losses to fire and logging have brought the estimated AAC down to 22.1 million cubic meters, and intensive commercial logging has brought the actual harvest level up to 20.3 million cubic meters.[24] And even that margin disguises the reality of available wood. The province's FMAs commit more of the province than is currently being logged. This is partly due to the lag time in building new mills, with logging to commence once the mills are up and running, and partly due to the fact that the FMAs allow the companies to average the AAC over a five-year period, allowing for front- or end-loading, depending on mill requirements. The *existing* FMAs have committed 99.6 percent of all the estimated coniferous forest and 88.6 percent of the deciduous trees.[25] And the province is still negotiating to give out more FMAs!

In response, a 1995 federal-provincial government study urged caution regarding any further FMAs: "Further allocations of the few remaining uncommitted public forests in Alberta is inadvisable and not consistent with the current national and international directions in forest stewardship."[26] The Environment Minister Ty Lund dismissed the study as one man's opinion. In fact, it was the work of twenty-one scientists.[27]

As John McInnis, former associate director of environmental research and studies at the University of Alberta, remarked, "In some cases the forest service has come close to admitting they may have allocated more trees than actually exist for harvest."[28]

The situation is made worse by logging on private land, none of which is regulated or inventoried. While many provinces make an effort to include private lands in their AAC, Alberta does not.[29] Although only 4 percent of Alberta's forests are privately owned, in recent years they have been heavily over-cut.[30] Many farmers still clear their land for grazing. Conversion of forest to agricultural land is not the only problem. When pulp prices went sky-high in the mid-1990s, and British Columbia, just over the mountains, began running out of wood for its mills, large-scale clear-cutting of private land became a serious environmental threat. No one knows how much wood left Alberta during this period, unprocessed, for mills to the west and in Montana to the south. In 1994–95, the amount of wood cut from private lands was estimated at approximately 2.3 million cubic meters, but it could be more.[31] In the first half of 1995, three million dollars' worth of timber crossed the border into British Columbia *every two days*.[32]

Even after nearly doubling stumpage rates in 1994, the province of Alberta only collects $10 to $12 per cubic meter in stumpage for its coniferous wood, whereas B.C. mills were offering $48.75 per cubic meter, *at the stump*.[33] Cheap wood from private land in Alberta has been a windfall for the B.C. forest industry. Even after the costs of transportation, it is cheaper than logging locally.

The irony is that small local mills are the most adversely affected, both by the huge FMAs and by the rape of the privately held forest land. These mills are nearly wholly dependent on sales from private woodlots, as virtually all of the Crown land is tied up in the large FMAs—and private landowners are able to ask the market price for wood. The large mills have the advantage of a guaranteed low price, a fraction of the market prices private landowners are obtaining. The small mills also produce about nine times more jobs per tree logged than do the high-tech multinational mills. And yet, it is the small mills that are having significant difficulty maintaining a wood supply.

Can this picture get worse?

With nearly 90 percent of the allocated AAC in the hands of about sixteen companies, with unreliable data and inflated wood-supply numbers, the forest industry could still be reoriented to sustainability—with strong, consistent government regulation and ecologically sound management. Of course, it is futile to close the barn door after the horse is gone, but at least a conscientious provincial chief forester could insist on better inventory data and reduce AACs as the wood supply dwindles. This is, after all, the first time Alberta's boreal has ever been cut. It has the advantage that centuries of damage have not already been done to its forests.

In fact, a government forest service study in 1991 came to the conclusion that significant budgetary increases were necessary if the forest service was to cope with the runaway increase in logging. Without an increase of forty million dollars by the

1992–93 budget, the report warned, "the Alberta Forest Service will be unable to monitor and enforce the environmental standards promised by the Government of Alberta to its citizens. . . . [and that] insufficient staffing will prevent the division from protecting forests from large scale environmental damage."[34]

Environmental impacts

Environmental damage had already begun. Biodiversity was threatened, with plants and animals dependent on the boreal becoming rare or endangered. In Alberta's forests, the yellow Indian tansy and the cypripedium orchid, rare plants of the boreal, are threatened.[35] The wood bison is currently found only in captivity in Alberta. Its once thundering masses have been reduced to a captive herd in Elk Island National Park and Wood Bison National Park. The grizzly bear, bobcat and Canada lynx are in trouble; so too are the trumpeter swan, whooping crane and wolverine.

Currently, no legislation at either the federal or the provincial level is in force to protect endangered species in Alberta. On September 8, 1995, Premier Ralph Klein met with environmental groups and promised that Alberta would bring in its own endangered species legislation. The premier specifically assured the environmental groups that the legislation would protect not only endangered species, but their habitat as well. But the amendments to the Alberta Wildlife Act will not protect anything. They merely require that the minister establish an advisory committee on endangered species, with its own subsidiary scientific advisory body.

Similarly, Alberta has not fulfilled its promise to protect 12 percent of its representative ecoregions. Protected areas have actually been undermined as standards are relaxed to allow resource development within parks. Legislative reform is necessary, as existing parks legislation does not prohibit industrial development. Roads and five wells have gone into Dinosaur Provincial Park. Offroad vehicle use is occurring in Lakeland Provincial Park, and logging is being considered. Cypress Hills Provincial Park is also facing threats of logging and intensified agriculture.[36]

As logging removes the habitat of endangered species, no legal tools will be available to prevent extinctions, and few protected areas have been established. No Noah has emerged to build an ark against the development deluge.

The commitment to logging virtually all of Alberta's forests on a rotational basis will ultimately eliminate all old-growth aspen and coniferous ecosystems. A Canadian Wildlife Service study concluded that "intensive forest harvest (clearcut logging of sixty- to seventy-year rotations) in boreal mixed wood forests, by simplifying the structure of young stands and reducing the frequency of old stands, will not maintain the abundance of flora and fauna at levels found in unmanaged forests."[37]

But the "environmental damage" of which the forest service warned is not only damage affecting what the industry calls "non-timber values." It is affecting the ability of the forest to grow new trees. There are huge areas of backlogged, not satisfactorily restocked (NSR) land. The most recent federal report, *The State of Canada's Forests, 1996-1997*, puts the unstocked harvested Crown land at 37 percent.[38] The coniferous land base alone where natural regeneration has failed to succeed following clear-cutting has reached 247,486 hectares. Moreover, Alberta has a regeneration problem similar to that of the Newfoundland kalmia barrens. A grass called *calamagrotis* is extremely invasive, growing in sites after clear-cutting. A 1984 study found that 33 percent of the second-growth conifers were having serious difficulty as a result of the spread of calamagrotis.[39] Interestingly, foresters speculate that the grass, like certain insects and disease, does not do well after fires; but it thrives after clear-cuts.

The provincial policy of replacing conifer forests with new conifer forests is constantly undermined by the natural process of succession, which government foresters are desperate to avoid. According to one forest service spokesman: "The profuse regeneration capabilities of many deciduous species . . . can limit successful regeneration and a return to pure coniferous areas following harvest."[40] In other words, just as in every other province, clear-cut logging leads to species conversion.

In simple economic terms, maintaining a timber supply on publicly owned land requires strict government regulation. But any notion of effective regulation is the stuff of pipe dreams. The February 21, 1996, budget for the Province of Alberta delivered a very serious blow to the environment, just as Premier Mike Harris's government had done in Ontario that same spring. Six hundred staff positions and $123 million were cut from the Alberta Environmental Protection budget over a three-year period. The forest service, far from getting the increased resources it had insisted were necessary, has been reduced by $42 million, with a 13 percent cut in staffing.

Even before the cuts, the will to enforce the law had been doubtful. Of twenty-three mill enforcement actions for pollution violations between January 1989 and April 1996, only four resulted in prosecutions. The provincial registry of pollution offenses fails even to mention twenty-two violations of effluent guidelines by Millar Western's Whitecourt pulp mill. Procter & Gamble's bleached kraft pulp mill accumulated 167 complaints before any charges were laid. But even though fines of $140,000 were levied, the government happily renewed Procter & Gamble's license, just in time for them to sell to Weyerhaeuser.[41]

But the lack of regulation does not end with the budgetary axe. The whole thrust of new forest legislation is toward deregulation and industry self-regulation. In November 1995, the government released its "Regulatory Reform Report." It sets out a plan for a three-year program of delegation of enforcement activity to the forest industry, of streamlining the approval process for a range of industrial activities, and, of course, of cutting enforcement costs.

Under Regulatory Reform, the industry will be in charge of timber production audits, FMA planning, the establishment of seeding standards, and other silviculture decisions. The industry is to monitor itself, keep its own records, and report from its own data. Looming large in Alberta and across the country is the notion that industry self-regulation can be coupled with voluntary programs, such as the Canadian Standards Association (CSA) "Sustainable Forest Management" certification scheme. A CSA certification would mean nothing in terms of actually knowing that the logging had been ecologically sound. It would merely mean that the company in question had bought into a process of environmental improvement, with targets it set for itself.

Deregulating the pollution control requirements through reduced enforcement has been defended by government with the suggestion that citizen watchdogs will replace government regulators. But according to one Alberta environmental group, relaying public complaints to the government is useless. When the Pembina Institute followed up on previously filed complaints, they were told that no one had investigated them because there was no staff to do the work.[42] Similarly, the Minister of Environmental Protection has admitted that, of seventy calls received between March 1995 and May 1996 reporting poor logging practices on private lands, only five had been investigated.[43]

Alberta's current political agenda is geared toward industry self-regulation. And what does that finally mean, in plain language? That decisions about whether Alberta's public forests are to be sustainably managed will be made in Japan.

12

British Columbia

British Columbia is a land of superlatives: the most active waves of any sea coast in the world, the greatest seismic action, the tallest and oldest trees, and Canada's greatest biodiversity. It has more distinct ecosystems than any other province, embracing Canada's only true desert in the south and glaciers in the mountains.[1] Only in British Columbia can you ski one day and sail the next, in a land of mountain and sea; of ice and garden. As the tourist ads proclaim, it is "Super Natural British Columbia."

It has ancient coastal temperate rainforests, luxuriant with green—cedar, spruce, creepers, ferns and lichens. Mosses cover fallen trees in fertile, moist and lush profusion, and new trees sprout from the fallen trunks of the old giants. It has record-setting biomass; the heaviest in the world: forests of rare Garry oak, boreal forest to the north and montane in the interior. But British Columbia also sets another kind of record—the only evidence of human activity visible from outer space, along with the Great Wall of China and the burning Amazon, is the scarred landscape of British Columbia clear-cuts.

Record-setting protests, too: a thousand people arrested in Clayoquot Sound. More flashpoints per square kilometer than any other Canadian province. The names are like an incantation: Carmanah, Meares Island, Gwaii Haanas (South Moresby) and Lyell Island, the Stein, the Kitlope, Khutzeymateen, the Walbran. That all but Meares have now been saved is a miracle. A tribute to public pressure and political will. But the industry cry goes out that the environmentalists' agenda is unending. How many forests have to be "saved"? Where are they supposed to log? Environmentalists feel beleaguered. We have won so many battles. Why do we still feel we are losing the war?

Because we *are* losing the war. So long as survival of ecosystems rests on the setting aside of fragments of the original forest, the forest loses. As long as everything outside

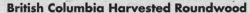

British Columbia Harvested Roundwood

SOURCE: Compendium of Canadian Forestry Statistics 1995.

those fragments is viewed as actual or potential industrial forest, to be managed as fiber farms for a second-growth timber supply, then British Columbia's never-logged forests will inevitably experience the same degradation and decline as has been seen across Canada. The difference is that British Columbia still has options; it still has significant areas of intact primeval forest; it has a choice.

In the beginning . . .

In the beginning, the forests of British Columbia were the homelands of populous and cultured peoples. The indigenous nations of British Columbia interacted with the ecosystems that supported them, reflecting their surroundings in the totems, clan lines and kinship, in celebration and offerings, in their artistry and dance.

There were sea people and forest people. The coastal First Nations plied the ocean waters in huge, intricately carved and ornamented war canoes, each made from a single giant cedar tree. Materials for longhouses and poles were taken from the forest by these aboriginal coastal dwellers. The Interior tribes also found their needs met by the vast expanses of forest, its wildlife and fish.

The first settlers and explorers gained riches through the exploitation of fur, opening trading posts in the eighteenth century. The first sawmill followed, built by the fur empire of the Hudson's Bay Company in 1848. The forests of New Brunswick and

BRITISH COLUMBIA	(1995)
Forest Land in million hectares	60.6
Stocked Harvested Crown Land in hectares	2,614,000
Area Logged in hectares	189,608
Volume Logged in million cubic meters	74.5
Annual Allowable Cut in million cubic meters	71.6

SOURCE: Natural Resources Canada, Canadian Forest Service, *The State of Canada's Forests, 1996-1997* (Ottawa, 1997). These are federal government summaries, based on provincial government data. The figures are not necessarily accurate.

Nova Scotia were felled to build ships for the British Navy, but the first logging boom on the West Coast was driven by the gold rush. San Francisco's nearly insatiable appetite for building materials demanded imports from as far away as Maine.[2] Other mills followed and with them legendary stories of the West Coast giants. The first commercially valuable tree was Douglas fir, the tallest tree in Canada. One ancient Douglas fir, well over 1,100 years old, was measured after it finally fell to the forest floor. It was three hundred feet (90m) tall and forty-five feet (14 m) around its base. Douglas fir produced excellent lumber, as well as masts and planking for shipbuilding. Today, less than 1 percent of the original coastal old-growth Douglas fir forests remain.

Production levels of the early B.C. forest industry were astonishing. One of the first large lumber camps at English Bay, built within the shadows of what are now the highrises of downtown Vancouver, produced nine million board feet of Douglas fir from only eighty acres (32 ha). The forests that used to ring English Bay became the paneling and stairs of English churches and the beams of the Imperial Palace in Peking.[3]

BRITISH COLUMBIA CORPORATE PLAYERS

MacMillan Bloedel
Slocan Forest Products
Harmac
Interfor
Crestbrook Forest Industries
Weldwood of Canada
Western Forest Products
Fletcher-Challenge
Lignum
Louisiana-Pacific

Regulating the timber boom

With 95 percent of the forest owned by the Crown, the government instituted a timber licensing system in the mid-1880s. The first stumpage rate in B.C. was fifteen cents per tree.

Some government reports were unhappy with how the benefits from logging were being distributed. In 1905, one such report noted:

> In a sense, the lumber industry in British Columbia has not been a prosperous one, though owners of mills and timber limits, as a rule, have grown into wealth.[4]

The timber licenses were easy to obtain and as the shortages of wood elsewhere, particularly in the U.S., became pronounced, the B.C. forests were not only staked by mills, they were claimed by timber speculators. By 1910, the bonanza in "timber-staking" was out of control, warranting the province's first Royal Commission on Forests. Foresters in the province warned that if speculative timber staking and uncontrolled logging were allowed to continue, British Columbia could run out of wood.[5]

The Report of the Royal Commission resulted in the province's first Forest Act in 1912. Timber Sale Licences were legislated, based on a process of competitive bidding for small to medium-sized blocks of timber.[6] In advance of putting a parcel of forest up to bid, it had to be cruised and surveyed. All costs of classifying, surveying and advertising the Timber Sale Licences were paid by the winning bidder. The licenses were only for three to four years, so the forest was not tied up in long-term commitments. Other than a grandfathering provision for hand-loggers working small areas along the coast, Timber Sale Licences became the province's only form of tenure.[7]

All of that changed in 1945 with the recommendations of the next B.C. Royal Commission, chaired by Mr. Justice Gordon Sloan. It largely reflected the vision of the provincial Chief Forester, C.D. Orchard. Orchard was a proponent of sustained-yield forest management in the tradition of Pinchot and Fernow. He favored long-term leases, to be called Tree Farm Licences (TFLs), over the Timber Sales arrangements that had prevailed since 1912. What Orchard had envisioned was a system that distributed several hundred long-term Tree Farm Licences fairly among the applicants who qualified for them.[8] Instead, the opportunity to gain perpetual access, as it was initially granted, over huge areas of the province was seized by the companies with the political and financial wherewithal to make a killing. Large corporations saw the TFLs as a way to raise capital to build pulp and lumber complexes. And as the new legislation made the granting of TFLs a matter purely within the discretion of the Minister of Forests, the whole system was virtually designed to reward corruption.

By the time the first round of major land-grab TFLs had been issued, the Minister of Forests, R.E. Sommers, had been jailed. Sommers was convicted of accepting bribes to grant a TFL to B.C. Forest Products. The provincial Chief Forester, C.D. Orchard, had opposed issuing the TFL on the grounds that it would constitute "a dangerous over-cut . . . a timber grab and legalized liquidation." But the minister had overruled his Chief Forester, granting B.C. Forest Products the desired TFL. Several years later, evidence of a $30,000 payment from B.C. Forest Products to Sommers finally came to light. The minister went to jail, but B.C. Forest Products was acquitted, and all the TFLs issued by Minister Sommers remained valid. Moreover, the pattern was set. Substantial TFLs and other forest tenures were to continue to be granted to large companies, often based and financed from outside B.C.

The big prize: Corporate windfalls in British Columbia

In an atmosphere of political payoffs, scandals and sleaze, the granting of British Columbia's forests to private interests has always been a high-stakes game. And no wonder: nearly half of all the wood logged in Canada comes from British Columbia forests.[9] In the 1990s, anywhere from 160,000 to 200,000 hectares was logged every year, 92 percent by clear-cutting.[10]

Rates of cut have increased dramatically from pre-1970 levels. The cut rate doubled between 1950 and 1975, rising to about fifty million cubic meters annually. By the late 1970s, it had grown by another 40 percent, to approximately seventy million cubic meters. The B.C. government allows the industry to over-cut the AAC in any given year, so long as the averages over a five-year period fall within AAC limits—which means that in some years, the B.C. Crown land forests have experienced rates of cut above eighty million cubic meters.[11]

The 1996 AAC was set at 71.3 million cubic meters—or more than the total logged in Quebec, Ontario, New Brunswick, Manitoba and Saskatchewan combined.[12]

British Columbia, with a total area of over ninety-five million hectares, has roughly sixty million hectares of forest. The forested area runs the gamut from the coastal temperate rainforest, containing some of the world's most valuable timber, to the northern boreal, an open subalpine forest of stunted small trees on rocky and boggy soils, to inaccessible forests on steep slopes, and otherwise uncommercial forest. Some of these areas are removed in the "netting down" process: protected areas are supposed to be removed from calculations of the forest land base before the process of establishing cut levels begins (so the AAC is set only on "net," not "gross" holdings). In British

Columbia, substantially more forest has been protected than in other provinces. However, the total area of forests protected is inadequate—only a little over 7 percent of the forest land.[13] Nearly 69 percent of the protected areas are non-forested, or contain only high-elevation forests, primarily alpine, rock and ice. Less than 6 percent of protected areas are low-elevation forests.[14]

Even within British Columbia's so-called protected areas of forest, much is in bogs and rocky zones that were never commercially viable in any event. Of the 8.6 percent of the coastal western hemlock zone which has been protected on Vancouver Island, much is of the bog variety, with stunted trees, not the towering old-growth Sitka spruce and western red cedar.[15]

It is not hard to see why it is easier to create parks in areas dominated by rock and ice than in forested areas. Most valuable forest ecosystems are already locked up in long-term leases to forest companies. While historically the fees companies paid for the right to cut forests did not approach market value, the province has at times in the past interpreted the leases as requiring compensation to forest companies for areas converted to parks. When South Moresby in the Queen Charlotte Islands was set aside as Gwaii Haanas National Park, Western Forest Products negotiated tens of millions of dollars in compensation for a lease they had received for only tens of thousands. Reflecting the perverse dynamic of arranging for protected-area status, as the provincial and federal government neared successful completion of negotiations to protect the ancient forest giants of Gwaii Haanas, the logging contractor moved to triple shifts, logging around the clock, to clear-cut as much of Lyell Island as he possibly could before the lease was revoked.[16] The logged areas of Lyell Island remain today as mute testimony to the destructive clear-cutting legacy of Western Forest Products.

Ninety-six percent of the ninety-five-million-hectare land base of the province is owned by the Crown, 3 percent by the forest industry, and 1 percent by private owners.[17] The sixty-million-hectare forest area is netted down to determine the productive operable forest base. Once reductions have been made to allow for inoperable and inaccessible areas—the largest reductions—protected areas are also subtracted. The remainder is the productive forest land base, estimated to be between eighteen and twenty-one million hectares.[18]

By 1970, the corporate control of the forest was fairly well established. Most of the Crown forest is in the hands of powerful multinationals, who have access to huge tracts of forest on very easy terms. Since 1976, the twenty largest forest companies have increased their control of harvesting rights from 74 percent to 86 percent. The ten biggest forest companies have maintained a fairly steady 60 percent control over the forest from 1976 to the present.[19]

Among many instruments for giving away forests in B.C. are "Tree Farm Licences"

(TFLs). By 1970, there were thirty-four issued, covering approximately four million hectares of some of the most productive Crown land, and providing 26 percent of B.C.'s total forest cut. In the same period, between 1950 and 1975, logging more than doubled. The integrated companies producing lumber and pulp and paper were able to put smaller, lower-quality logs to economic use, with the result that the cuts in some TFLs increased by as much as 600 percent—and all in the name of sustained-yield forest management.[20] *Overall, the cut increased from thirty million cubic meters in 1960 to ninety million cubic meters by 1990.*[21]

Concentration of corporate power came in for criticism in the fourth of B.C.'s royal commissions, a one-man inquiry by the respected resource economist Peter Pearse in 1975. The Commission was established by the left-wing government of Premier Dave Barrett and the New Democratic Party. In the wild world of B.C. politics, by the time Pearse issued his findings, the government was back in the hands of the far-right Social Credit Party. His report highlighted the remarkable degree of power and control over the industry by a handful of companies. On the B.C. coast, for example, the largest ten companies controlled 86 percent of the AAC.

In the Interior, the ten largest companies held rights to 53 percent of the AAC. On a province-wide basis, nearly 100 percent of the pulp industry, 94 percent of the paper production capacity, 55 percent of lumber and 90 percent of plywood were in the hands of the twenty-seven largest forestry companies. All told, this same twenty-seven firms had rights to 80 percent of the provincial AAC.[22] Pearse wrote:

> The forest policies we have pursued have not . . . been neutral; while they
> have not been deliberately biased to the disadvantage of smaller, non-
> integrated firms and potential new firms, there can be little doubt that they
> have nevertheless accelerated the consolidation of the industry into fewer,
> larger, and more integrated enterprises.[23]

Pearse's solution was to break the stranglehold of the industry giants through competitive bidding for timber sales and rights, as well as making tenure less permanent. Two years after the report was issued, the new Minister of Forests, Tom Waterland, introduced new forest legislation. Whereas Pearse had recommended reducing the term of TFLs to fifteen years, Waterland settled on twenty-five years, on renewable terms. While TFLs remained a powerful form of tenure across the landscape, they were not the only way in which B.C. allocated rights over publicly held timber. B.C. has more instruments for tenure arrangements over Crown land and greater complexity than any other Canadian province.[24] The volume-based forest licences are the most common form of tenure, but there are also Tree Farm licenses, Timber Supply Areas and a few remaining timber berths as well. Other recommendations of the Pearse Commission to break up corporate concentration and to increase competition in the log market were defeated by industry opposition.

By 1986, Waterland was forced to resign from cabinet, following revelations that he held a $20,000 personal investment in Western Forest Products, a company to which he had issued TFLs and in whose favor he had made decisions as minister. Other cabinet colleagues were also enmeshed in the scandal, having made personal investments in the province's forest industry. Stephen Rogers, later to rejoin cabinet as Environment Minister, briefly resigned over his $100,000 Western Forest Products investment.[25]

The politics of the Socred government in the early 1980s was one of wholehearted support for the industry. When an economic downturn adversely affected the corporate bottom line, forest service officials were instructed to turn a blind eye to logging infractions. Whole valleys and mountains were clear-cut. Excess slash, cutting through streams, and waste above departmental guidelines were all allowed, through a policy of "sympathetic administration," as the government approvingly termed it. The policy was described as an "interim" approach to the economic difficulties of the industry. What it meant was "anything goes," and what went was the old-growth forest and ecological non-timber values. The abusive clear-cuts in old-growth were described as "relaxed utilization of the over-mature."[26]

In this same period, the government laid off about one-third of its forest staff and combined ranger districts into larger forest districts. Many of British Columbia's current pressing forestry and ecological disasters can be laid at the door of "sympathetic administration." This period of willful negligence resulted in significant areas of non-regenerating NSR land, destroyed watersheds, over-cutting, landslides and devastated fish habitat. Since then, governments have created large *post facto* subsidies to remedy the wanton destruction and short-term profit of the era of sympathetic administration. The first of these programs was the Federal Regional Development Agreement funds, totaling five hundred million dollars in B.C., much of which went to planting the NSR lands. Now the government has created Forest Renewal BC, to attempt rehabilitation of forested land and fish habitat. Up to 4 billion dollars in tax revenue, largely generated by increased stumpage rates, will be spent in a last-ditch effort to bring back ecosystems in which salmon once thrived.

Efforts to enforce the few laws that existed were thwarted. Canada's strongest environmental law is the federal Fisheries Act. Under that law, destruction of fish habitat or placing nearly any substance in water in which fish live is a federal offense. One of the few times the federal Department of Fisheries and Oceans invoked the law, in an attempt to protect a B.C. salmon stream from clear-cut damage, was in 1977, when Queen Charlotte Timber, a wholly owned subsidiary of the giant Japanese corporation

C. Itoh, was planning to clear-cut along Riley Creek, on northern Graham Island within the Queen Charlotte Islands.

Federal fisheries officials, recognizing that Riley Creek was a significant salmon spawning ground, with steep unstable slopes prone to slides, ordered a halt to logging. Queen Charlotte Timber ignored the order and began logging the creek's fragile slopes. In a rare display of federal muscle, possibly unique in Canadian history, the federal fisheries officers sent in the RCMP to halt the illegal logging. The forest industry in B.C. rallied around the company to ensure that the Fisheries Act was never again used to protect salmon streams or interfere with logging. Loggers were flown in by helicopter to replace men arrested for ignoring the fisheries order. Political pressure mounted and charges against Queen Charlotte Timber were stayed by the provincial attorney general. Logging went ahead in Riley Creek. That fall, massive landslides—one of them was 2,000 feet long, 200 feet wide and 5 feet deep—destroyed the fish habitat of Riley Creek.[27]

But if governments were unwilling to protect the forest environment, public concern about the environmental impacts of logging was growing. Other resource users, including fishermen, guide outfitters, tourism operators, and trappers, were worried that their economic base was being degraded by poor forestry practice. Loggers became concerned about the increased mechanization and resulting job losses, and, perhaps more fundamentally, Commissioner Pearse's report had drawn public attention to the fact that the current AAC actually exceeded the sustainable level. The term "fall-down effect" came into more common parlance. Some British Columbians began to realize that logging rates would have to be reduced once all the high-volume old growth was gone. As Ian Miller of the B.C. Forest Service described this period: "The physical and economic boundaries of timber supply were no longer on the horizon, they were already becoming limiting."[28]

More fundamentally, British Columbians began to fight to protect the last remaining wilderness areas from the impact of industrial forestry.

British Columbia's vanishing wilderness

In British Columbia, substantially more forest has been protected than in other provinces. However, the total area of forests protected is well under 10 percent of the forest land, and not all of the protected forest area was commercially viable in any event, making protection much easier.[29]

Magnificent forest ecosystems of temperate rainforest, old-growth Douglas fir, interior montane, and boreal have been eliminated in the last half-century. Using state-of-the-art satellite-mapping techniques, the Sierra Club of British Columbia has determined how much original forest remains on Vancouver Island. The results are startling. By 1990, nearly half of the ancient temperate rainforest extant on the Island in 1954 had been logged.[30] Even those areas not completely logged have suffered serious fragmentation. Similar satellite mapping of Haida Gwaii (the Queen Charlotte Islands) shows the same pattern of lost old growth. As of 1992, most watersheds on Vancouver Island, the south mainland coast, the plains of northeast British Columbia east of the Rockies, and the interior plateaus from the U.S. border to two-thirds of the distance to the Yukon border were no longer undeveloped. The remaining untouched watersheds are largely confined to higher-elevation mountainous areas and the far north.[31]

The most recent Sierra Club mapping of all of the British Columbia coastal temperate rainforest, released in March 1997, demonstrates an increased level of logging.[32] Over half of the ancient temperate rainforest along the B.C. coast has been cut. The southwest corner of the province has been stripped of its exceptional old trees, including over 70 percent of the forests on Vancouver Island.[33] All major salmon rivers have been logged and the most productive forests are gone.

In the southern interior, there were once 208 undisturbed watersheds of 5,000 hectares or larger. Currently, only two of these remain undeveloped.[34] The situation is not much better along the south coast. The rich primary coastal watersheds, those where the land mass is completely within the watershed of a stream draining to the ocean, were prime targets for logging. The volumes that can be logged from temperate rainforests are beyond anything found in the rest of the country. These wet coastal forests have very little fire history. Disturbances were chiefly through the action of strong storms, or through the process of old giants keeling over, creating openings of sunlight for the young growth below. Currently, only five of the eighty-four primary large (over five-thousand hectare) coastal watersheds on the south mainland coast remain unlogged. On Vancouver Island, only five out of ninety remain undeveloped.[35]

The mapping exercise has focused attention on the last major intact area of coastal temperate rainforest. Located on the remote central coast of the province is significant habitat for salmon, grizzly and an extremely rare population of white-colored black bears. The Kermode or "spirit" bear is found primarily on the island of Princess Royal and the valleys of the adjacent mainland coast. Logging threatens its habitat.

Currently, support is growing for the proposed 265,000 hectare Spirit Bear Park, to encompass much of Princess Royal Island, as well as neighboring islands, part of the mainland and interconnecting seas. Such habitat protection is crucial for the survival of the Kermode bear and other endangered creatures.

The area known to forest companies as the "Mid-Coast Timber Supply Area" has been more aptly proclaimed the "Great Bear Rainforest" by Greenpeace and other B.C. environmental groups. Fighting to protect this area from unsustainable rates of logging will likely catapult B.C. forest practices back into the international headlines. The logging rates have been set at one million cubic meters a year, despite the fact that the Chief Forester has acknowledged that the long-term harvest level is approximately half that.[36]

A 1990 report for Conservation International by forest consultant Keith Moore, now chair of the Forest Practices Board, confirmed that, "virtually every watershed on the entire south coast, including Vancouver Island, that was identified as unlogged has had logging plans proposed in the recent past."[37]

A B.C. Ministry of Forests report on old growth set out the liquidation policy of the provincial government:

> Within the over-all policy of achieving sustained yield, it appears the *province's implicit old-growth forest policy is to liquidate it in favour of young forest plantations.* The lack of an explicit recognition of the non-timber values within old-growth forests is resulting in continuing conflicts over specific old-growth stands. These conflicts will become increasingly bitter as old-growth forests disappear (emphasis added).[38]

In the face of these short-sighted policies, it is no wonder that the fight to save areas such as Clayoquot Sound has taken on such urgency and ignited such passion. Of those few remaining unlogged watersheds on Vancouver Island, three are in Clayoquot Sound. The other two are the Klaskish and the East Rivers to the north and adjacent to the Brooks Peninsula Provincial Park on the west coast of Vancouver Island. In September 1997 logging was approved in the Klaskish. The two watersheds of the Klaskish and the East harbor the last remaining wild chinook salmon runs on the north island and an abundant population of the endangered marbled murrelet. South of Clayoquot, on southern Vancouver Island, *at current rates of logging, all of the old-growth forests, other than those areas in parks, will be logged out by 2001.*[39] Coastal old-growth Douglas fir is almost completely wiped out, with less than 1 percent protected.

Biodiversity at risk

As the forest disappears, woodland creatures lose their home. Loss of the forests' old-growth characteristics has huge implications for biological diversity, as has been seen in every other province. For much of British Columbia, new logging continues to move into pristine forests—some of the last remaining ancient temperate rainforests on earth. These areas are home to grizzly, salmon, marbled murrelet, northern goshawk and cougar. So, too, is logging destroying habitat in the older montane and boreal forest ecoregions.

A large number of British Columbia forest creatures are dependent on the structural characteristics of the ancient forest. More than 65 percent of Vancouver Island's bird species, as well as more than 80 percent of mammals, and many amphibians and reptiles, require old-growth habitat. Seventy percent of these forests are already logged and the remaining forests are severely fragmented. The connections between flora and fauna are intricate and intriguing. The endangered marbled murrelet, for example, nests in the mossy forest, tumbling to the ground as a hatchling and heading straight to the sea.[40] The marten and the long-eared Keene's myotis bat are also old-growth-dependent and in decline. In B.C., the grizzly bear is in serious trouble, losing ground as access roads, logging roads and clear-cuts fragment and destroy habitat. The rare Kermode bear is threatened, as logging removes its home.

In 1996, three new forest-dependent species were added to the national endangered-species list. Of these, two are in British Columbia—the Queen Charlotte Islands goshawk and the cryptic paw lichen.[41] And numerous plant species have already joined the extirpated column in the endangered-species list.

The loss of old-growth deciduous forests has caused declines in numerous species, including the yellow-breasted chat, Lewis's woodpecker and Vaux's swift. The rare Garry oak forests, reduced to less than 5 percent of their original range, harbor a unique insect, the robber fly, which disappears with its habitat. Most of this forest loss is due to urbanization.

Meanwhile, the rate of cut in southeastern B.C. is also endangering the woodland caribou (mountain ecotype). More than half of their habitat has been removed. And as old-growth forests disappear, the new growth managed on planned rotations of clear-cuts will never again provide the habitat that was lost when the ancient forest was felled. The woodland caribou are dependent on lichen that grow only in the ancient forest. Forests on a permanent cycle of logging at "maturity" will never develop the characteristics of the natural forest. It takes 350 years for coastal clear-cut forests to reach the first stages of old growth. The caribou in the Chilcotin are especially at risk; they roam an area of two extinct volcanoes, the Itcha and Ilgachuz. The Itcha-Ilgachuz herd belong to a distinct ecotype known as the northern caribou. This internationally significant herd of fifteen hundred caribou is at risk as clear-cut logging threatens the lichen-bearing forests upon which it depends for sustenance.[42]

Of particular concern in British Columbia has been the destruction of critical fish habitat. As the East Coast cod fishery collapsed, there were drastic declines in specific runs and races of salmon, the economic mainstay of the West Coast commercial, sport and aboriginal fishery. While many factors have played a role, primarily over-fishing and increased water temperatures consistent with climate change, clear-cut logging operations have been a major contributing factor. An independent audit of logging operations commissioned by the province in 1992 found that of the twenty-one Vancouver Island clear-cuts surveyed, every one had caused a major or moderate impact on stream quality. Damage was so substantial from clear-cut logging that 35 percent of the streams in the studied clear-cuts had "complete habitat loss." More than 90 percent of the streams had been polluted to some extent by logging debris.[43]

A provincial government review in 1994 found that hundreds of streams on the coast had been degraded by clear-cutting. Clear-cutting can increase the severity of flooding, alter stream flows, cause channel instability and increase erosion. Logging roads, in particular, have been identified as a cause of landslides, erosion, and the clogging and destruction of what was once ideal fish-spawning habitat. Even siltation can clog the stream, coating fish eggs and alevin and thereby reducing reproductive success.[44] There have been 142 documented salmon and trout stock extinctions in the Yukon and British Columbia associated with habitat degradation from logging, urbanization and hydropower developments. Currently, a further 624 stocks are considered at "high risk."[45]

Neither British Columbia nor the federal government has any legislation to protect these endangered species.

While the plight of the endangered spotted owl is well known, fewer people are aware that the canopy of a temperate old-growth forest offers unique conditions for an amazing array of insect life. In fact, when the Western Canada Wilderness Committee built the world's first ancient-temperate-forest-canopy research station in the treetops of the Carmanah Valley, scientists identified sixty-seven species previously unknown in the world. According to Neville Winchester, a key insect researcher, a further three hundred insect species are still under review and may be unique. Ultimately, based on the research thus far, Dr. Winchester estimates that more than six hundred species previously unknown to science will be identified. These are predator and parasitoid species that prey on forest pests and are an integral part of the forest ecology. Canopy-dwelling insects of the ancient forest help maintain forest health.[46]

Recently, lichen expert Trevor Goward announced that he had established a new class of old-growth forests, which he calls "antique oroboreal rainforests." Based in part on the presence of lichens, and their abundance and diversity, Goward has determined that the oldest inland rainforests have apparently been standing in place for a thousand years or more, and are probably much older than the oldest trees within them. The presence of certain lichen structures is an indicator for ancient forests because such stratified lichen appear only in forests that have not seen a disturbance for hundreds of years. While the forest service declares a forest "mature" and ready for logging at sixty years, the forest continues to change and develop old-growth characteristics long after that. In fact, it has been found that a five-hundred-year-old forest will contain significantly more and different lichens, including rare species, than a relatively "young" two-hundred-year-old forest. Notes Goward, "By their very patterns of distribution, these old-growth-dependent lichens are powerful allies in our efforts to locate and set aside the oldest of our old-growth forests."[47]

As logging moves ever farther north, the pressure is being felt even in the Yukon and northern British Columbia. The impacts on wildlife and old growth are predictable. A government study in British Columbia concluded: "The clear-cutting silvicultural system that is typically used in the range of the two ecotypes of caribou . . . in British Columbia is not compatible with maintaining their habitat."[48]

As the evidence of wilderness and habitat loss, clogged streams and endangered species grew in the public consciousness, protests erupted on the logging roads.

The battle for Clayoquot Sound

Clayoquot Sound has been one of the most contentious areas in the B.C. forest for over a decade. In 1984, the Nuu-Chah-Nulth and local residents launched the first forest blockade in British Columbia's history against MacMillan Bloedel's logging on Meares Island, within Clayoquot Sound. After successfully obtaining an injunction to protect Meares Island's forests, pending resolution of their land claim, the Nuu-Chah-Nulth declared Meares Island a "Tribal Park" in 1985.

The controversy on Meares Island was quickly overshadowed by Haida blockades on Lyell Island in the Queen Charlottes (Haida Gwaii) and by protests by the Lillooet people of the Stein Valley. Clayoquot Sound flared again in the late 1980s as clear-cut logging continued to push into pristine areas. A new logging road into Sulphur Passage, the entrance to the Shelter Inlet and the Megin Valley, was blockaded, and arrests were made in the summer of 1988. But "Clayoquot Sound" did not become a household name in Canada until the summer of 1993. When the B.C. government announced on April 13, 1993, that 70 percent of Clayoquot Sound would be logged, the Friends of Clayoquot Sound launched an enormous campaign of non-violent civil disobedience to create global awareness of the threat. In all, nearly a thousand people were arrested at the Kennedy Lake blockades. The protest reverberated around the world.

Following a ruling by the B.C. ombudsman that the government had failed adequately to consult with the Nuu-Chah-Nulth, an interim measures agreement (IMA) was negotiated through forty days of intensive discussion and signed in the spring of 1994, giving greater control and rights of veto to First Nations over land-use decisions in Clayoquot. Among other things, the agreement with the First Nations called for protection of critical areas of salmon habitat, as Clayoquot Sound is an important area for numerous salmon runs. It also called for protection of "culturally modified trees," those old trees that, through test holes or bark or plant removal, presented evidence of Nuu-Chah-Nulth traditional use and occupation of the area.[49]

As a result of the interim measures agreement, a central regional board (CRB), a local community-based group, was created to review all resource-development plans in Clayoquot. Membership of the CRB is divided equally between provincial and First Nations appointees. As all decisions of the CRB must be by consensus, the First Nations have, in essence, secured a veto.

The most high-profile effort in British Columbia to assess the impacts of clear-cutting and present logging practices and to make recommendations for ecologically appropriate logging was the Clayoquot Sound Scientific Panel, with co-chairs Dr. Fred Bunnell, wildlife biologist of the University of British Columbia, and Dr. Richard Atleo, a respected hereditary chief from Ahousat in Clayoquot Sound. The panel was convened by the embattled NDP government of Mike Harcourt in June 1993, as a response to the public outcry over the government's announcement of clear-cut logging of 70 percent of the Sound's big-tree forests. The panel brought together renowned scientists and native elders, but they were given a mandate only to identify *how* logging could be made ecologically sound, not *whether* it should take place at all.

The final recommendations of the panel, published in several volumes, were released in 1995. In July 1995, the Harcourt government accepted all 128 recommendations, including a moratorium on logging in pristine watersheds until extensive inventories could be conducted. In accepting the recommendations, the minister stated that it signified the end of clear-cutting in Clayoquot Sound. The panel recommended a system they called "variable retention silviculture," where logging approximates the small openings that occur in a natural forest when old giants die and fall to the forest floor. The panel recommended that no opening, or clearing, should be more than two tree lengths from the next area of standing forest. It also called for a full inventory of the biological characteristics of the forest before logging plans could be approved.

The most significant aspect of the panel's report, however, was not in the nuts and bolts of the specific recommendations, but in the approach recommended to exploiting a natural resource. It could apply to forest ecosystems far beyond the temperate rainforest, and to ecosystems beyond forests—fisheries and agriculture. In its approach, the Scientific Panel called for the application of the precautionary principle—that every decision affecting complex ecosystems about which we fundamentally know so little be approached with caution. In terms of logging operations, in the words of panel chair Dr. Fred Bunnell, traditional forest practice was "turned on its head."[50]

The panel recommended that, when cut plans were prepared, rather than deciding what the industry wanted taken out of the forest, decisions should be based first on what should remain. They were to identify, first, what needed to be retained to protect other values, and then what could be logged. This is fundamentally different from the way logging is currently conducted in B.C. As in every other province, decisions are driven by the rate of cut, with "non-timber" values viewed as a constraint on logging. In essence, the panel's recommendations recognized that, whereas foresters may be able to regrow trees, they cannot regrow a forest under the industrial-forest model. The panel's recommendations would ensure that forest management is based on sustaining the ecosystem, not on meeting the needs of the mills.

These recommendations, fully supported by the Nuu-Chah-Nulth Central Region Tribal Council, slowed the rate of logging in the Sound. But despite these parallel accomplishments, and the commitment of the provincial government to implement all of the Scientific Panel's recommendations, clear-cut logging has not ended in Clayoquot Sound. Just as the Scientific Panel report is a blueprint for ecological forest practices, so too is its implementation a blueprint for loopholes you can drive a logging truck through. The forest industries that hold rights within Clayoquot Sound, MacMillan Bloedel and Interfor, have interpreted the "no more than two tree heights" opening guideline as permission for long ribbon-like clear-cuts, each devastating areas four very tall tree lengths in width. They are long, stringy clear-cuts that do not resemble normal forest disturbance, with predictable ecological impacts.

But substantial progress is being made in moving Clayoquot Sound toward United Nations Biosphere Reserve status. The environmental community, industry, and members of local communities are working constructively with the Nuu-Chah-Nulth and the government toward a result that may increase protection in Clayoquot Sound, while maintaining locally sustainable economic activity in the region.

In April 1997, a step was taken toward tenure reform with the creation of an industry–First Nations joint venture. MacMillan Bloedel and the Central Region Tribes of the Nuu-Chah-Nulth Tribal Council established a new joint venture company, 51 percent owned by the Nuu-Chah-Nulth and 49 percent by MacBlo. Both have pledged to support the venture financially. They plan to log up to 400,000 cubic meters a year from the northern part of MacBlo's TFL, cutting to Clayoquot Sound Scientific Panel standards. The first two years of the joint venture will concentrate on inventory, training and the exploration of value-added opportunities. The fate of pristine areas will be decided after inventories of all forest values have been conducted and areas are set aside to protect fish, water, soils, cultural features and biodiversity.

Many observers credit the controversy over Clayoquot Sound, and the international black eye it gave the B.C. government, with a host of protected areas. It can also be argued that the public spotlight it directed on logging practices led to the most sweeping reform efforts in decades.

Taming the monster . . . Reforming B.C. logging practices

Faced with the legacy of "sympathetic administration" and over-cutting, the government of former Premier Mike Harcourt made valiant efforts, both to protect more forest and to reform the practice of logging across the landscape. Unfortunately, those efforts were continually undermined by a recalcitrant bureaucracy and a rebellious forest industry used to having its own way.

The Harcourt government created a host of new regulations, laws and acronyms. Announcing the proposed Forest Practices Code in November 1993, Harcourt declared, "Our objective is to dramatically change the way B.C.'s forests are managed and to better protect both the environment and wildlife. Until now, the attitude has been that the forests were there to be exploited. Those days are over."[51]

The Forest Practices Code, launched in June 1995 with promises to implement it fully by June 1997, was supposed to dictate biodiversity protection as an aspect of forest management, with far stricter rules for protecting riparian zones and the structural characteristics of old growth. Along with the Code came a Forest Practices Board to respond to public complaints about Code violations. It established Forest Renewal BC (FRBC) to fund intensive silviculture, rehabilitation, research and inventory efforts, with revenues gained from increasing stumpage rates by 80 percent. Overall, FRBC was to reinvest about $400 million a year in forest renewal. The government brought in a program of watershed restoration, to rehabilitate degraded fish habitat. The head of the Watershed Restoration Program has estimated the cost of attempting to rehabilitate the province's most abused watersheds at one to four billion dollars. For many watersheds, of course, it is too late.

Harcourt's Forest Minister, Andrew Petter, used terms often heard recently from finance ministers explaining to a skeptical public that cutbacks now are the price for profligate spending in the past. The deficit Petter had to attack was ecological. Ecological deficits are harder to erase than fiscal ones.

Petter explained that decades of mismanagement and over-cutting had created a situation requiring dramatic reforms. Overall, new Code measures to reduce the environmental damage of logging were predicted to reduce the cut rate by 6 percent—on top of the expected reductions due to a Timber Supply Review. Petter made a commitment to the loggers' union, the IWA-Canada, that the 6-percent estimate would be the cap on impacts.

In February 1996 the government released a Timber Supply Analysis that provided an estimate of the Code's impact. To no one's surprise it matched the political commitment to only a 6 percent impact on the short-term timber supply. While the overall provincial impact was predicted to be approximately 8 percent, this was reduced by 2 percent for increased logging in scenic areas using more sensitive techniques.

Implementation of the Forest Practices Code has been sabotaged by government's determination to hold the reduction of the AAC to no more than 6 percent. Thus, Code requirements for protection of biodiversity and other non-timber values are immediately undercut by an artificial directive to hold the Code's impact on timber supply at a certain level. Biodiversity goals set in 1995 stipulated only that in 10 percent of the forest, biodiversity will be a high priority in forest management. Even with 10 percent of the forest to be considered "high emphasis" for biodiversity, the requirements of many key species were never considered in the Code. Chief Forester Larry Pederson admitted that nobody knows what impact protecting the grizzly bear or spotted owl would have on timber supply.[52] Outside the 10 percent "high emphasis" areas, 90 percent of the landscape will see considerable risk to biodiversity.

In "low emphasis" biodiversity areas, covering 45 percent of the forest, the impact on biodiversity, according to the Code's Biodiversity Guidebook, will be significant: "The pattern of natural biodiversity will be significantly altered and the risk of some native species being unable to survive in the area will be relatively high."[52]

Disillusioned after one year of working with the Forest Practices Code, former Sierra Legal Defence Fund executive director Greg McDade wrote: "All in all, measured by change on the ground, the Code has been a sham, successful merely as a tranquillizer for public concern."[53]

Industry has played a difficult public-relations game. Out of one side of its mouth, the forest industry tries to benefit from the Code's "strict protection of biodiversity" goals. It is extremely useful in speaking tours through Europe and the United States to quote from the Code's sustainability rhetoric and commitment that logging not interfere with the spiritual values of forests. Out of the other side of its mouth, industry has opposed the Code, arguing that it has been too costly and that the wood supply will be jeopardized.

While the Forest Practices Code remains a progressive piece of legislation, superior to any found in the rest of the country, it is seriously threatened. Environmental groups are struggling to ensure that the promise of the Code is met in its implementation.

New premier Glen Clark at the helm of the NDP government issued warnings to the forest industry that it must process more wood in B.C., increasing employment through "value-added" activities. Clark signed a "Jobs and Timber Accord" with industry, in which industry committed to create twenty-one thousand new forest industry jobs. The government has responded to increased public awareness that the drastic losses in forest industry employment relate far more to mechanization than to environmental programs.

These two issues are being played off against each other. Premier Clark's political future lies in creating more jobs. This provides leverage for the industry, which can ask for concessions in return for delivering on that promise. The increased stumpage rates, which have been funding the Forest Renewal BC rehabilitation and silviculture efforts, and the Forest Practices Code are the targets of aggressive industry propagandizing. And all this is against a backdrop of falling global prices for pulp in 1996–97. For the first time in years, MacMillan Bloedel posted losses in each quarter.[54] Repap was forced to declare bankruptcy over its B.C. operations, as part of its failed restructuring in the abortive bid by Avenor to buy Repap's assets from coast to coast. Overall, B.C. pulp company operations lost $625 million in 1996.[55] The plywood sector has had trouble as well. When Evans Forest Products of Golden, B.C., was on the verge of bankruptcy in spring 1997, Glen Clark delivered fourteen million dollars in subsidies as well as twisting arms in the trade unions to gain wage concessions. Mill owner Georges St. Laurent, an Oregon banker, reciprocated with commitments to keep the mill open and install twenty-five million dollars' worth of new equipment.[56] Clark has also bailed out the failing Skeena Cellulose Inc. mill by $240 million.

As profits have fallen, the Code has become the industry's scapegoat. A study jointly commissioned by the provincial government and the industry claimed that the cost per log had increased 75 percent in four years, and the industry used that figure to lobby hard for concessions.[57] The study, conducted by KPMG, had been done using extremely subjective techniques. Lacking accounting systems that allowed any objective assessment of what operations actually cost, KPMG conducted the study via questionnaires sent to timber companies. This questionable method led to claims that costs had increased from an average $49.57 per log in 1992 to a 1997 average of $86.74. The bulk of the increase was attributed to higher stumpage and royalty fees.

For many years, British Columbia's stumpage rate was so low that even producing a volume of timber equal to the rest of the Canadian provinces combined, the government still lost money on forestry. The stumpage collected did not even offset the cost of running the forest service. As recently as the early 1980s, the average stumpage rate to a large forest company was less than $2 per cubic meter. In 1993–94, stumpage rates were substantially increased. Currently the government collects approximately $25 per cubic meter from the major forest companies and $40 per cubic meter from smaller companies.[58] Even these increased rates are estimated to be approximately half what forest companies would be paying for similar wood in the U.S.[59] The increased stumpage rates are, at long last, sufficient to ensure that government forest revenues actually exceed forest costs. At the same time, of course, government is making more investments in the forests.

The increased price for logs was also blamed on the Code, with an average $12.22

per log in Code-related costs. But the biggest increase attributable to Code requirements was for road-building. Companies operating on the coast claimed the price per log had increased $7.80, solely due to the more careful road-building required on steep slopes in coastal forests.

Environmental groups in B.C. pointed to a different study, undertaken by Price Waterhouse, which supported the argument that it was companies operating in areas they had largely logged out that faced higher costs in logging remote and inaccessible forests.[60] "The truth is that many companies have already mowed down the best old-growth forests, and what remains is poor quality wood that is in remote and expensive-to-access terrain," said Sierra Club's Conservation Chair, Vicky Husband.[61]

For all the industry uproar about the Forest Practices Code, it has not resulted in a single charge being laid in the years it has been in effect. But a study by the Sierra Legal Defence Fund found abundant evidence of Code violations, including 83 percent of streams in 1996 cutblocks being clear-cut right to their banks.[62]

Old habits die hard. The B.C. industry is accustomed to cheap wood, cozy deals and lax regulation. For years, government caved in to whatever industry demanded. For generations, British Columbians had been conditioned to believe that their bread and butter, whether they were personally in the forest industry or not, relied on the forest industry. The slogan was that "fifty cents out of every dollar" came from forestry. The truism wasn't true. A recent economic analysis found that since 1970 the contribution of the forest industry to the provincial economy dropped from approximately 11 to 8 percent. The 50 percent figure was a convenient myth. Over the same period, logging increased by 40 percent, but as mechanization reduced the number of people required per unit of production, employment remained stable.[63]

Higher stumpage and Code requirements are the target of a well-organized industry campaign. While the Clark government is of the same political stripe as the previous Harcourt government, the green shade is fading. One of Clark's key supporters is the head of the B.C. Federation of Labour, Ken Georgetti, who has argued that help to the forest industry must come before job creation. "I think we have to turn a little less green, a little more brown," he said.[64] The browning of B.C.'s forest policy will have predictable and disastrous results.

When will British Columbia run out of wood?

As clear-cutting has increased, so too in absolute terms has the area logged. The debate about whether this is an over-cut comes back to the question of whether the Long Term Harvest Level (LTHL) is itself sustainable. Bearing in mind that everyone expects the "fall-down effect" to reduce drastically what is available to the industry, is it reasonable to cut at levels that, even according to the government, exceed the LTHL by nearly twenty million cubic meters a year?

British Columbia is ahead of every other province in acknowledging the need to rethink its wood supply and recalculate its AAC. The only problem is that after all the hoopla, the rate of cut has been reduced by just under half of one percent province-wide and the liquidation of the old-growth primary forests continues.

In 1984, the provincial government issued a timber supply analysis which candidly admitted, "*British Columbia's forests are commonly thought to be managed under a policy of constant production over time. This is not true*" (emphasis added).[65]

It went on to explain the reality that, once the old-growth forest was liquidated, harvest levels would have to fall: "Many future second-growth stands will yield smaller harvests at maturity than the existing old-growth forests. Application of the sustained yield concept must, therefore, allow for making a transition from using an accumulated inventory of mature timber to relying on annual production from second growth."[66] The policy of liquidating old growth, creating logging rates that could not possibly be maintained into the future, was a policy of planned over-cut. British Columbians began to realize that logging rates would have to be reduced once all the high-volume old growth was gone.

In 1991, the government conducted a review of the timber supply and the management process for granting AACs. The study found that:

Allowable annual cuts were based on outdated information and management practices;

There was a lack of recognition of non-timber resources and values such as fish and wildlife habitats, biodiversity, visual quality, recreation, and sensitive resources such as community watersheds;

Forest Service Staff had a poor understanding of inventory and timber supply analysis applications.[67]

Perhaps the most stunning conclusion noted in the report was that "there is a perception among many staff that AACs are too high."[68]

As a result of this study, in 1992 the NDP brought in legislation requiring the Chief Forester to review and set new AACs every five years. Since then, the provincial Chief Forester has been conducting a Timber Supply Review. Reduced levels of cut are now viewed as inevitable as the AAC is significantly higher than the long-term harvest level (LTHL) in many areas. In fact, the 1996 provincial AAC was 71.3 million cubic meters, while the forest service recently calculated the LTHL at 51 million cubic meters.[69]

In 1993, Sierra Club issued a court challenge to MacMillan Bloedel's AAC for TFL 44. The Forest Act at that time required the Chief Forester to set "an allowable cut that he determines may be sustained from the tree farm licence area."[70] The Sierra Club argued that setting an AAC that was *higher* than a cutting level that could be sustained indefinitely violated the act. The provincial Chief Forester, MacMillan Bloedel, and the pro-industry International Woodworkers of America, Canadian branch, disagreed. Government and industry argued that "sustained" meant sustaining the cut through higher rates to remove old growth, eventually lowering the cut level to one that could be sustained in the long run. Harking back to the Fernow model of the "normal" forest, old-growth forest was described as "non-interest-earning capital in an interest-bearing account." Therefore, cutting out all the old-growth and then reducing the cut levels to accommodate the smaller volumes of the second-growth forest meets the goal of "sustained yield." The court accepted the Chief Forester's view.[71]

Decisions about the appropriate level of cut are first based on the inventory. In British Columbia, as in every other province in Canada, the inventory is not reliable. A 1990 government-appointed Forest Resources Commission concluded that the inventory was out of date and weak, and could not be relied upon for accurate information at the stand level. The commission commented that inventory information on non-timber values "is a disgrace."[72] Since then work has accelerated to improve the quality and coverage of the inventory.[73] Spot-check audits have been conducted to assess the accuracy of the inventory information.

There is a serious backlog of areas classified as not satisfactorily restocked (NSR). In fact, over 20 percent of the area logged between 1976 and 1985 was degraded. In 1995, 27 percent of harvested Crown land was considered "understocked." Over 90 percent of all logging in B.C. was by clear-cutting and still is. Worse still, the industry prefers "progressive" clear-cut, where an entire valley or mountain is denuded in a series of large clear-cuts, one after the other. Soil degradation, landslides and poor regeneration were are the result. A 1988 government-funded Forest Resource Development Agreement (FRDA) study concluded that the potential annual loss in future timber productivity to the B.C. economy due to soil degradation was approximately $80 million per year, and growing. By the year 2000, soil degradation could be leading to potential future *annual* productivity losses to the provincial economy of over $200 million.[74] Although the area categorized as NSR land has dropped substantially since 1988, it still remains high. As of 1995, it was officially reported as over one million hectares of the logged-over Crown land.[75]

Wood shortages

The debate about whether B.C. is over-cutting depends on the availability of the second-growth forest once the old growth has been totally liquidated. The AAC will fall, but by how much? The answer to that question is hardly reassuring. There are clear indications, from the government's own Timber Supply Review, that the old-growth forest will run out *before* adequate regrowth has occurred in the logged-over areas.

In 1981, the then Deputy Minister of Forests, currently the president of the Council of Forest Industries, Mike Apsey, warned that there would be "local shortages in every region of the province within the next twenty years."[76]

The reality of wood shortages has arrived in B.C. On Vancouver Island, some mills have closed, and others are importing wood from neighboring provinces, as far away as Saskatchewan and the Yukon. The mills have overbuilt capacity, considerably above what the B.C. forests can continue to produce. In 1990, it was estimated that the capacity of B.C. mills exceeded the AAC by about 20 percent. In the Interior, capacity exceeded supply by 30 percent. These supply shortages are occurring while the province is still over-cutting, based on the higher AAC achieved through the liquidation of old growth. Once the AAC begins to drop, many more mill closures will be inevitable.

Despite widespread acknowledgement that the inventory is faulty, the Timber Supply Review process is based on an inventory that relies on less than 1-percent-accurate coverage of the province. The Chief Forester uses those data to calculate the appropriate AAC. Moreover, the B.C. inventory approach relies on a volume-based analysis. A recent review of the timber-supply analysis process shows that government forestry staff had recommended a different approach. They recommend that analysis be spatially based. The rationale was that the volume-based analysis relied on outdated inventories, whereas a spatial analysis could rely on maps, providing a more accurate and environmentally sensitive approach. By using GIS technology and Forest Renewal funds, it would be possible to map what an area will look like in twenty years' time. But, despite the weakness of the volume-based approach, that is still the only analysis used in the Timber Supply Review process.[77] As the Chief Forester began his next round of reviews, environmental groups joined the staffs of both the forest and environment departments in calling for a spatial approach.

In some cases, Chief Forester Larry Pederson has angered industry with significant reductions in the AAC. In the Fraser Timber Supply Area (TSA), for example, Pederson's July 1996 inventory audit found that timber volumes in the area had been overestimated by 23 percent. Logging rates had been reduced in April 1995 by 12 percent, based on the suspicion that the volumes had been overestimated. Further reductions in cut for the Fraser TSA are likely. But Pederson hastened to reassure industry that "the lower estimate does not necessarily mean a corresponding 23 percent reduction in the AAC."[78] Industry spokesperson Les Kiss of the Coast Forest and Lumber Association commented, "I hope people don't think this means forest companies have over-harvested."[79]

Setting the AAC is not simply a technical process. It is also political. Part of the Chief Forester's mandate is to consider social and economic issues. The review of the Williams Lake Timber Supply Area, in the Cariboo-Chilcotin region of the province, resulted in a minor reduction of only 4 percent. The rate of cut remains 35 percent higher than the Long Term Harvest Level (LTHL) estimated by the Ministry of Forests. Pederson's rationale for keeping the AACs high in the Williams Lake area is clearly the economic dependence of the local mills—four sawmills, a plywood and veneer mill and six "value-added" manufacturing plants—on rates of over-cut established during temporary beetle-wood salvage. Commenting on the Williams Lake decision, B.C. environmentalist Jim Cooperman wrote, "Timber companies are stealing from British Columbia's future."[80]

A similar timber review for the Kingcome Timber Supply Area on northern Vancouver Island and portions of the adjacent mainland has also created controversy. The Timber Supply Review in July 1995 determined that the AAC in the Kingcome TSA was 65 percent too high. This conclusion did not include the impact of the new Forest Practices Code or proposed protected areas. Interfor, with cutting rights in the TSA, vigorously opposed the recommended reduction to its AAC. Interestingly, Interfor did not debate the reality of wood shortages. Instead, the company argued for a smaller reduction of 15 percent in the AAC, coupled with the usual magic panaceas of increased silviculture to allow continued over-cutting. The Sierra Club believes a 75 percent reduction is required. But the Chief Forester reduced the cut by only 25 percent.[81]

While AACs in southern B.C. are going down, they are being radically increased in the north. British Columbia's last unlogged frontiers are being opened to logging. A 13.5-million-hectare area, the Cassiar Timber Supply Area, is also known as the Serengeti of the North. Far from most industrialized development, in the northwestern corner of the province, this huge area boasts an amazing richness of wildlife, from enormous herds of caribou to black and grizzly bear, to Dall sheep and mountain goat. The forests of the Cassiar had always been too remote to be considered commercially viable. But with timber shortages to the south, the boreal and coastal forests of the Cassiar are becoming more attractive to logging companies. Just as in the forests of Labrador, there are real concerns in northern British Columbia that logging cannot be sustainable. The region's harsh climate and short growing season mean that regrowth will be slow. The region is already feeling the impact from increased logging roads, affecting critical habitat of wildlife. Chief Forester Pederson's Timber Supply Analysis ordered the AAC increased from 140,000 cubic meters to 400,000 cubic meters—an almost threefold increase.[82]

Logging is also set to increase in the northeastern interior forest of the Mackenzie Timber Supply Area of over six million hectares. Effective September 1, 1996, the Chief Forester has approved a fifty-thousand-cubic-meter increase in logging, bringing the AAC to nearly three million cubic meters for the TSA.[83]

Despite imminent timber shortfalls and dwindling old growth, overall B.C.'s AAC has remained more or less stable, increasing between 1993 and 1994 from 71.9 million cubic meters to 72.4 million cubic meters, and going down to 71.3 million cubic meters in 1996.[84]

And the B.C. government seems determined to make the situation worse. In 1996 an amendment to the Forest Act was passed, putting B.C. on the road to greater shortages. Bill 7's amendments brought to B.C. the allowable-cut effect that has justified over-cutting across Canada. The amendment, called "Innovative Forestry Practices," will allow license-holders to increase the AAC in exchange for intensive silviculture. Greenpeace forest campaigner Karen Mahon attacked the bill, saying: "According to the government's own statistics the cut is already 30 percent over the sustainable level. This Bill is based on a faulty premise and amounts to short-term gain for long-term pain."[85]

Exhausting the inexhaustible

British Columbia has a policy of deliberate over-cutting and liquidation of old growth. The unsustainable rates of logging are locked into the system through mill overcapacity. Despite efforts under the Forest Practices Code and the Timber Supply Review, B.C. forest policy is a recipe for economic and ecological disaster.

British Columbia already has wood shortages due to substantial over-cutting. In most of the Timber Supply Areas on the B.C. coast, the government's own analysis confirms that the rate of cut is 25 to 65 percent too high. The provincial AAC of approximately seventy-one million cubic meters is higher than the government's designated Long Term Harvest Level (LTHL). And the LTHL itself is arguably too high at fifty-six million cubic meters. Overcapacity of mills and a historic industry stranglehold on the provincial governments, of all political stripes, reduces the likelihood of courageous decisions now.

The reality is that industrial logging practices are wholly incompatible with healthy, self-renewing forests. Ecologists have known this for years. It is only recently that wood shortages should make the same point evident to economists.

13

Yukon and Northwest Territories

The legends of Canada's North are filled with the Klondike Gold Rush of 1898. The words of Robert Service resonate for southern Canadians when they think of the Yukon: "There are strange things done in the midnight sun by the men who moil for gold . . ."[1]

The two territories of the Yukon and Northwest Territories encompass Canada's circumpolar reaches. They have a small population clustered around the territorial capitals of Whitehorse and Yellowknife, with smaller towns and hamlets of Dene and Inuit living closer to the land. Increasingly, enormous tracts of territory are being ceded to First Nations self-government. But so far, no forest areas have been conveyed to Inuit or Dene rule. The fact that even these marginal northern boreal forests are under logging pressure is a sure sign of wood shortages to the south.

Most of the Northwest Territories and the Yukon is a land of white—snow, ice and thundering herds of muskoxen. In the Northwest Territories, out of a vast region of 326 million hectares, only 61 million hectares are forested. In the neighboring Yukon Territory to the west, roughly 60 percent of the 48.4-million-hectare territory is forested, sharing ecosystem characteristics with the forests of Alaska and northern British Columbia.

A government report in 1981 noting that the timber in the Yukon and Northwest Territories was largely inaccessible, physically and economically, concluded: "There is little likelihood of major forest industry development in the Territories during the next two decades."[2]

Just as in Labrador, it always seemed that one would have to be desperate to consider logging in Yukon.

But logging pressures have built in the last two decades. Initially it was sawmills for local supply; one large one in the Watson Lake area, with another eighteen smaller

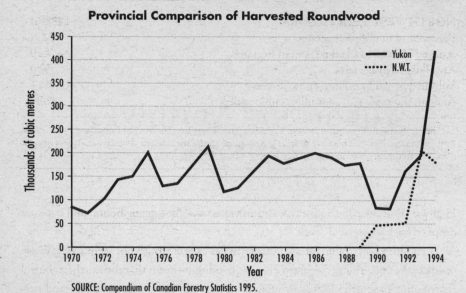

Provincial Comparison of Harvested Roundwood

SOURCE: Compendium of Canadian Forestry Statistics 1995.

sawmills meeting local needs. But in the 1990s, something unprecedented began to happen to the Yukon woods and the forest managers realized they had better catch up with the oncoming assault.

YUKON

The forests of the Yukon, comprising 5 percent of Canada's total forest land, are over-whelmingly coniferous, with a substantial predominance of white spruce. The current estimates of species composition place white spruce at 306 million cubic meters, with the next most prevalent species, lodgepole pine, at only 75 million cubic meters.[3] Of the Yukon's entire forested area, only 20 to 30 percent, 7.6 million hectares, is considered commercially valuable.[4] These productive forests are found in the south, particularly in the southeast, and in riparian zones.

Logging is not new in the Yukon. The Gold Rush created the first short-lived boom in clearing the northern boreal ecoregion for fuel to power stern-wheelers, and building supplies for tent floors and early settlements in 1898. Primitive sawmills provided whipsawed lumber along the water route between Lake Bennett and Dawson City.[5] At the peak of the Yukon Gold Rush, loggers chewed through 210,000 cubic meters of forest in one year.[6] But by 1902, logging rates had plummeted, staying below 60,000 cubic meters for the next forty years. In 1944, another brief spike appears in the logging charts of the Yukon, as timber was required for the construction of the Alaska

NORTHWEST TERRITORIES	(1995)
Forest Land in million hectares	61.4
Stocked Harvested Crown Land in hectares	440
Area Logged in hectares	500
Volume Logged in million cubic meters	0.11
Annual Allowable Cut in million cubic meters	0.24

SOURCE: Natural Resources Canada, Canadian Forest Service, *The State of Canada's Forests, 1996-1997* (Ottawa, 1997). These are federal government summaries, based on provincial government data. The figures are not necessarily accurate.

Highway. But, once the highway was finished, so was the logging boom, and cut rates dropped back to previous levels.[7]

A commercially viable forest industry in the Yukon would not seem a very likely prospect. For one thing, the harsh climatic conditions mean that the northern boreal ecoregion is extremely slow-growing and fragile. Soils are low in nutrients, and permafrost conditions militate against any forestry. The cold soil temperatures and short growing season have a major impact on the physiology of the boreal. Water uptake is slowed, and the forests' animal population is far smaller than those of warmer climates, which means that the litter of organic material on the forest floor is broken down very slowly, and the availability of nutrients to the trees is low.[8] But as the forces of history and dwindling resources collide, even the Yukon is being clear-cut.

Ownership, jurisdiction and the state of forest management in the Yukon

The administration of Canada's two territories breaks nearly every rule about federal and provincial relations. As the territories are almost autonomous jurisdictions, negotiations for territorial rule over natural resources are an apparently never-ending process. In the Yukon, transfer of jurisdiction over forests has been promised for years, but remains stalled in the details. This is further complicated by substantial negotiations to turn over enormous chunks of land to aboriginal self-rule. As of November 1997, six such agreements for self-government in the Yukon have been completed. The remaining eight Yukon First Nations are still in the negotiating process. First Nations represent another level of government. Once the land claims are settled, the First Nations determine for themselves the nature and extent of resource extraction on their land.

For the time being, despite the existence of an elected legislature, the real power in

YUKON	(1995)
Forest Land in million hectares	27.5
Stocked Harvested Crown Land in hectares	3,600
Area Logged in hectares	833
Volume Logged in million cubic meters	0.19
Annual Allowable Cut in million cubic meters	0.01

SOURCE: Natural Resources Canada, Canadian Forest Service, *The State of Canada's Forests, 1996-1997* (Ottawa, 1997). These are federal government summaries, based on provincial government data. The figures are not necessarily accurate. We are unable to determine why the Volume Logged is so far above the Annual Allowable Cut.

the North is still the federal government. And the single most powerful decision-making body is the Department of Indian Affairs and Northern Development (DIAND). The federal government owns 100 percent of the forested land. And that effectively makes the Minister of DIAND Yukon's Minister of Forests. When one considers the relatively larger resources available to the federal government, the state of forest information and regulation is appalling.

The Yukon had no forest inventory, no annual allowable cut (AAC), and no forest policy when the government set an annual allocation of 450,000 cubic meters. Nevertheless, the government had set an annual allocation of 450,000 cubic meters. Efforts to develop an inventory began recently, but as of 1995 one federal forestry official estimated, "At the rate we're going, we may have a first pass of the Yukon's forest inventory within the next decade."[9]

For decades, the resource regulations were based on what was designed for the mining industry at the turn of the century. Archaic regulations conspired with benign neglect of the forests. Stumpage rates until August 1995 were set at the rock-bottom price of twenty cents a cubic meter. There were no requirements for reforestation, no long-term tenure arrangements, and little regulation of forest operations.

In other words, the Yukon was in a perfect state for a jurisdiction without a forest industry. But suddenly, in the early 1990s, the Yukon's forest sparked a second resource rush. In April 1995, a federal government discussion paper on a proposed forest policy put it this way: "Today's challenges are upon us. Improved markets for forest prod-

YUKON CORPORATE PLAYERS
Trans North Lumber
Saber Lumber
Discovery Forest Products
Romeo Leduc
Canyon Custom Cuts
Kaska Forest Products
Yukon River Timber

ucts, fiber shortages within parts of Western Canada, coupled with low stumpage prices for Yukon timber, are creating unprecedented demands and pressures on the Yukon forest resource."[10]

The value of forest products in the Yukon in 1992 was four million dollars; just two years later, it had more than doubled, to ten million.[11] A 1995 letter from former federal Indian and Northern Affairs Minister Ron Irwin to former Yukon Government Leader John Ostashek put the situation in perspective:

> Only two years ago, there were 30 to 40 applications for commercial timber permits for 30,000 to 50,000 cubic meters of wood. *This year, there are 1,300 applications for the 450,000 cubic meters of available timber* (emphasis added).[12]

Playing catch-up

The federal regulators started to realize that they were woefully behind the oncoming rush of timber-hungry industries. Logs were being cut and shipped unprocessed to Alaska and to British Columbia, and demand was sharply increasing from year to year. In response, the federal Department of Indian and Northern Affairs dispatched a bureaucrat to Whitehorse to draft a forestry policy. Gary Miltenberger, regional manager of Forest Resources for DIAND, told local media that Yukon's forest regulations were "very simplistic and sadly out-dated."[13]

Virtually immediately, Miltenberger had to deal with demands for increased logging and schemes for export of wood chips to Alaska. First Nations objected to any clear-cutting on territory that was likely to fall within their self-government regimes, while the previous territorial government wondered if federal bureaucrats weren't taking too long in clearing the way for development.

In fact, the territorial government was part owner of one of the development proponents, the Yukon Development Corporation, which entered into a joint venture with a private company called Envirochip to clear-cut nine blocks of the White Mountain for wood chips. The chips were destined for export to Alaska. In 1993, after the companies had spent $700,000 on the wood-chip scheme, the application was withdrawn due to a public outcry over clear-cutting green timber instead of using waste wood to produce chips for export.

To exert some control over the new timber rush, the federal government placed a moratorium on the export of raw logs from the Yukon out of Canada. But no one could stop the ongoing export to British Columbia. Even including the cost of transporting wood from the Yukon to southern mills, Yukon wood was still a bargain.

Stopping the flow to Alaska was proving difficult as wood cut for other purposes than timber was being trucked out; a contractor clearing 160 hectares for a sewage lagoon near Whitehorse was caught by angry town residents and sawmill owners selling the wood to Alaska. One local contractor told the press, "I'll stand buck naked in the middle of the road if that's what it takes to stop those trucks. It's not right. That wood should go to locals."[14]

One timber license, to a First-Nations-controlled corporation, Kaska Forest Resources, specifically allows the export of raw logs—the only exemption from the export moratorium. Tempers flared in 1993, when Kaska, in partnership with Rayonier Canada of B.C., proposed five years' worth of logging for export to Alaska, with the eventual goal of building a mill in the Yukon that would process small-diameter pine logs.[15] Other logging can be done under agricultural permits and through road-building contracts. Even mining claims include the timber rights, and so the government has been unable to completely stop the clearing of Yukon forests for B.C. and Alaskan mills.

A second moratorium was declared in the spring of 1995 on the issuing of any new Commercial Timber Permits (CTPs) and Timber Harvest Agreements (THAs). Logging pressure in the Yukon closely parallels the increased demand for fiber in northern B.C.

In August 1995, the federal Minister of DIAND came forward with the first attempts at modern forest regulation for the Yukon. The interim forest policy established that the two types of tenure agreements would continue: Timber Harvest Agreements (THAs), negotiable for up to five years, and the more common Commercial Timber Permits (CTP), which allow up to two years' access to no more than 15,000 cubic meters per year. The CTPs in true Yukon gold rush fashion were to be allocated based on a lottery system where names are literally drawn from a drum of hopeful logging contestants. Meanwhile, the Timber Harvest Agreements cover a larger area. In 1995, Kaska Forest Resources was the only holder of a THA.

Under the new policy, stumpage rates jumped from twenty cents a cubic meter to $5 per cubic meter for wood utilized in the Yukon, and $10 per cubic meter for unprocessed wood for export. The funds raised will be placed in a reforestation fund, to begin to address the backlog of NSR lands from previous logging.[16] No tree planting had been done in the Yukon until 1992. Virtually the entire budget of government forest management had been spent on fire protection. As fires have been increasing in recent years with more and larger areas consumed, the territorial governments have become concerned about accepting this responsibility without adequate financial assistance. Far more forest has been burned than felled. In 1994, Yukon lost over 400,000 hectares to fire, and over 2,000 to logging.[17]

The timber rush

Between 1988 and 1994 the area harvested jumped from 465 hectares to 2,056 hectares, with logging volumes increasing from 160,000 cubic meters in 1993 to more than double that in just one year—390,000 cubic meters were logged in 1994. Meanwhile, the mill capacity in the Yukon remained at approximately 155,000 cubic meters, demonstrating that more than half of Yukon logging goes to feed mills in B.C., Alberta and Alaska.[18]

There is also pressure for industrial expansion within the Yukon. In the spring of 1996, a new company based in Watson Lake, Liard Pulp and Lumber, announced its intention to build a sawmill, pulp mill and plywood plant, with annual wood-supply requirements of 350,000 cubic meters of wood—an amount nearly equal to the entire volume logged in the unprecedented clear-cutting of 1994! Watson Lake in southeastern Yukon is the district with the most merchantable timber. The five million hectares of forest in the Watson Lake district accounted for 86 percent of the 1994–95 logging.[19]

Fortunately, federal officials have taken a cautious approach to the new mill complex. They recognize that they lack the most basic information on which to base expanded industrial capacity. The inventory is still incomplete. Moreover, as logging in the Yukon takes place on federal land, new mills and forest projects must undergo an environmental assessment pursuant to the federal Canadian Environmental Assessment Act. This particular proposal was called into question by the Liard First Nations and federal officials who have doubted the business experience of the mill-complex proponent. Liard Pulp and Lumber (CPL), lacking the necessary $165 million for the mill, believed the capital would be raised just as soon as the government gave them access to the forest. In fact, the concerns of the First Nations were borne out by events. LPL did go into business, but was bankrupt a year later, leaving a trail of creditors and earning the new LPL acronym, "Let's pay later."

Despite the fact that logging had been at low levels until the early 1990s, the Yukon already had a backlog of over two thousand hectares of NSR lands by 1993. Since increasingly large expanses are logged every year, it is likely that this area will increase sharply. As ecologically disastrous as clear-cutting is in ecosystems across Canada, it is completely untenable in the Yukon, with its poor, fragile soils and permafrost conditions. Logging plans involve the usual ninety-year rotation, with the expectation that Yukon forests will re-establish themselves within that time.

Foresters probably know less about the dynamics of the northern boreal forest than about any ecoregion on earth. Ecological studies of the Yukon forest are fairly recent and point to some particular problems in clear-cutting Yukon's forests.

Meanwhile, clear-cut logging is wholly incompatible with the biodiversity of the North. The caribou are integral to the lives of the northern peoples. Those who now fight for the trees can learn much from the efforts of the more northern Gwich'in, who have been at the forefront of efforts to prevent oil-and-gas development on the Alaska side of the border, in the Arctic National Wildlife Refuge. The sensitive calving grounds of the Porcupine caribou herds are within those lands, and, as the Gwich'in say, "The caribou are our life."

Further south, First Nations are dependent on the woodland caribou herds of the Yukon and northern British Columbia. A government study in British Columbia concluded: "The clear-cutting silvicultural system that is typically used in the range of the two ecotypes of caribou . . . in British Columbia is not compatible with maintaining their habitat."[20] This conclusion also applies to the southern Yukon.

The removal of old growth also threatens the pine marten. While in the rest of Canada threats to marten habitat are seen as a biodiversity concern, in the Yukon they are also an economic concern to First Nations. The marten is the most important fur-bearing mammal harvested by Watson Lake area trappers. The forests along rivers and streams, the riparian zones, are also home to songbirds found nowhere else in the Yukon. But it is precisely these riparian zones that have the most productive forests.

Northern lights

Of all the jurisdictions in Canada, the Yukon government may be the most likely to learn the lessons of previous devastation to the south. On September 30, 1996, a new territorial government with strong environmental principles came to power. One of their first actions was to create a Yukon Forest Commission. The Commission is tasked with developing a forest-management policy before the federal government devolves control over natural resources to the territorial government in spring of 1998. In February 1997, a tripartite devolution agreement was signed by the federal Department of Indian and Northern Affairs, the territorial government and the Council of Yukon First Nations.[21]

As well, the government established a citizen-led Yukon Forest Advisory Council, including representatives of industry, conservation groups, other forest users and all levels of government—First Nations, territorial and federal.

While control over the forest is still in federal hands, and logging continues to be allowed in the absence of any resource or land-use planning, there are hopeful signs. The head of the Yukon Forest Commission, Dennis Fentie, is the member of the legislature for Watson Lake. While only time will tell if the territorial government will be able to avoid the mistakes of provincial governments, Fentie's approach inspires confidence. He has set three goals for Yukon forest management: protecting the forest, building a better understanding of forest ecosystems, and strengthening the ability to manage the forest. Recognizing errors in other jurisdictions, he has set forth a commitment to identify protected areas *before* they become locked-up in long-term forest licenses.

"We are in a unique situation in the Yukon," Fentie said in a speech in March 1997. "Our ecosystems are relatively undisturbed compared with the rest of North America. We have an opportunity to manage them in a way that will not simply save them from the devastation faced in other regions, but will actually preserve them in their natural state."[22]

THE NORTHWEST TERRITORIES

Much of what has been said about the Yukon applies equally to the Northwest Territories, in terms of both biodiversity and ecosystem characteristics, as well as powers of the federal government, the territorial government and First Nations. In the Territories, a frontier attitude still reigns, and wildcat resource exploitation can still grip like a fever.

The most recent experience in the Northwest Territories (NWT) has been the extensive mineral claiming and exploration by the diamond mining industry. Environmental assessments have been wholly inadequate. First Nations, environmental groups and Canada's most distinguished scientists have expressed outrage, but the South African diamond prospectors are digging up the terrain with an intensity that reminds northerners of Gold Rush days.

The pressures on the NWT forests have also increased, but not as drastically as those in the Yukon. Still, logging in the NWT has jumped considerably over the same period as in the Yukon.

The forest of the Northwest Territories

Out of an enormous area of 342 million hectares, only 61 million hectares are forested. Within that, just over 14 million hectares could be considered at all commercially viable. The forests are owned by the federal government, but considered in territorial control. While the rates of logging are low, it must be remembered that the productive forest land happens also to be the richest area for northern boreal biodiversity. The riparian zones are fertile habitat for a range of wildlife. Logging roads do the same damage as in southern Canada, increasing access by hunters and disruption to the wilderness.

As in the Yukon, stumpage rates in the NWT constitute a subsidy to industrial forestry. In 1993–94, for example, the government collected $189,000 in stumpage and reforestation levies, while spending $518,000 in forest management costs. This figure is exclusive of fire protection costs, which are primarily directed to protecting people and property rather than forests.[23]

In 1988 a total area of 399 hectares was logged. By 1994, logging had increased to 604 hectares. The NWT has set an annual allowable cut at 300,000 cubic meters, and as of 1994 was logging about half that.

Even though the basic research has not yet been done on forest regeneration in conditions like those found in the Yukon and the NWT, the logging in the NWT is 100 percent clear-cutting.[24] Clear-cutting is likely responsible for the highest percentage of any jurisdiction in Canada of NSR lands within logged-over areas. Fully 85 percent of the NWT harvested areas are reported to be "understocked."[25] But despite the recent increases in logging, and the unsustainable reliance on clear-cutting, the forests of the NWT remain one of the only forest ecosystems in Canada not yet overexploited.

III

WHERE DO WE GO FROM HERE?

Throughout this book, an analogy has been drawn between current conditions in Canada's forests and those that led to the collapse of the East Coast cod fishery. With the advantage of hindsight, many people can now see what could have been done to prevent the loss of the fishery. There were too many fish plants. Some should have been closed. Far too much damage was being done by draggers. If draggers had been banned outright, the fish catch would have been cut in half, but only 10 percent of the workforce would have been affected. The industry was over-subsidized and over-capitalized. Economic ambitions should have been aligned with conservation goals.

Much was learned from the collapse of the East Coast fishery—through autopsies. Canada's forests need a proper diagnosis *before* it is too late. Canada will not run out of wood in 1998 or 1999. Indeed, in many specific areas and a number of forest companies, improvements have been made. Road-building, in general, has become more careful, particularly as performed by the larger companies. Some of the big forest companies have started employing forest biologists to assist in maintaining habitat for certain species, such as moose and marten. Some are opening up their management methods through public advisory committees. Such changes might make a difference, if the scale and pace of logging across Canada could also be controlled.

Every indicator points to significant wood-shortages across the country within fifteen to twenty years. British Columbia is already importing wood from the Yukon and the prairie provinces. New Brunswick is importing from Nova Scotia and Prince Edward Island. Quebec is importing from Maine and New Brunswick, and Newfoundland is gearing up to clear-cut the remote and marginal forests of Labrador. Across the board, there are far more mills than Canadian forests can feed.

The overcapacity of mills is becoming a competitive disadvantage. As provincial governments bail out old mills, newer facilities are kept out. In British Columbia, for example, where the wood supply is completely committed, the government's determination to subsidize old mills may cost jobs. "Provincial government policy that favors preserving jobs in obsolete sawmills is discouraging a sixty million dollar investment," said the president of Primex Forest Products, George Malpass, in April 1997.[1]

The second-growth forests will not have the same volume as the primary forest. Nor will they have the same biodiversity. Production levels will fall, and technology will shift to the current "weed" species. After aspen, maybe someone will figure out how to make building materials from raspberry bushes. Given Canada's forest history, the industry will keep moving through the ecosystem to species of less economic and ecological value.

That historical pattern can be changed. Canadians have a right to demand that forest management not be dictated by the interests of a small group of multinationals. The goal of forest management should be to create the maximum economic value to

Canadian society, while maintaining critical ecological functions, including carbon sequestration and protection of biodiversity.

The debate needs to move to fundamentals. The reliability of inventories needs urgent reassessment. The questionable assumptions that go into the annual allowable cut calculations need to be laid bare. Subsidies, in all forms, must stop.

The federal government should take responsibility, not for the forest resource, which is provincial, but for the potential national economic disaster that sudden mill closures and wood shortages will have on Canadian society. A national review of wood supply needs to be undertaken with full involvement of all stakeholders—industry, government, environmental groups, labor unions and the public. First Nations must have a prominent role.

The rate of cut must be re-examined. The wisdom of premising today's rate of cut on unproven benefits from future silviculture, the "allowable cut effect," should be a priority item for review. Justifying current over-cutting on the basis of speculative future efforts is more than a gamble. It is voodoo forestry.

Relying on smoke-and-mirrors analyses, every jurisdiction in Canada is playing the same game. Over-cutting is a critical issue everywhere. Sierra Club of Canada believes that, nation-wide, the cut is currently *at least* 30 percent too high.

The precautionary principle adopted at the Earth Summit in Rio in 1992 needs to be invoked constantly. Foresters like to believe that they can make management decisions based on their vast knowledge and expertise. Just as fisheries scientists were confident in their theories, so foresters, with confidence in their expertise, set logging rates at the upper end of what they hope is available. Given what humanity does not know about forests, any land-use and management decisions need to be premised on our collective ignorance rather than on presumptions of knowledge. Pumping up the estimates of what we hope may be available in order to deliver wood to the mills now is a dangerous course. We need to reassess our wood supply, including healthy margins for error. The allowable cut effect is wholly incompatible with the precautionary principle. In fact, it has entrenched risky behavior as the norm, for decades.

We must anticipate an inevitable level of climate change in practical ways, and begin serious efforts to reduce fossil fuel emissions now. To ensure the survival of key ecosystems, large tracts of wilderness must be set aside, with usable north-south corridors, as buffers against sudden climate change. An element of the precautionary principle must be to recognize the enormous value of the northern boreal to global climatic balance. We cannot afford to drain our carbon sink for cheap paper.

As the wood-supply crunch hits, some process will be needed to equitably decide which mills remain open and which must be shut down. B.C.'s Forest Minister David

Zirnhelt has already acknowledged that there is too much capacity in sawmilling and that older mills may have to close.[2] It will of course be politically difficult to make such decisions, but once a sound information base is agreed upon by all participants, it should be apparent that the approaching shortages will have serious economic impacts. If these can be managed in such a way as to protect workers and forest-dependent communities, the hardship experienced by the small coastal communities of Newfoundland need not be repeated. Those mills demonstrating high levels of labor-intensity, value-added and modern pollution control should be assured wood supply, as less environmentally responsible mills go under. Worker relocation, retraining and unemployment insurance should be devised in advance, so that large and ineffectual subsidy programs can be avoided. In the event that mills are forced to close, due to a wood shortage, funds should be collected now from the forest industry in order to assure that its misuse of the resource will not lead to economic hardship for employees.

Canadian provinces should immediately increase stumpage rates to reflect the full costs of logging. Internalized costs will increase the cost of forest products and ensure that sufficient revenues are collected to protect other resources and values associated with forests.

Individual citizens can support the transition to sustainably logged forest products. As a first step, consumption levels must be reduced. Currently, it is estimated that global demand for wood products will increase by 56 percent by the year 2010![3] That trend spells disaster for forests around the world. Think about your consumption. Whether you live in Canada or the United States, you are doing your part to deforest the world. Choices about consumption of paper and wood products matter. Do you need paper towels and serviettes? Cloth does as well (or better). Disposable diapers, instead of cotton, increase deforestation and solid waste. Avoid excess packaging. Seek out products in bulk. Re-use your own containers. Re-use envelopes. Consumers should avoid any unnecessary paper products, recycle waste paper and insist on recycled content in their purchases. Concerned citizens should "vote with their pocketbook," creating a market demand for environmentally sustainable wood products, even if at a slightly higher cost. We can also help drive the market for "tree-free" products of agricultural waste, hemp, kenaf or straw paper. Within Canada, the potential for non-THC hemp to replace tobacco as a crop in southern Canada could alleviate the strain on tobacco farmers *and* the forests.

The goal of the new era of forest management should be to reduce the cut substantially, while ensuring that employment is maintained and, ideally, expanded, in a new sustainable forest industry. As the Pulp and Paper Workers of Canada has said, "We need to create more jobs while cutting fewer trees."[4]

We need to hear more about those individual forest owners who are demonstrating sustainable forest management on their lands through selection logging. Leonard Otis, a seventy-two-year-old Quebec farmer, has husbanded his 283 hectares of forest land for forty years, providing a steady flow of wood products to sawmills and pulp mills, while producing $200,000 worth of maple syrup every year.[5] Merv Wilkinson in British Columbia is another venerable example of long-term forest stewardship, producing high-value forest products through selection logging of his British Columbia forest.

One of the best-known North American examples of community forestry is the Menominee forest in northeast Wisconsin. It is the first commercial forest operation in the United States to receive certification as sustainably managed. It is owned and managed by the people of the Menominee Nation. In 1854, when the lands were established as a reservation for the Menominee, it was estimated the land contained one and a half billion board feet of usable timber. More than a hundred years later, in 1988, two billion board feet of timber had been logged, yet the estimate of timber volume available for logging remained at least as high as it had been in 1854. The Menominee maintain their own mill and run their own woodlands operation, employing nearly five hundred people on a full-time basis.[6] If the Algonquin of Barriere Lake are allowed to move from the painstaking development of the Integrated Resource Management Plan to its implementation, Canada may well have another example to lead the world.

Meanwhile, communities are coming to grips with the necessity of planning new approaches to economically viable and ecologically sustainable forestry. The Slocan Valley in British Columbia, for example, is at a turning point. All evidence points to critical timber shortages as clear-cutting significantly above sustainable levels continues, and pristine areas are opened to industrial forestry. Community conflict has escalated. Thirty-five local residents, part of a blockade by 350, were arrested in the summer of 1997. They were protesting to protect their water supply from planned logging. As one arrestee, Eloise Charest, said, "When they are down to your watersheds, they have logged everything else around."[7] Yet an alternative vision has been promoted by the Slocan Valley Watershed Alliance and the Silva Forest Foundation. In August 1996, Herb Hammond, one of Canada's leading ecological foresters, unveiled a comprehensive ecosystem-based plan for the valley. The goal of the plan is to provide enhanced economic opportunities for the area through environmentally integrated activities. It sets standards for "ecologically responsible forest use that leaves a fully functioning forest after logging." Water quality, tourism values and "wildcrafting," the collection of non-timber forest products such as mushrooms, are all protected.

"The plan maintains logging and milling jobs, even though the allowable annual cut is greatly reduced," Hammond said. In fact, the plan would reduce the AAC for the area to 10 percent of what the government currently projects as the allowable harvest over the next one hundred years. But jobs would be maintained, even at one-tenth the rate of cut. Hammond explained, "This is possible because logging is done with small machines that require more people to cut fewer trees, and because value is added to wood products before they leave the local area. This means that far more people can be employed cutting and milling much less wood than is currently cut."[8]

Instead of racing for the bottom, this approach means racing for the top. If the ecosystem-based approach advocated by Hammond was applied across the country, Canada would no longer export low-value, unprocessed forest products. Everything about Canadian forest products would aim for quality, in both economic and ecological terms. Canadian forest products would no longer come from clear-cuts. Canadian forest products would qualify for every possible eco-labeling scheme, guaranteeing markets in Europe, with a "green premium."

While it is unrealistic to expect clear-cutting to end overnight, the phase-out of this disastrous practice should begin immediately. In its place, the recommendations of the Clayoquot Sound Scientific Panel should be pursued across Canada. At the heart of the report was the idea that logging plans should focus on what must be left undisturbed to maintain the ecological integrity of the forest. The type of logging recommended to replace clear-cutting was a "variable retention silviculture system." This involves leaving different amounts of the forest intact, depending on the ecoregion, landscape and topography. Some areas might have large clearings, being essentially modified clear-cuts. But selection logging would be the preferred mode of harvest. By maintaining forest form, function and productivity, selection logging will routinely yield more timber than the initial stocking would have, within less time than it takes industrial forestry to "rotate" the forest. Methods of selection logging apply to all forest types in Canada.

The training of operators will be critical to ensure that selection logging in the new millennium is nothing like the high-grading of the past. The simple rule of thumb that *the first cut takes out the lower-value species* would work toward continual ecosystem enhancement and avoid a repetition of past errors.

Labor-intensive silviculture would largely replace mechanized harvesting. To those who respond that such recommendations come from a Luddite perspective, remember that the mechanized industrial approach destroyed the East Coast fishery and is changing Canada from a land of abundant forest resources to a nation with a wood shortage. Some high-tech mechanization will be part of selection logging as well, avoiding the physical dangers of the logging of yesteryear.

Canadian society needs to examine the economic, ecological and social costs of an energy-intensive, capital-intensive approach to forestry. Industry will have to have a large role in redesigning the system. In order to maintain Canadian markets, the tax system will have to be reformed to ensure that Canadian forest companies can compete, even as they shift to a quality-driven product.

What if we're wrong?

Just as environmentalists urge the industry and government regulators to stop exaggerating the wood supply to justify over-cutting now, it is fair for the reader to ask, what if environmentalists are wrong about forest management? Knowing that inventories are hopelessly inaccurate, could it not be that the faulty data are obscuring not bad news, but good, and a larger wood supply than was imagined?

It is possible, but not likely. Still, *all* possibilities should be discussed. The hope in writing this book is for a fuller and better public debate about forest management, forest preservation and forest exploitation. Ironically, I actually have higher expectations for leadership from within the forest industry than from government. There are many industry "insiders" who know that the cut is dangerously high and that there are too many mills. Many are genuinely trying to improve forest practices, even if environmental groups do not yet see the results of their efforts. A respectful dialogue between industry and environmentalists will do more to advance the sustainability of Canada's forests than any number of political public-relations exercises.

Strong evidence from government and industry sources throughout this book makes the case that Canada's forests are being over-cut. The rate of over-cutting threatens the economic base of the forest industry as well as irreplaceable forest biodiversity, wildlife and fish habitat, and the myriad of ecological functions offered to us free by a healthy forest. The humbling experience of walking through a grove of venerable trees—hearing birds in the canopy overhead, listening to a brook gurgling over the pebbles, and smelling the deep richness of layers of moss—is beyond economic valuation.

A national overview is required. Otherwise, each province will continue to lay plans based on the vain hope that when the wood-supply crunch hits fiber supplies can be boosted through silvicultural alchemy, or imported from a neighboring province. No one is looking at the big picture, assessing what is a truly sustainable level of logging to supply what number of mills. No one is assessing the loss of habitat, of species, of sacred creation. And so new mills are added, more logging roads are driven through wilderness, more forest is clear-cut by fewer and fewer workers. At some point, there will be nowhere to go to borrow wood, and the green mantle will be so reduced worldwide as to affect all life on this planet. We are at the cutting edge.

Afterword

The Earth Must Slow Down

I am one of several founders of Canada's Endangered Spaces campaign, which was launched by World Wildlife Fund Canada (WWF) in September 1989 with the publication of *Endangered Spaces: The Future for Canada's Wilderness*. I have supported this campaign primarily through WWF and also through the Canadian Parks and Wilderness Society (CPAWS—a co-founder of the campaign), the Sierra Club of Canada and the Sierra Club of British Columbia.

It is significant that the WWF, CPAWS, and the Sierra Club are heavily involved with the forest industry in the "war in the woods." Arlin Hackman of WWF summed up the situation in *Timber Supply and Endangered Spaces*:

> *The Endangered Spaces goal will be difficult if not impossible to attain if the vice-grip of industrial demand on forest land, as expressed in approved harvest levels, is not relaxed.* More than any other simple factor, it is the volume of timber extraction permitted from the forest, as well as rights and expectations about future volumes, which fundamentally constrain options for new protected areas in Canada's forests today.

During the past twenty-five years, I have traveled extensively in the parks and wilderness areas of western North America. I have prowled around numerous clear-cuts. Most clear-cuts are industrial wastelands. My first real exposure to this issue came during the mid-1980s campaign to create a national park on South Moresby, a part of British Columbia's Queen Charlotte Islands. At that time, Canadians watched and read about logging companies working around the clock to mutilate as much of the landscape as they could, before the national park reserve was declared in 1987. My visits to the Queen Charlottes revealed the typical clear-cut scenario—logging roads,

228 AT THE CUTTING EDGE

landslides, the absence of real buffer zones near rivers and oceans, industrial debris, logging debris, slash burns, etc. The most damaging aspect of the clear cutting was the combination of improperly built roads and careless cutting practices, which were probably illegal and which effectively ended the life of salmon streams.

>—+—◆>—O—<◆+—<

As an environmentalist, people ask me what is the fundamental environmental problem and what is the solution to it? While there are many serious environmental problems, the fundamental problem is the world's population explosion.

Most North Americans are aware of this explosion. However, as a group, in our day-to-day lives, we tend to deny the problem it poses and pursue endless growth for its own sake.

As a result of the population explosion there is a never-ending worldwide demand for products from the forest and the ocean. The consequence is the destruction of forests and the collapse of many of the world's fisheries. Resources that have always been renewable, when used in moderation, have become non-renewable.

What are the dimensions of the population problem? It isn't easy to count all of the world's people. It is also difficult to estimate the gross national product of any nation, let alone that of the world as a whole. However, these issues are subject to serious study and it is possible to arrive at a consensus position that is adequate for our purpose.

In 1994, David Suzuki presented an estimate of world population growth:

Year	World Population	Years to Add One Billion
0	250,000,000	From the beginning of time
1850	1,000,000,000	N/A
1930	2,000,000,000	80
1958	3,000,000,000	28
1974	4,000,000,000	16
1988	5,000,000,000	14
1998(Est'd)	6,000,000,000	10
2050(Est'd)	10,000,000,000	N/A

Using the latest information from Worldwatch Institute, we can amend Suzuki's numbers.

2000(Est'd)	6,000,000,000	12
2043(Est'd)	12,000,000,000	N/A

There are several factors influencing my amendments. The world's population exploded after 1950, reaching a peak annual growth rate of 2.2 percent in the mid-1960s. Recently, growth has slowed to 1.6 percent (which doubles world population every forty-three years) or perhaps to 1.4 percent. This reduced rate of growth is the reason why Suzuki's estimate in 1994 that world population would hit 6,000,000,000 in 1998 was a bit off, and it now appears that the world will hit 6,000,000,000 in 2000. I use the 1.6 percent multiple to arrive at my estimate of 12,000,000,000 by 2043. It is of interest that it was once predicted that the annual increase in world population would soon hit 100,000,000. With the fall in rate of increase to 1.6 percent, annual growth has declined from an average of 86,000,000 in 1987–90 to an average of 81,000,000 in 1992–95. Another observation is that the world is now adding approximately 1,000,000,000 people every ten years and if world population growth can be held at that level, then there will be "only" 10,000,000,000 by 2040, which was Suzuki's projection for 2050.

A frequently asked question is, how many people can the world support? Of course, there is no answer. Those who try to find an answer use a series of guesses and value judgments in addition to whatever factual information they can find to make an educated guess. The real question is, how many people can the planet support *at what standard of living?* Do the world's people want to be moderately rich or very poor? Joel Cohen outlined the parameters of the problem:

> In 1992, the 830 million people in the world's richest countries enjoyed an average annual income of $22,000 U.S.—a truly astounding achievement. But the almost 2.6 billion people in the middle-income countries received only $1,600. The more than 2 billion people in the poorest countries lived on an average income of $400, or a dollar a day.

In answer to the question "how many people can the planet sustain indefinitely?" David Suzuki quotes E. O. Wilson, a Harvard professor who said: "'At the present level of North American consumption, perhaps 200 million.'" Suzuki adds that, "Crude as it is, the conclusion is inescapable: 'there are far too many people on Earth.'"

Paul and Anne Ehrlich provide a different but still very bracing message about population and the environment. They write:

> When is an area overpopulated? When its population can't be maintained without rapidly depleting nonrenewable resources (or converting renewable resources into nonrenewable ones) and without degrading the capacity of the environment to support the population. In short, if the long-term carrying

capacity of an area is clearly being degraded by its current human occupants, that area is overpopulated. *By this standard, the entire planet and virtually every nation is already vastly overpopulated.*

The concept of the Earth's carrying capacity is extremely important. We should be aware of the relevant questions and answers—even if many of the world's political leaders are not concerned about this issue (for example, former U.S. presidents Reagan and Bush, both of whom opposed measures designed to help limit population growth, including birth control and abortion).

The world's population exploded between 1950 and 1997. Fortunately for humanity, on a worldwide basis, the economy also grew. In many cases, the rate of increase in the production of goods exceeded the rate of population growth. According to the Worldwatch Institute, per capita income increased from $1,925 to $4,846, using constant 1995 U.S. dollars.

That is the good news. The bad news is that since about 1985 a number of indicators have become negative. The world's population has continued to grow, but for a number of products the world's production has declined on a per capita basis and possibly even on an absolute basis. Using fish as an example, the world's catch in 1950 was 19.2 million tons (21.1 million imperial tons); in 1994 it rose to 91.0 million tons (100.1 million tons). On a per capita basis, the catch rose from 7.5 kilograms per person (16.5 pounds per person) to a peak of 17.2 kilograms per person (38 pounds per person) in 1988, falling to 15.9 kilograms per person (35 pounds per person) in 1995. A number of the world's fisheries have collapsed. There is great fear that more fisheries will collapse and that worldwide fish production will decline. North America's cod and salmon are an important part of the story.

In 1990, Anita Gordon and David Suzuki wrote: "Food scarcity is emerging as the most profound and immediate consequence of global environmental degradation. It is already affecting the welfare of hundreds of millions of people, and will begin to affect North Americans directly in this decade."

As the 1990s draw to a close, we can illustrate Gordon and Suzuki's prediction that North Americans will be directly affected. In 1992, after years of mismanagement and disbelief as to what was happening, Canada was forced to close its northern cod fishery (there is no sign of recovery). During the summer of 1997, Canada and the United States had a most unseemly "salmon war" on the West Coast and it appears that the real loser is the salmon. A combination of overfishing, dams and industrial pollution has virtually eliminated the salmon from much of the West Coast. It may be that humanity is hell-bent on eliminating the rest of the salmon.

>─◄►─◦─◄►─◄

Subsidies are complex oddities. Elizabeth May's text deals with a number of these issues and it is not my purpose to duplicate her work. However, it is my belief that the Canadian forest industry is the recipient of massive public subsidization. I also believe that one result of this subsidization is the rapid, wanton destruction of our scarce forest resource.

Worldwatch Institute outlines aspects of the subsidy phenomenon:

A subsidy is defined here as a government policy that alters market risks, rewards, and costs in ways that favor certain activities or groups. The most visible subsidies are direct government payments that help hold down prices for consumers or prop them up for producers. Subsidies also take a dizzying variety of less obvious forms—ones that can be just as costly and are actually more popular with politicians because of their low visibility.

Around the world, government policies shunt at least $500 billion U.S. a year toward activities that harm the environment, from overfishing to overgrazing. The full amount may be much greater: few countries have ever tried to assess the magnitude of the subsidies they create.

Worldwatch then gives examples of specific forest subsidies:

Government timber sales in parts of the United States and Australia, especially where young trees or steep terrain make logging expensive, bring in less than agencies spend administering the concessions, particularly building logging roads. Annual losses on forest administration hovered in the range of $300-400 million U.S. in the United States in the early nineties. In effect the general taxpayer is paying timber companies to raze public forests. The biggest money-loser is the Tongass National Forest in Alaska, the world's largest remaining temperate rain forest. Providing roads and other services to private clear-cutting operations there cost the government $389 million between 1982 and 1988, yet earned it only $32 million. In the Australian state of Victoria, the pattern is strikingly similar; there the government is losing some $170 million U.S. a year on net.

In Canada, there is no comprehensive analysis of the subsides paid to the forest industry. This is a field that begs investigation. What we do have is a large number of stories—many recounted by Elizabeth May—that show us the tip of the iceberg.

It is important to recognize that in addition to cash subsidies, the forest industry also receives immense intangible subsidization. The forest industry does immeasurable, often intangible damage to the environment, and forest companies do not have to pay for this damage. For example:

1. A clearcut creates a wasteland and is harmful to native wildlife and biodiversity.
2. Forest operations cause pollution of many kinds—from the toxic spraying of forests to the poisonous effluent from pulp and paper mills, which among other things, often makes fisheries unusable.
3. Traditionally, forest companies in Canada have not been responsible for cleaning up the mess they leave (the not sufficiently re-stocked problem).
4. Forest operations have had a tremendous negative impact on the lives of some of Canada's Native people.
5. It is generally accepted that the forest industry has a negative impact on the tourist industry.

The fishing industry and the forest industry in Canada are far from being the same, but there are important parallels:

1. Both industries are heavily subsidized.
2. Both industries are overcapitalized. (There are more hooks, nets, boats and fish processing plants than there are fish to be caught, and there are more chain saws, feller bunchers, sawmills and pulp and paper mills than there are trees to be cut.)
3. Both industries harvest their product in a manner that is cruel and wasteful.

During the 1990s, it has been fashionable in North America for governments to slash their levels of spending in the name of fiscal responsibility. In the forest, we continue to subsidize the destruction of a scarce natural resource. We should stop subsidizing this industry. We should let it bear its own costs and stand on its own feet.

>⊶⊷⊙⊶⊷⊰

The concept of responsibility for corporations and the individuals who manage them provides fuel for never-ending debate. Nineteen ninety-seven was the year the American tobacco industry was exposed. It was finally revealed that tobacco companies had lied both to the American public and to Congress for an extended period of time. As we go to print, penalties in the hundreds of billions of dollars are being argued.

Adam Zimmerman has just written his memoir *Who's in Charge Here, Anyway?* Zimmerman spent more than thirty years near or at the center of power in Canada's largest forest companies, including ten years as president, COO, CEO and chairman of Noranda Forest and MacMillan Bloedel. Zimmerman is an interesting character. Although he worked for powerful forest companies, he is also a longtime member of the executive committee of WWF and a supporter of the Endangered Spaces program. He tells us that his wife and four children told him "in no uncertain terms that they were less than proud of what I and my company were doing." Writing about his early days in the 1960s, Zimmerman admits that:

> Forestry practices were rather more careless and far more wasteful. Loggers left behind massive quantities of debris and neglected such problems as stream-bank erosion and landslides that stemmed from logging-road construction. Reforestation took place, but not nearly as diligently as it should have. The concept of sustainable yield was more honoured in the breach than in the observance.

It is easy to agree with Zimmerman's views of the early days, but I do not understand his comments about the situation in the forests in the 1990s. He remarks, "I've said to countless audiences that forestry firms in particular should be saluted as exemplars of environmentally sound behaviour. They produce no waste that goes untreated or remains unaccounted for. They have to—they're closely watched, quantified on a daily basis, and regulated into the ground." Zimmerman then goes on to say that "Nothing is perfect, but on balance, no better forestry is being generally practised anywhere in the world" than in Canada.

Unfortunately, environmentalists do not share his current optimism about the industry. With regard to the quality of Canada's forestry, the Sierra Club has published *Clearcut: The Tragedy of Industrial Forestry*, which exposes industry practices across North America. Similarly, M. Patricia Marchak, dean of arts at the University of British Columbia, has written a trenchant treatise, *Logging the Globe*. She concludes that "Despite its rich resource base and low population density, Canada's record of forest management is appalling."

In the 1990s, British Columbia and its forest companies make the claim that they have taken steps to improve performance in the forest. However, there is a growing list of field audits and analyses by the province's environmental watchdogs indicating that the fox still lives in the chicken coop. The British Columbia Environmental Network, B.C. Wild, Greenpeace, the Sierra Club, and the Sierra Legal Defence Fund have searched long and hard for evidence of improvement. Sadly, they conclude that as 1997 comes to a close it is still business as usual in the province's forests.

Just as it is fashionable in the 1990s for governments to reduce spending, it is also fashionable in both Canada and the United States to deregulate industry and to make governments smaller. However, based on the evidence, forest companies, perhaps like the tobacco companies, seem unable to do either what they pledge to do or even what is required of them by law. While companies in the forest industry continually plead for fewer restrictions on their operations—that's deregulation—it is clear that the laws governing their activities need to be strengthened and enforced in a meaningful manner. Experience has shown that in the case of the forest industry self-regulation is a bad joke.

Glen W. Davis

Notes

Introduction

1. Roderick Nash, *Wilderness and the American Mind* (New Haven, Conn.: Yale University Press, 1967), pp. 134-5.
2. Samuel P. Hayes, *Conservation and the Gospel of Efficiency* (Cambridge, Mass.: Harvard University Press, 1972), p. 42.
3. Nash, *Wilderness and the American Mind*, p. 188.

PART I

Chapters 1 to 7

1. Canadian Forest Service, Department of Natural Resources, *The State of Canada's Forests, 1995-1996* (Ottawa, 1996), p. 92; data based on employment in 1995.
2. J. Cooperman, "British Columbia's Forest Crisis: A B.C. Environmental Network Forest Caucus Discussion Paper," *British Columbia Environmental Report*, undated.
3. D. Bryant et al., *The Last Frontier Forests: Ecosystems and Economies on the Edge* (Washington: World Resources Institute, 1997), p. 21.
4. Canadian Forest Service, Department of Natural Resources, *The State of Canada's Forests, 1995-1996* (Ottawa, 1996).
5. Canadian Forest Service, Department of Natural Resources, *The State of Canada's Forests, 1994* (Ottawa, 1995), p. 84.
6. Canadian Forest Service, Natural Resources Canada, *The State of Canada's Forests, 1993* (Ottawa, 1994), p. 91.
7. A. Nikiforuk and E. Struzik, "The Great Forest Sell-Off," *Globe and Mail Report on Business*, November 1989.
8. L.A. Sandberg, ed., *Trouble in the Woods: Forest Policy and Social Conflict in Nova Scotia and New Brunswick* (Fredericton: Acadiensis Press, 1992), p. 5.

9. E. May, *Paradise Won: The Struggle for South Moresby* (Toronto: McClelland & Stewart, 1990).

10. D. Sullivan, *Suspension of Liquidation of Canadian Lumber Is Critical to Provide Short-term Relief to the U.S. Lumber Industry*, pp. 11-12.

11. Ibid., pp. 13-14.

12. Environment Probe is a project of Energy Probe, a Toronto-based environmental non-government organization, which has championed the use of market forces and private property rights for environmental protection.

13. Quoted in Terry Glavin "Much ado about APEC," *Globe and Mail*, Nov. 7, 1997, p. A23.

14. Canadian Press, "Nova Scotia tree-cutting assailed: Government not protecting resource, independent foresters say," *Globe and Mail*, March 28, 1997.

15. Environment Canada, *Building Momentum: Sustainable Development in Canada*, Canada's submission to the fifth Session of the United Nations Commission on Sustainable Development, April 7-25, 1997, p. 18.

16. A. Swift, "Americans, Canadians at odds over 'sustainable forestry' plan," *Ottawa Citizen*, February 1, 1997, p. H3. The minister clarified her remarks in a letter to Sierra Club asserting that nations using trade barriers based on sustainable forest practices were the target of her remarks, not environmental groups. Nevertheless, it is clear that the federal role in forestry is one of defending industry interests in a global propaganda war.

17. Environment Canada, "Forests," *State of the Environment Bulletin* No. 95.4 (Summer 1995); Environment Canada for 1950 and 1970; 1994 data from Canadian Forest Service, Department of Natural Resources, *The State of Canada's Forests, 1995-1996* (Ottawa, 1996).

18. Environment Canada, "Forests," *State of the Environment Bulletin*; Canadian Forest Service, Natural Resources Canada, *The State of Canada's Forests*, 1996-1997 (Ottawa, 1997).

19. Quoted in Okanagan TSA Rationale, 1996, p. 19.

20. Canadian Forest Service, Department of Natural Resources, *The State of Canada's Forests, 1991* (Ottawa, 1992), p. 41.

21. *Broken Promises: The truth about what's happening to British Columbia's forests*, Greenpeace Report, April 1997. Ninety-seven percent of the Forest Alliance's funds are from the forest industry.

22. Ibid., p. 20.

23. Credit for unmasking industry myths goes particularly to Herb Hammond, *Seeing the Forest Among the Trees: The Case for Holistic Forest Use* (Vancouver: Polestar Press, 1991); Mitch Lansky, *Beyond the Beauty Strip* (Gardiner, Maine: Tilbury House, 1992); and Dr. Chris Pielou, "A Clear-Cut Decision," *Nature Canada*, Spring 1996.

24. R. Locke, "Regeneration Status of Black Spruce and Balsam Fir sites after cutting in district 12," *Silviculture Notebook*, No. 3 (St. John's: Newfoundland Forest Service, 1994).

25. T.J. Carleton and P. MacLellan, "Woody Vegetation Responses to Fire Versus Clear-cut Logging: A Comparative Survey in the Central Canadian Boreal Forest," *Ecoscience*, 1/2 (1994).

26. Official number: Canadian Forest Service, Department of Natural Resources, *The State of Canada's Forests 1995-1996* (Ottawa, 1996). Actual area: 2,487,167 (6,145,705 acres) or 18 percent of harvested Crown land, based on 1992 data. The same 1992 data were used in the *State of the Forest Report, 1994*. Unofficial number: two million hectare NSR acknowledged by B.C. government, but not included in the one million hectare NSR level.

27. Nova Scotia Department of Lands and Forests, *The Forest Resources of Nova Scotia* (Halifax, 1958), p. 59.

28. Ibid., p. 60.

29. Canadian Forest Service, Department of Natural Resources, *The State of Canada's Forests, 1994* (Ottawa, 1995).

30. Royal Commission on Forest Protection and Management, *Report of the Royal Commission* (St. John's: Queen's Printer, 1981).

31. Hammond, Herb, *Seeing the Forest Among the Trees: The Case for Holistic Forest Use* (Vancouver: Polestar Press, 1991), p. 62.

32. B. Devall, ed., *Clearcut: The Tragedy of Industrial Forestry* (San Francisco: Sierra Club Books, 1993), p. 26.

33. I am grateful to Dr. Chris Pielou for pointing this out.

34. Clayoquot Sound Scientific Panel, cited in *Broken Promises: The truth about what's happening to British Columbia's forests*, Greenpeace Report, April 1997, p. 9.

35. B. Freedman et al., "Forestry Practices and Biodiversity, with Particular Reference to the Maritime Provinces of Eastern Canada," *Environment Review* 2 (1994), 54.

36. Chris Maser, "Ancient Forests: Priceless Treasures," *The Mushroom Journal*, Fall 1988.

37. G.R. Parker, D.G. Kimball and B. Dalzcll, *Bird Communities Breeding in Selected Spruce and Pine Plantations in New Brunswick* (Publication: Canadian Field Naturalist, 108/1, 1994).

38. Pielou, "A Clear-Cut Decision," *Nature Canada*, p. 23.

39. B. Freedman et al. "Forestry Practices and Biodiversity, with Particular Reference to the Maritime Provinces of Eastern Canada," *Environmental Review* 2 (1994).

40. R. Silen, *Nitrogen, Corn and Forest Genetics*, U.S. Department of Agriculture Forest Service, Pacific North West Range Experiment Station, General Technical Report, PNW137, June 1982.

41. P. Moore, *Pacific Spirit: The Forest Reborn* (West Vancouver: Terra Bella Publishers, 1995).

42. Pielou, "A Clear-Cut Decision," *Nature Canada*, p. 25.

43. Canadian Council of Forest Ministers, *Compendium of Forestry Statistics 1994* (Ottawa, 1995), p. 88.

44. "Protected areas" for this purpose is defined in conformity with the International Union for the Conservation of Nature (IUCN) protected levels 1,2 and 3, i.e., no logging.

45. K. Lewis and S. Westmacott, "Protected Areas Strategy Provincial Overview and Status Report" (draft), B.C. Land Use Coordination Office (Victoria, 1996).

46. Debate on *Face-Off*, CBC Newsworld, January 3, 1996.

47. Hammond, *Seeing the Forest Among the Trees*, p. 62.

48. M. Reeder, "Individual Tree Selection: More than forestry without chemicals," *Journal of Pesticide Reform*, Vol. 8, No. 3, Fall 1988.

49. Ibid., p. 2.

50. Hammond, *Seeing the Forest Among the Trees*, p. 63.

51. Paul Hawken, *The Ecology of Commerce* (New York: Harper Business, 1993).

52. Wayne Roberts, *Get a Life!* (Toronto: Get A Life Publishing House, 1995).

53. M. Rauter, *Expert Panel on Information Technology Development and Use*. Presentation by the president of Ontario Forest Industries Association. *Proceedings Decision Support— 2001*, Vol. 2, 17th Annual Geographic Information Seminar Resource Technology 1994, Symposium. (Toronto, September 12-16, 1995) eds., J.M. Power, M. Strome and T.C. Daniel (Bethesda, Maryland: American Society for Photogrammetry and Remote Sensing), pp. 1111-1116. Sponsored by the Canadian Forest Service, the Ontario Ministry of Natural Resources and the Resource Technology Institute.

54. J. Swift, *Cut and Run: The Assault on Canada's Forests* (Toronto: Between the Lines, 1983), p. 139.

55. M. McCormack, "Overview," *Proceedings of the Conference on the Impacts of Intensive Harvesting, January 22, 1990* (Fredericton: Forestry Canada, Maritime Region, 1991). The discussion of the evolution of logging technology is based on Dr. McCormack's paper, especially Figure 5.

56. Environment Canada, "Forests," *State of the Environment Bulletin*.

57. Statistics Canada, *Principle Statistics in the Logging Industry, 1967-1995*, Cat. no. 25-201 (Ottawa: Minister of Supply and Services, January 1996). Note that the figures from 1967-1987 and 1987-1993 are not completely comparable as, after 1987, the data collected included more small operators. In other words, if the data were readjusted to take this factor into account, the job-loss figures would be greater.

58. Forest Allies (Box 300, Jamestown, Newfoundland, A0C 1V0), *Wood Consumption Increases . . . Jobs Decrease*, Factsheet 1995. (originally in cords: 200,000 cords = 724,920 cubic meters; 900,000 cords = 3,262,140 cubic meters).

59. Cited in Wildlands League, *Cutting the Future out of Prosperity?*, Forest Diversity/Community Survival Series, Factsheet 2, 1995.

60. Ibid. Wildlands League sources for these statistics were drawn from Statistics Canada, *Canadian Forestry Statistics*, Cat. no. 25-202 (Ottawa: Minister of Supply and Services, 1996); Forestry Canada, *Selected Forestry Statistics, 1988*, Info Report E-X-41 (Ottawa, 1989); Forestry Canada, *Selected Forest Statistics, 1991*, Info Report E-X-46 (Ottawa, 1992); and Price Waterhouse, *The Canadian Pulp and Paper Industry: A Focus on Human Resources* (Ottawa: Minister of Supply and Services, 1994).

61. Quoted in Sierra Club of Canada, *Forests,* Factsheet (1996).

62. J. Berthiaume, *Research Note: Evolution of Employment in the Forestry Industry between 1970 and 1992* (Ottawa: Economic Studies Division, Canadian Forest Service, August 1993).

63. R. Wood, "Analysis of the Forest Industry Employment Situation in Port Alberni," *Forest Planning Canada* 8/2 (March/April 1992).

64. Statistics Canada, *Canadian Forestry Statistics*, Cat. no. 25-202; Price Waterhouse, *The Forest Industry of British Columbia* (1993-94 annual).

65. Price Waterhouse, *The Canadian Pulp and Paper Industry*.

66. Cited by Wildlands League, *A New Appetite in the Forest*, Forest Diversity/Community Survival Series, Factsheet 3 (1995).

67. K. Drushka, *Stumped: The Forest Industry in Transition* (Vancouver: Douglas & McIntyre, 1985), p. 23.

68. N.S. Nicholas et al., "The reliability of tree crown position classification," *Canadian Journal of Forest Research*, Vol. 21, 1991, p. 699.

69. R.E. McRoberts et al., "Variation in forest inventory field measurements," *Canadian Journal of Forest Research*, Vol. 24, 1994, p. 1766.

70. Ibid., p. 1769; for similar studies and conclusions. See also G. Gertner et al., "Effects of measurement errors on an individual tree-based growth projection system," *Canadian Journal of Forest Research*, Vol. 14, 1984, p. 311; S.A. Omule, "Personal Bias in Forest Measurements," *The Forestry Chronicle*, October 1980, p. 222; W. Dahms, "Correction for a possible bias in developing site index curves from sectioned tree data," *Journal of Forestry*, January 1963, p. 25.

71. S. Magnussen, "Recovering time trends in dominant height from stem analysis," *Canadian Journal of Forest Research*, Vol. 26, 1996, pp. 9-22; Abstract: "Site-index curves derived from stem analysis of trees with dominant height at the time of selection will underestimate dominant height of young trees and thus over-estimate the performance and yield expectations of young stands."

72. Drushka, *Stumped*, p. 34.

73. Manitoba, "An Action Plan for a Network of Protected Areas—1996-1998," Manitoba Department of Natural resources, p. 104.

74. Forestry Canada, *The State of Canada's Forests, 1992* (Ottawa, 1993), p. 109.

75. C. Pielou, Speech to the University of British Columbia Law School conference on Biodiversity and the Law, *Nature Canada*.

76. D. MacKay, *The MacMillan Bloedel Story—Empire of Wood* (Vancouver: Douglas & McIntyre, 1982), p. 335.

77. Ibid., p. 336.

78. D.H. Kuhnke, *Silvicultural Statistics for Canada: an 11-year summary* (Ottawa: Forestry Canada, 1989), p. 12.

79. Environment Canada, "Forests," *State of the Environment Bulletin* (90 percent of all forest logged in Canada every year has never previously been commercially logged).

80. Report of the British Columbia Royal Commission on Forestry, "Timber Rights and Forest Policy," 1976, Vol. 1, at p. 228.

81. T. Clark, "Timber Supply and Endangered Spaces," A World Wildlife Discussion Paper (Toronto: World Wildlife Fund Canada, 1996), p. 54.

82. Forestry Canada, *The State of Canada's Forests* (Ottawa, 1990), pp. 32-33.

83. D.L. Booth, "The Sustainability of Canada's Timber Supply," Policy and Economics Directorate (Ottawa: Forestry Canada, June 1993), p. 3.

84. *20 Year Forestry Development Plan 1990-2009* (Government of Newfoundland, Feb. 1992), p. 67.

85. T. Clark, "Timber Supply and Endangered Spaces," a World Wildlife Fund discussion paper (1995), quoting Ray Addison on the philosophy of the 1945 Sloan Commission, p. 47.

86. M. Ross, *Forest Management in Canada* (Calgary: Canadian Institute of Resources Law, 1995), p. 90.

87. Sierra Club of Canada, *Forest Fires and Climate Change*, Factsheet (1996).

88. Ibid.

89. Quoted in M. Lansky, *Beyond the Beauty Strip* (Camden East: Old Bridge Press, 1993), p. 277.

90. Ibid., citing D. Cayle, "From Commons to Catastrophe: The Destruction of the Forests," Transcript, Part V (Toronto: Canadian Broadcasting Corporation, 1989).

91. D. Lachance et al., *Health of Sugar Maples in Canada*, Info Report ST-X-10 (Ottawa: Canadian Forest Service, Natural Resources Canada, 1995).

92. J.P. Hall et al., "Health of North American Forests" (Ottawa: Canadian Forest Service, Natural Resources Canada, 1996).

93. J. Hoddinott, "Global Warming and the Forest Flora," *Boreal Conference Proceedings* (Athabasca: Athabasca University, 1992), pp. 172-178.

94. Shawna L. Naidu et al., "The Effects of Ultraviolet-B Radiation on Photosynthesis of Different Aged Needles in Field-Grown Loblolly Pine," *Tree Physiology* 12 (1993), 151-162.

95. R. Prins and D.G. Roberts, *The Role of Forests in Global Warming: A Problem Analysis* (Ottawa: Economic Studies Division, Forestry Canada, March 1991), p. 7.

96. M. Apps and W. Kurz, "Retrospective Assessment of Carbon Flows in Canadian Boreal Forests," in M.J. Apps and D.T. Price, eds., *Forest Ecosystems, Forest Management and the Global Carbon Cycle Series*, Vol. 18 (Heidelberg: Springer-Verlag, 1995).

97. "Global warming and Canada's forest fires," *Globe and Mail*, July 10, 1995.

98. Canadian Forest Service, Department of Natural Resources, *The State of Canada's Forests, 1995-1996* (Ottawa, 1996).

99. J. Saunders, "Forest fires raise expensive questions," *Globe and Mail*, July 20, 1995, quoting Dr. Jag Maini, former Assistant Deputy Minister, Forestry Canada.

100. D. Bueckert, "Fire fumes burn hole in ozone, experts say," *Ottawa Citizen*, June 27, 1995; Carbon figures, R. Gelbspan, *The Heat Is On* (Reading: Addison-Wesley, 1997).

101. M. Harmon et al., "Effects on Carbon Storage of Conversion of Old-Growth Forests to Young Forests," *Science* 247 (February 9, 1990), 699.

102. A.M. Gordon et al., "Seasonal Patterns of Soil Respiration and CO2 Following Harvesting in White Spruce Forests of Interior Alaska," *Canadian Journal of Forest Research* 17 (1987), 304-319, cited in Greenpeace International, *The Carbon Bomb: Climate Change and the Fate of the Northern Boreal Forests* (Toronto, 1994).

103. R. Hornung, "Corporate Action on Climate Change—1996: An Independent Review" (Alberta: The Pembina Institute, April 1997), p. 39.

104. W. Troyer, *No Safe Place* (Toronto: Clarke Irwin, 1977).

105. W. Sinclair, *Controlling Pollution from Canadian Pulp Manufacturers: A Federal Perspective* (Ottawa: Environment Canada, March 1990).

106. Ibid., p. 34.

107. T. Colborn, D. Dumanoski and J. Peterson Myers, *Our Stolen Future* (New York: Dutton, 1996).

108. During this period, I was Senior Policy Advisor to the federal minister. This is personal recollection of events. Dr. Ranata Kroesa of Greenpeace did an invaluable service in running the tests and in sharing her results before releasing them.

109. D. Meagher, "Restrict pulp mills' organochlorines," *Fredericton Daily Gleaner,* September 1, 1989.

110. J. Myrden, "Stora tops pulp mill pollution list," *Chronicle-Herald*, October 1, 1988, cited in Green Web Bulletin 26.

111. J. Myrden, "Stora tops mill pollution list," *Chronicle-Herald*, March 17, 1989.

112. Myrden, "Stora tops pulp mill pollution list," *Chronicle-Herald.*

113. Canadian Forest Service, Department of Natural Resources, *The State of Canada's Forests 1993; Fourth Report to Parliament* (Ottawa, 1993), p. 107.

114. Colborn, Dumanoski and Peterson Myers, *Our Stolen Future.*

115. Northern River Basins Study, "Some Fish Under Stress and Nutrients Affect River System," *River Views*, Winter 1996.

116. Colborn, Dumanoski and Myers, *Our Stolen Future.*

117. Canadian Forest Service, Department of Natural Resources, *The State of Canada's Forests, 1993* (Ottawa, 1994).

118. See Part II, Chapter 5, on Manitoba for details.

119. Canadian Forest Service, Department of Natural Resources, *The State of Canada's Forests, 1995-1996* (Ottawa, 1996), p. 62.

120. Ibid., p. 53.

121. J. Cartwright, "Can Canada Afford Its Forest Industry?" *Policy Options* 17(9), November 1996, pp. 15-18.

122. G. Kuehne, "On the Softwood Lumber Tariff—An Update," *Forest Planning Canada* 7/3 (September/October 1991).

123. Adam Zimmerman, *Who's in Charge Here, Anyway?* (Toronto: Stoddart Publishing, 1997), p. 78.

124. Ibid.

125. Zimmerman, *Who's in Charge Here, Anyway?*

126. E. May, *Paradise Won: The Struggle for South Moresby* (Toronto: McClelland & Stewart, 1990), p. 164.

127. K. Drushka, *Stumped*, p. 279.

128. Coalition for Fair Lumber Imports, "Suspension of Liquidation on Canadian Lumber is Critical to Provide Short-Term Relief to the U.S. Lumber Industry," 1995.

129. G. Shannon, "It's time to solve the softwood issue," *Globe and Mail Report on Business*, August 1, 1996.

130. Zimmerman, *Who's in Charge Here, Anyway?*, p. 103.

131. P. Lush, "Lumber shipments flooding into U.S.," *Globe and Mail Report on Business*, July 4, 1996.

132. See Part II, Chapter 2, on Nova Scotia.

133. Sean Silcoff, "Ontario accused of dragging heels on smog reduction," *Globe and Mail*, June 13, 1996.

134. I was approached to sit on the Canadian Standards Association forest-certification advisory committee, but declined in view of time constraints. I became extremely dissatisfied with the CSA only after I learned I was being listed as a committee member who consistently sent regrets for not attending meetings. Subsequently I asked the CSA to remove my name from the members' list, only to discover I was then listed as an associate member. Monte Hummel of the World Wildlife Fund had a similar experience.

135. C. Elliott and A. Hackman, "Current Issues in Forest Certification in Canada," a World Wildlife Fund Canada discussion paper (Toronto, April 1996).

136. The six criteria under CCFM for sustainable forest management are: conserving biodiversity, maintaining and enhancing forest ecosystems, conserving soil and water, contributing to global ecological cycles, providing multiple benefits to society and accepting society's responsibility for sustainable development. A seventh criterion, relating to the rights of aboriginal peoples, was rejected by the CCFM. Thus, there are no specific obligations to First Nations in the CSA process.

137. Elliott and Hackman, "Current Issues in Forest Certification in Canada," Appendix 6.

PART II

Chapter 8: Atlantic Provinces

Newfoundland

1. "Newfoundland 20 Year Forest Plan," reported shortfalls of 10-15 percent in 1992; the most recent Forestry Development Plan for 1996-2015, still in draft, reported shortfalls of 27 percent.

2. Farley Mowat, *Sea of Slaughter* (Toronto: McClelland & Stewart, 1984).

3. W. Meades, "Stability in the Boreal Forest/Ericaceous Dwarf-Shrub Heath Ecotone of Eastern Newfoundland" (St. John's: Forestry Canada, Proc. Of 1989, IURFO Working Party 51, 05-2, Information Report N-X-271, 1986) and "Successional Status of Ericaceous Dwarf-Shrub Heath in Eastern Newfoundland," Doctoral Dissertation (University of Connecticut, 1986).

4. Poole Royal Commission, *Royal Commission on Forestry Report* (St. John's: David R. Thistle, 1955), p. 10.

5. John Gray, *The Trees Behind the Shore: The Forests and Forest Industries of Newfoundland and Labrador* (St. John's: Economic Council of Canada, 1981), p. 17.

6. Gray, *The Trees Behind the Shore,* p. 16.

7. A "board foot" is a timber term for a piece of wood one inch thick and one foot square. It takes 4.6 cubic meters of round logs to make 1000 board feet of lumber.

8. D. Haley and M.K. Luckert, *Forest Tenures in Canada: A Framework for Policy Analysis,* Information Report E-X-43 (Ottawa: Forestry Canada, 1990) p. 99.

9. Gray, *The Trees Behind the Shore,* p. 18.

10. Greg Mitchell, "Newfoundland's Giant Trees of the Past," *Newfoundland and Labrador Environment Network News* (January 1996), citing Anglican Bishop Edward Field's travels of 1849.

11. Poole Royal Commission, *Royal Commission on Forestry Report*. The Poole Royal Commission is cited as the source for the six-million-board-feet-per-year figure, and a Ph.D. thesis "Public Timber Allocation Policy in Newfoundland," University of British Columbia, by John Munroe is credited for the 1884 and 1910 production levels.

12. See Part I, Chapter 2: Myths, Propaganda and Half-Truths.

13. R. Locke, "Regeneration Status of Black Spruce and Balsam Fir sites after cutting in district 12," *Silviculture Notebook*, No. 3 (May 1994), published by the Newfoundland Forest Service.

14. Canadian Forest Service, Department of Natural Resources, *The State of Canada's Forests, 1995-1996* (Ottawa, 1996), actual area: 2,487,167 hectares, or 18 percent of harvested Crown land, based on 1992 data. The same 1992 data were used in the 1994 *State of the Forests* report.

15. Canadian Forest Service, Department of Natural Resources, *The State of Canada's Forests, 1994* (Ottawa, 1995), p. 89, not updated from the 1993 data in the more recent 1995-1996 *State of the Forests* report.

16. G. Mitchell, "Newfoundland's Newest Endangered Species," *Newfoundland and Labrador Environment Network News* 7/3 (April 1996).

17. Greg Mitchell, referring to Upper Glide, Pikes Brook and Copper Lakes, to be logged by Kruger (Corner Brook Pulp and Paper) Newfoundland.

18. The federal government's endangered-species legislation, Bill C-65, died on the Order Paper in spring 1997. In any event, it would not have protected the pine marten.

19. Gray, *The Trees Behind the Shore*, p. 5.

20. Canadian Forest Service, *State of Canada's Forests, 1994*, p. 89.

21. Government of Newfoundland and Labrador, *20 Year Forestry Development Plan 1990-2009* (St. John's, February 1992).

22. Government of Newfoundland and Labrador, *20 Year Forestry Development Plan, 1990-2009*, pp. 2-4.

23. Gray, *The Trees Behind the Shore*, p. 20.

24. Government of Newfoundland and Labrador, *20 Year Forestry Development Plan, 1996-2015*, October 1996, p. 84.

25. Canadian Council of Forest Ministers, *Compendium of Canadian Forestry Statistics, 1994* (Ottawa, 1995), p. 60; the 964,000 cubic meter figure is from 1993.

26. Government of Newfoundland and Labrador, *20 Year Forestry Development Plan, 1990-2009*, p. 85.

27. "Government shall issue to the Company licenses ... to cut timber on all or any part, as requested by the Company": The Labrador Linerboard Limited Agreement Act, 1979, Chapter 11, Statutes of Newfoundland, section 1(2), at p. xxv.

28. Timber Licence, Province of Newfoundland: Agreement between Newfoundland and Abitibi Paper Company Ltd., November 2, 1987.

29. Gray, *The Trees Behind the Shore*, p. 23.

30. Personal communication from Greg Mitchell, logging contractor.

31. Government of Newfoundland and Labrador, *20 Year Forestry Development Plan, 1990-2009*, p. 69.

32. Canadian Forest Service, Department of Natural Resources, *The State of Canada's Forests, 1994* (Ottawa, 1994), p. 89. Data from 1993 used in Canadian Forest Service, Department of Natural Resources, *The State of Canada's Forests, 1995-1996* (Ottawa, 1996).

33. M. von Mirbach, *Newfoundland's Wood Supply: A Critique of the Assumptions Used in the "20 Year Forestry Development Plan, 1990-2009,"* Humber Environment Action Group, November 1993.

34. Poole Royal Commission, *Report of the Royal Commission on Forest Protection and Management* (St. John's: Queen's Printer, 1955), pp. 14-15: figure was stated as 805,000 cords. Since 2.2 cubic meters makes up to one cord, the metric figure is 1.6 million cubic meters.

35. Government of Newfoundland and Labrador, *20 Year Forestry Development Plan, 1996-2015*, October 1996, p. 84.

36. Quoted in Larry Innes, "Adaptive Mismanagement Proposed for Nitassinan Forests," American Indian Heritage web site, "aihf@dgsys.com" or "www.indians.org."

37. Ibid.

38. Statistics are from Newfoundland Forest Service, *Forest Management* (St. John's, 1995).

Nova Scotia

1. Nova Scotia Department of Lands and Forests, *The Forest Resources of Nova Scotia* (Halifax, 1958).

2. Ibid.

3. Quoted in K. Drushka, *Stumped: The Forest Industry in Transition*, (Vancouver: Douglas & McIntyre, 1985), p. 27.

4. L. Anders Sandberg, "Forest Policy in Nova Scotia: The Big Lease, Cape Breton Island, 1899-1960," in L.A. Sandberg, ed., *Trouble in the Woods: Forest Policy and Social Conflict in Nova Scotia and New Brunswick* (Fredericton: Acadiensis, 1992), p. 65. (25 cm = 10 inches)

5. Andrew D. Rodgers, *Bernhard Edward Fernow* (Durham: Forest History Society, 1992).

6. Quoted in Nova Scotia Department of Lands and Forests, *The Forest Resources of Nova Scotia*, p. 1.

7. Ibid., p. 55.

8. Sandberg, "Forest Policy in Nova Scotia," pp. 65-89.

9. Quoted in L. Anders Sandberg, "Introduction: Dependent Development and Client States," in Sandberg, ed., *Trouble in the Woods*, at p. 78.

10. Nova Scotia Department of Lands and Forests, *The Forest Resources of Nova Scotia*, p. 62.

11. Ibid.

12. Ibid, pp. 63-64.

13. John S. Donaldson, General Manager of Halifax Power and Pulp Co. Ltd, of Sheet Harbour, N.S., cited in *Pulp and Paper Primer: Nova Scotia*, Bulletin 26, Green Web, Saltsprings, Pictou County, N.S., April 1991.

14. Quoted in H. Thurston, "Nova Scotia: Squandering Tomorrow," in A. Schneider, ed., *Deforestation and "Development" in Canada and the Tropics* (Sydney: University College of Cape Breton, 1989), p. 163; originally published as "Prest's Last Stand," in *Harrowsmith* 50 (August/September 1983).

15. Quoted in ibid.

16. E. May, *Budworm Battles* (Tantallon: Four East, 1982).

17. L.A. Sandberg, ed., *Trouble in the Woods*, especially P. Clancy, "The Politics of Pulpwood Marketing in Nova Scotia, 1960-1985."

18. May, *Budworm Battles.*

19. Quoted in ibid., p. 31.

20. Quoted in Farley Mowat, Introduction, in E. May, *Paradise Won: The Struggle for South Moresby* (Toronto: McClelland & Stewart, 1990).

21. Stora Kopparberg, *Annual Report*, 1992.

22. C. Shaw, "Stora announces $650 m plant," *Chronicle-Herald*, December 12, 1995.

23. Ron Stang, "Environmentalist's claims 'ridiculous,' says Stora president," *Cape Breton Post*, July 6, 1988.

24. Quoted in K. Cox, "Cape Breton forestry program stirs debate," *Globe and Mail*, November 6, 1991.

25. Quoted in D. MacNeil, "Fight for the Keppoch," *Cape Breton Post*, October 26, 1991.

26. P. Neily, "Nova Scotia Status Report on Timber Supply," in Natural Resources Canada, ed., *Timber Supply in Canada* (Ottawa: Canada Communication Group, 1994), p. 64.

27. Forestry Canada and Nova Scotia Department of Natural Resources, *Nova Scotia's Forest Management Strategy*, printed under the Canada-Nova Scotia Cooperation Agreement for Forestry Development, July 1994, p. 2.

28. ATI Consulting Corp., Inc., "CAFD 2: Evaluation of the Canada-Nova Scotia Cooperation Agreement for Forestry Development, 1991-1995," March 1995, pp. A6-10.

29. Neily, "Nova Scotia Status Report on Timber Supply."

30. Total area harvested: Forestry Canada, *The State of Forestry in Canada, 1990, First Report to Parliament* (Ottawa, 1990), p. 12; demand for wood to mills: Gardner Pinfold Consulting Economists, *An Evaluation of the Forest Resource Development Agreement and the Forest Renewal Agreement*, prepared for the Nova Scotia Department of Lands and Forests and the Canadian Forestry Service, March 1987.

31. Canadian Forest Service, Department of Natural Resources, *The State of Canada's Forests, 1996-1997* (Ottawa, 1997), p. 104.

32. Gardner Pinfold Consulting Economists, *An Evaluation of the Forest Resource Development Agreement and the Forest Renewal Agreement*, pp. 106-108.

33. Observations based on a series of workshops held with stakeholders in the Maritime forest industry on the subject of small private woodlots organized by the National Round Table on Environment and Economy (workshops held through winter/spring of 1996-97; I was a member of the NRTEE Taskforce on Small Private Woodlots and Vice-Chair of the NRTEE through this period).

34. Keith Elwood, Representative of Nova Scotia Joint Venture, "Presentation to the National Round Table on Environment and Economy: Panel Discussion on Private Woodlots," Miramichi, New Brunswick, May 24, 1996.

35. ATI Consulting Corp., Inc., "CAFD 2," Ex-3 and p. 96.

36. Ibid., p. 103.

37. Canadian Press, "Nova Scotia tree-cutting assailed: Government not protecting resource, independent foresters say," *Globe and Mail*, March 28, 1997

38. Canadian Forest Service, Natural Resources Canada, *The State of Canada's Forests, 1996-1997* (Ottawa, 1997).

39. Nova Scotia's Future Forest Alliance, "Fantasy Gardens East: Nova Scotia's Annual Allowable Cut," Information Report No. 1, 1990.

New Brunswick

1. R. Foot, "Timber Land," *The New Brunswick Reader*, February 17, 1996, p. 8.

2. M. Betts and D. Coon, *Working with the Woods: Restoring the Forest and Communities in New Brunswick*, (Fredericton: Conservation Council of New Brunswick, 1996), citing Webster (1991).

3. Timber Management Branch, Department of Natural Resources and Energy, *New Brunswick Forest Inventory (1986) Report*, 1989, p. 23.

4. R. Foot, "Fibre Crunch: Now," *The New Brunswick Reader*, March 2, 1992, p. 8.

5. Betts and Coon, *Working with the Woods*.

6. Quoted in Foot, "Fibre Crunch: Now," p. 8.

7. Quoted in L. Anders Sandberg, "Introduction: Dependent Development and Client States," in L.A. Sandberg, ed., *Trouble in the Woods: Forest Policy and Social Conflict in Nova Scotia and New Brunswick* (Fredericton: Acadiensis, 1992), p. 6.

8. Bill Parenteau, "Pulpwood Marketing in New Brunswick," in Sandberg, ed., *Trouble in the Woods*, p. 117.

9. Ibid., pp. 95-96.

10. Ibid., pp. 116-117.

11. Quoted in ibid., p. 122.

12. Steve Llewellyn, "We're talking about resource being destroyed," *Fredericton Daily Gleaner*, September 22, 1995.

13. R. Foot, "Fibre Crunch: 2015," *The New Brunswick Reader*, March 2, 1996, p. 6.

14. R. Foot, "Timber Land," p. 11.

15. Quoted in E. May, *Budworm Battles* (Tantallon: Four East, 1980), p. 46.

16. Ibid.

17. Ibid.

18. Quoted in ibid., p. 26.

19. The federal decision on fenitrothion left the door open to its use against insects other than budworm if an economically acceptable alternative insecticide could not be found.

20. Personal communication from David Coon, Conservation Council of New Brunswick.

21. Compiled from data from the Department of Natural Resources and Energy, Timber Management Branch, *Annual Reports, 1952 to 1994*.

22. Private communication, Department of Natural Resources official interview with Matthew Betts.

23. R. Clearwater and D. Coon, "Biodiversity Primer 1995" (Conservation Council of New Brunswick, 1995).

24. B. Freedman et al., "Forestry practices and biodiversity, with particular reference to the Maritime Provinces of eastern Canada," *Environmental Review* 2 (1994).

25. Ibid.

26. R. Foot, "Timber Land," p. 7.

27. New Brunswick Department of Natural Resources, *Forest Management Plan Highlights, 1992*, Crown License 1-10.

28. Fish and Wildlife Branch, Department of Natural Resources, *Management of Forest Habitat in New Brunswick* (Fredericton, 1995).

29. New Brunswick Department of Natural Resources, *Forest Management Plan Highlights, 1992*, Crown License 1-10.

30. Fish and Wildlife Branch, Department of Natural Resources, *Management of Forest Habitat in New Brunswick* (Fredericton, 1995).

31. Quoted in R. Foot, "The endangered spaces debate," *The New Brunswick Reader*, March 2, 1996, p. 12.

32. R. Foot, "Timber Land," p. 9.

33. Ibid., p. 10.

34. T. Clark, *Timber Supply and Endangered Spaces: A World Wildlife Fund Canada Discussion Paper* (Toronto: World Wildlife Fund, 1996), p. 55.

35. Canadian Forest Service, Department of Natural Resources, *The State of Canada's Forests, 1994* (Ottawa, 1994) and *The State of Canada's Forests, 1996-1997* (Ottawa, 1997).

36. Timber Management Branch, Department of Natural Resources and Energy, *Annual Reports*.

37. Queen's-Charlotte Forest Management Plan, 1992, Crown Licence no. 6.

38. T. Erdle, "Timber Management in New Brunswick," in D. Brand, ed., *Canada's Timber Resources: Proceedings of a National Conference*, held June 1990 at the Victoria Conference Centre, Victoria (Chalk River: Petawawa National Forestry Institute, 1991), Petawawa National Forestry Institute, Information Report PI-X-101 (Fredericton, 1994), p. 94.

39. Queen's-Charlotte Forest Management Plan, 1992, Crown Licence no. 6, p. 26.

40. See Part 1, Chapter 2: Myths, Propaganda and Half-Truths on mechanization and job loss.

41. Peter DeMarsh, Presentation to the National Round Table on the Environment and the Economy, Miramichi, New Brunswick, May 24, 1996.

42. Private communication: Department of Natural Resources official interview with Matthew Betts.

43. Janice Harvey, "The Ugly Truth about Our Clearcutting Policy," *Telegraph-Journal*, June 12, 1996.

44. R. Foot, "The miller's tale," *Telegraph-Journal*, April 20, 1996.

45. T. Erdle, "Timber Management in New Brunswick," p. 8.

46. Ibid, p. 8.

47. *Report of the Partnership for Sustainable Coastal Communities and Marine Ecosystems* (Ottawa: National Round Table on the Environment and Economy, Fall 1995).

Prince Edward Island

1. Canadian Forest Service, Department of Natural Resources, *The State of Canada's Forests, 1994* (Ottawa, 1994), p. 89.

2. Personal communication from Gary Schneider, Environmental Coalition of Prince Edward Island, 1996.

3. Department of Agriculture, Fisheries and Forestry, Forestry Division, *Report on Forest Resource Issues, An Update of the 1990 Forest Inventory* (Charlottetown, August 1995).

4. Information from the National Round Table on Environment and Economy, "State of the Debate Report on Maritime Small Woodlots," work in progress, spring 1997.

5. PEI Forestry Branch, press release, "Forestry Cuts its own Future," quoted in the *Guardian*, February 1, 1996.

6. G. Schneider, "Acadian Calamity," *Rural Delivery*, March 1990, p. 32.

7. Ibid., p. 33.

Chapter 9: Quebec

1. Ministry of Natural Resources, *Quebec's Forests: Ecology—Biodiversity—Forest resource protection* (Government of Quebec, June 1996).

2. Hugh Gray, letters from Canada written in 1806, 1807 and 1808, cited in A.R.M. Lower, *North American Assault on Canadian Forests* (New York: Greenwood Press, 1938).

3. M. Ross, *Forest Management in Canada* (Calgary: Canadian Institute of Resources Law, 1995), p. 65.

4. J. Cooperman, "Cutting Down Canada," in B. Devall, ed., *Clearcut: The Tragedy of Industrial Forestry* (San Francisco: Sierra Club Books, 1993).

5. Pierre Dubois, "Une 'old-growth' québécoise au Témiscamingue," *Forêt conservation* 59/5 (September 1992).

6. Ross, *Forest Management in Canada*, p. 207.

7. D. Lachance et al., *Health of Sugar Maples in Canada*, Info Report ST-X-10 (Ottawa: Canadian Forest Service, Natural Resources Canada, 1995).

8. J. Gauvin, "Forest Development in Quebec: New Models on the Horizon?" in Natural Resources Canada, ed., *Timber Supply in Canada* (Ottawa: Canada Communications Group, 1994), p. 158.

9. Mitch Lansky, *Beyond the Beauty Strip: Saving What's Left of Our Forests* (Gardiner: Tilbury House, 1992), p. 47.

10. Cooperman, "Cutting Down Canada."

11. Lansky, *Beyond the Beauty Strip*, p. 206.

12. Cooperman, "Cutting Down Canada."

13. Ross, *Forest Management in Canada*, p. 80.

14. Felice Page, "Cultural Clearcuts: the Sociology of Timber Communities in the Pacific Northwest," in Devall, ed., *Clearcut*, p. 162.

15. D. Haley and M.K. Luckert, *Forest Tenures in Canada: A Framework for Policy Analysis*, Information Report E-X-43 (Ottawa: Forestry Canada, 1990), p. 76.

16. Gauvin, "Forest Development in Quebec," pp. 203-209.

17. Ross, *Forest Management in Canada*, pp. 80-81.

18. Miller Freeman Inc., *Company Profiles: Abitibi-Price* (St. John's, 1994).

19. J. MacFarland, "An unusual team, on paper," *The Globe and Mail Report on Business*, February 19, 1997, p. B-1.

20. Miller Freeman Inc., *Company Profiles: Kruger* (St. John's, 1994).

21. Allan Swift, "Stumpage fees puts lumber industry at risk," *The Ottawa Citizen*, April 23, 1997, p. C4.

22. Grand Council of the Cree, *Crees and Trees* (Ottawa, 1996), p. 4.

23. While the companies are to be responsible for planting, the province provides the seedlings and restocks for NSR (not satisfactorily restocked) areas: Haley and Luckert, *Forest Tenures in Canada*, p. 75.

24. "La Forêt publiques: Nouvelles règles du jeu," *Forêt conservation* supplement (September 1987); my translation.

25. J. Dufour, "Towards Sustainability of Canada's Forests," p. 100.

26. Dufour, quoting Vanier at p. 199.

27. Boyce Richardson, *The Algonquins Defend the Forest*, National Film Board video, Barriere Lake, Quebec, 1990.

28. World Commission on Environment and Development, *Our Common Future* (New York: Oxford University Press, 1987), p. 116.

29. E. May, "Cultural Survival Canada Report—Algonquins of Barriere Lake," *Cultural Survival Quarterly* 15/2 (1991), 79.

30. In this period, 1991-92, I worked for the Algonquins of Barriere Lake in the implementation phase of the agreement. I was constantly amazed by their patience and forbearance in the face of the complete unreliability of any government assurance. I honestly do not know how they kept such a principled focus on the outcome of the Trilateral Agreement during the face of daily provocative actions. The conflict that centered on the existing permits finally resulted in arbitration. At this writing, the Integrated Resource Management Plan is on hold due to the uncertainty about Band Council leadership.

31. Tony Wawatie, "Algonquins of Barriere Lake—Update," April 1997, unpublished.

32. Vincent Malenfant Inc., *Economic Output from the James Bay Forest*, Forest Economics report commissioned by the Grand Council of the Cree, July 1996.

33. Grand Council of the Cree, *Crees and Trees*, p. 1.

34. G. Drouin, "Les parcs, trois ans plus tard," *Forêt conservation* 61/6 (March/April 1995), 23.

35. Canadian Forest Service, Department of Natural Resources, *The State of Canada's Forests, 1991* (Ottawa, 1992), pp. 12, 16.

36. Ministère du Loisir, de la Chasse et de la Pêche (Ministère de l'Environnement et de la Faune), *Liste des espèces de la faune vertébrée susceptible d'être désignée menacée ou vulnérable* (Quebec: Gouvernement du Québec, 1992).

37. The other Canadian provinces to ban 2,4,5-T use were Ontario and Saskatchewan.

38. Ross, *Forest Management in Canada*, p. 164.

39. Personal communication with Henri Jacob, Regroupement Écologiste de Val d'Or et Environs, 1996.

40. Grand Council of the Cree, *Crees and Trees*, p. 10.

41. Canadian Forest Service, Department of Natural Resources, *The State of Canada's Forests, 1996-1997* (Ottawa, 1997).

42. P. Dubois, "Bilan environnemental de la forêt québécoise," document synthèse, Bureau d'audiences publiques sur l'environnement, May 1991.

43. Miller Freeman Inc., *Company Profiles: Kruger* (St. John's, 1993), p. 380.

44. Clark, *Timber Supply and Endangered Spaces*.

45. The figures for 1993 are from Canadian Forest Service, Department of Natural Resources, *The State of Canada's Forests, 1994*; the figure for 1995 is from Canadian Forest Service, Department of Natural Resources, *The State of Canada's Forests, 1996-1997*.

46. Ross, *Forest Management in Canada*, p. 212.

47. Douglas Williams and Jordan S. Tanz, "Summary and Analysis of Provincial and Territorial Timber Supply Status Reports," in Natural Resources Canada, ed., *Timber Supply in Canada* (Ottawa: Canada Communication Group, 1994), where Quebec is not mentioned.

48. Swift, "Stumpage fees puts lumber industry at risk," p. C4.

49. Ibid.

Chapter 10: Ontario

1. Jimmy Kennedy, "Teddy Bears Picnic."

2. Canadian Forest Service, Natural Resources Canada, *The State of Canada's Forests, 1995-1996* (Ottawa, 1996), p. 95.

3. The Ministry of Northern Development and Mines is overseeing a development initiative for the north. While logging is not the focal point, it is considered possible within the planning process.

4. Canadian Forest Service, Natural Resources Canada, *The State of Canada's Forests, 1994* (Ottawa, 1995), p. 22.

5. B. Bynes, "Saving the Countryside: Conserving Rural Character and the Countryside of Southern Ontario," Conservation Council of Ontario, 1994.

6. G.M. Allen, P.F.J. Eagles and S.D. Price, "Conserving Carolinian Canada" (Waterloo: University of Waterloo Press, 1990).

7. A. Jamieson, *Winter Studies and Summer Rambles* (1836-37), p. 6.

8. J. Theberge, *Legacy: The Natural History of Ontario* (Toronto: McClelland & Stewart, 1989).

9. The provincial government Old Growth Forest Policy Advisory Committee estimated the proportion of old-growth red and white pine in the pre-settlement forest at 30-40 percent. (Ontario Ministry of Natural Resources, *Interim Report on Conserving Old Growth Red and White Pine* (Toronto, 1993).) The figure is probably conservative as others have estimated the original proportion at 50-60 percent. See: P.A. Quinby, "Old Growth Eastern White Pine—An Endangered Ecosystem," *Forest Landscape Baselines*, 2 (1993).

10. R.H. Bonnycastle, *Canada and the Canadians in 1846* (London, 1846) cited in Quinby, ibid.

11. Old Growth Public Advisory Committee, Ontario Ministry of Natural Resources, *Interim Report on Conserving Old Growth Red and White Pine* (Toronto, 1993).

12. Wildlands League, *Eastern White Pine Forests in Ontario, Ecology, Threats and Survival*, Forest Ecology Series, Factsheet 1, 1995.

13. From a letter written in 1871 by Sir John A. Macdonald, cited in *Forest History* 11/3 (New Haven: Forest History Society, 1968: National Archives of Canada C3207).

14. "Ontario," in Department of Energy and Resource Management, *Mississippi Valley Conservation Report 1970*.

15. Macdonald, cited in *Forest History* 11/3.

16. B. Fernow, "Forest Resources and Forestry in Ontario," in Adam Short and Arthur G. Doughty, *Canada and its Provinces* (Toronto: Publisher's Association of Canada, 1912), Vol. 18, p. 599.

17. L.L. Rogers and E.L. Lindquist, *Supercanopy White Pine and Wildlife*, White Pine Symposium Proceedings, Minnesota, U.S.A., 1992.

18. M. Stabb, *Ontario's Old Growth: a learner's handbook* (Ottawa: Canadian Nature Federation, 1996).

19. C. Wilkins, "Beset by disease, Ontario's provincial tree is not regenerating," *Canadian Geographic* 114: 59-66, 1991.

20. G.P. Buchert, "Genetics of white pine and the implications for management and conservation," *The Forestry Chronicle* 70: 4, pp. 427-432, 1994.

21. T.J. Carleton, and P. MacLellan, "Woody vegetation responses to fire versus clear-cut logging: a comparative survey in the central Canadian boreal forest," *Ecoscience* 1(2) 1994, cited with more details in Part I, Chapter 2: Myths, Propaganda and Half-Truths.

22. K. Hearnden, Chair, *Report on the Status of Forest Regeneration*, Ontario Independent Forest Audit Committee, 1992.

23. A. Perera, Ontario Forest Research Institute, paper presented at "Global to Local: Ecological Land Classification Conference," 1994.

24. Ibid.

25. Wildlife Habitat Canada, *The Status of Wildlife Habitat in Canada: Realities and Visions* (Ottawa, July 1991).

26. F.T. Flemming and K. Kloski, *Moose Habitat studies and Moose Management Unit 40, with particular reference to the effects on roads and cutovers* (Temagami: Ontario Ministry of Natural Resources, 1976).

27. "Strategy to halt decline in moose populations," MNR Fact Sheet, March 1997. The study encompassed Wildlife Management Units 38, 39, 40 and 41.

28. Personal communication with Tim Gray, WWF Endangered Spaces Coordinator for Ontario.

29. B. Hodgins and J. Benidickson, *The Temagami Experience* (Toronto: University of Toronto Press, 1989).

30. Ibid., p. 293.

31. Ibid.

32. Ibid.

33. T. Gray, "Temagami Update: What's it going to be, Mr. Harris?" *Wildland News*, Summer 1996; most recent information from personal communication from T. Gray.

34. P. Quinby et al., *An Ancient Forest Atlas of the Lake Temagami Site Region (4E)* (Ottawa: Canadian Nature Federation, April 1996).

35. Canadian Forest Service, Natural Resources Canada, *The State of Canada's Forests, 1994* (Ottawa, 1995), p. 91.

36. Ross, *Forest Management in Canada*.

37. B. Callaghan, "Ontario Status Report," in Natural Resources Canada, ed., *Timber Supply in Canada* (Ottawa: Canada Communications Group, 1994).

38. Canadian Forest Service, Natural Resources Canada, *Compendium of Canadian Forestry Statistics, 1994* (Ottawa: Canadian Council of Forest Ministers, 1995).

39. K.A. Armson, "Forest Management in Ontario," Ontario Ministry of Natural Resources (Toronto: Queen's Park Press, 1976).

40. G. Baskerville, "An Audit of the Crown Forests of Ontario," Ontario Ministry of Natural Resources, (Toronto: Queens Printer for Ontario, 1986), cited by Marcelo Levy, "Timber Supply in Ontario: Environmentally Sensitive and Transparent," in Natural Resources Canada, ed., *Timber Supply in Canada*.

41. Levy, "Timber Supply in Ontario," citing the Lakehead Report to the Royal Commission on the Northern Environment and the Baskerville audit (1986).

42. Callaghan, "Ontario Status Report," p. A-71.

43. R. Sawn, "Legal Implications of the Crown Forest Sustainability Act," in *Operating under Ontario's New Crown Forest Sustainability Act* (Toronto: Insight, 1995).

44. Personal communication from Tim Gray, Wildlands League. The original target was April 1, 1997, but it has been extended by one year.

45. D. Haley and M. Luckert, *Forest Tenures in Canada: A Framework for Policy Analysis*, Information Report E-X-43 (Ottawa: Forestry Canada, 1990). Subsidies are over $40,000 per kilometer for primary roads, $12,000 per kilometer for secondary roads and $471 per kilometer for annual maintenance.

46. Ibid.

47. Ontario Ministry of Natural Resources, *Forest Values: Sustainable Forestry Programme, Forest Management Accounting Framework* (Toronto, 1993). Expenditures averaged $267 million/year over the same period.

48. The renewal charges per cubic meter were: $11.00 for red and white pine; $6.00 for all other conifers; $0.50 for poplar and birch; $8.00 for grade-1 hardwoods; and $1.50 for grade-2 hardwoods.

49. If the market price goes above a certain ceiling, the government's share of industry windfall profits drops to 10 percent.

50. Ontario Ministry of Natural Resources, "Ontario Restructures Forest Management," news release, April 1996.

51. Gray, "Temagami Update."

52. Ross, *Forest Management in Canada*, citing the brief from the Forest for Tomorrow coalition before the Class Environmental Assessment.

53. T. Clark, *Timber Supply and Endangered Spaces: A World Wildlife Fund Canada Discussion Paper* (Toronto: World Wildlife Fund, 1996), citing Ontario Environmental Assessment Board, Reasons for Decision: Class Environmental Assessment, 1994.

54. Canadian Forest Service, Natural Resources Canada, *The State of Canada's Forests, 1994* (Ottawa, 1994), p. 8. The report claims that the 115 requirements of the Ontario Class Environmental Assessment "will change the way forests are managed."

55. M. Kaiser, "Ontario's New Reality: The Timber E.A. and the Crown Forest Act," *Canadian Forest Industries*, March 1996, p. 34.

56. Bill 171, An Act to revise the Crown Timber Act to provide for the sustainability of Crown forests in Ontario, Statutes of Ontario, 1994.

57. T. Gray, "Is Corporate Ownership and the End of Wilderness Ontario's Forest Future?" Wildlands League, April 1997.

58. Ontario's Forest Products Industry, *Hard Choices—Bright Prospects*, Forest Industry Action Group, OMNR, 1993.

59. Numbers derived from: D. Frood and L. Sanders, "Lean and Mean: The Woodland Labyrinth of Ken Buchanan," Northern Insights for the Canadian Paperworkers Union, Thunder Bay, 1992.

60. The E.B. Eddy Group, *A Question of Balance: Third Status Report on Sustainable Development*, December 1996.

61. Frood and Sanders, "Lean and Mean."

62. J. Geddes, *Financial Post*, January 20, 1989.

63. Forest Management Agreements, Five-Year Reviews 1987-1992, OMNR, 1995.

64. Levy, "Timber Supply in Ontario," p. 78, citing Bob Carman, "New Forest Industry/Ontario Government Relationship," Treasury Board presentation, 1994.

65. Mike Innes, Abitibi-Price, "Perspective on Eastern Canada's Timber Supply," Natural Resources Canada, ed., *Timber Supply in Canada*, p. 74.

66. Ontario Ministry of Natural Resources, *Ontario Forest Products and Timber Resource Analysis*, vols. 1 and 2 (1992), cited in Levy, "Timber Supply in Ontario," p. 79.

67. Wildlands League, *Cutting the Future out of Prosperity?*, Forest Diversity/Community Survival Series, Factsheet 2, 1995.

68. Canadian Forest Service, *Compendium of Canadian Forestry Statistics, 1994*: 90 percent. Wildlands League, op. cit: 91 percent in 1996.

69. B. Callaghan, "Ontario Status Report: Assessing Ontario's Timber Supply Future," in Natural Resources Canada, ed., *Timber Supply in Canada*, p. A-74.

70. Ibid., p. A-83.

71. Ibid., p. A-74.

72. Ontario Ministry of Natural Resources, "Forest Industry Developments," press release, February 16, 1995.

73. Ontario Ministry of Natural Resources, "$9 Million Investment Will Help Create 40 New Jobs in Hearst," press release, December 16, 1994.

74. Ontario Ministry of Natural Resources, "Forest Industry Developments."

75. R. Forrest, "Jury Out on Ontario Forest Act," *Logging and Sawmilling Journal* 26/1 (February/March 1995).

76. Ibid.

77. Callaghan, "Ontario Status Report," p. A-81.

Chapter 11: Prairies

Manitoba

1. D. Haley and M.K. Luckert, *Forest Tenures in Canada: A Framework for Policy Analysis*, Information Report E-X-43 (Ottawa: Forestry Canada, 1990), p. 9.

2. V. Werier, "Keeping data from public shows up in Repap fiasco," *Winnipeg Free Press*, May 13, 1989.

3. Ibid.

4. J. Saunders, "Petty ponders sale of Repap," *Globe and Mail Report on Business*, July 16, 1996, p. B-1.

5. R. Foot, "Fibre Crunch: Now," *The New Brunswick Reader*, March 2, 1996, p. 5.

6. Quoted in V. Werier, "Manfor decision raises environmental concerns," *Winnipeg Free Press*, March 25, 1989.

7. Werier, "Keeping data from public shows up in Repap fiasco."

8. Quoted in Werier, "Manfor decision raises environmental concerns."

9. Roy Adams, ed., *Proceedings of the Aspen Symposium*, Natural Resource Research Institute (Duluth, Minnesota, July 25-27, 1989).

10. D. Sullivan, "Louisiana-Pacific's Forest Management License: Not a Clear-Cut Issue," *Canadian Dimension*, April/May 1995.

11. Ibid.

12. "Repap and Manitoba Finalize Development Agreement," Manitoba Government news release, November 6, 1995.

13. P. Lush, "Repap close to the financial brink: Sources say company must find buyer or obtain more credit next week—otherwise it could go under," *Globe and Mail Report on Business*, April 11, 1997, p. B1.

14. D. Kuxhaus, "Repap wins injunction," *Winnipeg Free Press*, April 2, 1996; A. Bray, "Band halts Repap road," *Winnipeg Free Press*, April 9, 1996.

15. D. Sullivan, "Manitoba whitewashes environmental process," *Canadian Dimension*, October/November 1994.

16. Quoted in *Louisiana-Pacific: A Report on the Company's Environmental Policies and Practices* (New York: Council on Economic Priorities, Corporate Environmental Clearing House, May 1992).

17. See discussion of doubling the AAC for hardwood in Part I, Chapter 3: "Over-Cutting and How It Is Justified in Canada."

18. Manitoba news release, November 6, 1995.

19. R. Lamont, "Manitoba Status Report," *Timber Supply in Canada*, pp. A-84-92.

20. Ibid.

21. KPMG Management Consulting, "Manitoba's Forest Plan: Report to Manitoba Natural Resources," 1995, funded by Canada-Manitoba Partnership Agreement in Forestry.

22. "Pitre Honoured with Gift of Appreciation," *The Community Voice*, Pine Falls, Manitoba, September 8, 1994.

23. KPMG, "Manitoba's Forest Plan."

24. D. Sullivan, "Louisiana-Pacific's Forest Management Licence Agreement: Analysis and Implications," Manitoba's Future Forest Alliance, December 11, 1994.

25. Letter to Sierra Club of Canada, from The Hon. Glen Cummings, Minister of Natural Resources, March 18, 1997.

26. KPMG, *Manitoba's Forest Plan; Towards Ecosystem-Based Management*, 1995, pp. 4-58.

27. Williams, "Paper trail of broken promises."

28. Repap, 1997 Annual Operating Plan.

29. KPMG, *Manitoba's Forest Plan*, p. 4-10, and *Status of Wildlife*, Five Year Report to the Legislature on Wildlife 1987-1992.

30. "The First 5-Year Review of Manitoba's Forest Royalty System," Manitoba Natural Resources, Forestry, September 1986.

31. Ibid., pp. 3-25.

32. Letter from Dr. R.A. Westwood, A/Director of Forestry, Department of Natural Resources, Manitoba, to Don Sullivan, April 5, 1996.

33. D. Soprovich, "A submission to the Clean Environment Commission," November 23, 1996.

34. "Environment Canada's Response to Louisiana-Pacific Canada Ltd., Letter of January 3, 1996," Environment Canada, Prairie and Northern Region, January 18, 1996, at p. 8.

35. A. Santin, "Swan River biologist sacked after faulting province over L-P."

36. Letter from W.J. Ball, Manitoba District Office, Forestry Canada, Department of Natural Resources, to Dr. Floyd Phillips, Chairman, Forestry Technical Advisory Committee, August 17, 1995.

37. Letter from J.W. Ball, Forestry Canada, to Larry Strachan, Director Environment Act, Manitoba Department of Environment, December 15, 1995.

38. Ibid., p. 2.

39. Ibid.

40. Ball, letter to Strachan, December 15, 1995: "I apologise for not appearing at the CEC environmental review hearings as previously agreed; however, I received instructions that Thursday morning [the day he was to have testified] not to appear."

Saskatchewan

1. J.H. Richards and K.I. Fung, "Natural History of Saskatchewan Forest," in R.T. Coupland and J.S. Rowe., eds., *Atlas of Saskatchewan* (Saskatoon: University of Saskatchewan Press, 1969).

2. R.T. Coupland and J.S. Rowe, "Early history of logging in Saskatchewan," in Coupland and Rowe, eds., *Atlas of Saskatchewan*.

3. National Research Council, Canadian Forest Service, *Saskatchewan Environment and Resource Management: Focus on Forests in Saskatchewan*, 1994, draft.

4. Draft Concept Plan for Forest Management in the Hudson Bay and Cumberland House Supply Areas, Forestry Branch, Saskatchewan Environment and Resource Management, August 1994.

5. Delcan Western Ltd., *State of the Resource Report* (Prince Albert: Saskatchewan Environment and Resource Management, April 1993), Figure 5-13, p. 143.

6. Environmental Impact Statement for Oriented Strand Board Plant (Hudson Bay, Saskatchewan, September 29, 1995), p. 1.9.

7. "Weyerhaeuser Canada Ltd.—Prince Albert Pulp Company Ltd. and UCFS Paper Mill Development," Government-Weyerhaeuser Agreement, September 8, 1986, Vol. 1.

8. *The Norsask Forest Management Project*, Vol. 3: *Technical summary*, November 1995; MISTIK Management Ltd., Meadow Lake, Saskatchewan, and Crown Investment Corporation of Saskatchewan, *Annual Report, 1995*.

9. D. Haley and M.K. Luckert, *Forest Tenures in Canada: A Framework for Policy Analysis*, Information Report E-X-43 (Ottawa: Forestry Canada, 1990), p. 54.

10. Province of Saskatchewan, *Stumpage Fees and Reforestation Fees, 1996* (Saskatoon, 1996).

11. Delcan Western Ltd., *State of the Resource Report* (Prince Albert: Saskatchewan Environment and Resource Management, April 1993), p. 145.

12. Isidore Campbell, Jobs and Environment Conference 1994, *Employment and Sustainable Development: Opportunities for Canada* (Winnipeg: International Institute for Sustainable Development).

13. Action Alert from Protectors of Mother Earth, undated.

14. P. Hanley, "Forest Adventure faces legal morass," *Saskatoon Star-Phoenix*, November 2, 1992.

15. Delcan Western Ltd., *State of the Resource Report*, p. 41.

16. M. Fitzsimmons, "Community Review—Forested Farmland," *Saskatchewan Biodiversity Conference*, Regina, April 11-13, p. 1-2.

17. David Lindenas, "Saskatchewan Status Report," in Natural Resources Canada, ed., *Timber Supply in Canada* (Ottawa: Canada Communications Group, 1994), p. A-93.

18. L. Lawton, *A Status Report of Protected Areas in Saskatchewan* (Saskatoon: Saskatchewan Environment and Resource Management, October 1993).

19. C. Varcoe, "New Forestry Law may force Weyerhaeuser to kill expansion," *Regina Leader-Post*, March 18-22, 1996.

20. B. Bradon, "Timber companies fuming," *Saskatoon Star-Phoenix*, March 15, 1996, front page.

21. Varcoe, "New Forestry Law may force Weyerhaeuser to kill expansion."

22. Bradon, "Timber companies fuming."

23. Personal communication from Joys Dancer. "An Act respecting the Management of Forest Resources," assented to June 25, 1996. Implementation of increased stumpage fees will be determined through ongoing negotiations of the FMLAs.

24. Lindenas, "Saskatchewan Status Report," p. A-93.

25. Delcan Western Ltd. et al., *State of the Resource Report*, Province of Saskatchewan Integrated Forest Resources Management Plan (Prince Albert, April 1993), section 4.1.6.

26. Canadian Forest Service, Department of Natural Resources, *The State of Canada's Forests, 1996-1997* (Ottawa, 1997), p. 92.

27. Delcan Western Ltd., *State of the Resource Report*.

28. Again, the provincial 1993 review concluded: "Definite softwood supply shortages occur in the southeastern portion of the commercial Forest Zone ... the young age classes are under-represented ... and a large component of NSR (Not Satisfactorily Restocked) land is present in this area ... This pattern suggests a history of severe softwood over-cutting in the last fifty years and minimal softwood reforestation ... the bulk of the uncommitted (to FMLAs) area is in the eastern portion, most seriously over-cut in the past and under significant commercial pressure:" Delcan Western Ltd., *State of the Resource Report*, pp. 143-44. Other government documents acknowledge the problem as well: "Some of this surplus (above harvest level) timber is located in remote areas and its harvest is not, at present, economically feasible. At the same time, some regions of the province are experiencing shortages of harvestable conifers." *Saskatchewan Forests*, Saskatchewan-Canada Partnership Agreements (Saskatoon, Environment Canada, March 1994). "Over-utilization of the timber resource is currently limited to our eastern timber supply areas. In this area softwood harvest levels exceed softwood (AAC) primarily because the existing mill facilities cannot utilize the small softwood timber." Lindenas, "Saskatchewan Status Report," p. A-100.

29. Delcan Western Ltd., *State of the Resource Report*, p. 121.

30. Personal communication: interview by Joys Dancer with Forestry Board representative.

31. Chris Varcoe, "Hudson Bay Sawmill delayed one year," *Saskatoon Star-Phoenix*, February 20, 1996, p. C10.

32. A. Gore, *Earth in the Balance: Ecology and the Human Spirit* (Boston, New York, London: Houghton Mifflin Company, 1992), p. 191, see also H. Daly, and John B. Cobb, *For the Common Good* (Boston: Beacon Press, 1989).

Alberta

1. B. Devall, ed., *Clearcut: The Tragedy of Industrial Forestry* (San Francisco: Sierra Club Books, 1993), p. 154.

2. C. Henderson, "Status Report on Alberta," in Natural Resources Canada, ed., *Timber Supply in Canada* (Ottawa: Canada Communication Group, 1994), p. A-10.

3. Canadian Forest Service, Natural Resources Canada, Canadian Council of Forest Ministers, *Compendium of Canadian Forestry Statistics 1994* (Ottawa, 1995).

4. M. Ross, *Forest Management in Canada*, p. 85.

5. A. Nikiforuk and E. Struzik, "The Great Forest Sell-Off," *Report on Business Magazine*, November 1989.

6. Henderson, "Status Report on Alberta," p. A-10.

7. J. McInnis, "The Sale of Alberta's Forests," *NeWest Review* 20/5 (June/July 1995).

8. *Alberta Environmental Protection Annual Reports, 1994/1995* and *Forest, Lands and Wildlife Annual Reports 1991/1992*.

10. B. Sadler, "International Study of the Effectiveness of Environmental Assessment: Final Report," *Canadian Environmental Assessment Agency, International Association for Impact Assessment* (Ottawa, June 1996), p. 213.

10. Based on 1993 prices: Jim Cooperman, "Cutting Down Canada," in Devall, ed., *Clearcut*, p. 57.

11. J. Goddard, *Last Stand of the Lubicon Cree* (Vancouver: Douglas & McIntyre, 1992). Although I refer to Goddard's work, I do not condone his vicious and inaccurate attack on Farley Mowat.

12. McInnis, "The Sale of Alberta's Forests," and personal communication.

13. Ibid.

14. Cooperman, "Cutting Down Canada," p. 57.

15. Canadian Forest Service, Department of Natural Resources, *The State of Canada's Forests, 1996-1997* (Ottawa, 1997).

16. Henderson, "Status Report on Alberta."

17. Alberta Lands and Wildlife Department, *Impact of Forest Industry Development on the Alberta Forest Service* (Edmonton, 1991).

18. Henderson, "Status Report on Alberta," pp. A-111 and A-110.

19. Alberta-Pacific, 1995 Detailed Forest Management Plan.

20. D. Haley and M.K. Luckert, *Forest Tenures in Canada: A Framework for Policy Analysis*, Information Report E-X-43 (Ottawa: Forestry Canada, 1990).

21. D. Dancik et al., *Forest Management in Alberta, Report of the Expert Review Panel* (Edmonton: Alberta Energy/Forestry, Lands and Wildlife, 1990), p. 26.

22. McInnis, "The Sale of Alberta's Forests."

23. Ibid., p. 9.

24. Canadian Forest Service, Department of Natural Resources, *The State of Canada's Forests, 1996-1997* (Ottawa, 1997).

25. Alberta Liberal Caucus press release, January 24, 1995.

26. J.B. Stelfox, *Relationships between Stand Age, Stand Structure, and Biodiversity in Aspen Mixedwood Stands in Alberta* (Vegreville and Edmonton: Alberta Environmental Center and the Canadian Forest Service, 1995).

27. Canadian Broadcasting Corporation, "The Great Northern Forest," *The Nature of Things* (Sun. April 13, 1997).

28. McInnis, "The Sale of Alberta's Forests," p. 8.

29. Newfoundland, Prince Edward Island, Nova Scotia, New Brunswick, Quebec and Manitoba include private lands in the AACs; Alberta, Ontario, Saskatchewan and British Columbia do not: Canadian Forest Service, Department of Natural Resources, *The State of Canada's Forests, 1995-1996.*

30. McInnis, "The Sale of Alberta's Forests," p. 8.

31. Alberta Environmental Protection, "Alberta's Timber Supply," *Forestry in Alberta Fact Sheet* (Forest Management Division, Land and Forest Service, May 1996), No. 003.

32. Nikiforuk, "The Great Alberta Timber Rush," excerpts from an article that appeared in *The Georgia Strait*, in "Logging and Private Land: Not in my Own Backyard," Western Canada Wilderness Committee, Boreal Forest Campaign, *Educational Report* 14/8 (Summer 1995).

33. B.C. mills were offering $65 per tonne at the stump in 1994. Converting on the basis of 1 cubic meter equaling 750 kilograms of conifer produces $48.75. Source: Ken Glover, Alberta Provincial Government Private Woodlot Program, 1995, Ministry of Forests (personal communication with Karen Baltgailis, Western Canada Wilderness Committee, Edmonton).

34. Impact of Forest Industry Development on the Alberta Forest Service.

35. Cooperman, "Cutting Down Canada," in Devall, ed., *Clearcut*, p. 57.

36. Sierra Club of Canada, *Rio Report Card 1996* (Ottawa, June 11, 1996).

37. J. Stelfox, "Effect of Clear Cut Logging and Scarification on Wildlife Habitats in West Central Alberta," Canadian Wildlife Service, 1984, p. 271.

38. Canadian Forest Service, Department of Natural Resources, *The State of Canada's Forests, 1996-1997.*

39. V. Lieffers and E. MacDonald, "Ecology and Control Strategies for Calamagrotis Canadensis in Boreal Forest Sites," National Research Council of Canada, 23 (September 1993).

40. Henderson, "Status Report on Alberta," p. 86.

41. Alberta Environmental Protection, *Summary of Joint LSF/F and W Enforcement Activities* (March 6, 1995—May 1, 1995); R. Volman, "City not told about Mill's pollution violations," *Fort McMurray Today*, July 2, 1992; Alberta Environmental Protection, Enforcement History Report, 1988-1996.

42. T. Marr-Laing, "Regulatory Reform: Deregulation by any other name," *Environment Network News*, No. 44, March /April 1996.

43. *Pollution Control Division Enforcement Action report*, September 1, 1993 to December 31, 1994.

Chapter 12: British Columbia

1. B.C. Ministry of the Environment, Lands and Parks/Environment Canada, *State of the Environment Report for British Columbia*, 1994.

2. D. MacKay, *Empire of Wood—The MacMillan Bloedel Story* (Vancouver: Douglas & McIntyre, 1982).

3. Ibid.

4. Ibid, p. 19.

5. K. Drushka, *Stumped: The Forest Industry in Transition.*

6. John Gray, "Royal Commission and Forest Policy in British Columbia: A Review of the Pearse Report," *Canadian Public Policy*, 3 (1977), p. 218.

7. Drushka, *Stumped.*

8. Drushka, *Stumped*, p. 74.

9. Canadian Council of Forest Ministers, *Compendium of Canadian Forestry Statistics, 1994* (Ottawa, 1995).

10. B.C. Ministry of Forests, *Annual Reports*. 1991-92: 166,000 hectares; 1992-93: 196,000 hectares; 1993-94: 180,000; and 1994-95: 160,000 hectares plus another 30,000 hectares on private land.

11. B.C. Ministry of Forests, Annual Reports, 1971-1993/94.

12. In British Columbia, the total harvest always exceeds the AAC as the latter does not include logging on private and unregulated Crown land.

13. B.C. Ministry of Forests, *Forest Range and Recreation Resource Analysis and Addendum* (Victoria, 1994).

14. Land Use Coordination Office, "Protected High Elevation, Low Elevation and Non-Forested Areas of B.C.: Provincial Summary," *Land Use Coordination Office Report, 1997*.

15. J. Cooperman, "B.C.'s Old Growth Forest Crisis," *British Columbia Environmental Report*, Summer 1996.

16. E. May, *Paradise Won*.

17. Forest Resources Commission, *The Future of Our Forests* (Victoria, 1991).

18. B.C. Forest Sector Strategy Committee, Resource Working Group, *Interim and Final Reports*, 1994.

19. Forest Resources Commission, *The Future of Our Forests*, April 1991.

20. Drushka, *Stumped*.

21. Ministry of Forests Annual Reports, includes private lands.

22. Gray, "Royal Commission and Forest Policy in British Columbia."

23. Quoted in Drushka, *Stumped*, p. 84.

24. D. Haley and M.K. Luckert, *Forest Tenures in Canada*, p. 99.

25. May, *Paradise Won*, p. 131.

26. Ibid., p. 53.

27. Ibid.

28. Ian Miller, "British Columbia Status Report on Timber Supply," in Natural Resources Canada, ed., *Timber Supply in Canada* (Ottawa: Canada Communication Group, 1994), p. A-129.

29. B.C. Ministry of Forests, *Forest Range and Recreation Resource Analysis and Addendum* (Victoria, 1994).

30. Sierra Club of Western Canada, *Ancient Rainforests at Risk* (Victoria, 1993).

31. B.C. Ministry of Forests, *An Inventory of Undeveloped Watersheds in British Columbia*, Recreation Branch Technical Report (Victoria, 1992), p. 2.

32. The term "coast" encompasses the coastal fringe, not including Vancouver Island or Haida Gwaii (the Queen Charlottes). Sierra Club mapping of the coastal forest is of the larger area, encompassing both Vancouver Island and Haida Gwaii.

33. Sierra Club of British Columbia, "Half of B.C.'s Ancient Temperate Rainforest Gone," press release, March 19, 1997; data based on satellite information and six years of mapping and research.

34. T. Jones and F. Depey, "An Inventory of Undeveloped Watersheds in the Southern Interior of British Columbia," unpublished report, 1991.

35. K. Moore, "An Inventory of Watersheds in the Coastal Temperate Forests of British Columbia," *Earthlife/Ecotrust*, 1991.

36. V. Palmer, "Government's own forests reports show Greenpeace has a point," *Vancouver Sun*, April 22, 1997. LRHL estimated at 550,000 cubic meters.

37. K. Moore, "Where Is It and How Much Is Left? The State of Temperate Rainforest in British Columbia," *Forest Planning Canada* 6/4 (1990), 17.

38. Ibid., citing B.C. Ministry of Forests, *Executive Summary: Towards an Old-Growth Strategy*, March 1990.

39. Jim Cooperman, "Cutting Down Canada," 1993 Sierra Club Mapping Project Report, p. 32.

40. May, *Paradise Won*.

41. Canadian Forest Service, Department of Natural Resources, *The State of Canada's Forests, 1995-1996* (Ottawa, 1996).

42. *Overcutting the Chilcotin: Putting at Risk Southern B.C.'s Great Herd*, published by BC Wild, 1997.

43. R. Tripp, "Findings from the Application and Effectiveness of the Coastal Fisheries Forestry Guidelines in Selected Cutblocks on Vancouver Island, 1992," cited in BC Wild, "Forest Practices in British Columbia: Not a World Class Act" (Vancouver: BC Wild, 1995).

44. Ministry of Environment, Land and Parks; Ministry of Forests; and Department of Fisheries and Oceans, *A Preliminary List of Watershed Assessment, Restoration and Evaluation Projects for the Watershed Restoration Program* (Vancouver, 1994).

45. T.L. Slaney, K.D. Hyatt et al, "Status of Anadromous Salmon and Trout in B.C. and the Yukon," *American Fisheries Society Journal*, 21, 10, pp. 20-35.

46. I. Harding and E. McCullum, eds., *Biodiversity in British Columbia*, p. 263; and personal communication with Jim Cooperman.

47. Communication with the author. See also T. Goward and A. MacKinnon, "B.C.'s Inland Rainforests," *The Log* (Fall 1996) 13; T. Goward, "Lichens of British Columbia: rare species and priorities for inventory," Research Branch, B.C. Ministry of Forests and Habitat Protection Branch, B.C. Ministry of Environment, Lands and Parks, Working Paper (Victoria: 08/1996).

48. H. Armleder and S. Stevenson, "Silvicultural Systems to Maintain Caribou Habitat in Managed British Columbia Forests," in Land Management Handbook, *Innovative Silvicultural Systems in Boreal Forests* (Victoria: B.C. Ministry of Forests, 1986), p. 83.

49. G. Hamilton, "Clayoquot Sound's quieter, gentler face of logging," *Vancouver Sun*, June 29, 1996.

50. *Vancouver Sun*, November 10, 1993.

51. G. Hamilton, "Forest code change allows more logging," *Vancouver Sun*, Business section, March 2, 1996.

52. Forest Practices Code, Biodiversity Guidebook.

53. G. McDade, "B.C.'s Forest 'Clearcutting' Code," guest editorial, *British Columbia Environmental Report*, Summer 1996.

54. C. Osterman, "MacBlo set to report record large losses," *Globe and Mail Report on Business*, February 7, 1997, p. B-2.

55. Price Waterhouse report, March 4, 1997, cited in B.C. Environmental Network Forest Caucus news release, "Environmentalists tell industry, don't destroy the environment to make a profit," March 1, 1997.

56. M. Cernetig, "Under Siege," *Globe and Mail Report on Business Magazine*, May 1997, p. 51.

57. P. Lush, "Cost of B.C. logs soars 75% in 4 years: study: Industry blames provincial forest policy, higher stumpage, royalty and compliance fees," *Globe and Mail Report on Business*, April 7, 1997, p. B-5.

58. The smaller companies pay more stumpage, as they have historically, but they are not required to plant and thin. The requirement to return a forest to "free to grow" conditions increases the cost for large companies.

59. *Broken Promises: The truth about what's happening to British Columbia's forests*, Greenpeace, April 1997.

60. The solid wood portion of the B.C. industry was profitable with profits of $475 million, in a year when pulp companies lost $625 million. Companies operating in the Interior also made a profit of $510 million. The average cost per log in the Interior was just four dollars above costs in Ontario and Quebec. It was only companies operating on the coast, along the steeper slopes, who lost money.

61. B.C. Environmental Network Forest Caucus news release, "Environmentalists tell industry, don't destroy the environment to make a profit."

62. *Broken Promises: The truth about what's happening to British Columbia's forests*, Greenpeace, April 1997.

63. R. Schwindt and T. Heaps, *Chopping up the Money Tree: Distributing The Wealth from British Columbia's Forests*, The David Suzuki Foundation, June 1996.

64. Cernetig, "Under Siege," p. 56.

65. B.C. Ministry of Forests, *Range and Timber Analysis* (Victoria, 1984), cited in J. Cooperman, "The Elephant under the Table: A Critique of B.C.'s Timber Supply Review," *British Columbia Environmental Report* 5/3 (September 1994), 7.

66. Ibid.

67. Ian Miller, "British Columbia Status Report on Timber Supply," p. A-131.

68. J. Cooperman, "The Elephant under the Table," B.C. Ministry of Forests, *Review of the Timber Supply Analysis Process for B.C. Timber Supply Areas: Final Report* (Victoria, March 1991), p. 4.

69. B.C. Ministry of Forests, Timber Supply Review documentation, 1995-1996; K.L. Runyon, *Canada's Timber Supply: Current Status and Outlook*, Forestry Canada Information Report E-X-45.

70. Revised Statutes of B.C., 1979, c. 140, section 28(g)(i).

71. *Sierra Club of Western Canada* v. *British Columbia (Chief Forester)*, (1993), 13 C.E.L.R. (N.S.) 13 (B.C.S.C.) .

72. Forest Resources Commission, *The Future of Our Forests* (Victoria, 1991).

73. B.C. Ministry of Forests, *Annual Report 1993/94* (Victoria, 1991).

74. G. Utzig and M. Walmsley, *Evaluation of Soil Degradation as a Factor Affecting Forest Productivity in British Columbia—A Problem Analysis*, FRDA Report 025.

75. *Environment on the Brink*, Forest Policy Watch, March 1997. This figure does not include a further approximate two million hectares of pre-1982 NSR land included on the Inventory Branch database. Much of this two million hectares is considered non-commercial, although regrowth is occurring in some areas.

76. Drushka, *Stumped*, p. 116.

77. Jim Cooperman, "End the Overcut!," editorial, *The British Columbia Environmental Report*, Spring 1997, p. 2.

78. B.C. Ministry of Forests, "Audit Results Show Fraser TSA Inventory is Overestimated," news release, July 16, 1996.

79. B. Bouw, "Fraser area tree harvest slashed again," *Vancouver Sun*, July 17, 1996.

80. Cooperman, "End the Overcut!"

81. Sierra Club of British Columbia files.

82. BC Wild, "The Cassiar," March 1996; "Begging Questions: The Cassiar Timber Supply Analysis and the Ruin of B.C.'s Northwest Wilderness," February 1995 (Forestry pamphlets).

83. B.C. Ministry of Forests, "New Allowable Annual Cut Announced for Mackenzie Timber Supply Area," news release, July 17, 1996.

84. 1993 AAC: Canadian Forest Service, Department of Natural Resources, *The State of Canada's Forests, 1994*; 1994 AAC: Canadian Forest Service, Department of Natural Resources, *The State of Canada's Forests, 1995-1996*; 1996 AAC: B.C. Ministry of Forests, Timber Supply Review documentation, 1995-96.

85. B.C. Environmental Network Forest Caucus, "Putting the Cart before the Horse," news release, July 24, 1996.

Chapter 13: Yukon and Northwest Territories

1. Robert Service, "The Cremation of Sam McGee."

2. "A Forest Sector Strategy for Canada," Discussion Paper, Ministry of Environment, 1981; cited in R. Grenier, "In Search of a Forest Policy for the Yukon and the Northwest Territories," submitted to the Northern Renewable Resources Branch, Indian and Northern Affairs, December 1982.

3. Canadian Forestry Service, Whitehorse, *Yukon Forestry Fact Sheet*.

4. Forestry Canada, *The State of Forestry in Canada, 1990: First Report to Parliament*, (Ottawa, 1990), p. 16.

5. Department of Indian and Northern Affairs, "Yukon Development Strategy: Forestry," in *Yukon 2000—Building the Future* (Whitehorse, October 23, 1986).

6. C. Heartwell, *The Forest Industry in the Economy of the Yukon*, prepared for Department of Renewable Resources; Government of Yukon, Department of Economic Development; Indian and Northern Affairs Canada, Forestry Canada, February 1988.

7. Heartwell, *The Forest Industry in the Economy of the Yukon*.

8. H. Hammond, "The Boreal Forest: Options for Ecologically Responsible Human Use," paper prepared for the Yukon Conservation Society, April 1994.

9. Don White, "State of Yukon's Forests," *Symposium Proceedings for Yukon Forests: A Sustainable Resource, February 2-4, 1995* (Whitehorse: Government of Yukon), p. 11.

10. Indian and Northern Affairs Canada, *Discussion Paper on Policy Changes to Stumpage Pricing, Reforestation and Forest Tenure in the Yukon* (Ottawa, April 26, 1995), p. 1.

11. Yukon Council on the Economy and the Environment, "The Future of Yukon's Forests: Conference Summary," Watson Lake, Yukon, November 4-5, 1995.

12. The Honourable Ron Irwin, letter to Government Leader John Ostashek, published in the *Whitehorse Star*, November 20, 1995.

13. L. Jenkins, "Mountain clear-cutting proposal is called off," *Whitehorse Star*, November 24, 1993.

14. R. Mostyn, "Logs still being exported despite ban," *Yukon News*, May 26, 1995, quoting Jerry Armstrong, local contractor.

15. L. Jenkins, "Logging companies grilled about plans," *Whitehorse Star*, March 30, 1994.

16. Indian and Northern Affairs Canada, "Announcement of Interim Yukon Forest Policy, including a Yukon Forestry Advisory Committee and the Edward Elijah Smith Reforestation Program," communique (Whitehorse, August 4, 1995).

17. Canadian Forest Service, Department of Natural Resources, *The State of Canada's Forests, 1995-1996* (Ottawa, 1996).

18. Figures on volume and areas logged are from Forestry Canada, *The State of Forestry in Canada: 1990 Report to Parliament* (Ottawa, 1990) and Canadian Forest Service, Department of Natural Resources, *The State of Canada's Forests, 1994* and *The State of Canada's Forests, 1995-1996* (Ottawa, 1996).

19. Watson Lake Management Office, Yukon Forest Management Plan (Sertling Wood Group Corp., August 1991).

20. H. Armleder, and S. Stevenson, "Silvicultural Systems to Maintain Caribou Habitat in Managed British Columbia Forests," *Innovative Silvicultural Systems in Boreal Forests*, p. 83

21. Yukon Government News Release, "Governments agree to further work on devolution," February 3, 1997.

22. Dennis Fentie, "Ecosystems know no political boundaries," speech by the Yukon Forest Commissioner, delivered at Ecosystem Management Workshop, March 24, 1997.

23. Canadian Council of Forest Ministers, National Forestry Database, *1995 Compendium of Canadian Forestry Statistics* (Ottawa, 1996).

24. Ibid.

25. Canadian Forest Service, Natural Resources Canada, *The State of Canada's Forests, 1996-1997* (Ottawa, 1997).

PART III: Where Do We Go from Here?

1. G. Hamilton, "Primex discouraged by NDP," *Vancouver Sun*, April 25, 1997, p. E1.

2. Ibid.

3. D. Bryant, Daniel Nielsen, Laura Tangley, *The Last Frontier Forests: Ecosystems and Economies on the Edge* (Washington: World Resources Institute, 1997).

4. Sierra Club of Canada, "Forests," factsheet (Ottawa, 1995).

5. Wildlands League. "Ecological Forestry … A Cut Above"; Fact Sheet #6, Forest Diversity and Community Survival, Toronto, 1995.

6. Wildlands League, Fact sheet #6; also read about this success story in Paul Hawken's *Ecology of Commerce*.

7. "Slocan Residents, Behind Bars for Water," B.C. Environmental Report, (Fall 1997) 8, No. 3, p. 7.

8. Slocan Valley Watershed Alliance and Silva Forest Foundation, "Ecosystem-Based Planning Provides Win/Win Solution to Logging Conflicts," press release, August 15, 1996.

Appendices

	Guidelines/ Regulations*	Limits on Size of Clear-cuts	Steep Slope Restrictions
NFLD Provincial Crown land	Guidelines 1994	None	Increased buffers on steepest slopes
Private land	None	None	N/A
PEI Provincial Crown land	None	None	N/A
Private land	None		
NS Provincial Crown land	Regulations established in 1989 Guidelines	Not to exceed 50 ha without the incorporation of wildlife corridors	Slopes >10° and <30° must have a 1 m buffer on either side
Private land	Guidelines	None	None
NB Provincial Crown land	Guidelines	Limited to 100 ha, effective in 1993	Slopes are harvested at >50%. Cutting on slopes is allowed if the environment is protected and if there is a 90% restocking rate on such slopes (major companies have said in the next 5 yrs. they may be doing more steep slope harvesting)
Private land	None		
QUEBEC Provincial Crown land	1987 Forest Act, 1994 Forest Protection Strategy	Adjacent clear-cuts must be separated by a corridor of 60 m if neither clear-cut exceeds 150 ha If one of the areas exceeds 150 ha, then a corridor of 100 m is required Cutblock not to exceed 250 ha (since 1988)	
Private land	None		
ONTARIO Provincial Crown land	Guidelines since 1988 Crown Forest Sustainability Act (April 1, 1995)—the forest industry is required to conduct and pay for the renewal of all areas harvested	Boreal—Moose habitat guidelines: 80,130 ha in prime areas (exceptions permitted). Great Lakes-St. Lawrence: Deer habitat guidelines: in preparation, size limits not specified	Slopes: 0–15% 16–30% 31–45% 46–60%
Private land	Trees Act (1946) in Great Lakes-St. Lawrence and deciduous forest regions only		

Buffer Zones and Wildlife Corridors	Restrictions on Herbicides or Pesticides	Percentage of Area Clear-cut
20 m buffer on streams	None	100%
None		
Guidelines are in place for the delineation of buffer areas	None	100%
50 m buffer width required with unique wildlife habitat. 20 m buffer zone required on each side of an aquatic resource	N/A	100%
None		
15 m machine exclusion zones are required adjacent to streams greater than 0.5 m in width 75 m are now required on streams within designated watersheds	Restrictions on aerial application of pesticides Dept. of the Environment sets limits for forest spraying on a permit-by-permit basis No limits on areas where herbicides are applied; the public reimburses herbiciding on Crown land	90%
	Total elimination of chemical herbicide and insecticide by the year 2001	80.5%

Buffer Width: 30 m
                  50 m
                  70 m
                  90 m
(buffer may increase or decrease—areas assessed on an individual basis)
		91%

*Guidelines are not legally binding. Regulations are, but enforcement is uneven.

	Guidelines/ Regulations*	Limits on Size of Clear-cuts	Steep Slope Restrictions
MB Provincial Crown land	Regulations	Cutblocks limited to 100 ha	N/A
Private land	None		
SASK Provincial Crown land	Forest Management Act (1996)	Guidelines also address buffer areas and adjacent clear-cuts. Cutblocks limited to: softwoods: approx. 40 ha; hardwood: approx. 120 ha	N/A
Private land	None		
ALBERTA Provincial Crown land	Guidelines since 1966	Hardwood: no more than 60 ha, but may vary up to 100 ha. Softwood: Pine blocks; same as deciduous. Spruce blocks: patches and blocks to a max. of 24 ha, or strips to a max. of 32 ha. Not more than 20–30%	N/A
Private land	None		
BC Provincial Crown land	Forest Practices Code of B.C. (June 1995), Operational Planning Regulation	Max. cutblock size— 40 ha for Vancouver, Kamloops and Nelson regions; 60 ha for Prince George, Cariboo, Prince Rupert regions (these max. can be changed by district managers if cutblocks have ragged edges and green tree retention)	Terrain stability field assessments are requirements where slopes are greater than 60%, where areas have been identified as unstable, or are prone to landslides
Private land	None		
NWT Provincial Crown land	Adopted in 1987, legislation states that unless timber operators regenerate all cutover lands in a manner satisfactory to a forest management officer, they must pay a reforestation fee	Max. cutblock size: 50 ha Where a stand or group of stands exceeds 50 ha, the stands are divided into blocks or strips	None
Private land	None		
YUKON Provincial Crown land	None	Max. cutblock size: 15 ha (Timber Permits) Max. cutblock size: 40 ha (Timber Harvest Agreement)	None
Private land	None		

Buffer Zones and Wildlife Corridors	Restrictions on Herbicides or Pesticides	Percentage of Area Clear-cut
	Rules relating to wildlife corridors and fish protection procedures for stream crossings	100%
Guidelines address buffer areas and adjacent clear-cuts		100%
Buffer zones beside streams	Not traditionally used There is a push from Monsanto to use Round-up (active ingredient glyposate) which kills calamagrotis	100%
Buffer zones beside streams Wildlife corridors are not yet required	No spraying less than 100 m upslope from community watershed intakes 10 m pesticide-free zone from community watershed streams Pesticide-use—Permits are needed before any spraying can occur	92%
None	None	100%
None	None	100%

Employment Figures for Forest Industry (Canada)

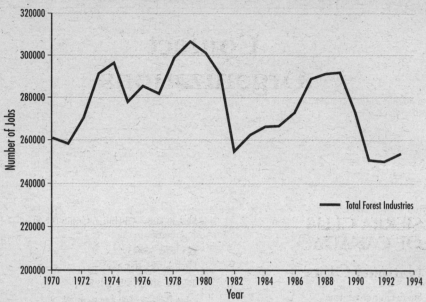

── Total Forest Industries

Total Harvested Roundwood (Canada)

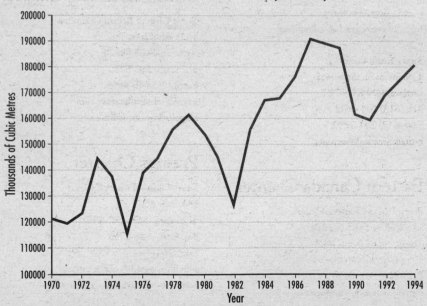

SOURCE: Compendium of Canadian Forestry Statistics 1995.

Contact Organizations

SIERRA CLUB OF CANADA
National Office

Sierra Club of Canada
1 Nicholas St,. Suite 412
Ottawa, ON K1N 7B7
Tel: (613) 241-4611
Fax: (613) 241-2292
e-mail: sierra@web.net
http://www.sierraclub.ca/national

Sierra Youth Coalition
1 Nicholas St,. Suite 412
Ottawa, ON K1N 7B7
Tel: (613) 241-4611
Fax: (613) 241-2292
e-mail: sierrayc@web.net

Eastern Canada Chapter

Sierra Club of Eastern Canada
517 College St., Suite 204
Toronto, ON M6G 4A2
Tel: (416) 960-9606
Fax: (416) 960-0020
e-mail: sierraec@interlog.com
http://www.sierraclub.ca/eastern

Sierra Club—Chebucto Group (Halifax)—
   Atlantic
P.O. Box 36093
Halifax, NS B3J 3S9
Tel/Fax: (902) 492-1995
e-mail: pfalvo@chebucto.ns.ca
http://www.chebucto.ns.ca/Environment/Sierra/

British Columbia Chapter

Sierra Club of British Columbia
1525 Amelia St.
Victoria, BC V8W 2K1
Tel: (205) 386-5255
Fax: (205) 386-4453
e-mail: scbc@islandnet.com
http://www.sierraclub.ca/bc

Prairies Chapter

Sierra Club—Prairies Chapter
P.O. Box 2268
Winnipeg, MB R3C 4A6
Tel: (204) 444-2750
Fax: (204) 444-3763
e-mail: hebertjl@mbnet.mb.ca
http://www.sierraclub.ca/prairie/

SIERRA CLUB— UNITED STATES

Sierra Club National Headquarters

85 Second St., 2nd Floor
San Francisco, CA
94105-3441 U.S.A.
Tel: (415) 977-5500 or 977-5653
Fax: (415) 977-5799
http://www.sierraclub.org

Sierra Club D.C.
408 C St., N.E.
Washington, D.C.
20002 U.S.A.
Tel: (202) 547-1141
Fax: (202) 547-6009
e-mail: scdcl@igc.apc.org

NATIONAL GROUPS

Assembly of First Nations
1 Nicholas St., Suite 1002
Ottawa, ON K1N 7B7
Tel: (613) 241-6789
Fax: (613) 241-5808

Canadian Environmental Network
Forest Caucus
945 Wellington St., Suite 1004
Ottawa, ON K1Y 2X5
Tel: (613) 728-9810
Fax: (613) 728-2963
e-mail: cen@web.net, caucus2@web.net

Canadian Nature Federation
1 Nicholas St., Suite 606
Ottawa, ON K1N 7B7
Tel: (613) 562-3447
Fax: (613) 562-3371
e-mail: cnf@web.net

Canadian Parks and Wilderness
Society (CPAWS)
401 Richmond St. West, Suite 380
Toronto, ON M5V 3A8
Tel: (416) 979-2720
Fax: (416) 979-3155
e-mail: cpaws@web.net

Grand Council of the Crees
24 Bayswater Ave.
Ottawa, ON K1Y 2E4
Tel: (613) 761-1655
Fax: (613) 761-1388

Greenpeace Canada
250 Dundas St. West, Suite 605
Toronto, ON M5T 2Z5
Tel: (416) 597-8408
Fax: (416) 597-8422

Sierra Legal Defence Fund
131 Water St., Suite 214
Vancouver, BC V6B 4M3
Tel: (604) 685-5618
Fax: (604) 685-7813
e-mail: sldf@wimsey.com

Taiga Rescue Network
c/o Don Sullivan
2–70 Albert St.
Winnipeg, MB R3B 1E7
Tel: (204) 947-3081
Fax: (204) 947-3076
e- mail: sullivan@mbnet.mb.ca

World Wildlife Fund Canada
90 Eglinton Ave. East, Suite 504
Toronto, ON M4P 2Z7
Tel: (416) 489-8800, 1-800-26-PANDA
Fax: (416) 489-3611
e-mail: panda@www.wwfcanada.org

NEWFOUNDLAND & LABRADOR

Central Avalon
  Environmental Association
P.O. Box 16, Conception Harbour
Conception Bay, NF A0A 1Z0
Tel: (709) 229-6206
Fax: (709) 229-4781
e-mail: econway@nfld.com

Humber Environment
  Action Group
P.O. Box 1143
Corner Brook, NF A2H 6T2
Tel/Fax: (709) 634-2520

Innu Nation
P.O. Box 119
Sheshatshiu, Labrador
A0P 1M0
Tel: (709) 497-8398
Fax: (709) 497-8396
e-mail: innuenv@web.net

NOVA SCOTIA

Ecoforestry School in the Maritimes
RR#2, New Germany, NS B0R 1E0
Tel: (902) 543-0122
Fax: (902) 543-9950
e-mail: windhors@fox.nstn.ca

Ecology Action Centre
1568 Argyle St., Suite 31
Halifax, NS B3J 2B3
Tel: (902) 429-2202
Fax: (902) 422-6410
e-mail: eac.hfx@istar.ca

Margaree Environmental Association
P.O. Box 617
Margaree Forks, NS B0E 2A0
Tel: (902) 258-3354/248-2573

Nova Scotia Coalition for
  Alternatives to Pesticides
RR#1, Baddeck, NS
B0E 1B0
Tel: (902) 295-3053
Fax: (902) 295-2766

NEW BRUNSWICK

Conservation Council of
  New Brunswick
180 St. John Street
Fredericton, NB E3B 4A9
Tel: (506) 458-8747
Fax: (506) 458-1047
e-mail: ccnbcoon@nbnet.nb.ca

Fallsbrook Centre
RR#2, Hartland, NB E0J 1N0
Tel: (506) 375-8143
Fax: (506) 375-4221
e-mail: fbcja@web.net

PRINCE EDWARD ISLAND

Environmental Coalition of
  Prince Edward Island
81 Prince Street
Charlottetown, P.E.I. C1A 4R3
Tel: (902) 566-4696
Fax: (902) 368-7180

QUEBEC

Algonquin of Barriere Lake
Kitiganik—Rapid Lake
La Vérendrye, PQ J0W 2C0
Tel/Fax: (819) 824-1734

Regroupement Écologiste de
  Val d'Or et Environs (REVE)
C.P. 605
Val d'Or, PQ J9P 4P6
Tel: (819) 738-5261
Fax: (819) 825-5361
e-mail: reve@web.net

L'Union québécoise pour
  la conservation de la nature
690 Grande-Allée Est, Bureau 420
Quebec, PQ G1R 2K5
Tel: (418) 648-2104
Fax: (418) 648-0991
e-mail: ecogroupe@uqcn.qc.ca

ONTARIO

Earthroots
401 Richmond St. West, Suite 410
Toronto, ON M5V 3A8
Tel: (416) 599-0152
Fax: (416) 340-2429
e-mail: eroots@web.net

Northwatch
P.O. Box 282
North Bay, ON P1B 8H2
Tel: (705) 497-0373
Fax: (705) 476-7060

Federation of Ontario Naturalists
355 Lesmill Rd.
Don Mills, ON M3B 2W8
Tel: (416) 444-8419
Fax: (416) 444-9866

Ontario Public Interest Research Group
Carleton—Forest Working Group
326 Unicentre, Carleton University
1125 Colonel By Drive
Ottawa, ON K1S 5B6
Tel: (613) 520-2757
Fax: (613) 520-3989

Wildlands League
401 Richmond St. West, Suite 380
Toronto, ON M5V 3A8
Tel: (416) 971-9453
Fax: (416) 979-3155
e-mail: wildland@web.apc.org

MANITOBA

Manitoba Future Forest Alliance
270 Albert St.
Winnipeg, MB R3B 1E7
Tel: (204) 947-3081
Fax: (204) 947-3076

Manitoba Naturalists Society
63 Albert St., Suite 401
Winnipeg, MB R3B 1G4
Tel/Fax: (204) 943-9029

SASKATCHEWAN

Saskatchewan Forest
  Conservation Network
Box 359
Glauslyn, SK S0M 0Y0
Tel: (306) 342-4689

Saskatchewan Environmental Society
P.O. Box 1372
Saskatoon, SK S7K 3N9
Tel: (306) 665-1915
Fax: (306) 665-2128
e-mail: saskenv@link.ca

ALBERTA

Alberta Wilderness Association
P.O. Box 6398, Stn. D
Calgary, AB T2P 2E1
Tel: (403) 283-2025
Fax: (403) 270-2743

Bow Valley Naturalists
Box 1693
Banff, AB T0L 0C0
Tel/Fax: (403) 762-4160
e-mail: mcivor@telusplanet.net

Friends of the Athabasca
P.O. Box 1351
Athabasca, AB T0G 0B0

Western Canada Wilderness Committee
Suite 310, 10168—100 A St.
Edmonton, AB T5J 0R6
Tel: (403) 420-1001
Fax: (403) 420-1475
e-mail: wcwcab@web.apc.org

BRITISH COLUMBIA

B.C. Wild
Box 2241, Main Post Office
Vancouver, BC V6B 3W2
Tel: (604) 669-4802
Fax: (604) 669-6833

Cariboo Horse Loggers
P.O. Box 4321
Quesnel, BC V2J 3J3
Tel/Fax: (250) 747-3363

East Kootenay Environmental Society
Cranbrook/Kimberley Branch
P.O. Box 8
Kimberley, BC V1A 2Y5
Tel: (250) 427-2535
Fax: (250) 427-3535
e-mail: ekes@cyberlink.bc.ca

Friends of Clayoquot Sound
P.O. Box 489
Tofino, BC V0R 2Z0
Tel: (250) 725-2527
Fax: (250) 725-2527
e-mail: focs@web.apc.org

Silva Forest Foundation
3301 Coch Siting Rd.
Slocan Park, BC V0G 2E0
Tel: (250) 226-7770
Fax: (250) 226-7446

Valhalla Wilderness Society
P.O. Box 329
New Denver, BC V0G 1S0
Tel: (250) 358-2333
Fax: (250) 358-7950
e-mail: vws@web.net

Western Canada Wilderness Committee
20 Water Street
Vancouver, BC V6B 1A4
Tel: (604) 683-8220
Fax: (604) 683-8229
e-mail: wc2wild@web.net
http://www.webnetwcwild/welcome.html

YUKON

Canadian Parks and Wilderness Society
Yukon Chapter
30 Dawson Rd.
Whitehorse, YK Y1A 5T6
Tel/Fax: (403) 668-6321

Yukon Conservation Society
P.O. Box 4163
Whitehorse, YK Y1A 3T3
Tel: (403) 668-5678
Fax: (403) 668-6637
e-mail: ycs@polarcom.com

Biographies of Researchers

National Research Coordinator

ERICA KONRAD

Erica Konrad was the coordinator of the forest campaign for the Sierra Club of Canada and assisted Elizabeth May in all facets of the book. She holds an Honours B.A. in Environmental Studies and Environmental Resource Management from the University of Toronto. Erica conducted research on a federal level and coordinated the provincial and territorial research. She also assisted in the editing, layout and design. Currently, Erica resides in Fernie, B.C., where she is actively involved in environmental issues with the East Kootenay Environmental Society.

Newfoundland

GREG MITCHELL

Greg Mitchell was born in Corner Brook and grew up in Curling, Newfoundland. After a short stint on the "mainland" in Toronto, he entered Memorial University in 1970 where he acquired a B.Sc. (Hon.) in Biology. Following graduation, he worked for two years as an Instructional Assistant with the Biology Department at the newly opened Sir Wilfred Grenfell College in Corner Brook. In 1977, after building a sawmill and clearing land, he and his wife, Lynn, began mixed farming near Gillams in the Bay of Islands. For the past ten years, his prime concern has been logging. He was Chair of the first environmental group, Ecowatch, at Corner Brook in 1976 and is presently a member of the Humber Environment Action Group, Forest Allies and coordinator of the Forest Caucus for the Newfoundland and Labrador Environment Network. He is also very active in the Humber River Allies, a group fighting a proposal by Kruger Inc. to construct a large hydroelectric dam on the doorstep of Gros Morne National Park. Greg presently resides at Gillams with his wife and daughter, Emily. They spend their free time cruising western Newfoundland in their boat, the *Lady L.*

Nova Scotia

CHARLIE RESTINO

Charlie Restino first became aware of the diversity of eastern temperate forests as a child through the influence of the father of a close friend, a forester who would lead groups of neighborhood kids on hikes through the woods, helping identify the myriad of plant and tree species. For the past 25 years, he has been involved in forestry as a woodlot manager on Cape Breton Island. During this time, he has carried out extensive commercial harvesting of trees from severely degraded woodlands, while remaining focused on the critical need to develop economically and ecologically sound silvicultural methods of promoting the restoration of shade-dependent species. In 1976, he joined the Cape Breton Landowners Against the Spray to prevent the spraying of forest biocides on the island. In 1986, Charlie became executive director of the Nova Scotia Coalition for Alternatives to Pesticides. He remains active in the Taiga Rescue Network, Canadian and Nova Scotia Environmental Network's Forest Caucuses, and other organizations dedicated to ecological and social justice. Charlie has published in *Alternatives Magazine, Wild Earth, The Northern Forest Forum* and other publications. He lives in Baddeck, Nova Scotia.

New Brunswick
MATTHEW BETTS
Matthew Betts is an environmental researcher and consultant from Fairvale, New Brunswick. He has his Master's degree in Regional Planning and Resource Development from the University of Waterloo, Ontario. Currently, Matthew is on the board of directors of the Conservation Council of New Brunswick and is studying forestry at the University of New Brunswick.

Prince Edward Island
GARY SCHNEIDER
Gary Schneider is a coordinator of the Environmental Coalition of Prince Edward Island. His interests in forest restoration, wildlife habitat improvement and conservation issues were the foundations of the Macphail Woods Ecological Forestry Project in Orwell. He has written extensively on growing and restoring the native Acadian forest and leads many of the nature tours and workshops at Macphail Woods.

The Environmental Coalition of Prince Edward Island was formed in 1989. It is active in many areas of environmental protection and education, including forest restoration, pesticide reduction, composting, recycling and development. The organization has earned various provincial awards and continues to be at the forefront of environmental protection in the province.

RUTH RICHMAN
Ruth Richman graduated with Honours from the Maritime Forest Ranger School in Fredericton, New Brunswick, in 1987. She became a technician after many years of tree-planting and two as a power-saw operator. While working for the P.E.I. Forestry Branch for five years (seasonal), she volunteered some time with the Macphail Woods Ecological Forestry Project. In 1995 she was employed by Macphail Woods to help with all aspects of the project including the native tree and shrub nursery, writing and editing, and workshops and tours.

Quebec
PIERRE DUBOIS
Natif de Rivière-à-Pierre, comte de Portneuf, à quelque 100 km au nord-ouest de Québec, Pierre Dubois vit dans la région de Québec. Ingénieur forestier, il est connu du milieu forestier québécois à titre de journaliste, et surtout de contestataire de la foresterie industrielle existante. Il fut engagé socialement plusieurs années au sein de groupes communautaires, syndicaux et environnementaux.

A titre de journaliste indépendant, il écrit dans la plupart des médias qui s'intéressent à la forêt au Quebec. Il est également l'auteur de <<Les vrais maîtres de la forêt québécoise>>, un livre publié en 1996 qui dénonce la mainmise industrielle sur la forêt québécoise. Pierre Dubois continue aujourd'hui d'être journaliste, en plus d'etre consultant en foresterie.

HENRI JACOB

Originaire d'Abitibi, pays forestier au nord-ouest du Québec, Henri Jacob y a passé la plus grande partie de sa vie à militer en faveur d'une utilisation plus écologique et plus équitable des ressources naturelles.

Impliqué depuis plus de vingts ans dans différents organismes écologistes, il défend avec conviction le droit des citoyens à participer aux multiples débâts environnementaux qui détermineront l'héritage que nous laisseront à nos enfants.

Militant acharné, il a aussi travaillé depuis plus de quinze ans au développement du Réseau québécoise des groupes écologistes (RQGE) et du Réseau canadien de l'environnement (RCE).

Henri a travaillé à vulgariser et à rendre accessible la cartographie écologique comme outil de gestion de nos ressources.

Avec le Regroupement écologiste Val d'Or et environs (Le REVE), il a développé un réseau de sentiers d'interprétation du milieu naturel, l'École Buissonnière.

Ontario

TIM GRAY

Tim Gray is the executive director of the Wildlands League, a chapter of the Canadian Parks and Wilderness Society. Formed in 1968, the League has a twenty-eight-year history of involvement in protecting key elements of Ontario's natural heritage and working to encourage sustainable resource use. The League has fought long and successfully to protect Quetico, Killarney and Algonquin provincial parks.

Tim holds an undergraduate degree in Biology from Wilfrid Laurier University and an M.Sc. in Botany/Environmental Studies from the University of Toronto. He haas been working for the Wildlands League since 1980. He has acted as co-chair of the Forests for Tomorrow Coalition in the Provincial Timber Class Environmental Assessment hearing and served as a member of the Ontario-cabinet-appointed Old Growth Forest Policy Advisory Committee. He has also spent the greater part of the last five years traveling the highways and forests of the province, working to conserve lakes, rivers and forests. Current commitments include his role as the Ontario coordinator of World Wildlife Fund's national Endangered Spaces Campaign and a member of the University of Toronto's Faculty of Forestry Advisory Committee.

LORNE JOHNSON

Lorne Johnson is a consulting forest economist who works for the Wildlands League. At present, he is coordinating the development of forest management standards for the Great Lakes–St. Lawrence Forest Region of Ontario. These standards will be used by Forest Stewardship Council (FSC) accredited certifiers in their audits of forest operations in the region. In addition to his work on forest certification, Lorne has been organizing "character" log and wood auctions in Central Ontario for the last few years with an aim to improve the wood flow and prices for wood products.

Manitoba

DON SULLIVAN

Don Sullivan is an award-winning environmental writer, researcher, photographer and activist. He is the spokesperson for the Manitoba Future Forest Alliance, a coalition of organizations that have been actively involved in exposing the environmental impacts associated with the recently licensed Louisiana-Pacific oriented strand board plant in western Manitoba. Don was the recipient of the 1995 Manitoba Eco-Network Award for his outstanding contribution to the awareness and protection of Manitoba's environment. Currently, Don has been hired as the new North American Coordinator for the Taiga Rescue Network, an international network located in Jokkmokk, Sweden, which includes some 130 organizations, individuals and scientists who work exclusively on boreal forest issues in Europe, North America and Russia. Don also was the lead project coordinator for the North American Forest Forum held in September of 1996, which was endorsed by over thirty organizations and attracted some 150 environmentalists, First Nations representatives, and youth from across Canada, the United States and Mexico to discuss forest-related issues in North America.

Saskatchewan

JOYS DANCER

Joys Dancer lives in a solar-powered, wood-heated house in an alternative community on the southern edge of the boreal forest in northwest Saskatchewan. She works on forestry and political issues and community development as a musician through involvement in the Saskatchewan Forest Conservation Network, the local forest advisory council and a twinning project with an indigenous group in Costa Rica, focused on community-based environmental and cultural impact assessment.

Alberta

KAREN BALTGAILIS

Karen Baltgailis has produced two videos critiquing Alberta and British Columbia forestry, and offering economic and environmental alternatives. Both videos are in use in the Alberta school system, and the second, *A Cut Above*, won a 1996 award for inspiration. Karen also researched the Canadian portion of the Taiga Rescue Network's recently published international report on sustainable forestry in the boreal. She has also worked as a campaigner for the Western Canada Wilderness Committee in Edmonton.

ERIN McGREGOR

Erin McGregor was born and raised in rural Alberta. She currently lives in Edmonton and works for the Western Canada Wilderness Committee.

British Columbia

JIM COOPERMAN

Jim Cooperman has been a resident of the Shuswap area for twenty-five years. He and his wife, Kathleen, have a small farm and five children. Jim acquired his Bachelor's degree from the University of California at Berkeley and a teaching credential from Simon Fraser University. His past occupations included teaching, log building, construction and some logging as well as operating a small sawmill with partners for over ten years. In the 1980s he researched and wrote local North Shuswap history and helped edit a local history journal. Jim began conservation work in 1989 by helping to organize the Shuswap Environmental Action Society (SEAS). He has concentrated on writing and editing in his work as an environmentalist. Currently, Jim works provincially with the B.C. Environmental Network, serving three years on the steering committee and now in his seventh year as coordinator of the forest caucus and editor of the B.C. Environmental Report. He has also edited three editions of the Shuswap Eco-Watch, nine Shuswap Conservation Notes columns, and he wrote the chapter on Canada for the exhibit-format book, *Clearcut, The Tragedy of Industrial Forestry*.

Yukon

LAUREL JENKINS

Laurel Jenkins is the office manager and researcher for CPAWS-Yukon and the Endangered Spaces Campaign. Before joining CPAWS she was a reporter with the *Whitehorse Star* covering environmental and resource issues throughout the Yukon. Laurel is active in the Yukon's environmental education association and also works on consumer utilities issues.

JURI PEEPRE

Juri Peepre is the national president of the Canadian Parks and Wilderness Society and a former chair of the Yukon CPAWS chapter. He also coordinates the Yukon Wildlands Project and the World Wildlife Fund Endangered Spaces campaign in the Yukon. Juri serves on the board of the North American Wildlands Project and is active in the Yellowstone to Yukon Biodiversity Strategy.

Before moving to the Yukon he was chair of the Outdoor Recreation Council of British Columbia. He became a full-time environmentalist in 1995 after fifteen years consulting in protected areas and environmental planning.

Bibliography

Algonquin Wildlands League. *Wilderness Now: A Statement of Principles and Policies of the Algonquin Wildlands League*. Toronto: 1972.

Brown, Lester R., Christopher Flavin and Hilary French. *State of the World 1997: A Worldwatch Institute Report on Progress Toward a Sustainable Society*. New York: Worldwatch Institute/W.W. Norton, 1997.

Brown, Lester R. and Hal Kane. *Full House: Reassessing the Earth's Population Carrying Capacity*. Worldwatch Environmental Alert Series. New York: W.W. Norton, 1994.

Brown, Lester R., Michael Renner and Christopher Flavin. *Vital Signs 1997: The Environmental Trends That Are Shaping Our Future*. New York: Worldwatch Institute/W.W. Norton, 1997.

Carson Rachel L. *Silent Spring*. Boston: Houghton Mifflin, 1962.

Clark, Tom. *Timber Supply and Endangered Spaces*. A World Wildlife Fund Canada Discussion Paper.

Cohen, Joel E. *How Many People Can the Earth Support?*. New York: W.W. Norton, 1995.

Devall, Bill, ed. *Clearcut: The Tragedy of Industrial Forestry*. San Francisco: Sierra Club Books/Earth Island Press, 1993.

Drushka, Ken. *Stumped: The Forest Industry in Transition*. Vancouver: Douglas & McIntyre, 1985.

Ehrlich, Paul R. and Anne H. Ehrlich. *The Population Explosion*. New York: Touchstone, Simon & Schuster, 1990.

Gordon, Anita and David Suzuki. *It's a Matter of Survival*. Toronto: Stoddart, 1990.

Hammond, Herb. *Seeing the Forest Among the Trees: The Case for Wholistic Forest Use*. Vancouver: Polestar Press, 1991.

Hodgins, Bruce and Jamie Benidickson. *The Temagami Experience*. Toronto: University of Toronto Press, 1989.

Howard, Ross. *Poisons in Public: Case Studies of Environmental Pollution in Canada*. Toronto: James Lorimer, 1980.

Hummel, Monte, ed. *Endangered Spaces: The Future for Canada's Wilderness*. Toronto: Key Porter Books, 1989.

Hummel, Monte, ed. *Protecting Canada's Endangered Spaces: An Owner's Manual.* Toronto: Key Porter Books, 1995.

Kimmins, Hamish. *Balancing Act: Environmental Issues in Forestry.* Vancouver: University of British Columbia Press, 1992.

Lansky, Mitch. *Beyond the Beauty Strip: Saving What's Left of Our Forests.* Gardiner, Maine: Tilbury House, 1992.

Marchak, M. Patricia. *Logging the Globe.* Montreal and Kingston: McGill-Queen's University Press, 1995.

Maser, Chris. *The Redesigned Forest.* San Pedro, California: R. & E. Miles, 1988.

May, Elizabeth. *Budworm Battles.* Tantallon, N.S.: Four East Publishers, 1982.

May, Elizabeth. *Paradise Won: The Struggle for South Moresby.* Toronto: McClelland & Stewart, 1990.

Meyer, William B. *Human Impact on The Earth.* Cambridge: Cambridge University Press, 1996.

M'Gonigle, Michael and Ben Parfitt. *Forestopia: A Practical Guide to the New Forest Economy.* Madeira Park, B.C.: Harbour Publishing, 1994.

Ross, Monique. *Forest Management in Canada.* Calgary: Canadian Institute of Resources Law, 1995.

Stream Protection Under the Code: The Destruction Continues. Sierra Legal Defence Fund, February 1997.

Suzuki, David. *Time to Change.* Toronto: Stoddart, 1994.

Swift, Jamie. *Cut and Run: The Assault on Canada's Forests.* Toronto: Between the Lines, 1983.

Troyer, Warner. *No Safe Place.* Toronto: Clarke, Irwin, 1977.

Zimmerman, Adam. *Who's in Charge Here, Anyway?: Reflections from a Life in Business.* Toronto: Stoddart, 1997.

Index

Note: Page numbers in **bold** indicate a chart.

sustainable development:
    Manitoba, 156; Quebec, 121;
    Saskatchewan, 169-70
Sustainable Forest Licences (SFLs), 141,
    144
Sustainable Forest Management
    Certification, 59-60
sustainable-yield forest management, xiii,
    38, 59-60, 158, 222
Swift, Jamie, 27

T

taxation system, and forest industry, 26
tax reform, ecological, 26
Techfor Sask, 165
technology:
    and clear-cut logging, 10; and collapse
    of fishery, xiv, 13
    See also mechanization
Temagami, 136-9
Teme-augama Anishnabai, 137-8
temperate old-growth forest, B.C., 64, 192
tenure system:
    British Columbia, 199; Quebec, 118-
    19
The Pas mill, 150-2, 158
timber harvest, annual area (1920-1994), **9**
Timber Harvest Agreements (THAs), 214
timber licenses:
    Alberta, 174; British Columbia, 187,
    190-1, 208; New Brunswick, 106-7;
    Newfoundland, 69, 74; Ontario, 141;
    Quebec, 120; Yukon, 213
timber limits, Ontario, 133
timber supply, 34, 182, 200
    analysis, 200, 204, 208; review, 200,
    204, 206, 207
Timber Supply and Forest Management
    Agreements (TSFMAs), 119
Timber Supply Area (TSA), 190, 206-8
Tobin, Brian, 77
Tonene, Chief, 137
Tothill, J.D., 80, 101
tourism:
    Alberta, 172; and logging, 137, 140
toxic chemicals, pollution from, 46-50

Tree Farm Licences (TFLs), 5, 187-8, 189-
    90
tree-length logging, 27
tree planting, unreliability of, 36
tree species:
    estimates, 33; Ontario, 132; under-uti-
    lized, 34
The Trees Behind the Shore (Gray), 73
Trilateral Agreement, Quebec, 122-3
Trouble in the Woods (Sandberg), 82
Troyer, Warner, 45
tundra, Manitoba, 149
*20 Year Forestry Development Plan 1990-
    2009*, 75

U

under-utilized:
    hardwood, 34-5, 109-10, 160; tree
    species, 34
uneven-aged forest management system,
    23-4
United Nations:
    Biosphere Reserve status, 199;
    Commission on Sustainable
    Development, 7; Convention for the
    Protection of Biodiversity, 24-5, 157
United States:
    Environmental Protection Agency, 90;
    forest products exports and imports,
    51-6, 127; Securities and Exchange
    Commission, 152
UNOCAL, 175-6

V

Vanier, D., 120
Van Weizsacher, Ernst, 26
variable retention silviculture system, 198,
    224
Voisey's Bay, 76
voluntary certification schemes, 58, 61
Voluntary Challenge Registry (VCR), 44
voluntary measures, to pollution control,
    48-9
Vrancart, Ron, 148